Banking Reforms in South-East Europe

NEW HORIZONS IN MONEY AND FINANCE

Series Editor: Mervyn K. Lewis, *University of South Australia*

This important series is designed to make a significant contribution to the shaping and development of thinking in finance. The series will provide an invaluable forum for the publication of high quality works of scholarship on a breadth of topics ranging from financial markets and financial systems to monetary policy and banking reform, and will show the diversity of theory, issues and practices.

The focus of the series is on the development and application of new original ideas in finance. Rigorous and often path-breaking in its approach, it will pay particular attention to the international and comparative dimension of finance and will include innovative theoretical and empirical work from both well-established authors and the new generation of scholars.

Titles in the series include:

Banking Reforms in South-East Europe
Edited by Zeljko Sevic

Russian Banking
Evolution, Problems and Prospects
Edited by David Lane

Banking Reforms in South-East Europe

Edited by

Željko Šević

The Business School
University of Greenwich, London, UK

NEW HORIZONS IN MONEY AND FINANCE

Edward Elgar
Cheltenham, UK • Northampton, MA, USA

Published by
Edward Elgar Publishing Limited
Glensanda House
Montpellier Parade
Cheltenham
Glos GL50 1UA
UK

Edward Elgar Publishing, Inc.
136 West Street
Suite 202
Northampton
Massachusetts 01060
USA

A catalogue record for this book
is available from the British Library

Library of Congress Cataloguing in Publication Data
Banking reforms in South-East Europe/ edited by Zeljko Sevic.
p. cm. — (New horizons in money and finance series)
Includes index.
1. Banks and banking—Balkan Peninsula—Congresses. I. Sevic, Zeljko, 1968– II. Series.

HG3214 .B36 2002
332.1'09496—dc21

2002022246

ISBN 1 84064 377 3

Printed and bound in Great Britain by MPG Books Ltd, Bodmin, Cornwall

Contents

Tables vii
Figures xi
Contributors xiii
Preface and Acknowledgements xix

1. Assessing the Banking Reforms in South-East Europe 1
Željko Šević

PART ONE: GENERAL AND THEORETICAL ISSUES

2. Economic Reform in South-East European Countries in Transition 19
Davor Savin
3. The Role of the Stability Pact in Financial Sector Reform in South-East Europe 47
Fabrizio Saccomanni
4. Governance Structures 79
Mervyn K. Lewis
5. Central Bank Reform in South-East Europe: Recent Developments and Prospects 99
Željko Šević
6. Currency Boards and Currency Arrangements in Transition Economies 125
Mervyn K. Lewis
7. Comparative Models of Banking Reform 147
Djordje Djukić
8. Banking Reform in South-East European Countries in the Light of the Central European Experience 163
Sonya Dilova-Kirkowa and Andy W. Mullineux

PART TWO: COUNTRY STUDIES

9. Banking Reform in Albania 187
Fiqiri Baholli and Amika Stavri

10. Banking Reform in Bosnia and Herzegovina 207
Jean Tesche
11. The Banking System in Bulgaria 219
Guglielmo Maria Caporale, Kalin Hristov, Jeffrey B. Miller, Nickolay Nenovsky and Boris Petrov
12. Reforming the Banking System in Croatia and its Broader Macroeconomic Environment 241
Radmila Jovančević
13. Banking Reform in Macedonia 261
Gligor Bišev
14. Banking Reform in Romania 285
Claudiu Doltu
15. Reforming the Banking System in Yugoslavia 309
Yoji Koyama, Goran Pitić, Jelena Galić and Aleksandar Šević

Index 331

Tables

2.1	Methods of privatisation in medium-sized and large enterprises	33
2.2	Growth in real GDP in Central and East European countries	35
2.3	Corruption index, 1999	37
2.4	Stabilisation lags in Central and East European countries	39
3.1	EBRD banking and financial sector reform indexes	58
3A.1	Financial institutions in Albania, 1995–1999	69
3A.2	Financial institutions in the Federation, 1995–1998	70
3A.3	Financial institutions in Republika Srpska, 1995–1998	70
3A.4	Financial institutions in Bulgaria, 1995–1999	72
3A.5	Financial institutions in Croatia, 1995–1999	73
3A.6	Financial institutions in Macedonia, 1995–1999	75
3A.7	Financial institutions in Romania, 1995–1999	76
6.1	Features of existing currency boards	126
6.2	Bilateral and trade-weighted exchange rate movements, June 1997 to March 1998	134
6.3	Exchange rate regimes of EU candidate countries in Central and Eastern Europe, as of 14 November 1999	140
6.4	Exchange rate arrangements of national currencies, 1986–1999	141
7.1	A comparison of centralised and decentralised approaches to banking sector restructuring	149
8.1	Financial development in selected transition economies, 1993–1998	166
8.2	Savings and investment in selected transition economies, 1993–1998	168
8.3	Interest spreads in selected transition economies, 1992–1998	176
8.4	Average interest spreads and annual inflation rate in selected countries from Central and South-East Europe, 1992–1998	177
9.1	Banking system in Albania, end of 1998	192
9.2	Banking products in Albania	193
9.3	Statutory ratios in Albania, 1994–1998	194
9.4	Balance sheet ratios and share of treasury bills in Albania, end of June 1999	194
9.5	Savings of citizens in Albania, 1994–1998	195
10.1	GDP of Bosnia and Herzegovina, 1995-1998	209

10.2	Banking system in Bosnia and Herzegovina, 1996–1999	211
10.3	Assets and demand deposits in the banking system of Bosnia and Herzegovina, 1997–1999	212
10.4	Bank loans and deposit rates in Bosnia and Herzegovina, 31 December 1998 and 30 September 1999	213
10.5	Money supply and foreign assets and liabilities in Bosnia and Herzegovina, 1997–1999	214
11.1	Basic economic indicators of Bulgaria, 1991–1999	221
11.2	Development of the banking system in Bulgaria, 1990–1999	224
11.3	Financial sector aggregates in Bulgaria, 1991–1999	226
11.4	Payments in Bulgaria handled by BISERA, 1993–1999	229
11.5	Credit portfolio of Bulgarian commercial banks, 1993–1999	233
11.6	Budget deficit and debt ratios in Bulgaria, 1991–1999	235
12.1	Main economic indicators of the Croatian economy, 1994–1999	242
12.2	Number of banks in Croatia, 1993–1999	246
12.3	Credit rates of Croatian banks,1993–1999	247
12.4	Savings of citizens in Croatia, 1994–1999	249
12.5	International reserves of the CNB and DMBs, 1993–1998	251
12.6	Classification of bank credit portfolios in Croatia, 1995–1998	255
12.7	Percentage of foreign assets in the nine largest Croatian banks, 1998 and 2000	257
13.1	Number of financial institutions in Macedonia, 1992–1999	263
13.2	Total assets of banks and the depth of the financial market in Macedonia, 1992–1998	267
13.3	Ownership structure of Macedonian banks as of 31 December 1999	269
13.4	Total deposits and savings of citizens in Macedonia, 1994–1999	270
13.5	Projected and achieved growth rates of inflation and money supply in Macedonia (in per cent, annually), 1992-1999	273
13.6	Bad-debt ratios for Macedonian banks, 1992–1999	277
13.7	Statutory ratios and Cook ratio in Macedonian banks, 1994–1999	278
14.1	Romania's GDP growth, 1990–1999	286
14.2	Inflation rate in Romania, 1990–1999	286
14.3	Romanian exchange rate ROL/USD, 1990–1999	286
14.4	Romanian government fiscal position, 1990–1999	287
14.5	Current account deficit in Romania, 1990–1999	287
14.6	Number of Romanian banks by type of capital, 1991–1999	290
14.7	Position held by state-owned banks in Romania, 1991–1998	291
14.8	Segmentation of the Romanian banking system as of	

	31 December 1998	292
14.9	Total assets in the Romanian banking system, 1991–1999	293
14.10	Household savings in Romania, 1994–1999	295
14.11	Bad-debt situation in Romania's banking system, 1994–1999	299
14.12	Standard banking products offered by Romanian banks	302
14.13	The scale of banking in the Romanian economy, 1992–1999	303
14.14	Developments of the key financial indicators in Romanian banks, 1998–1999	303
14.15	Sources of finance for real sector investments in Romania, 1994–1998	304
15.1	Yugoslavia's main economic indicators, 1994–1999	310
15.2	Banking products offered in Yugoslavia	314
15.3	Savings of citizens in Yugoslavia, 1994–1999	323
15.4	Statutory ratios in Yugoslav banks, 1994–1999	324

Figures

2.1	Private sector share in GDP, 1999	21
2.2	Transition indicators, 1999	23
2.3	Explaining recession: initial conditions and real GDP growth	26
2.4	Index of real GDP, 1989–1999	27
4.1	Corporate governance relationships	84
8.1	Average share of savings, investment and FDI to GDP in eight transition economies, 1992–1998	169
8.2	Institutional index and non-performing loans in 1998	172
8.3	Corporate governance index and the unofficial economy	174
9.1	M2 and M3 growth in Albania, December 1994 to October 1999	197
9.2	Short-term deposit interest rates in Albania, July 1992 to June 1999	198
9.3	The payments system in Albania	201
12.1	Money supply, deposit money and cash balances in Croatia, April 1994 to February 2000	252
12.2	Monetary aggregate M4 in Croatia, April 1994 to February 2000	253
13.1	Lending, deposit and interest rate spreads in Macedonia, 1995–1999	271
13.2	Money supply, exchange rate and rate of inflation in Macedonia, 1995–1999	274
14.1	Average interest for non-banking customers (1991–2000)	294
14.2	Average interest rate (1996–2000)	294
14.3	Average interest rate for interbank operations (1996–2000)	294
14.4	Growth rates of M1 and M2 monetary aggregates in Romania, 1990–2000	297
14.5	Key elements of the Romanian central bank's payments system	300
14.6	Real loan growth and bank capitalisation in Romania, 1991–1999	301
15.1	Relative weight of assets of Yugoslav banks and non-bank financial institutions, 1994–1999	314
15.2	Comparison of 'old' and 'new' Yugoslav banks in terms of assets, equity and profit	315
15.3	Placements of the NBY, 1994–1999	317

15.4 M1 and M2 annual growth in Yugoslavia, 1995–1999 319
15.5 Banks' interest rate margin in Yugoslavia, December 1998 to December 1999 325
15.6 Banks' liquidity rate in Yugoslavia, December 1997 to December 1999 326

Contributors

Fiqiri Baholli is currently Acting Director of the Public Relations Department. He holds a BSc degree in Economics from the University of Tirana and, since 1989, he has worked for the Bank of Albania (formerly the State Bank of Albania). He has published widely in leading Albanian professional and academic journals, and prepared a number of policy-oriented publications for the Bank of Albania. At the time of writing a chapter for this book Mr Baholli was the Director of the Monetary Policy Department in the Bank of Albania.

Gligor Bišev is the Managing Director of the Stopanska Banka in Skopje, Macedonia. Until September 2000 he was the Deputy Governor of the National Bank of the Republic of Macedonia, the institution in charge of the operation of banking supervision and monetary policy. He is also a Professor of Economics at the University of Skopje, Faculty of Economics. He has published a number of papers in Macedonian, Yugoslav and international journals, and attended both academic and professional courses in EU countries and the USA. Professor Bišev holds a BSc(Econ), an MSc(Econ) and a PhD(Econ) from the University of Skopje.

Guglielmo Maria Caporale is Professor of Economics and Finance and the Director of the Centre for Monetary and Financial Economics at South Bank University, London. Formerly he was a Research Officer at the National Institute of Economic and Social Research (NIESR) in London; a Research Fellow and then a Senior Research Fellow at the Centre for Economic Forecasting (CEF) at the London Business School (LBS); and Professor of Economics at the University of East London (UEL). He holds a *Laurea* from the University of Rome and an MSc and a PhD from the University of London – London School of Economics (LSE). He has written extensively on econometrics, macro modelling, macroeconomics and international finance.

Sonya Dilova-Kirkowa has recently completed her PhD thesis entitled 'Banking Reform in Transition Economies: The Case of Bulgaria' at the University of Birmingham Centre for Russian and Eastern European Studies. Her works have been published both in Bulgaria and abroad. She holds an MSc degree from Sofia University 'St. Kliment Ohridski', and prior to coming to the UK to pursue higher studies, she was with the Bulgarian government's Foreign

Investment Agency as a chief expert in the Projects Department.

Djordje Djukić is a Professor of Economics and Banking and Director of Postgraduate Studies in Monetary, Banking and Financial Management in the Faculty of Economics at the University of Belgrade. He is also a visiting professor in the Faculty of Economics at the University of Montenegro in Podgorica. He holds a BSc(Econ), an MSc(Econ) and a PhD(Econ) from the University of Belgrade. He was also a recipient of a Fulbright fellowship for postdoctoral study in monetary economics at Stanford University, USA (1988/89). Professor Djukić has published five books (two of which he has co-authored) and numerous articles in Yugoslav and international professional and academic journals. His main research interests lie in monetary theory and policy, banking, financial markets, inflation and anti-inflation policy theory and comparative finances.

Claudiu Doltu is a Senior Lecturer in Economics in the Economics and Economic Policy Department at the Academy of Economic Studies in Bucharest. He has published two books, one of which won the most outstanding economics book prize of the Romanian Academy of Sciences. He has also published widely in Romanian professional and academic journals. Dr Doltu writes in the popular press, on the performance of the Romanian economy and the financial system. He holds an MSc and a PhD from the Romanian Academy of Sciences. He is also the current Vice-President of the Romanian Institute for Human Studies, and he acts as a consultant for a number of international donor agencies including USAID, the World Bank and the United Nations Development Programme (UNDP).

Jelena Galić is a Research Associate at the Economics Institute in Belgrade. She has authored the book *Monetarna vlast u zemljama u tranziciji* [Monetary Authority in Countries in Transition], and has published a number of papers in Yugoslavia. She has also contributed to a number of international publications. She holds a BA and an MSc, both in Economics, from the University of Belgrade where she is currently studying for a PhD degree.

Kalin Hristov is a Teaching Assistant in the Department of Economics at the University of National and World Economy, Sofia, and an Expert in the Monetary and Analysis Division at the Bulgarian National Bank. He has published papers in many Bulgarian journals on macroeconomics, microeconomics, monetary economics, and the economics of transition. He holds an MSc in Economics from the University of National and World Economy in Sofia.

Radmila Jovančević is an Associate Professor of Macroeconomics and the Croatian Economy in the Faculty of Economics at the University of Zagreb. She has published widely in Croatian and Yugoslav professional and academic journals and acted as a consultant for the World Bank and Croatian Central Bureau of Statistics. She also advises the Croatian government on European issues. Dr Jovančević holds a BSc, an MSc and a PhD, all in Economics from the University of Zagreb. Recently her research interests have focused on the economics of the European Union, EU enlargement, international economic integration and competition and trade liberalisation.

Yoji Koyama is a Professor of Russian and East European Economies at Niigata University's Faculty of Economics. A graduate from the University of Tokyo, he was a visiting scholar in Belgrade from October 1978 to March 1980, under the Yugoslav government fellowship scheme. He is a leading Japanese specialist in East European Area Studies. He authored a seminal book (in Japanese) on the Yugoslav economic experience entitled: *Self-managing Socialism*: *Regime of the 1974 Constitution in the Former Yugoslavia*, Niigata University, 1995. He holds a BSc(IER) and a PhD in Economics from the University of Tokyo, a leading Japanese educational institution.

Mervyn K. Lewis is the National Australia Bank Professor of Banking and Finance in the School of International Business at the University of South Australia in Adelaide. Previously he was the Midland Bank Professor of Money and Banking at the University of Nottingham and Reader in Economics and Associate Dean at the University of Adelaide. He was elected a Fellow of the Academy of Social Sciences in Australia (FASSA) in 1986. He has written numerous papers for leading academic and professional journals and authored or edited more than thirteen books. Recently his research interests have focused on Islamic economics and finance and theory of monetary policy. He holds a BEc(Hons) and a PhD in Economics from the University of Adelaide. His book *Monetary Economics* (co-authored with Paul Mizen) was published in 2000, and represents a recent major work in monetary economics.

Jeffrey B. Miller is a Professor of Economics at the University of Delaware. Recently he has worked extensively on the Bulgarian economy and co-edited a book, *The Bulgarian Economy: Lessons from Reform during Early Transition* (with Derek Jones), Ashgate, 1997. He was an adviser to the Bulgarian National Bank and Director of the University of Delaware Coalition Project. Professor Miller also held visiting positions at many universities in the US and abroad, and was a Professor at the US Naval Academy in Annapolis. He holds a BA degree from Amherst College and MS and PhD degrees from the University of Pennsylvania.

Andy W. Mullineux is Professor of Money and Banking in the Department of Economics at the University of Birmingham, and served as Head of School of

Social Sciences from 1 August 1997 to 31 July 2000. He has written or edited 11 books and four more are at various stages of preparation. He has also published widely in refereed academic and professional journals. His expertise lies in the fields of business cycle theory, monetary policy, banking regulation and supervision and banking sector restructuring in Central and Eastern Europe and East and South-East Asia.

Nikolay Nenovsky is an Assistant Professor in Economics in the Department of Finance at the University of National and World Economy, Sofia, and the Head of the Monetary and Analysis Division at the Bulgarian National Bank. He has published extensively in Bulgaria and abroad. He holds Masters degrees in Economics from Moscow State University 'M. Lomonossov' and the University of Poitiers, a DEA in Economics from Nancy University and a PhD from the Institute of Economics at the Bulgarian Academy of Sciences. He was also a visiting scholar at Geneva University and the University of Paris I (Sorbonne-Panthéon).

Boris Petrov is currently a Research Analyst in the Monetary and Financial Analysis Division at the Bulgarian National Bank and a Teaching Assistant in the Department of Finance at the University of National and World Economy in Sofia. He has recently co-authored a book, *Bulgarian National Bank 1879–1999* (with R. Avramov, V. Dimitrov, L. Dimova, H. Yanovski and G. Vandalova). His research interests are in monetary economics, international finance, macroeconomics, the economics of transition and the theory of banking. He holds an MSc in Finance from the University of National and World Economy in Sofia.

Goran Pitić is currently the Minister of Foreign Economic Relations in the government of the Republic of Serbia. He also holds a Chair at the University of Belgrade where he teaches Economic History and Macroeconomic Theory. He is the past Director of the Centre for Economic Research at the Economics Institute in Belgrade, a leading Yugoslav economics think-tank, and former Senior Manager at Deloitte & Touche's Belgrade office. He holds a BSc(Econ), an MSc and a PhD from the University of Belgrade and an MA in Economics from the University of Toronto. Professor Pitić is a leading Yugoslav economist of the younger generation, with a vast experience of consulting assignments in both the private and public sector. He is also involved in building an alternative educational network in Serbia, and many other 'social outreach' projects.

Fabrizio Saccomanni is Central Director for International Affairs at the Bank of Italy and has served, since September 1999, as Chairman of the Working Table on Economic Reconstruction, Development and Co-operation of the Stability Pact for South-Eastern Europe. Mr Saccomanni holds a

Masters in Economics from Bocconi University (Milan) and has done postgraduate work in international economics at Princeton University. He was seconded by the Bank of Italy to the International Monetary Fund from 1970 to 1975 and currently represents the Bank of Italy in several international bodies, including the Economic and Financial Committee of the European Union, the International Relations Committee of the European Central Bank and the Committee on the Global Financial System of the Bank for International Settlements.

Davor Savin is a Professor of Economics at the University of Maribor (Slovenia) where he is the Director of the Banking and Finance Institute in the Faculty of Economics. He was a senior civil servant in charge of economic policy analysis and implementation in the Federal Assembly of the former Yugoslavia, where he was a Chief Economic Adviser to the President. He published widely in Yugoslav professional and academic journals prior to the dissolution of the country. He is Editor-in-Chief of a leading Slovenian economic journal *'Naše gospodarstvo/Our Economy'*, which under his editorship began publishing papers in English and German in addition to Slovenian. He was an adviser to the Slovenian government and the Slovenian central bank, as well as a number of other countries in the region. Professor Savin holds a BSc, an MSc and a PhD, all in Economics, from the University of Belgrade.

Aleksandar Šević is a Research Fellow in the Economics Institute in Belgrade, a leading Yugoslav institution for economic research. He holds a BSc(Hon) in Economics, *summa cum laude*, from the University of Belgrade and an MA in International (Economic) Development from the International University of Japan. Currently he is a doctoral candidate in the Nanyang Business School at Nanyang Technological University in Singapore. He has been a consultant to many public and private organisations in Yugoslavia, usually acting as an academic secretary to various project teams. His papers have been published in both Yugoslav and international journals and his monograph '*Thailand's FDI Policy and its Impact on the Development of SMEs*' was published by the Balkan Centre for Public Policy and Related Studies in 1999.

Željko Šević, the editor of this book, is a Principal Lecturer in Accounting and Finance and the Head of the Accounting and Finance Department in the University of Greenwich Business School, where he teaches a wide range of postgraduate courses in accounting and finance. He holds an LLB(Hons), an LLM, an MSc and an SJD (all *summa cum laude*) from the University of Belgrade and a PhD(FinEcon) from the University of Dundee. To date he has published more than fifty papers and two books in Serbo-Croatian. Dr Šević also gained experience working in the public service and private sector, before becoming a full-time academic. His strategic research interests are focused on a wide range of subjects including, among others, bank and financial management, organisational accounting and finance, law and economics, public administration/public policy and public sector finance and accounting. Dr Šević is also a Recurrent Visiting Professor of Accounting, Finance and Public Policy in the European Centre for Peace and Development (ECPD) of the University for Peace established by the United Nations.

Amika Stavri is an independent consultant based in Canada. Until recently she was the Division Chief of the Monetary Programming and Analysis Division in the Monetary Policy Department at the Bank of Albania. She holds a BSc in Economics from the University of Tirana and an MBA jointly offered by the University of Lincoln, Nebraska and the University of Tirana. She has prepared a number of analytical studies for the Bank of Albania and many international donor agencies.

Jean Tesche is a Senior Tax Adviser with the US Treasury, based in Budapest. She was a Resident Tax Adviser to the Croatian Minister of Finance through a US Treasury International Technical Assistance Program, following her mission in Sarajevo in a similar capacity as a Resident Adviser in the Federal Ministry of Finance of Bosnia and Herzegovina in Sarajevo from 1996 to 2000. In addition to providing assistance in Croatia, she has provided tax policy and technical assistance in Slovenia, Macedonia, Montenegro, Kosovo, Bulgaria, Romania and both ethnic entities in Bosnia and Herzegovina (the Bosnian Federation and Republika Srpska). Dr Tesche taught at Emory University, Economics Department, from 1988 to 1995, prior to joining the US Treasury. She holds a BA in Russian from the University of Oregon and an MBA and a PhD in Economics from Columbia University in New York.

Preface and Acknowledgements

This book is the final result of a project undertaken to examine changes that have occurred in the banking sectors of the South-East European transitional economies since late 1998. The project was initiated by the University of Greenwich Business School (Accounting and Finance Subject Group, at the time), the Balkan Centre for Public Policy and Related Studies, and the Humanities Research Centre from Sofia, and commenced with a conference, 'Banking Reform in South-East European Transitional Economies', held in Sofia in June 1999. The conference was funded by a World Bank conference grant though the Economic Institute/Centre for Economic Research and Graduate Education (EI/CERGE), following public competition. After the conference, the participants agreed to form an *ad hoc* research group and to prepare a number of country studies and technical papers related to vital issues in the banking system reform in the transition countries of South-East Europe.

The chapters were finalised during 1999 and 2000 and their ultimate versions are published in this book. In terms of legal regulations and quantitative data, the chapters depict the real and true situation as it was in mid to late 2000. All the contributors and the project director/book editor are very grateful to the World Bank Group and EI/CERGE for their generous support, which allowed the implementation of this valuable project, and Edward Elgar for agreeing to publish this book. It was a pleasure to co-operate first with Dymphna Evans, and later with Francine O'Sullivan and Alex Minton as commissioning editors. Susan Hammant, and later Suzanne Mursell did a very good job as copy editors, working on many versions of this book. Their editorial support proved to be invaluable, and they have contributed greatly to the final layout of this book.

The editor would like to thank Mrs Annette Bowen who painstakingly checked the manuscripts, and did her best to improve the quality of the written word. Mrs Barbara Green also assisted with the proof-reading of many versions of the chapters. Mrs Azlina Mohamed Noor Beg assisted in formatting the book and proof-reading the drafts, and deserves credit for the final layout. Dr Guglielmo M. Volpe of the University of North London provided advanced computer support and helped in formatting complex tables and figures. Professor David M. Kemme, of the University of Memphis, looked critically at the final manuscript and provided invaluable comments that have contributed significantly to the overall quality of the book. My colleagues, Ronald P. McIver and John O. Smullen, have helped me greatly with editing the language.

Last but not least, the final version of the book was produced by Miss Jelena Zekić who visited the Accounting and Finance Department from September 2001 to April 2002 as a Chevening Visiting Fellow. Jelena painstakingly typed in all corrections suggested by the anonymous referees and various copy editors. The final layout of this book goes, to a large extent, to her credit. Edouard Mambu ma Khenzu, a PhD student working with the Editor, checked references and consistency of referencing throughout this book, with the persistence of an experienced senior civil servant (as Edouard has occupied important positions in many Zairian governments since the mid 1960s).

Series editor Professor Mervyn K. Lewis helped with a number of useful comments and guidance which certainly shaped the book. The editor is sure that all contributors will join him in thanking Mervyn for his invaluable assistance – and patience. All involved learned a lot from Mervyn during these three years.

Thanks also go to all in-country referees who reviewed the chapters and pointed out areas for improvement, as well as to those referees who worked for Edward Elgar in assessing the suitability of text topics and the conclusions reached. All these people, although by definition anonymous, have built a great deal of themselves into this book. As a collective effort, all good points should be attributed both as a group and individually to the authors, while the editor accepts sole responsibility for all the shortcomings. His great hope is that all his future enterprises will show continuous improvement.

1. Assessing the Banking Reforms in South-East Europe

Željko Šević

The Balkan peninsula has long been a border between different cultures, empires, religions and so on. The feature was both a blessing and a curse. The former because it enabled the region to develop a very specific mix of different cultures, social attitudes, social values and organisational patterns, and the latter because armed conflicts are the rule rather than the exception in this area. Because of its unique position, the Balkans demonstrated a greater variety of political, social and economic systems than any other region of a similar size. However, following the dissolution of the former Yugoslav Federation, some of the countries that have emerged are not, technically speaking, in the Balkans. Slovenia is now regarded as a Central European country, while the Croatians are dissatisfied that Croatia is placed in the group of Balkan countries. In part in response to the break-up of the former Yugoslav Federation, a more fashionable term 'South-East European countries' has emerged in the 1990s, covering the Balkan states (plus Slovenia).[1]

The South-East European (SEE) region includes, besides the republics of the former Yugoslavia (Bosnia and Herzegovina, Croatia, Macedonia, Montenegro and Serbia, two of which, Serbia and Montenegro, form the *new* Federal Republic of Yugoslavia), Albania, Bulgaria, Greece, Romania and Turkey. Greece and Turkey are two medium-developed market(-oriented) economies, Greece even being a member of the European Union (EU), while both countries are members of the North Atlantic Treaty Organisation (NATO) defence alliance. All the other SEE countries are transitional economies, subject to a painful process of economic and social transformation. All these countries (with the exception of Greece and Turkey, which are not included in this study), were so-called socialist economies. Nevertheless, there have been far too many differences among them for them to be analysed as a single unit.

Throughout its socialist period, Albania was subjected to the single will of a dictator (first Enver Hoxha and then his successors), relatively isolated until the 1990s and at odds even with other socialist countries, denouncing them as revisionist and 'quasi-capitalist'. The poorest country in Europe alternated between an elected position of self-isolation and short periods of co-operation, first with the Russians and then with the Chinese. Finally, a decade before the collapse of the socialist regime, it was in chosen self-isolation, with many citizens fleeing the country, mostly to inhabit the border areas of the southern Serbian province of Kosmet (Kosovo and Metohija). Little news was heard from or about Albania until the fall of Communism and the increasing civil unrest in the first half of the 1990s, followed by an armed rebellion in 1997, provoked by the failure of the so-called 'pyramid schemes', operated by some of the savings banks. Until the very end of their rule, Albania's communists continued to impose the most orthodox communist system and the classic Stalinist economic blueprint. Agriculture, traditionally the dominant branch of the Albanian economy, was literally destroyed during the communist period, and failed to produce any surpluses. Collectivisation, although undertaken early in the process of building a socialist society, was not a success. Despite negative trends no reform attempts were made to improve the overall situation, in contrast to all other socialist countries which, on a regular basis, tried to improve and strengthen the socialist system (although no attempt was made to change its intrinsic nature: the property rights system and high centralisation, which required the serious limitation of social and personal initiative and freedom).

Bulgaria was, according to many, the closest Soviet ally, and embraced the classic Soviet blueprint. Many reforms introduced in other socialist countries in the 1960s and 1970s completely bypassed Bulgaria, which utilised a classic command economy concept until the early 1990s. Its close relationship with the Soviet Union had its roots in the historically good relations it had enjoyed with tsarist Russia. Russia saw Bulgaria as a key factor for its presence and influence in the Balkans, and Bulgaria maintained that position throughout the socialist period. An additional problem for Bulgaria was its long-standing leader (Todor Zhivkov), who towards the end of his rule lost any semblance of reality, and was the main obstacle to any kind of much-needed reform.

Romania, in contrast, had a fairly unique position within the 'community of socialist states' comparable, to some extent, to the French position within NATO. Romania had, at first sight, an independent foreign policy, with no Russian troops on its territories, yet it also had a unique political system with a classic dictatorship at its core. Nicolae Ceauşescu and his family were incontestable rulers of the country, who advocated a policy of no foreign debt and, to a great extent, an autarchic economic policy. Of course, such an isolationist policy had huge negative effects on the living standards of the population, and adversely affected the country's growth prospects. Finally, at the end of the 1980s there was a shortage of all consumer goods, which was an instrumental factor in the serious civil unrest in 1987, and the demise of the Ceauşescu regime.

The former Socialist Federal Republic of Yugoslavia saw itself unequivocally as a socialist country, positioned somewhere between West and East. Theoretically, it built a kind of socialism that was different from that of other socialist countries. People enjoyed many freedoms, such as the freedom of movement and employment mobility. The control over the social life of citizens was negligible compared to a classic socialist blueprint. The economic sphere was subject to vast decentralisation and the presence of a 'self-management concept', in which workers were *de jure* able to exercise decision-making rights. Although, theoretically, this was a well-established concept, in practice it did not work because of an unsustainable legal framework and the lack of strong political will to sustain any changes. The socialist rulers saw the danger of opening up the economy and introducing full market relationships among economic agents, realising that with the introduction of market forces they would lose their dominant social position, which was based on a system of immense discretionary power. However, the obstruction of the establishment ('nomenclature') of the full market relationship was accomplished through the segmentation of the market (which is not inherently a bad thing) and the devolution of the federal state (Djurić, 1971a; 1971b).[2] The republics took over most of the original functions of the state, while the Federation became a forum for the reconciliation of regularly emerging adversarial positions (Šević, 1996b). In most cases, a unanimous vote was required for the adoption of a law or policy measure and this led eventually to the disintegration of the country. Instead of continuing with the real market reforms initiated in 1987, Yugoslavia became immersed in a civil war, which lasted for almost five years. Even now, the whole territory of the former Yugoslavia (with the notable exception of Slovenia) is regarded as a high-risk and unstable area. Perceptions, however, may change in the near future following the change of government in Belgrade in October 2000, when the Serbian leader Slobodan Milošević who had been unchallenged for more than a decade was replaced by Dr Vojislav Koštunica. Koštunica has a reputation for being a 'moderate nationalist', but is also a firm advocate of democracy and 'participative public policy' practices.

Thus, there are many differences in the *modus operandi* of SEE countries, but when it comes to a quantitative analysis of their performance they are fairly similar, or even 'convergent' with one another. Slovenia, again, is an exception, being the richest of all the former socialist countries, with an economic structure comparable to a median EU member country (for example, the Netherlands (Šević, 1997)).

The banking system must reflect its wider environment (see Šević, 1999). In all countries, except the republics of the former Yugoslavia, a classic one-tier, monobank system was in place. At the core of the system was the State Bank, which was at the same time the central monetary authority and a large commercial banking conglomerate. There were also other banks, but they were of no importance to households and citizens, as they served certain branches of the economy exclusively. Nevertheless, *stricto lege*, those few banks that existed under socialism could not really be called 'banks', as they operated only as adjuncts of the State Bank. All monetary flows were initiated by the State Bank, and would end in the State Bank. Money in a classic socialist financial system had predominantly an accounting role; credits were granted automatically as required, with the State Bank controlling the whole financial system (Šević, 1999). From the very beginning of the transition process, banking reform was somewhat neglected. It was the general belief that the real sector should be restructured first and only then would the issues of financial system reform be addressed (for example, see Blanchard et al., 1990; Fischer and Gelb, 1990, 1991; Hinds, 1990a 1990b; Calvo and Frenkel, 1991),[3] although there were exceptions to this main approach (see van Wijnbergen, 1994). However, the initial move was really made at the very outset of transition. The State Bank was relieved of its commercial banking functions and retained only its central banking functions. This structural reorganisation occurred in 1987, in most CEE countries. Parts of the State Bank which operated with (externally assigned) 'clients' from the real sector of the economy became independent banks, although they were still state owned. Retaining only monetary policy and banking supervisory duties, the State Bank was soon renamed the central bank, national bank, or the bank of a particular country (for instance, Bank of Albania). Since all the Balkan countries, except Yugoslavia, were unique states, this task was not particularly difficult in purely technical terms. The case of the former socialist Yugoslavia differed significantly, as expected.

Yugoslavia introduced a two-tier banking system in the mid 1960s as part of a very ambitious economic reform project, which aimed to open up Yugoslavia and its economy to the international market. Yugoslav citizens were able to travel abroad without any restrictions, go to work outside the country, and transfer their income to and from the country, with virtually no limitation. Private foreign exchange accounts that paid some interest in the deposit currency were allowed. Simultaneously with the establishment of a two-tier banking system, the interbank market was introduced, followed by the opening of a foreign exchange market in the early 1970s. On a political level, overall decentralisation was introduced. However, the process of decentralisation of the economy unfortunately precipitated the disintegration of the country. The achievements of the previous socialist reform, begun in 1987, did not last long, as the former socialist Yugoslavia disintegrated in the flames of civil war. One of the many irrational decentralisation actions taken was the creation of the system of central banks headed by the National Bank of Yugoslavia (NBY). The Yugoslav system of central banks was very ineffective as the NBY was merely *primus inter pares*. The bank could not enforce any of its decisions, as the republican/provincial central banks were in fact accountable only to the respective republican/provincial parliaments (Šević, 1995a). Therefore, when their independence was declared, the former Yugoslav republics simply promulgated their 'national banks' into newly independent central banks, either changing the name (Slovenia) or even without any name change (all other republics, except Bosnia and Herzegovina). In Bosnia and Herzegovina the Law on Central Banks was imposed externally, following the Dayton Peace Agreement of 1995 (see Tesche in this volume), and the central monetary authority is called the Central Bank of Bosnia and Herzegovina (CBBH).

Nevertheless, despite all these differences, there is a shared experience with the banking reform in the SEE transitional economies. It differs from the countries of Central Europe, which opted for significantly different models. With the exception of Slovenia, all SEE countries are in the early-to-middle stages of transition, with many macroeconomic imbalances yet to be tackled by the policy formulators. Even Slovenia, according to some analysts (EBRD, 1997, 1999), will have to speed up the privatisation process in order to be recognised as a true 'advanced transitional economy'. Starting from 1996–97, the SEE countries began the ambitious process of ownership transformation in the banking sector. But, despite the emergence of new banking entities, there is still much to be done in the old banks. State-owned banks still experience the problem of deficits in their balance sheets which contain a considerable proportion of bad debts. Proposals by some scholars to cancel all bank credits at the beginning of transition (for example, see Mayer and Vives, 1993) were not accepted, and different approaches to the cleaning of the balance sheet were put forward and finally applied. Djukić in this volume analyses the pros and cons of different approaches (centralised versus decentralised) to banking rehabilitation. The experience of more-advanced transitional economies (Hungary, Poland, the Czech Republic) demonstrates that both models can be equally successful, but that their combination probably gives the best results (as demonstrated by Dilova-Kirkowa and Mullineux in this volume).

The centralised approach has shown in its shortcomings the presence of increased moral hazard and adverse selection problems. The authorities in Hungary were forced to intervene three times over a short period to maintain systemic stability and, after each intervention, an injection of public money was required. A noticeable proportion of newly granted credits become new bad debts. The Polish decentralised approach required very pro-active behaviour on the part of the banks, and their involvement in the reconstruction of enterprises. The banks were recapitalised before they were required to deal with their bad debts. After the successful recapitalisation, they had to create a new department that would work on the liquidation of bad debts (the so-called 'workout' units).

Interestingly enough, the Polish model even allowed the banks some of the prerogatives of the courts, allowing them to effectively initiate the corporate restructuring of their respective debtors. The Estonian approach was fairly straightforward, but was applicable only in a relatively small country. Estonia emphasised 'close supervision' after some banks went bankrupt. Different parts of society bore the costs of the banks' bankruptcy, but in order to preserve respect for the financial system, the Estonian authorities were forced to provide effective and efficient banking supervision and close 'bad banks'. Although it is difficult to imagine the Estonian approach being applied anywhere in the Balkans, in fact it seems that Romania has recently (late 2000) opted for this approach (see Doltu in this volume). It is hoped that this will not create huge social unrest, as it did in Albania after the failure of a credit co-operative that set up a pyramid savings scheme. The Albanian situation in March–August 1997 has shown what can happen when there is a systemic failure and there are many, simultaneous large-scale bankruptcies (see *Vreme*, 10 May 1997). Financial system instability can eventually lead to government failure. Consequently, a state of lawlessness may prevail, at least for a while.

All SEE transitional economies have a bank-based financial system (Šević, 1996c, 2000a), which means that banks are dominant financial institutions and financial markets play only a supplementary role in the economy. Banks are at the core of the financial system, extending into all aspects of the real economy, financing expansion and growth (Cameron, 1992). The SEE countries consequently opted for a model of the universal bank, although according to the law in all of the countries, banks cannot be involved in the securities business directly, but only through a separate subsidiary. Banks are usually organised as a group, with a number of subsidiary companies attached to the core bank. Consistent with the German model, banks are heavily involved in corporate governance, maintaining a close relationship with the enterprises which are, at the same time, the banks' debtors. Most of the information obtained in a bank-based financial system is the result of this close relationship and may even be regarded as insider information (see Macey, 1991). However, in the existing financial system, financial markets are also necessary as they provide better information efficiency than banks (Šević, 2000a). It has been demonstrated that financial markets are becoming more important in raising capital (Mayer and Vives, 1993). Although regarded as more expensive than bank finance, market finance is attractive to a growing number of young entrepreneurs.

One of the main improvements that is urgently required in the national banking sector is privatisation. It is generally believed that state ownership is not efficient and therefore should be replaced, in full, by private ownership (see Šević, 1995b). This trend has recently started in many Balkan economies. In a classic Western market economy, banks are controlled by supervisory authorities, depositors and owners. Each of these players has their own agenda in mind. Supervisory authorities serve to protect the general public and its belief in the stability of the financial system. Depositors are concerned with the interest rate offered, the stability of the bank and the soundness of management, while the owners are interested in profitability, performance in the long run, and the sustainable stability of the institution. It is assumed that privatisation is socially beneficial and that it increases efficiency (Veljanovski, 1987), but it is difficult to find empirical proof (Davies, 1981). However, from a supervisor's point of view, privatisation delivers. In the case of private ownership, supervisors are there to protect depositors, while in the case of widely based public ownership they ought to protect depositors and the owner equally, that is, the state (government in Anglo-American political terminology), especially in the early years of transition. Despite a priori best intentions, it is impossible for a bank to be unbiased towards the state, and the state will always have priority. In fact, banking supervision will, within that framework, become a kind of state audit institution, preventing mismanagement of the banks for the benefit of the state, rather than the depositors. Also, it is easier to supervise private than state-owned banks. In the latter case, some kind of state interest usually emerges and supervisors may be politically required to tolerate a certain situation temporarily.

The central bank operating in a predominantly privately owned financial system can achieve its *operational independence* more easily (Šević, 1996a; 1999). The purpose of lender of last resort is not to save a particular failed bank, but to preserve confidence in the financial system (Šević, 1996a). If banks in the financial system are predominantly state owned, then the institution of temporary financial support changes its nature. The political factor becomes prevalent in deciding whether or not to save a certain institution. Despite the long-announced privatisation schemes, little has been done so far and it is evident that the privatisation of banks, and other financial institutions, is overdue in SEE transitional economies. Romania has plans for a complete and rapid privatisation of its financial institutions. In other countries, some stakes in banks have been sold to foreign or international strategic investors, mainly the European Bank for Reconstruction and Development (EBRD). In Yugoslavia, a number of foreign banks have had representative offices and branches since the 1970s, and some of these have continued to operate inside Yugoslavia in spite of international sanctions against the country (1992–2000). Even in Slovenia, the privatisation of banks is a very slow process.

A banking system in the early stages of transition usually faces a few particular problems. First of all, a significant proportion of loans are 'bad' or non-performing loans. Second, banks operate at excessively high intermediation spreads and lending rates, which can be seen as a consequence of a significant proportion of bad debts in each institution's balance sheet. Third, despite an increase in the number of privately owned newly created banks, real competition does not exist, because of the huge credit potential of 'old' (state-owned) banks and negligible credit abilities of small new banks. Fourth, the supervisory and deposit insurance systems are new and fragile, incapable of preventing fraudulent behaviour. Fifth, for some time the market will be highly concentrated (see Šević, 1999). Usually up to ten of the largest banks account for up to 80, or even 90, per cent of the entire national banking sector. In SEE transitional economies, the number of incorporated banks blossomed, together with the separation of the former central bank entities, into a number of independent banks (Bulgaria and Romania). In the former Yugoslav republics, the single, largest commercial bank that dominated the banking scene before the break-up of the former socialist Yugoslavia still dominates today in each respective republic. The situation is again somewhat different in Slovenia, where 'old' banks changed their name in order to avoid responsibility for the liabilities to entities based in other former Yugoslav republics.[4] However, all the liabilities to London Club[5] members were taken over by newly created banking entities.

The banking systems in SEE countries are not internationally competitive in terms of product variety, soundness and aggregate costs. Financial restructuring, which is usually stressed in analytical materials published in these countries, will have to be accompanied by organisational and strategic restructuring (Petrović, 1992). Although there are a number of foreign-owned banks in the Balkan countries, there is still a need to open up the sector to more intense foreign competition. Allowing the creation of foreign branches should reduce bureaucratic procedures in discharging banking deals, and increase competition within the domestic banking sector. Since all these countries have a large number of small banks in the banking system, increased international competition will certainly lead to rationalisation among small banks. The privatisation process must be re-initiated and its implementation should be rapid. The first target should be large banks, as they dominate the system, and their privatisation would spur that of other banks. However, experience in more-advanced transitional economies has shown that this process must be fully transparent and public scandals should be avoided at all cost. If any manipulation in the privatisation process is observed, it can endanger both a country's credit rating outside the country and public confidence in the financial system inside the country – and this is a very high price for the public to pay unnecessarily. The inclusion of one or even several strategic foreign investors improves corporate governance and is strongly recommended. The sale of state-owned banks for cash would help to balance public finance and to reduce public debt. Inclusion of foreign partners also supports the global integration processes as foreign banks bring expertise and higher standards to the domestic banking sector.

The interbank agreement on the maximum deposit interest rate that exists in most of these countries should be abolished as soon as possible. This kind of cartel behaviour is not compatible with the need to strengthen competition in the domestic banking market (Šević and Šević, 1998). Competition in deposit rates and in the credit market is instrumental in forcing banks to identify their areas of comparative advantage and to increase efficiency. An often neglected aspect of banking reform in the SEE countries is internal micro-restructuring in the banking system. Banks alone should analyse the market and offer new products and services. Internal restructuring requires a significant change in the way the bank operates, leading to increased profitability, a reduction of operating costs and an expansion in the range of activities from classic services to more sophisticated products and services in other areas. This requires significant policy changes within the bank, personnel changes including a reduction in the number of employees, the introduction of internal training programmes for those who remain with the bank and so on.

Bank mergers are to be expected as they sustain a consolidation of the banking sector. Small banks will either disappear or merge with larger and more successful banks. It is also possible that a number of small banks will merge and create a new, more successful and larger bank. Problems experienced by small banks can also be tackled in a more traditional way – through regulatory capture. Regulations can enforce divestment by existing state-owned entities, and encourage amalgamation by a tightening of licensing requirements (Rostowski, 1995) and an insistence on quick privatisation by the current owners of small banks.

At the macro level, the government must provide a sound macroeconomic framework. It is very difficult to plan anything in a constantly changing environment and SEE economies do not have a stable economic environment (see Savin in this volume). In the early years of transition, the excuse that macroeconomic instability is inherent to the transition process cannot hold when transition is in full swing. Therefore, governmental policy and measures must provide a good environment for business and enable full protection of lenders and depositors. Good and sound management decisions within a bank or the entire banking sector must be supported by policy measures such as the creation of a sound legal framework and a state that is effective in the implementation of adopted laws and regulations. Effective legal enforcement is still lacking in the SEE transitional economies. An increase in corruption also undermines achievements of legal reform, and threatens to reduce the countries' international credit ratings. Foreign investors may still have to be very cautious when working, or contemplating an investment, in these transitional economies.

Many argue that the introduction of a new deposit guarantee scheme is also of the utmost importance. There are various possibilities as to how to achieve this. One is to create a state fund, which most of the countries do not envisage in the future. Another is that only the banks should create a deposit guarantee fund and, if this is done, then it should improve the degree of competitive neutrality in the banking system. Third possibility is, for instance, embodied in Yugoslav law, whereby banks can *de jure* entrust this job to a private insurance company. However, currently, the deposits are guaranteed by the state, implicitly or explicitly. In the case of state-owned banks, the Treasury's responsibility is clearly assumed in all the countries. The failures of private banks (Yugoslavia, Romania) and savings schemes (Albania) have demonstrated that poor countries cannot guarantee the deposits effectively. After the bankruptcy of Dafiment Banka and Jugoskandik in Yugoslavia,[6] the Federal government did not reimburse the losses of small depositors. In contrast, some powerful public figures used their social influence to help themselves and their friends. In Albania, the huge losses of small depositors led to social unrest, governmental failure and foreign intervention to preserve some kind of social order (early 1997). But, despite these actions, the Albanian government did not succeed in securing effective power in the north of the country, where armed gangs roam the area. The experience with these failures has shown that supervision was mainly inadequate, and failed to provide timely detection not only of mismanagement, but also of the fraudulent behaviour of those who were entrusted with the duty of protecting the public interests.

Most if not all of the SEE transitional countries are hoping to join the European Union in the years to come. Therefore it is necessary to bring national legislation into line with EU requirements. Legal regulations have to be in line with the Capital Adequacy Directive, the Large Exposure Directive, the Directive on Supervision of Credit Institutions on a Consolidated Basis, the Directive on Annual Accounts and the Directive on Consolidated Accounts of Credit Institutions and Other Financial Institutions. A sound legal framework is a main prerequisite for the inclusion of the domestic banking sector into wider international markets. However, as many note (see Šević, 2003) the major problem of late transition starters is a huge discrepancy between 'legal system' (prescribed legal rules) and 'legal order' (that is, social behaviour under these rules). And, until this discrepancy is fully addressed it is difficult to talk about the rule of law and the legal protection of anybody's interests.

In this volume, the authors analyse a number of issues applied to their respective countries, or provide an expert's outside view of the process of banking transition in SEE transitional economies. The book is organised into two parts. Part One is devoted to general and theoretical issues, while in Part Two, a number of country studies are presented. In Chapter 2, Savin analyses the macroeconomic prerequisites for successful monetary policy implementation in transitional countries with particular attention being paid to Balkan economies and Slovenia. Savin gives an extensive overview of the economic transition process in CEE countries as a whole, and SEE transitional countries in particular. This is followed by a contribution by Saccomanni (Chapter 3), co-ordinator of the Stability Pact's economic roundtable, who gives an account of recent developments with the pact and what its influence may be on the course of future developments in South-East Europe.

In Chapter 4, Lewis analyses different types of governance structures, and gives a broad framework within which the corporate governance system in a particular country can be studied. In Chapter 5, Šević further analyses institutional developments and the law and finance framework for the operation of central banks in SEE transitional economies, focusing on their legal framework and current efficiency level. This is followed by another contribution by Lewis (Chapter 6), which looks at the viability of currency board arrangements (CBAs) in transitional economies. The Balkans have recently been very prone to CBAs, with two countries (Bosnia and Herzegovina, and Bulgaria) and two dependent territories (Kosovo and Montenegro) opting to introduce some kind of a currency board. However, it is not clear whether the current arrangements are really currency boards, or a clear case of 'dollarisation' ('euroisation').

In Chapter 7, Djukić discusses different models of bank consolidation and rehabilitation, examining the differences between centralised and decentralised approaches. He supports the application of some kind of eclectic approach, which may give the best results. Dilova-Kirkowa and Mullineux (Chapter 8) compare the experiences of the *more*-advanced transitional economies with the Balkans' banking experience, drawing some very interesting conclusions, with many policy recommendations to be followed.

Part Two of this volume begins with a contribution by Baholli and Stavri (Chapter 9) who analyse recent developments in the Albanian banking sector. They give a comprehensive account of the current situation, paying particular attention to payments system development, which is one of the burning problems facing Albanian banking. This is followed by a contribution by Tesche (Chapter 10), who details the events that led to the Dayton Peace Agreement and the creation of a new, modern central bank in Bosnia and Herzegovina. Tesche considers both ethnic entities, and presents developments in both the Croat–Muslim Federation and the Serb Republika Srpska.

In Chapter 11, Caporale, Hristov, Miller, Nenovsky and Petrov look at the overall performance of the Bulgarian banking sector, and the performance of the Bulgarian Monetary Board between 1997 and 2000, and provide us with a few guidelines for the future development in Bulgarian banking. Jovančević (Chapter 12) looks at the macroeconomic conditions in the Croatian economy to determine their influence in the reform processes in Croatian banking. In Chapter 13, Bišev gives an outline of the current situation in the Macedonian banking system, and points out where there is room for improvement. Building on the inherited foundations of the former Yugoslavia, the Macedonian banking system has achieved an admirable level of stability, although there is still much work to be done on the promotion of competitiveness, and the introduction of 'customer-focused' banking. In Chapter 14, Doltu analyses the most recent developments in Romanian banking, looking at the structure and performance of the changing financial institutions in Romania. The country studies' analysis concludes with an account of the current situation in the Yugoslav banking sector. Koyama, Pitić, Galić and Šević (Chapter 15) present a study of the Yugoslav banking sector and its performance with regard to the wider macroeconomic framework, concluding that real banking reform in Yugoslavia is still to be introduced. They argue that an eclectic approach to banking reform can yield the best results in Yugoslavia due to the country's specific situation.

This book provides a comprehensive assessment and review of recent developments in the banking sector in all SEE countries. It makes a series of policy recommendations as to how to improve the existing banking sector, increase its internal and international competitiveness, structure, efficiency and reduce the costs to customers. SEE transitional economies are still some way from a smoothly operating and stable banking system, but it is evident that in a few years this aim could be achieved if events do not take an unexpected course. There is still much to be done with the privatisation of banking entities, and certainly this is the most important task to be addressed in the near future. Many of the current problems will be solved if privatisation in the banking sector is introduced successfully. However, this is something that will have to be carefully observed, as many of the SEE countries see banking privatisation as an undermining of national sovereignty. This is a political issue that must remain outside the remit of our study, which is confined largely to economic dimensions. In economic terms, macroeconomic stability in most of the SEE countries must be achieved to deliver and sustain the creation of a stable and competitive banking environment. This is expected but, as is usual for the Balkans, not many would be ready to take a bet ... and nor are we.

NOTES

1. It is very difficult to define 'Central Europe'. Before the fall of Communism, Central European countries were East Germany, Poland, Czechoslovakia, Hungary, Romania and Bulgaria (*The Economist*, 2000). However, with the major political changes the situation has changed. Today Central European countries are Poland, the Czech Republic, Slovakia, Hungary and Slovenia. However, some German scholars would claim that Germany and Austria are also part of Central Europe, that is, they are Central European countries. For this group of countries, including Germany and former Austro-Hungarian Empire territories, now independent states, the historical term was *Mitteleuropa*. However, it seems that some political forces would rather forget the concept for the sake of a new European unity (*The Economist*, 2000).
2. Professor Djurić was a leading Yugoslav legal philosopher and Professor of Legal Theory in the Faculty of Law at the University of Belgrade. After the publication of these two articles he was arrested, tried and imprisoned for two years, for 'causing public unrest'. The relevant issue of the *Annals of the Faculty of Law*, a leading Yugoslav journal, was banned, confiscated and destroyed. A number of other professors were arrested, imprisoned or banned from teaching ('contact with students'). Professor Djurić's texts now read like a prophecy, as he clearly envisaged the break-up of the Socialist Federal Republic of Yugoslavia, and ethnic conflict (see Šević, 2002).
3. For a more detailed account of the relevant literature, see Šević (1999).
4. Ljubljanska banka changed its name to Nova Ljubljanska banka [New Ljubljana Bank] in order to avoid claims from the foreign exchange deposit account holders, who had opened accounts in the former Yugoslav Federation, and whose accounts were *de jure* insured by the National Bank of Yugoslavia. However, it seems that the NBY was a lead insurer on behalf of the system of central banks of the socialist republics and socialist autonomous provinces, acting as an undisclosed agent. It would be a very interesting issue to examine

the sole legal responsibility of the Yugoslav central bank, as this kind of responsibility could be faced by the European Central Bank acting on behalf of the European System of Central Banks.

5. 'London Club' is a term that denotes a group of commercial banks that granted credits to the former Socialist Federal Republic of Yugoslavia (SFRY). In contrast, the Paris Club refers to foreign governments that granted credits to SFRY.
6. Jugoskandik Ltd and Dafiment Banka Ltd in the Federal Republic of Yugoslavia (Serbia and Montenegro) were two banks that defrauded a large number of people in the mid-1990s in Yugoslavia. These two privately owned banks offered interest rates of 15 per cent per month for hard currency, in the period from 1992 to 1994. But, in 1994 both of them went bankrupt, and a number of small depositors suffered losses. Although, according to the law, the National Bank of Yugoslavia (that is, the Federation) guaranteed deposits, no action was taken and losses were not recovered. The amount that was left after bankruptcy was declared could cover only about 10 per cent of all deposits. But, it is more interesting to note how the relevant authorities did not take appropriate action. Jugoskandik was registered as a savings bank, and did not have a licence to accept foreign currency deposits. Later on it appeared that it had a 'franchise' for this kind of activity from the Bank of Private Economy [Banka privatne privrede] which was registered in Podgorica (Montenegro). Not long afterwards, the Bank of Private Economy also went bankrupt. But even four years after the scandal, a number of questions remain unanswered and a large number of small depositors have not been compensated. It is even unclear why the banking supervision inspectors did not spot irregularities in the course of their regular controlling visits. Finally, it was concluded that the scandal might involve a number of current politicians, and therefore everything necessary was done to hush it up (see Šević, 1999).

BIBLIOGRAPHY

Blanchard, O.J., R. Dornbusch, P. Krugman, R. Layard and L. Summers (1990), *Reform in Eastern Europe: Report of the Wider World Economy Group*, Helsinki: WIDER.

Calvo, G.A. and J.A. Frenkel (1991), 'From Centrally Planned to Market Economy', *IMF Staff Papers*, **38** (2), 268–99.

Cameron, R. (ed.) (1992), *Financing Industrialisation*, Aldershot: Edward Elgar.

Corbet, J. and C. Mayer (1990), 'Financial Reform in Eastern Europe: Progress with the Wrong Model', CEPR Discussion Paper, No. 603, London: Centre for Economic Policy Research.

Corbet, J. and C. Mayer (1991), 'Financial Reform in Eastern Europe: Progress with the Wrong Model', *Oxford Review of Economic Policy*, **7** (4), 57–75.

Davies, G. (1981), 'Property Rights and Economic Behavior in Private and Government Enterprises: The Case of Australia's Banking System', *Research in Law and Economics*, **3**, 112–42.

Djurić, M. (1971a), 'Smišljene smutnje' [Premeditated Discords], *Anali pravnog fakulteta/Annals of the Faculty of Law*, **21** (5–6), 230–33.

Djurić, M. (1971b), 'Odgovor lažnom svedoku' [The Reply to a False Eye-Witness], *Anali pravnog fakulteta/Annals of the Faculty of Law*, **21** (5-6), 344-45.

Economist, The (2000), 'Where is Central Europe', July 8–14, 49–50.

European Bank for Reconstruction and Development (EBRD), *Annual Report*, various issues.

Fischer, S. and A. Gelb (1990), 'Issues in Socialist Economy Reform', mimeo, Washington, DC: World Bank.

Fischer, S. and A. Gelb (1991), 'The Process of Socialist Economic Transformation', *Journal of Economic Perspectives*, **5** (4), 91–105.

Gros, D. and A. Steinherr (1995), *Winds of Change: Economic Transition in Central and Eastern Europe*, London: Longman.

Hinds, M. (1990a), *Issues in the Introduction of Market Forces in Eastern European Economies*, Washington, DC: World Bank.

Hinds, M. (1990b), *Issues in the Introduction of Market Forces in Eastern European Socialist Economies*, Internal Discussion Paper, Report No. IDP-0057, Washington, DC: World Bank.

Macey, J.R. (1991), *Insider Trading: Economics, Politics and Policy*, Washington, DC: AEI Press.

Mayer, C. and X. Vives (eds) (1993), *Capital Markets and Financial Intermediation*, Cambridge: Cambridge University Press for the Centre for Economic Policy Research.

Petrović, M. (1992), *Finansijsko restruktuiranje banaka (sa posebnim osvrtom na Jugoslaviju, 1989–jun 1991. godine)* [Banks' Financial Restructuring (with special reference to Yugoslavia, from 1989 to June 1991)], Belgrade: National Bank of Yugoslavia, Centre for Research.

Rostowski, J. (ed.) (1995), *Banking Reform in Central Europe and the Former Soviet Union*, Budapest: Central European University Press.

Šević, Ž. (1995a), 'Centralna monetarna vlast u Srbiji, odnosno Jugoslaviji: istorijska perspektiva' [Central Monetary Authority in Serbia, that is, Yugoslavia: A Historical Perspective], *Finansije*, **51** (5–6), 459–80.

Šević, Ž. (1995b), 'Svojinski oblici i efikasnost funkcionisanja bankarskog sistema', [Types of Property and Banking System Efficiency], *Pravni život*, **44** (9), 647–60.

Šević, Ž. (1996a), *Centralna banka: Položaj – organizacija – funkcije* [Central Bank: Position – Organisation – Functions], Belgrade: Čigoja štampa.

Šević, Ž. (1996b), 'Political Economy, Economics and Art of Negotiation and Reconciliation: The Production of Law and Legal Order in a Polycentric Federation of a Yugoslav Type', Paper presented at the 9th Maastricht Workshop on Law and Economics, Maastricht: University of Limburg, 3–6 April.

Šević, Ž. (1996c), *Financial Reform in a Transitional Economy: Some Conceptual Issues*, Tokyo and Belgrade: Ryoichi Sasakawa Young Leaders' Fellowship Fund and Yugoslav Association of Sasakawa Fellows.

Šević, Ž. (1997), 'Slovenia: Economic and Institutional Perspectives for Impending EU Membership', Paper presented at the European Union/University Association for Contemporary European Studies workshop 'East-Central Europe: Prospects for Accession to the European Union', Leicester: University of Leicester, 21–22 February.

Šević, Ž. (1999), *Bank Restructuring in Central and Eastern European Countries as a Part of Macroeconomic Changes towards Market Oriented Economies*, Belgrade: Balkan Center for Public Policy and Related Studies and Čigoja štampa.

Šević, Ž. (2000a), 'Problems of Institutional Design in Economic Development: Economic Structure and Financial System Concepts Revisited', *Naše gospodarstvo/Our Economy*, **46** (4), 467–86.

Šević, Ž. (2000b), 'Banking Reform in South-East European Transitional Economies: An Overview', *MOCT-MOST*, **10** (3/4), 271–83.

Šević, Ž. (2002), 'Reforming Post-Socialist Federations: Can It Really Work?', in R. Baker (ed.), *Transition from Authoritarianism: The Role of Civil Service*, Greenwich, CT: Greenwood Press, 275–90.

Šević, Ž. (2003), 'A Comparative Socio-legal Framework for Corporate Governance: The Issues of Property, Trust, Legal System, Legal Order and Public Policy', ongoing research for International Institute for Corporate Governance and Accountability Project on Modern Corporate Governance.

Šević, Ž. and A. Šević (1998), 'Monetary Policy in a Transitional Economy: Some Open Questions and the Experience', *Economic Systems*, **22** (3), 299–304.
van Wijnbergen, S. (1994), 'On the Role of Banks in Enterprise Restructuring: The Polish Example', CEPR Discussion Paper No. 898, London: Centre for Economic Policy Research.
Veljanovski, C. (1987), *Selling the State*, London: Nicholson.
Vreme, a leading Yugoslav independent political weekly, various issues.

PART ONE

General and Theoretical Issues

2. Economic Reform in South-East European Countries in Transition

Davor Savin

INTRODUCTION

The past decade of economic and social change in the Central and East European (CEE) countries has revealed two transitional patterns that arise in the process of moving from a planned to a market economy. The first pattern is seen in the more advanced countries, which have managed to carry out processes of an accelerated liberalisation and privatisation, as well as achieving wide-reaching macroeconomic stabilisation. This enabled the development of an institutional infrastructure to facilitate the emergence of the market and stimulate economic growth. In countries with a less-developed economy and more rudimentary infrastructure, processes for change were more modest in scope and accompanied by numerous political and other obstacles, structural weaknesses, the circumvention of legal rules, and considerable instability in output and prices. This last behaviour is the key feature of the second pattern of transition.

The first, more advanced economic transition pattern is found in Central European countries: Hungary, Poland, the Czech Republic, Slovakia and Slovenia. On the other hand, the transition in the South-East European (SEE) countries has followed to a great extent the second, more rigid, pattern. It must be noted, however, that besides some common characteristics, there are considerable differences between individual transitional countries, so that all generalisations should be treated with caution.

The European Bank for Reconstruction and Development classifies all the transition countries into two groups. The first group includes 'countries at advanced stages of transition', and the second, 'countries at less advanced stages of transition'. The criteria employed in this classification are based on qualitative assessments of particular areas of transition. These assessments provide transition indicators and concern three key elements: (a) enterprises; (b) markets and trade; and (c) financial institutions.

SEE countries: Albania, Bosnia and Herzegovina, Bulgaria, Croatia, the Former Yugoslav Republic (FYR) of Macedonia, Romania, and the Federal Republic (FR) of Yugoslavia, are placed in the second group. FR Yugoslavia is not at present a member of any international political or financial organisation, and it has not to date been dealt with in analytical reports by international institutions (the International Monetary Fund: IMF; the World Bank; the European Bank for Reconstruction and Development: EBRD; and so on). Consequently, it is difficult to compare this country's transition results with others in the SEE group. This is especially so because after nine years of economic sanctions, isolation and war damage, it is difficult to make any precise and comprehensive assessment of macroeconomic results or the process of transition there. Furthermore, certain fundamental statistical data have not been published for years, which greatly hampers any comparative analysis.

Some of the countries in the 'advanced' group will be mentioned briefly, for reference purposes, to allow some comparison of the transformation achieved by the two groups of transition countries.

INITIAL CONDITIONS

South-East Europe is the least-developed part of the continent. Historically, the region has only a slight tradition of a functioning democracy or an entrenched civil society. The state has stepped into the social vacuum instead. There was no real middle class, rather a more-or-less educated administrative class. Economically, South-East Europe did not experience the stable, sustained market development that the Central European countries had enjoyed (they were among the wealthiest in Europe up to the Second World War).

The historical legacy creates profound challenges for the region. It is for this reason that the initial conditions at the onset of the transition were of so much more importance here than in the other ex-socialist countries. Gross domestic product per capita (purchasing power parity (PPP) basis) was 33 per cent of the European Union (EU) average in 1990 but fell to just 24 per cent eight years later (put differently, these countries as a group would need more than 50 years of sustained 5 per cent GDP growth per annum to catch up with average GDP per capita in the EU).

As a whole, SEE economies have recovered only 75 per cent of their pre-transition income level (which explains the huge deterioration in living standards and the high unemployment). The total GDP of the region is USD 100 billion, one-third of the five Central European countries. Per capita income varies considerably – the highest is in Croatia: at USD 4,520, and the lowest in Albania: at USD 810 (World Bank data for 1998). There is no official figure for the per capita income in FR Yugoslavia, but it can be estimated at about USD 1,200 (and even less in 1999 due to the appreciation of the dollar against the German mark and its impact on GDP growth computations).

There has been some modest progress in establishing the legal and financial institutions essential for an efficient market mechanism. However, the socialist heritage has proved too deeply rooted to be easily replaced. Unlike the Central European countries, which were not as infused with ethnic tensions, some of the SEE countries encountered severe nationalist conflicts, which culminated in the war in Croatia and Bosnia and Herzegovina and the North Atlantic Treaty Organisation (NATO) assault on Serbia. Enormous damage was inflicted on capital assets and infrastructure, production fell, income was lost, and most importantly of all, social capital was badly impaired and the transition process was markedly retarded.

Figure 2.1 *Private sector share in GDP, 1999*

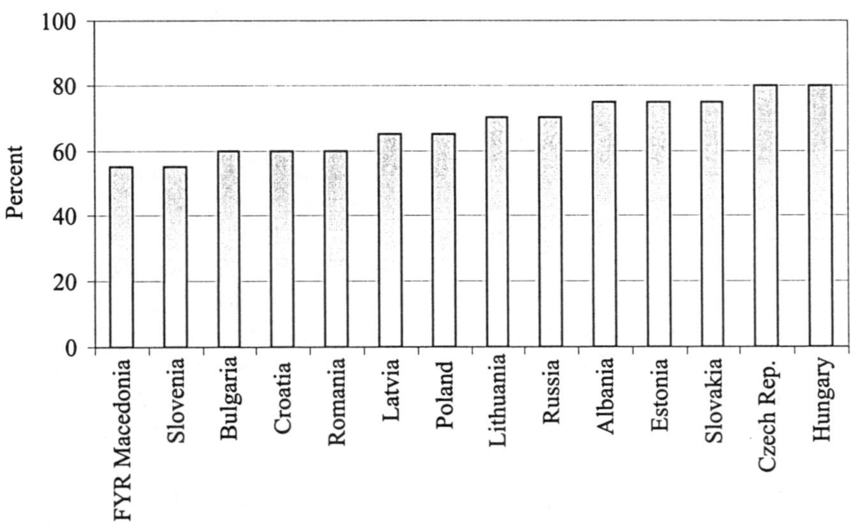

Source: EBRD.

The initial conditions of transition have proved to be particularly significant for the dynamics and quality of market reform. Some CEE countries had certain, if only rudimentary, market institutions in place even prior to launching reforms. Poland and Hungary had carried out partial market reforms during the 1980s, unlike Romania and Bulgaria. Hungary introduced a value-added tax in 1986, for example. The Czech Republic did this in 1993, and Slovenia only in 1999. Similarly, Hungary was the first CEE country to set up incentives for direct foreign investment back in the 1980s, which secured a significant inflow of capital from Western countries. In 1994 its private sector generated 55 per cent of GDP, compared with 40 per cent in Croatia, 35 per cent in Romania and 30 per cent in Slovenia. In 1999 the share of the private sector in GDP reached 80 per cent in both Hungary and the Czech Republic. In Bulgaria, Romania and Croatia the share was about 60 per cent (all data from 1999 World Bank statistics).

By the time ex-Yugoslav republics entered transition their enterprises had already been exposed to market influences, particularly in the foreign trade sector. All republics, however, were not equally successful in their economic development: Slovenia and Croatia were ahead. Yugoslav enterprises had become acquainted with Western markets and oriented towards importation of Western technology and know-how since the 1960s. Their industrial and farm exports went predominantly to West European markets. Other CEE countries had only limited forms of co-operation with industrialised economies outside the Council for Mutual Economic Assistance (COMECON). Furthermore, the self-management in former Yugoslavia was certainly a more advanced economic system (despite many and major drawbacks) than the system of central planning and broad state control of economic life that characterised other socialist economies. The economic structure of the latter countries was modelled on the Soviet system: extensive economic growth based on hypertrophied development of heavy industry and high dependence on raw materials and energy from the USSR.

Taken as a whole, the SEE countries lag behind the Central European countries in structural reforms and in building the systemic conditions for efficient market operation. The institutional framework for an unhindered competition relationship between economic agents has not been completed, banking has not been fully reformed, large-scale privatisation is incomplete and in some places has not even begun. Moreover, there are no developed financial markets, the tax systems are inefficient (and consequently budgets are not in balance) and wealth disparities are very pronounced.

The EBRD transition indicators for 1999, presented in Figure 2.2, show considerable differences between the Central and South-Eastern countries on several major transition characteristics. Transition indicators represent eight dimensions of transition: large-scale privatisation, small-scale privatisation, governance and enterprise restructuring, price liberalisation, trade and foreign exchange system, competition policy, banking reform and interest rate liberalisation, securities markets and non-bank financial institutions. These indicators cover a range of policy and institutional factors that determine the business climate. On a scale from 1 to 4+, the lowest point indicates little or no change from the previous socialist regime. The score 4+ represents the performance norm of advanced industrial countries.

Figure 2.2 *Transition indicators, 1999*

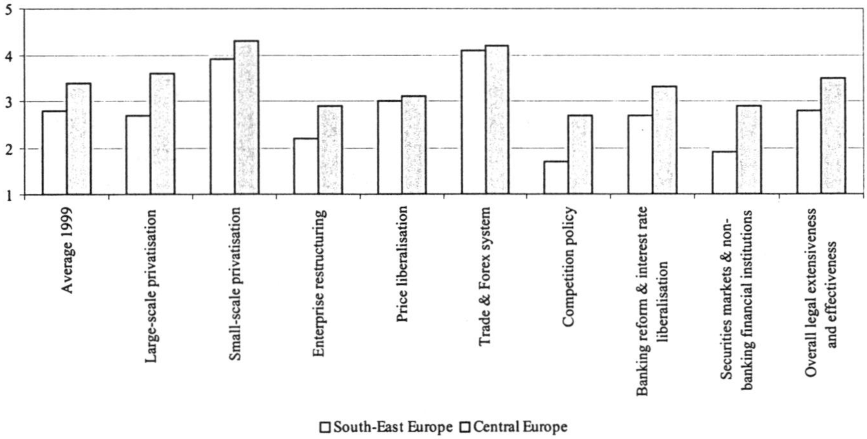

Source: EBRD.

In all of the CEE countries, the basic transition model involves the following components: privatising government-owned enterprises; liberalising prices and abandoning state subsidies as an integral part of the liberalisation of domestic trading; eliminating barriers to establishing new private companies and economic organisations; liberalising financial markets; loosening foreign trade by abolishing import and export permits and quotas, and closing down government-owned foreign trading enterprises; attaining effective enterprise management; and balancing state budgets by raising taxes and reducing over-scaled public sector consumption. In addition to this, some of the CEE countries immediately began structural reforms which encompassed: tax reform, reform of the banking system, designing industrial policies to differentiate between successful and unsuccessful businesses, halting the ecological damage caused by the extensive production system, evading monopolistic positions and establishing the rules of free competition on the market.

Low inflation, a stable exchange rate, and financial stabilisation in general have been put on the top of the reform agenda of all transitional economies, nevertheless these goals constitute intermediate objectives (in a conditional sense). The final goal should be stable and sustainable growth in GDP and growth in the standard of living. There is a tendency to equate the final and intermediate goals, which sometimes clouds the transition scorecard. The intermediate objectives are actually a means, a mode, to achieving the final goal, which is sustained growth. Frequently, more attention is given to the means to the final end than the end itself and this has often led to mistaken assessments of the success of transition policies.

Thus, for example, economic policy should not be evaluated solely on the basis of the share of the private sector in overall GDP, or the degree of liberalisation of the financial market but, above all, with regard to the results achieved in increasing productivity, competitiveness, and accordingly, growth in aggregate output. No matter how important a step privatisation is, the insistence on valid privatisation, for example, has sometimes borne a political imprint – an endeavour to have assets sold off as cheaply as possible. In some countries, powerful lobbies have advocated a policy of rapid sale of successful enterprises, because more cautious and slower privatisation would make it more difficult or impossible for the production and other assets available for privatisation to be bought up cheaply.

In brief, the process of transition has to be examined much more deeply than merely by a 'customary' scanning of data on the share of the private sector, the liberalisation of trade, or deregulation of the financial markets. These are merely intermediate objectives. They are important and necessary for attaining the final goals, but it is in terms of the final goals (sustained GDP and standard of living growth, and a more just distribution of the income thus generated) that the success of transition policies should be evaluated. This standpoint may be observed in the World Bank's present approach which, however, was not expounded at the time the transition process was launched. 'Our understanding of the instruments to promote well-functioning markets has ... improved, and we have broadened the objective of development to include other goals, such as sustainable development, egalitarian development, and democratic developments.' (Stiglitz, 1998, p. 1).

Transformation of the former centrally planned economies started in 1990. Poland was the first to commit to a free market with a 'big-bang' package programme launched in January 1990. Other countries in transition subsequently adopted similar packages, notwithstanding certain distinctive features. 'It was expected that the stabilisation programmes would restore external and internal balance in the countries, and also bring about a recession, which would bottom out in the one or two years following the inception of the programme. Then, it was anticipated, the structural transformation could really develop' (Lavigne, 1999, p. 113).

The results attained did not fulfil expectations or the theoretical convictions expounded at the start of transformation in the CEE countries. In most cases, inflation rose steeply as a direct consequence of various microeconomic and macroeconomic imbalances. Output dropped in all of the transitional countries, and the number of jobless climbed appreciably. Inequality in income distribution has increased, and social conflicts widened. Corruption is widespread throughout the ex-socialist countries, and the gap between haves and have-nots is broadening. Additionally, gaps in income have opened up between town and country.

LIBERALISATION AND STABILISATION

In all the SEE countries, liberalisation of the market has borne the same basic features, although there have been differences in its extent and dynamics. Like the Baltic and Central European countries, FYR Macedonia and Albania reduced state intervention and liberalised domestic prices in the very first phase of transition. Furthermore, they liberalised foreign trade and the foreign exchange market, though with less enthusiasm than they showed with liberalisation in the domestic domain. The EBRD defines a liberal market as one with a transition indicator score of three for price liberalisation (most prices were freed except for housing rents and infrastructure tariffs), and four for trade liberalisation (full current account convertibility).

In contrast to the rapid liberalisation in Albania and Macedonia, internal and external liberalisation was much slower and less complete in Bulgaria, Romania and FR Yugoslavia, especially with regard to trade and access to foreign exchange. Bulgaria, for example, attempted to liberalise domestic and foreign trade in the early stages of transition but could not complete the process because of inflation problems. The process of liberalisation was halted after three years, and was resumed only in 1999. Romania liberalised slowly and gradually. As a result of its peculiar conditions (involvement in wars in neighbouring countries, prolonged international sanctions, isolation from international political and economic affairs), FR Yugoslavia lags far behind other countries of the region. This is despite the fact that ex-Yugoslavia as a whole had enjoyed the highest level of liberalisation of CEE countries prior to the beginning of the process of political change and transition.

As with other aspects of transition, liberalisation was most rapid in the countries with the smallest structural imbalances and the highest degree of macroeconomic stability. However, a good starting position is not in itself sufficient to ensure sustained liberalisation. Similarly, a poorer starting position did not militate against liberalisation.

Figure 2.3 presents the correlation between the cumulative fall in GDP during the transition recession and a summary measure of initial conditions defined by the EBRD. These conditions are represented by the first principal component of a factor analysis, and are a weighted average of measures for the level of development, trade dependence on other socialist countries, macroeconomic disequilibria, and natural resource endowments according to the EBRD's methodology (1999, p. 30). The recession for each country is defined as the period from 1989 until the first year of positive economic growth. It is evident that favourable initial conditions are related to small cumulative declines in real GDP. Albania, FYR Macedonia, and FR Yugoslavia are not included as there are no measures of their initial conditions.

Figure 2.3 *Explaining recession: initial conditions and real GDP growth*

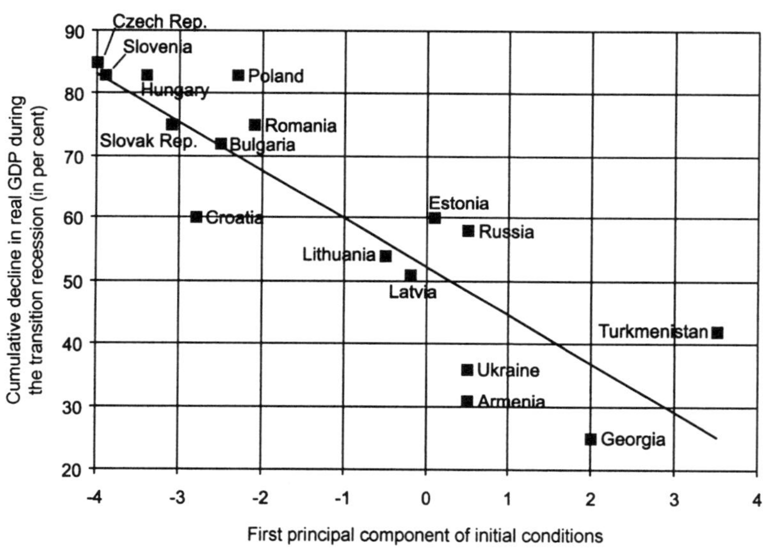

Source: EBRD.

Once central planning was abandoned and the transition process was launched, most of the countries of the region were confronted with rising inflation. However, disinflation followed fairly quickly and most of the countries achieved a 'moderate' level of inflation (that is, below 30 per cent per annum), by 1997. The median inflation rate went down from 84 per cent in 1992 to about 9 per cent in 1995 (even more rapid disinflation took place in the former Soviet Union countries, including Russia, where the median inflation rate fell from 1,210 per cent in 1992 to 60 per cent in 1995). But the decrease was not sustained and inflation has reappeared in some CEE countries. To measure the macroeconomic stabilisation of transition countries, the EBRD constructed an indicator composed of the number of years since the start of transition with a moderate rate of inflation and a sustainable fiscal deficit (less than 5 per cent of GDP). Price growth of 30 per cent was taken on the basis of empirical data as the cut-off point in view of earlier inflation impacts. The fiscal threshold used was the maximal fiscal deficit 'allowed' under an efficient stabilisation programme. The Central European transition countries, such as those in the Baltic, reached these stabilisation limits in half the period from the beginning of stabilisation whereas the SEE countries took much longer. The transition recession in South-East Europe lasted longer than in Central European countries, and the cumulative decline was about 30 per cent of the 1989 GDP level, twice the decline registered in Central Europe. (See Figure 2.4.)

Figure 2.4 *Index of real GDP, 1989–1999*

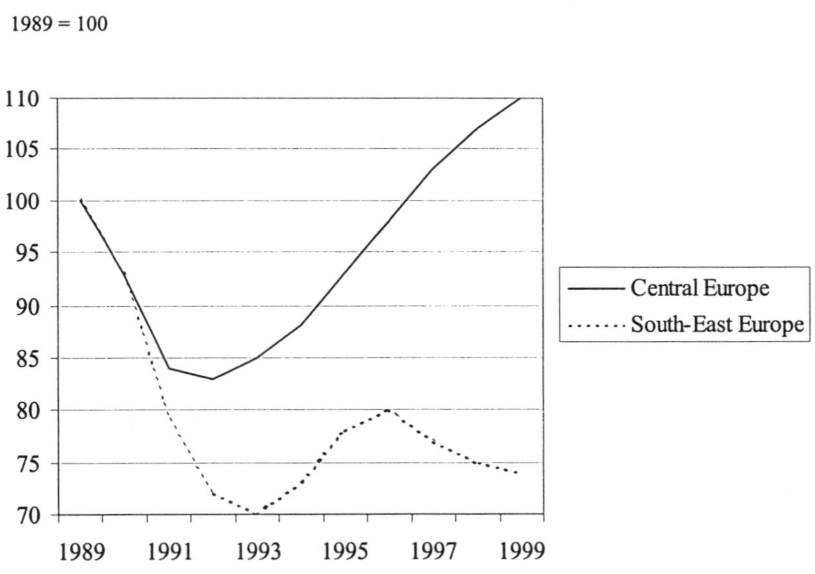

Note: Weighted averages; weights are computed from GDP in US dollars in 1989 at PPP exchange rates (for 1999 preliminary data).

Source: EBRD.

REFORMS IN SOUTH-EAST EUROPE

It was difficult for the SEE countries to carry out the stabilisation and liberalisation programmes simultaneously because, among other things, the state had to stop subsidising enterprises, which were then suddenly confronted with competition from private companies and imports. At the same time, because production flagged or was shut down, the tax base shrank and hence state budgets were crimped and state transfer payments reduced (this was particularly evident in lower pensions, and unemployment and other welfare benefits). Some countries, like Romania, cut back subsidies to inefficient enterprises from the state budget but the banking system continued to give significant loan support to businesses, which constituted a form of soft-budget constraint. Other forms of support such as non-payment of utility bills and tax arrears were applied in Albania and Bulgaria, while FR Yugoslavia resorted to each of these forms of subsidy to businesses.

Unlike most Central European countries, which managed to achieve macroeconomic stability by the mid-1990s, SEE countries were less successful until the end of the decade. Most countries from that region registered a significant economic instability, although we can see that economic growth in Albania, Bulgaria and Romania gradually began to show positive trends.

Albania's GDP rose by an average of 9 per cent per annum in 1993–96 but in 1997 it ran into serious difficulties due to the collapse of pyramid schemes. Total liabilities incurred by these schemes have been estimated at approximately 50 per cent of GDP. The consequences were very severe. With the loss of their savings, people spent less, and this had a negative impact on industry and construction. GDP was reduced by about 7 per cent that year, but thanks to a two-tier economic recovery programme in 1998 and 1999 (which was oriented towards three main goals: institution building and governance; economic and social policies; and revival of economic activities), it began to grow again by about 8 per cent per annum. At the same time, the inflation rate (based on consumer prices, end-year), which in 1997 was over 42 per cent, was reduced to about 9 per cent in 1998 and 2 per cent in 1999. Thanks to low inflation and regeneration of production, the exchange rate held steady (the exchange rate regime in Albania is a managed float).

Albania privatised small-scale enterprises in the first phase of transition. By mid-1998 about 479 small enterprises were still state owned, but by 1999 they were all sold, leased or closed down. A feature of Albanian enterprises is that most of them (about 98 per cent) employ ten or fewer workers. The main problem that the enterprises face, judging from various questionnaires, is a high rate of taxation and bureaucratic limitations, as well as competition from the informal sector. Large-scale privatisation has proceeded slowly. However, with the end of the Kosovo conflict, foreign investors have been attracted. The infrastructure, finance, mining and petroleum were offered for privatisation and the process of restructuring in these sectors is almost complete. In addition, the two large loss-making enterprises controlled by the Enterprise Restructuring Agency have been liquidated. The energy-production sector is state owned, inefficient and loss making. Because the criteria imposed by the World Bank and the EBRD were not adhered to, there have been no foreign investments in the energy sector. However, complete privatisation of this sector is already under way.

Bulgaria started its political transition at the end of 1989, but the initial market reform occurred two years later. The Bulgarian economy was almost entirely in state hands, prices were totally controlled, and external trade was oriented towards the former USSR, all of which made transition rather difficult. Between 1991 and 1996, progress in economic reforms was slow and often interrupted. The period of strict macroeconomic policy was followed by a period of 'adaptable' interventions, which was reflected in great oscillations in GDP growth (which fluctuated from 11.7 per cent in 1991 to 2.1 per cent in 1995) and inflation (339 per cent in 1991 to 33 per cent in 1995). Inconsistency in economic policy, high inflation and a fall in foreign currency reserves all resulted in a large depreciation of the exchange rate in the first months of 1997. In July of that year a currency board was introduced. The Bulgarian lev was fixed at BGL 1,000 to DEM 1. The results were impressive. Inflation was reduced from 528 per cent in June 1997, to less than 18 per cent in June 1998, foreign exchange reserves increased (from one month of imports to 6.5 months) and financial discipline was introduced in monetary and fiscal transactions.

Bulgaria speeded up the structural reform in 1997, when important steps were taken in privatisation, the introduction of legal rules aimed at strengthening market discipline, the reform of the banking system, and the liberalisation of agriculture and prices. The most important measure in the field of structural reform is privatisation of enterprises in state ownership. About a thousand of these enterprises were completely privatised by June 1998, and approximately the same number partially privatised. However, three-quarters of state-owned capital remains to be privatised. For those state enterprises that were too weak to be privatised, a programme of liquidation was established on the basis of which about a third of loss-making enterprises were shut down. The main methods of privatisation were direct privatisation through the Privatisation Agency or line ministries, privatisation through advisers, two rounds of mass privatisation, and the sale of shares on the Bulgarian Stock Exchange. By the end of 1998, about 80 per cent of agricultural land had been returned to private hands, and more than half of the agro-industrial companies had been privatised. Bank privatisation has started, but progress is slow. The third largest of the six remaining state-owned banks, Post Bank, was sold to a foreign investor at the end of 1998. From mid-1999 all prices were liberalised, with the exception of electricity, coal, postal services, gas and a few others, all of which remain under the control of state authorities.

The advance of privatisation was slower in Romania than in most other countries of South-East Europe. In 1996, over 75 per cent of the total book value of companies belonging to the State Ownership Fund were not privatised. In 1997, the Ministry of Privatisation was established. By 1999 the State Ownership Fund had about 5,500 enterprises under its supervision, all of which were supposed to be privatised.

At the beginning of 1997, a programme of reforms was started, which encompassed structural changes. Most prices, including the exchange rate, were liberalised and, within a year, more enterprises were privatised than in the previous six years. Banking laws that were supposed to ensure better regulation and supervision of banks were adopted. However, there is evidence of weaknesses in central bank independence and inflationary bailout operations have continued.

Romania experienced negative GDP growth rate in 1997–99, combined with high inflation (about 5 per cent a month), which directly contributed to a large depreciation of its currency, the leu (the average exchange rate against the US dollar in 1995 was 2,033 and three years later it was 8,881). Romania still faces many challenges before a complete structural reform has been accomplished in the enterprise and financial sectors, which is a condition for macroeconomic stabilisation.

The war in Bosnia and Herzegovina (BiH) devastated the country: about 250,000 people were killed and many hundreds of thousands left their homes or were forced out. Military clashes destroyed a considerable part of the available infrastructure and reduced GDP from USD 8.3 billion before the war to about USD 2 billion in 1995, while industrial production fell to about 10 per cent of its pre-war level. After the peace agreement, and with the assistance of the World Bank and other international institutions, a four-year programme of reconstruction was initiated. In mid-1997, the central bank was formed and the Convertible Mark (KM) introduced under the currency board principle at a rate of one KM per DEM.

In both political entities (Bosnian-Croat Federation and Republika Srpska), over 90 per cent of registered enterprises are private. These are small firms, mainly operating in trade, services and construction, whose creation was generously assisted by donations aimed at reconstructing the BiH economy. In 1999, auctions and tenders began for the sale of small-scale assets. It is likely that the sale will last for about three years. Unlike small-scale privatisation, large-scale privatisation ('privatisation through public offering of shares') is slow and controversial. Bank privatisation in both political entities has also begun and insolvent banks were to be shut down in 2000 (impaired assets and liabilities of banks have been transferred to the Finance Ministry, with their balance sheets reduced by 80 per cent).

FYR Macedonia introduced fairly widespread reforms, but the final results were unsatisfactory. Until 1995, GDP decreased, growth rate was below the SEE country average and it did not rise above 3 per cent per annum. Unemployment for the whole period of transition was high and has been about 35 per cent over the last few years. Inflation is low and in 1998 a negative rate was registered.

From 1994, Macedonia made an important step towards macroeconomic stabilisation and structural reforms. By mid-1998, about 95 per cent of all industry and trade enterprises were privatised, mostly through employee buy-outs. Agricultural enterprises were in fact privatised in full during 1998 and 1999. The trade regime was also greatly liberalised and important free-trade agreements have been made. Measures for strengthening the financial system were taken, but discipline in that field is still weak, as banks continue to support loss-making enterprises with modest debt-service capabilities (partly because banks have collected enterprise shares in debt–equity swaps). In 1998 a new bankruptcy law was passed, giving creditors more mechanisms to protect their interests and the number of bankruptcy cases was reduced. An important share of bad loans was transferred from banks to the Bank Rehabilitation Agency. Bank profitability increased markedly in 1997 and banks are now more or less capitalised. The share of bad loans in total loans was reduced from 70 per cent in 1992 to 36 per cent in 1998.

Macroeconomic policy is based on tight monetary and fiscal measures and on pegging the exchange rate to the German mark. The likelihood of maintaining a more or less fixed exchange rate is increased by a significant inflow of hard currency, because military personnel, foreign experts and journalists are stationed in Macedonia, and currency stability is also boosted by foreign aid. A stock exchange was established in 1996, but trading is still rather limited.

Croatia is the most-developed country within South-East Europe. The structure of its GDP is similar to the structure of output of developed nations (60 per cent services, 10 per cent agriculture). Foreign trade is higher than the value of GDP, which makes Croatia one of the most open economies of Central and East Europe.

In the period from 1991 to 1993, aggregate production had a negative growth rate, and from then on GDP grew, but at a relatively slow rate. Towards the end of 1993, Croatia launched a comprehensive exchange rate based stabilisation programme, thanks to which inflation was reduced (inflation was 938 per cent in 1992 and 1,150 per cent in 1993). Towards the end of 1994 the inflation rate was –3 per cent. One of the factors that had contributed to higher inflation was the denomination of prices in German marks. The government depreciated the nominal exchange rate parallel with inflation, which activated the spiral: prices–exchange rate–prices. The World Bank estimated that the Croatian stabilisation programme was one of the most successful in the region. But, in spite of advantageous macroeconomic factors, the economy did not manage to achieve higher growth rates.

Privatisation in Croatia occurred gradually. The primary method was the buy-out by the employees (management–employee buy-outs: MEBOs) and the second was voucher privatisation. 'The voucher privatisation programme in 1998 has reduced the residual holdings of the Croatian Privatisation Fund by almost half to 17 per cent of the book value of commercialised enterprises covered by the original privatisation law of 1991' (EBRD, 1999, p. 206). In the voucher privatisation process some 90 per cent of vouchers have been invested in seven privatisation and investment funds (of which two, the most liquid, are foreign owned). All the funds have traded at about 90 per cent discount on the face value of shares and vouchers, which was a consequence of the lower profitability of enterprises included in the Croatian privatisation programme.

PRIVATISATION

Privatisation involves a legal transfer of property rights from the state to private agents. The rights to decision making regarding economic and other managerial issues are transferred at the same time. In this sense privatisation is a component part of liberalisation and the stabilisation process and, in the political sense, represents a vehicle for the formation of a new class of entrepreneurs and capitalists. Moreover, privatisation also needs to be seen as a means for raising the efficiency of business operations through better management, lowered costs, and greater competitiveness.

Two different processes of privatisation may be observed in the SEE countries. The first is found in the retail trade and other small business sectors, where private firms sprouted spontaneously 'overnight', particularly in activities that called primarily for human capital rather than expensive investments. These were often activities that had been functioning as part of the underground economy even during the socialist period. 'Later on this type of entrepreneurship was supported by laws on "small privatisation", which meant the transfer of small state assets to private persons, mainly in trade and services, truck transport, construction, through sales of assets, by direct trade sales, by auctions officially not open to foreigners, and through leasing arrangements' (Lavigne, 1999, p. 165).

The process of large-scale privatisation (of big enterprises) was slower in all the SEE countries (and in the other transition countries, moreover). In fact, the mere act of privatisation, the transfer of state property to private hands, did not accomplish much. Many of the former state enterprises were burdened with old debts and dubious claims; they are often handicapped by outdated and unusable equipment. All the SEE countries are wrestling with governance problems and the problem of structural change in enterprises, both those that have been privatised and those still fully or partly in state hands.

Table 2.1 presents the methods of privatisation used for medium-sized and large enterprises. The countries of former Yugoslavia, which had a system of social property, that is formal management of enterprises by the employees, were compelled to adopt a privatisation method oriented towards insiders (vouchers and MEBOs). Like the Central European countries, the other SEE countries had greater scope for action in this regard, and they were not restricted to insider privatisation. Thus, for example, Hungary sold equity shares to strategic partners and privatised over 75 per cent of medium-sized and large state enterprises in this way.

Table 2.1 *Methods of privatisation in medium-sized and large enterprises*

CEE countries	EBRD indicator score[a]	Direct sales	Vouchers	MEBO[b]
Albania	2	–	Secondary	Primary
BiH[c]	2	Secondary	Primary	–
Bulgaria	3	Primary	Secondary	–
Croatia	3	–	Secondary	Primary
Czech Rep.	4	Secondary	Primary	–
Macedonia	3	Secondary	–	Primary
Hungary	4	Primary	–	Secondary
Romania	3–	Secondary	–	Primary
Slovenia	3+	–	Secondary	Primary

Notes:

[a] EBRD indicator score = progress in privatisation of medium-sized and large enterprises measured by transaction indicators; a score of two indicates that up to 25 per cent of state-owned enterprise assets have been privatised, a score of three indicates that up to 50 per cent of these assets have been privatised.

[b] MEBO = Management–employee buy-out.

[c] BiH = Bosnia and Herzegovina.

Source: EBRD (1999).

In its analysis of the conditions and circumstances influencing the transitional process, the EBRD employs the concept of *social capital*. This is defined as 'voluntary compliance with established laws, trust, co-operative behaviour and basic codes of conduct' (EBRD, 1999, pp. 5). In using the language of capital, the EBRD emphasises that it may be enhanced or eroded and that it can complement other factors of production, such as physical and human capital. The main idea is that with weak social capital, physical capital is misused or misappropriated and human capital can be wasted and worn out. Manifestations of weak social capital include bureaucratic interference of various kinds in economic life, corruption and other deficiencies in legal order, and unethical business practices, including poor corporate governance.

Differences in the development of social capital in the CEE countries help to explain to a considerable degree why advances along the path of transition have been different and why, even after a decade, some of the countries have made only modest progress. The degree of exposure to Western market culture and an acquaintance with the business principles of a modern, ordered economy have made it much easier and less painful for Hungary, Poland, the Czech Republic and Slovenia to implement transitional changes than was the case for underdeveloped countries that previously belonged to the Soviet Union, with its rigid central planning as the major mechanism for resource allocation.

With the sole exception of the former Yugoslavia, in all the socialist countries the means of production were owned by the state. In the former Yugoslavia the concept of 'social ownership' was introduced in 1950 as an integral part of the self-management economic system, which also contained substantial free-market elements (the fuzzy concept of social ownership, however, was never suitably defined, which resulted in considerable mystification and not a little confusion in the legal regulation of property rights).

TRANSITION RECESSION

Transition should be seen not as a single process but as two parallel and complementary processes. These are the processes that concurrently build democratic institutions and lay the foundations for a market economy. The first process is not complete without the second, and the second is not possible without the first. In countries that fail to build a legal infrastructure that ensures free initiative and democratic decision making, both in economic as well as in political affairs, the market cannot function smoothly. This is one of the reasons for the highly heterogeneous output performance of the CEE countries after 1995. Poland, Hungary, Slovenia and Slovakia continued along a steady growth path, while Bulgaria, Romania, and the Czech Republic registered a slowdown and in some years even a negative growth rate.

The transition reforms have progressed sufficiently to make the GDP figure for CEE countries more or less comparable to Western countries' output data. This was not the case for the old statistics on net material product. Estimates of real GDP or income (deflated by official prices) were misleading, since many goods and services registered in price index statistics were not always available at the 'formal' prices. Officially measured real incomes overstated the quantity of goods people could actually purchase with the available amount of money. Before price liberalisation, distribution plans (and queues) were the mechanism that allocated the available supply of goods. After liberalisation, all households tried simultaneously to get rid of their excess cash balances. This caused a rise in the average price level up to the point where the real value of the money held was consistent with the real balances households and enterprises need to finance their current transactions. Once the price level had increased to the new equilibrium level, the earlier surplus in money supply vanished. The correction of monetary overhang required a rise in the price level of between 30 and 55 per cent (in Russia, the necessary price jump was over 250 per cent). This explains why real income in all the European countries in transition fell by up to one-half or more.

Table 2.2 *Growth in real GDP in Central and East European countries*

	89	90	92	94	96	98	99	GDP 98/99
Albania	9.8	−10.0	−7.2	9.4	9.1	8.0	8.0	86
Bulgaria	0.5	−9.1	−7.3	1.8	−10.1	3.5	0.0	66
Croatia	−1.6	−7.1	−11.7	5.9	6.0	2.3	−0.5	78
Czech Republic	1.4	−1.2	−3.3	3.2	3.8	−2.3	0.0	95
FYRM*	0.9	−9.9	−8.0	−1.8	0.8	2.9	0.0	72
Hungary	0.7	−3.5	−3.1	2.9	1.3	5.1	3.0	95
Poland	0.2	−11.6	2.6	5.2	6.1	4.8	3.5	117
Romania	−5.8	−5.6	−8.8	3.9	4.1	−7.3	−4.0	76
Slovakia	1.4	−2.5	−6.5	4.9	6.6	4.4	1.8	100
Slovenia	−1.8	−4.7	−5.5	5.3	3.5	3.9	3.5	104

Note: * Former Yugoslav Republic of Macedonia.

Source: EBRD (1999).

By the end of 1999 the level of real GDP had surpassed the 1989 'base level' in only two countries: Poland and Slovenia. In Poland it has grown steadily for eight years, and in Slovenia for seven.

However, the main feature of the last decade was the CEE countries' growing lag behind the GDP of the Organisation for Economic Co-operation and Development (OECD) countries. According to EBRD data, the overall rate of GDP growth in transition countries declined from 5.5 per cent in 1995 to 4 per cent in 1996, 3.6 per cent in 1997, 2.4 per cent in 1998 and 1.6 per cent in 1999.

Several explanations have been offered for the decline in output at the initial stages of transition. They differ primarily according to the factors they treat as basic. Thus, for example, it is argued that the volume of output in industrial sectors with outdated technology and management, and an obsolete range of products, decreased at a faster pace than new sectors that had managed to modernise their technology, adapt their production processes and thereby raise output. GDP declined, says the other explanation, due to the break-up of the highly centralised and inefficient production network that could not adapt quickly to the decentralised system of decision making and operation under the new conditions. Moreover, in most cases, there was an abrupt move to a convertible currency with immediate adjustment of 'old system' prices that had been lower than those on the world market. Certain key input elements and raw materials became unaffordable as a consequence. At the same time, competition from imports grew and many companies that were still organised in the old way and had poorer technology could not counter it.

Another exposition emphasises the accumulation of stocks that could not be sold because of outdated product design and poor quality when Western imports competed directly against domestic products and consumer preferences switched to foreign goods. Unquestionably there was stockpiling, but it could not have lasted as long as the registered decline in GDP.

The reduction of commercial bank loans has also to be borne in mind. The new market orientation of banks in many SEE countries was reflected in fewer loans to companies that were not efficient enough and could not meet repayment terms. Real, positive interest rates were introduced, which dampened investments and consequently the growth of production in some sectors. However, here it should be recalled that production declined even in countries where the interest rate was negative, such as in Bulgaria and Romania. At the same time, in many of these countries the banks remained government owned and under state control, which preserved many previous bank–enterprise ties and prevented any appreciable tightening of lending conditions (the case of Bulgaria is again illustrative here). The banking systems in the SEE countries experienced a severe crisis in 1996 and 1997 because for years the banks had been financing the obsolete, inefficient and unprofitable state enterprises that did not settle their debts and so landed them in the red (quasi-fiscal deficits). This was the roundabout way used by governments to maintain soft-budget constraints for their enterprises.

A factor that has to be taken into account is the growth in the share of the unofficial economy registered in all SEE countries, which adversely affected statistically recorded output growth. Many production and trading activities went underground to evade taxes and bypass government regulations. The unofficial economy is oriented solely towards short-term profit, is not interested in investing in technology and development, and makes no contribution to budgetary revenues. As a rule, it is accompanied by corruption and bribery, spreads legal disorder and prevents, or at the very best hampers, the exercise of the rule of law in the economy. Moreover it damages the credibility of the market system.

The Transparency International Corruption Index for 1999 shows an exceptionally high level of corruption in many SEE countries, as can be seen from Table 2.3.

Table 2.3 *Corruption index, 1999*

Countries	Rank	Index	Countries	Rank	Index
Slovenia	25	6.0	Bulgaria	63	3.3
Estonia	27	5.7	Macedonia	63	3.3
Hungary	31	5.2	Romania	63	3.3
Czech Rep.	39	4.6	Croatia	74	2.7
Poland	44	4.2	Albania	84	2.3
Slovakia	53	3.7	Yugoslavia	90	2.0

Note: Rank among 99 countries with one being the country with the lowest perceived corruption (Denmark). The index is based on a one to ten scale, with ten indicating that business people face no corruption in dealings with public officials.

Source: Transparency International Website.

The economy of the SEE countries had recovered by the end of the 1990s, but growth is still weak and has not yet stabilized. One of the reasons is that these countries were unable to achieve constant and stable levels in productivity growth. In all transition countries a fall in productivity was a common feature in the first years of reform. However, productivity started to grow after the number of redundant employees was reduced (a smaller number of workers produced the same, or larger, output). Some Central European countries had marked productivity growth, resulting from the introduction of new technology and sophisticated equipment, as well as modern managerial methods. Thanks to this, their productivity was 50 per cent higher in 1998 than a decade earlier, while productivity in South-Eastern economies was still below the pre-transition levels. Weak productivity growth mirrors the lack of structural changes necessary for a more efficient production in the SEE countries.

Another factor contributing to weak productivity growth was investment in productive assets. The share of these investments in the GDP of South-East Europe fell from 23 per cent in 1991, to about 18 per cent in 1998 (the fall in investment-to-GDP ratio was especially marked in Bulgaria, Romania and Albania). In contrast to this, the average investment-to-GDP ratio in Central European countries increased in the same period from 19 per cent to 28 per cent, which was the main factor in productivity growth bouncing up.

It has to be emphasized that foreign direct investment as a percentage of GDP was only slightly lower in the SEE than in the CEE economies. Therefore, the revival of investment, and the consequent growth of productivity and output, depended on the level of domestic savings. This level constantly decreased through the 1990s: gross national savings as a percentage of GDP was 15 per cent in 1995 but only 12 per cent in 1999. Foreign savings made up the difference in the volume of realised investment, which was, in fact, the inverse of the current account deficit. These additional liabilities made the external debt of the SEE countries larger: in 1999 their debt-to-GDP ratio was more than 40 per cent and the debt–service ratio was more than 20 per cent.

TIMING OF REFORM

Economic policy as a factor that has directly affected the transition process in all the SEE countries deserves special attention. In the initial years of market reform one issue stood at the focal point of both general theoretical discussions and practical considerations: whether to embrace gradual or rapid reform.

The advocates of rapid transition stressed the need to make transition processes irreversible as quickly as possible in view of the entrenchment of the former system and its numerous supporters. These would thus be prevented from disrupting the transitional reform. Once reforms are under way they may be reversed or distorted by interest groups reacting to the initial costs of large-scale change. Furthermore, with rapid reform the period of uncertainty is much shorter than with gradual transformation. The view was that rapid transition could only be carried out by 'shock therapy', an expression used synonymously with 'big-bang' or 'single-burst' reform. The reform should comprise rapid price and foreign trade liberalisation, supplemented by a price stability programme, a quick move to current account convertibility, privatisation of state-owned enterprises, and comprehensive reform of the financial and legal systems.

The gradualists maintained that customs, institutions, the structure of the economy and the social infrastructure in the CEE countries were such that rapid changes were simply not feasible. Market institutions have to be *developed* in the former socialist countries; they cannot simply be *adopted* and transplanted from an advanced environment to one that is not. The development and upgrading of these institutions takes time. The experience of Poland, for example, shows that certain changes really can be carried out in a single stroke, and fairly rapidly. Liberalisation of prices as well as abolishing restrictions and limitations on small-scale enterprises, and the elimination of foreign exchange limits and controls are in principle possible via a one-off decision by the authorities. But most of the other essential reforms are extremely slow and time-consuming. Efficient management takes years to develop even when the enterprise is privatised rapidly. It also takes years to build market infrastructure, and the financial and legal systems. Changing regulations does not help much here: attitudes and customs have to be changed as well and there should be a complete understanding of the economic life that had taken shape in a wholly different way under a socialist, planned economy.

Distinguishing between rapid and gradual reforms has not proved useful in practice, however. Not one of the countries implemented rapid reform that encompassed 'current' and structural aspects at the same time. But, similarly, not one followed the gradualist model in the strict sense, in which 'slowness' in carrying out transitional changes would categorise them as gradual reformers. Instead, they followed different transition paths, both in terms of rapidity and sequence of steps. Some started on key stabilisation measures only long after the 'formal' commencement of transition processes, as Table 2.4 shows.

Table 2.4 *Stabilisation lags in Central and East European countries*

Country	Most serious stabilisation effort	Months from start of transition
Albania	August 1992	18
Bulgaria	February 1991	13
Croatia	November 1993	30
Czech Republic	January 1991	13
FYR Macedonia	January 1994	36
Hungary	March 1990	6
Poland	January 1990	6
Romania	September 1993	45
Slovenia	February 1992	8

Source: Adapted data from EBRD (1999).

The EBRD (1999, p. 103) notes:

> The gradual approach has too often been used as a rhetorical cover for preserving the *status quo* ... rather than a strategic plan for sequencing the numerous components of reform. In such cases the consequences of this approach have been unambiguously adverse. Lack of progress with privatisation has left firms in limbo and allowed incumbents to seize assets. Far from reducing the costs of transition, such an approach has imposed high costs on the population.

It has already been noted that in all the CEE countries, the shift to a market economy was accompanied by a rise in inflation. Reducing inflation depended on the strictness and completeness of the stabilisation measures undertaken, which helped some countries reduce the rate of growth of prices to less than 10 per cent per annum (Czech Republic, Slovakia, Slovenia, Croatia, FYR Macedonia). The key factor in disinflation was a restrictive monetary policy, especially the halting of the monetary financing of budget deficits. Because the disproportionate growth in the money supply was understood to be a major cause of inflation, most of the CEE countries committed themselves to a real positive interest rate policy. Positive interest, along with restrictive money supply targets, were the key instruments of disinflation policy. Of all the transition countries in Central and Eastern Europe only Bulgaria and Romania continued to face high inflation throughout transition, until just recently. The percentage change in consumer prices in 1997 in Bulgaria was 579 per cent; in the next two years, thanks primarily to the currency board introduced in mid-1997 and its tough fiscal policy, the inflation rate was reduced to 1 per cent in 1998 and 2 per cent in 1999.

Romania is still confronted with price rises of above 40 per cent per annum. This is a consequence of its failure to tighten financial discipline in the public sector. Some key loss makers are still receiving government financial assistance and there is wide toleration of tax arrears. Besides, Romania has not yet undertaken the structural reforms necessary to sustain GDP growth and the cost-reduction process.

After full employment under socialism, all SEE countries have registered mass unemployment in the two-digit range during transition. The exceptions are the Czech Republic and Romania. Baltic countries in transition have had relatively good unemployment figures.

In all the socialist countries, with the exception of the former Yugoslavia, the respective government controlled the economy more or less tightly. Economic agents enjoyed only restricted autonomy in decision making. The 'clearing of the markets' occurred through administered prices that were heavily distorted and could not optimise the allocation of productive resources or consumer goods. Socialist enterprises were notoriously insensitive to prices. The key to this unresponsiveness lay in the soft-budget constraints that prevailed in all these countries. Credit allocation was a byproduct of the central plan, and solvency was guaranteed through more or less direct subsidies and distorted prices. Getting soft loans was more important to socialist enterprises than looking after productivity growth and cutting costs. To this day, soft-budget constraints remain the factor determining the behaviour of firms in some countries in transition. Even when privatised, enterprises have not been subjected to hard-budget constraints owing to institutional weaknesses. Therefore, opportunities for unproductive profit seeking are in place, whereas incentives for enhancing efficiency do not have a prominent role yet.

BUILDING A FINANCIAL SYSTEM

Banks are the main institutions of the financial system of the South-East European countries. It is interesting that their role is more prominent here than in many developing countries with an efficient financial market. The banks evaluate the profitability of projects to be financed by assessing the borrower's creditworthiness, and also perform other significant financial functions, such as operating the clearing and payments system as well as the foreign exchange market. Consequently, the SEE countries' banking sector is the main institution for implementing monetary policy measures affecting market interest rates, the liquidity stance and economic activity as well.

In the former socialist countries, banks had special functions under the central plan system of allocation of economic and financial assets. Banks were in fact accounting agencies that implemented financial plans, held private savings deposits, and executed foreign payments. Banks have created and distributed bookkeeping claims to allow financing directed by the plan. The SEE countries entered transition with an inefficient financial system that had several drawbacks. The portfolios of commercial banks were dominated by non-performing ('bad') loans. A whole string of prerequisites necessary for market economies was missing: accounting standards, supervisory functions, legal regulation, proper supervision and specialised experts.

The legacies of central plan banking proved an exceptionally difficult burden for all countries in transition. As they became exposed to market conditions many enterprises simply could not continue producing and so defaulted on loans, which in turn impacted on the activities of the banks themselves. The growing stock of non-performing loans in the bank portfolios reduced the volume of credit available for good borrowers. Many of the SEE countries' banks restricted themselves to financing trade, or working capital, so that enterprises had no access to supplementary investment funds. This proved to be one of the factors contributing to slower economic growth than the available assets and labour force might otherwise have permitted. The form and magnitude of these problems differed from one transition country to the next, but they were pronounced in the SEE countries (some of the more-developed Central European countries managed to mitigate the effects of the inherited, inefficient financial system).

Apart from initial conditions, the absence or, at best, the slowing down of structural reforms is another crucial factor that contributed to modest economic results in the SEE countries. These countries did not really complete the process of building up a market economy. The average EBRD transition indicator for SEE countries was 2.19 in 1999 in contrast to 3.16 for the five Central European economies. The competition policy index for CEE countries was thus 3.0 against 1.9 for the SEE countries. The banking index for middle Europe was 3.2, and it was 2.1 for South-East Europe.

The liberalisation of the banking sector in SEE countries enabled the sprouting of a large number of small, poorly supervised, private banks with average low-skilled professional staff and inadequate loss-provisioning. The proportion of bad loans in the banks of SEE countries in 1998 and 1999 was between 11 per cent (in Croatia) and 91 per cent (in Albania, prior to the restructuring programme of the state-owned banks).

The required capital adequacy ratio was 8 per cent in these countries whereas Bulgaria and Croatia had 12 and 10 per cent, respectively. State assets dominate in the structure of banking assets. Their proportion is greatest in Albania – 90 per cent – while in Bulgaria it is 60 per cent, 75 per cent in Romania and 42 per cent in Croatia (there are no reliable data for BiH, FR Yugoslavia and FYR Macedonia). The regulatory framework of SEE countries was rated by the World Bank as 'acceptable' (FR Yugoslavia being an exception). However, important tasks remain to be fulfilled in monitoring and verifying loan classifications.

When a small number of banks dominate an economy, as is the case with the SEE countries, the competition mechanism does not work in a satisfactory way. This can jeopardise financial stability. Likewise, inefficient enterprises do not repay the credits (that is, the problem of bad loans, typical of the banking systems of ex-socialist countries). This, combined with the fact that transition banks are hugely leveraged, makes them vulnerable to various unpredictable disequilibrium factors. In such circumstances, even a minor problem of paying off savings deposits can lead to a 'run on the banks', which has already happened in certain countries.

A study conducted in 1996 on a sample of 29 bank insolvencies, showed that the following were the important contributory factors: terms of trade decline, economic recession, deficient bank management, poor supervision and political interference (Caprio and Klingebiel, 1996, p. 91).

Among South-East European countries, FYR Macedonia has been able to avoid the problems that have burdened Albania, FR Yugoslavia and Romania. Namely, in 1997, the operation of the largest savings bank was suspended when unreported deposits were found. There were some capital outflows after the suspension, but no other effects of financial activities were registered.

Bank liquidity problems appeared in Bulgaria at the end of 1995 when several banks were not able to settle their obligations as a result of the huge accumulation of bad loans. Trust in the banking system diminished, and the banks' deposit base was promptly reduced. This led to the closure of some banks. One year later, a run on the whole banking system occurred (in the first half of the year domestic currency deposits as a percentage of GDP were halved, and foreign currency withdrawals were about 40 per cent of deposits outstanding). The Bulgarian central bank supported the state banks facing the greatest strain and initiated the liquidation of several banks. GDP growth was 2.1 per cent before the banking crisis; in the year of crisis it collapsed to –11 per cent, and to –7 per cent in the year after the crisis.

In Albania, the 'pyramid saving schemes' attracted foreign currency deposits estimated at between 45 and 55 per cent of GDP in the period from 1994 to 1996. The legal system and existing regulatory network enabled these schemes. They collapsed at the beginning of 1997 when 'savings' companies were no longer capable of continuing to pull in new money with which the high interest payments for the previously deposited money were to be made (two private Yugoslav banks faced a similar problem, with their own style of saving schemes, resulting in their collapse following insolvency).

A sound banking system performs many crucial roles in the economy: from intermediation and facilitating payment flows, to maturity transformation and credit allocation. Banks serve an important function as allocators of financial resources and suppliers of liquidity. In transition countries with underdeveloped equity and capital markets, only banks can produce the necessary information and help reduce risks in different business and financial activities. Furthermore, they play an important role in enhancing financial discipline and so contribute to corporate governance. Since the market for corporate securities is limited in most SEE countries, a great proportion of lending is unsecuritised. Consequently, banks are the principal institution evaluating and supervising the magnitude of returns through the process of financing investment projects. The banks' efficiency in performing these tasks was a crucial determinant of the economic performance of the CEE countries from the beginning of transition. Several factors underpin this efficiency and the most important are the macroeconomic environment, the level of competition, a supportive legal framework, and a proper system of regulation and supervision. A common reason why the banks failed to perform their tasks effectively was interference by government authorities in banks' remit to secure financial assistance to inefficient state-owned enterprises, restrict ties with foreign banks, limit the flow of capital, and so on.

The lack of an efficient, market-based banking system proved a drawback for the implementation of monetary policy. That is, the transmission mechanism could not function without distortion because banks with weak balance sheets are less responsive to changes in mandatory reserves and interest rates. In the SEE countries, the institutional capacity of the financial system grew faster when a new banking system based on newly opened private banks was allowed to develop alongside the existing one. Similarly, it has been shown that the capacities of the financial system improved faster when new banks were allowed in than when the government attempted reform by merely restructuring existing state banks.

Extensive recourse to foreign means of payments – the phenomenon known as 'dollarisation'– was one of the factors hampering the orderly functioning of the financial system and directly impacting on the conduct of monetary policy. Previously, management of demand and supply of foreign currency had been concentrated in the central bank, which determined the allocation of foreign currency. Foreign currency holdings by domestic residents were restricted (however, dollarisation had officially been accepted in the pre-reform period in the former Yugoslavia, Poland and Hungary). It is noteworthy that liberalisation of the foreign exchange regime was one of the first steps taken at the very outset of the transition process in Central and Eastern Europe, whereas reform of the domestic financial system proceeded more slowly. One important reason for inducting foreign means of payment was that inflation had eroded the value of domestic currency.

Dollarisation has begun to decline with the process of stabilisation, and confidence in the domestic currency has revived as inflation has been tamed. The term 'dollarisation' refers to foreign cash currency circulating within the domestic economy and foreign exchange deposits held in domestic banks. Excluded, however, are the foreign currency deposits of nationals in banks abroad. The magnitude of these deposits is difficult to estimate and moreover they do not impact directly on the domestic economy (the World Bank defines the dollarisation ratio as the ratio of foreign exchange deposits to broad money supply, but excluding foreign cash in the domestic economy and deposits held at banks abroad, obviously because it is very difficult to estimate their volume).

All the transition countries, and the SEE countries could not have been an exception in this regard, had to ground reform of the financial system in the following basic tasks:

- to establish the central bank as a politically independent institution;
- to reduce the massive size of non-performing loans on bank balance sheets;
- to address the underdeveloped infrastructure and incentives for savings collection;

- to implement a legal framework for the entry of new banks and rehabilitation of existing banks;
- to develop non-bank financial institutions to complement commercial banks; and
- to bring the capital market to life.

BIBLIOGRAPHY

Atkinson, A.B. and J. Micklewright (1992), *Economic Transformation in Eastern Europe and the Distribution of Income*, Cambridge: Cambridge University Press.

Berg, A., E. Borensztein, R. Sahay and J. Zettelmeyer (1999), 'The evolution of output in transition economies: explaining the differences', IMF Working Paper, WP/99/73, Washington, DC: IMF.

Caprio, G. Jr and D. Klingebiel (1996), 'Bank Insolvency: Bad Luck, Bad Policy, or Bad Banking?', Annual World Bank Conference on Development Economics, Washington, DC: WB, pp. 5.

Christofferson, P. and P. Doyle (1998), 'From inflation to growth: eight years of transition', IMF Working paper, WP/98/100, Washington, DC: IMF.

Miklaszewska, E. (ed.) (1995), *Competitive Banking in Central and Eastern Europe*, Krakow: Jagielonian University Press.

De Melo, M., C. Denizer, A. Gelb and S. Tenev (1997), 'Circumstances and choice: the role of initial conditions and policies in transition economies', World Bank Policy Research Working Paper, No. 1866, Washington, DC: World Bank.

European Bank for Reconstruction and Development (EBRD)(1996), *Transition Report*, London: EBRD.

European Bank for Reconstruction and Development (EBRD)(1997), *Transition Report*, London: EBRD.

European Bank for Reconstruction and Development (EBRD)(1998), *Transition Report*, London: EBRD.

European Bank for Reconstruction and Development (EBRD)(1999), *Transition Report*, London: EBRD.

Fischer, S., R. Sahay and C.A. Vegh (1996), 'Stabilisation and growth in transition economies: the early experience', *Journal of Economic Perspectives*, **10**, pp. 45–66.

Fischer, S., R. Sahay and C.A. Vegh (1997), 'From transition to market: evidence and growth prospects', in S. Zecchini (ed.), *Lessons from the Economic Transition. Central and Eastern Europe in the 1990s*, Dordrecht: Kluwer Academic.

Gruszecki, T. and J. Winiecki (1991), 'Privatisation in East-Central Europe: a comparative perspective', *Aussenwirtschaft*, **46**, pp. 67–100.

Hinds, M.E. (1990), *Issues in the Introduction of Market Forces in Eastern European Socialist Economies*, Report No. IDP-0057, Washington, DC: World Bank.

International Monetary Fund (IMF)(1996), *Partnership for Sustainable Global Growth*, Interim Committee Declaration, September, Washington, DC: IMF.

Lavigne, M. (1999), *The Economics of Transition*, London: Macmillan.

Malinvaud, E., J.-C. Milleron, M. Nabli, A. Sen, A. Sengupta, N. Stern, J. Stiglitz and K. Suzumura (1997), *Development Strategy and the Management of the Market Economy*, Vol I, Oxford: Oxford University Press.

Milanović, B. (1996), 'Income, inequality and poverty during the transition', Transition Economies Division Research Paper Series, No. 11, Washington, DC: World Bank and Paris: OECD.
Nuti, D. Mario (1990), 'Crisis, reform and stabilisation in Central Eastern Europe: prospects and Western response', in *La Grande Europa. La Nuova Europa: Opportunita e Rischi*, Sienna: Monti Dei Paschi Di Sienna.
Organisation for Economic Co-operation and Development (OECD)(1997), *The New Banking Landscape in Central and Eastern Europe*, Paris: OECD.
Roland, G. and T. Verdier (1999), 'Transition and the output fall', *Economics of Transition*, **7**, pp. 1–28.
Rosati, D. (1994), 'Output decline during transition from plan to market', *Economics of Transition*, **2** (4), pp. 419–42.
Stern, N.H. (1992), *Le Rôle de l'État dans le Développement Économique/The Role of the State in Economic Development*, Lausanne: Editions Payout.
Stern, Nicholas (1996), 'The transition in Eastern Europe and the former Soviet Union: some strategic lessons from the experience of 25 countries over six years', Conference paper, OECD/CCET Colloquium, Paris.
Stern, Nicholas and Joseph E. Stiglitz (1997), 'A framework for a development strategy in a market economy: objectives, scope, institutions and instruments', EBRD Working Paper 20, London: EBRD.
Williamson, J. (1991), '*The economic opening of Eastern Europe*', Washington, DC: Institute for International Economics, *Policy Analysis*, **31**.
World Bank (1996), *From Plan to Market. World Development Report 1996*, Washington, DC: World Bank.
World Bank (1997), *World Development Report 1997*, New York: Oxford University Press.

3. The Role of the Stability Pact in Financial Sector Reform in South-East Europe

Fabrizio Saccomanni[1]

INTRODUCTION

The Stability Pact for South-East Europe was established in Cologne by the Group of Eight (G-8) Summit in June 1999 on the initiative of the European Union (EU) with the objective of restoring the conditions for a lasting peace and sustainable economic recovery in the region. The strategy was to be implemented by a joint effort of all Stability Pact participants (donor countries, international financial institutions and regional countries) to promote a rapid reconstruction of the main regional infrastructural networks (transport, energy, telecommunications, water) and a broad spectrum of structural reforms. The reform process was to lay the foundations for the development in the region of democratic societies, based on the rule of law, and of viable market-based open economic systems.

In order to fulfil its objectives the Stability Pact was expected to establish a number of consultative *fora*, involving all participating countries and institutions, where regional problems and requirements could be jointly examined with a view to the adoption of appropriate regional solutions. It is clear from the Stability Pact founding documents and from the Sarajevo Summit declaration of the Stability Pact Heads of State and Government of July 1999[2] that the new institution was to remain light and lean, without its own financial resources and operational structures, and entrusted essentially with a mandate to stimulate co-operation among participants through multilateral consultation, surveillance and peer pressure. The instructions were, simply stated, to avoid duplication of efforts and to exploit synergies among existing initiatives, thus creating added value for the international community strategy in South-East Europe.

The Stability Pact as an institution is managed by a special coordinator who chairs a Regional Table, the main political body of the Stability Pact, made up of ministers or deputy ministers of foreign affairs. Under the overall guidance of the Regional Table there are three working tables entrusted, respectively, with: democratisation and human rights (Working Table I); economic reconstruction, development and co-operation (Working Table II); and security issues (Working Table III).

Since its establishment, Working Table II has been active in both infrastructural reconstruction and institution building processes. A package of regional projects with an estimated cost of €1.7 billion, identified and agreed upon within Working Table II, has received the necessary financial support at a regional funding conference in Brussels in March 2000, where a total of €2.4 billion (also covering projects presented by Working Tables I and III) have been pledged by donor countries and international financial institutions. At its meeting in Skopje in February 2000, Working Table II agreed upon a series of objectives and procedures to create a climate attractive to foreign investment in the region which were embodied in a special instrument, the South-East Europe Compact for Reform, Investment, Integrity and Growth (Investment Compact).[3] The Investment Compact is now the framework for the reform process in the economic, legal and administrative fields.

The need to include financial sector reform in the context of the institution-building process in South-East Europe was widely recognised by the international community as a key medium-term objective in the process of economic rehabilitation of the region and an essential precondition for setting in motion a sustainable growth process. The objective of reform in this context could be defined as the set of measures needed to establish or re-establish an efficient and sound banking and financial system; to achieve these goals may require either adopting measures of financial consolidation and restructuring of ailing institutions, or introducing appropriate legislation in the field of banking and financial system regulation and supervision, or both. Financial sector reform was not included in the list of the specific tasks of the Stability Pact and the reason for the omission is probably the conviction that a politically delicate and technically difficult matter like financial sector reform should be left to specialised international institutions such as the International Monetary Fund (IMF), the World Bank, the European Bank for Reconstruction and Development (EBRD) and by the Commission of the European Union.

The experience gained in the context of Working Table II has, however, pointed to the need for a regional approach also in the field of financial sector reform precisely in order to complement the country-specific initiatives of specialised agencies. Moreover, the recent political developments in the region following the change of regime in the Federal Republic of Yugoslavia, where the banking and financial systems would most likely require a strong dose of restructuring following a decade of political and economic upheavals under a regime of pervasive state interference, have underlined the urgency to act in this field in order to speed up the process of the economic recovery and the resumption of foreign investment for the full South-East European region, including the Federal Republic of Yugoslavia. A proposal for a Stability Pact initiative in the financial sector was presented by the Greek government at the Working Table II meeting in Istanbul in October 2000 and has received broad support from regional countries.

The remainder of this chapter is organised as follows: the next section will briefly review the case for financial sector reform in the context of the strategy undertaken by the G-8 countries within the International Monetary Fund to build an 'international financial architecture' and of the process of gradual monetary and financial integration in the European Union; the third section will present a concise assessment of the initiatives currently undertaken in the financial sector by the major specialised international institutions; the fourth section will describe the current status of banks and financial markets in South-East Europe, outlining the policy challenges confronting the governments of the region; and the concluding section will identify the possible role that the Stability Pact would play in promoting financial sector reform.

One final introductory remark. The purpose of this chapter is not to carry out a new empirical investigation of the situation of the financial sector in South-East Europe. Rather, as stated in the mandate of the Stability Pact, the intention is to make use of available information and analysis, to stimulate a debate on issues of regional relevance, with the aim of mobilising the political and intellectual support necessary for a comprehensive and determined reform effort. It is argued, in particular, that Working Table II could play a role in promoting co-ordination and collaboration among regional countries and the relevant international financial institutions and in drawing the attention of private banks and financial intermediaries in Western Europe and other industrial countries to the business and investment opportunities offered by the reform process in the region. This is a contribution to that objective.

THE NEED FOR FINANCIAL SECTOR REFORM: THE INTERNATIONAL CONTEXT

When the Stability Pact was established the signatories were confronted with two major challenges: (i) to recreate the conditions for a resumption of growth in incomes and employment following a decade of conflicts which had resulted in a dramatic deterioration in living standards; and (ii) to set in motion in the region the process of transition towards a modern, competitive market economy which, after the fall of the Berlin Wall, had never really started because of the hostilities. In facing these challenges, the international community had to take stock of the lessons drawn from the difficulties experienced in the transition process by countries in Central and Eastern Europe, including Russia, and from the financial crisis suffered by emerging economies in Asia, Eastern Europe and Latin America during the 1990s.

The initiative taken by the European Union to launch the Stability Pact was based on the experience accumulated by the European Commission in dealing with Eastern European countries since 1990. It pointed to the need for a comprehensive strategy in which the financial assistance needed for reconstruction and relief would be coupled with a broad range of measures of institution building to promote democratisation, to establish law-based and market-oriented social and economic systems. In addition the Stability Pact was to provide a framework for the eventual integration of South-East Europe in the economic and trading system of the European Union and in the Euro-Atlantic structures.

As the Stability Pact organised its structures in the autumn of 1999, the evidence of ten years of transition strategies and policies was reviewed by the EBRD (1999). In its *Transition Report*, the EBRD concluded: that the process had turned out to be longer and more difficult than anticipated at the time of the collapse of the Berlin Wall; that liberalisation and privatisation, although necessary steps of the process, were not sufficient; and that a comprehensive strategy of institution building was required to support markets and private enterprises and to promote good governance in the state and in the corporate sectors.

At the same G-8 Summit that had launched the Stability Pact, the leaders endorsed a plan for reform of the international financial architecture designed to prevent the recurrent eruption of financial crises in emerging countries and their dissemination to international financial markets. The plan was in response to the series of episodes of turbulence which had characterised the 1990s, highlighting the volatility of capital flows and the vulnerability of the global financial system to the risks of contagion among the main debtor countries. Here again, as described in detail by Eichengreen (1999) and Saccomanni (2000), the plan assigned a major role to institution building, with the emphasis being on the need for effective prudential supervision on banking and financial markets, for improved lending and risk-management policies, for the introduction of internationally agreed standards for accounting, auditing and disclosure. The new architecture also provided indications for the choice of the exchange rate regime: emerging countries were advised to avoid exchange arrangements that may induce speculative capital flows and to adopt either a freely floating exchange rate or a currency board arrangement linked to a major reserve currency.

In the spring of 2000, the issue of strengthening the banking and financial system in countries of South-East Europe was indirectly addressed by the eurosystem, that is, the body comprising the European Central Bank and the national central banks that have adopted the euro, in the context of its discussion of the position to be taken on monetary issues *vis-à-vis* accession countries of the European Union. Such discussion had been prompted by unilateral developments in the exchange regime of a number of Eastern European countries as well as by the proposals elaborated by Emerson et al. (1999) and Gros (1999) within the Centre for European Policies Studies, a respected European 'think-tank'. The proposals called for, *inter alia*, the immediate adoption of euro-based currency board regimes by countries of the region as a step towards full euroisation by 1 January 2003.

The eurosystem formally took the position that the appropriateness of euro-based currency board arrangements would be decided on a case-by-case basis and that their adoption would be neither encouraged nor discouraged. The eurosystem, however, indicated that such arrangements cannot be regarded as a substitute for the two years' participation in the Exchange Rate Mechanism (ERM) of the European Union as envisaged by the Maastricht Treaty. Accession countries which have operated a euro-based currency board deemed to be sustainable might not be required to go through a double regime shift (from a currency board to the ERM, and from the ERM to the euro) in the process of adopting the euro. Thus accession countries may participate in the ERM with a currency board as a unilateral commitment provided there is a common accord with the eurosystem about the central parity against the euro.[4] The same position was confirmed by the EU Council of Economic and Financial Ministers in their report to the European Council in Nice on 13 December 2000. The report indicated that the only clear incompatibilities with the ERM are the cases of free floating, crawling pegs and pegs against anchors other than the euro.[5]

There is broad consensus, however, that a key prerequisite for the successful adoption of a currency board is the existence of a sound banking system, as the currency board implies that there would not be any creation of liquidity for the purpose of rescuing domestic banks in difficulties. This implies in turn that either there is a strong prudential supervision on the banking system in operation or there is a readiness to allow insolvent banks to fail. The eurosystem has indeed made clear that the adoption by any country of a euro-based currency board would not imply any responsibility for the European Central Bank to provide liquidity support to banking systems of such countries.

Therefore, all the lessons of the transition process in Eastern Europe and of the financial vicissitudes of emerging economies in the 1990s point to the need for banking and financial systems that are both efficient enough to support the development process of the economy and to attract foreign investment, and strong enough to manage the changes in credit and market risks that may arise from domestic and international financial turbulence. The evidence also shows that in the sequencing of the reform process, restructuring of the banking and financial system should take priority over other policy measures that may expose the economy to external factors of tension, such as the removal of exchange and capital restrictions and the adoption of a fixed exchange rate regime of any kind.[6]

In the drafting of a strategy for the international community in South-East Europe, financial sector reform was seen as an integral element of the policy agenda, but not one falling necessarily under the competence of the Stability Pact. At its first meeting in Bari in October 1999, Working Table II asked the World Bank to prepare a regional strategy paper outlining the key policy issues to be addressed by the region and the international community. The paper submitted to Working Table II by the World Bank (2000, pp. 11–12) identified the key components of a strategy for stability and prosperity as follows:

- *For the South-East European (SEE) countries*, there needs to be both a strong commitment towards political and social stability within the region and a determined effort to implement consistent macroeconomic stabilisation policies and deep structural, institutional, social and environmental reforms (for example, trade, privatisation, competition policy and financial sector reforms).
- *For the Stability Pact partners*, there needs to be parallel commitments both to providing a clear and credible roadmap for the eventual integration of the SEE countries into European and global structures and to providing financial and technical and political support to domestic reform programmes and regional initiatives.

Regarding financial sector reform in particular, the World Bank (2000, p. 14) indications were as follows:

- improve lending policies/practices and risk management of banks;
- manage foreign debt efficiently;
- improve bank governance through privatisation and strengthen supervision of banks and financial institutions;
- improve accounting and auditing practices, and adopt international accounting standards;

- strengthen the institutional/market framework, improve the technology of financial intermediaries and markets and enhance information transparency.

In its evaluation of the strategy, the World Bank paper underlined that the 'crucial incentive for success' would be provided by the economic and commercial integration of South-East Europe in European and global structures, without which the pursuit of sound macroeconomic and structural policies would not be sufficient to create the condition for growth and prosperity. From this point of view, a key role would be played by the European Union, through its Stabilisation and Association Agreements, in paving the way for the access of South-East Europe to the European single market and to the World Trade Organisation. The membership of the Stability Pact broadly endorsed the analysis of the World Bank and agreed that the Stability Pact structures should give priority attention to the identification of projects in their respective areas of competence which could be quickly brought to the attention of a donors' conference. Working Table II in particular was expected to identify infrastructural projects of a regional dimension and to promote reforms needed to create a favourable climate for foreign investment. Strategies to ensure macroeconomic stabilisation and structural reforms (including financial sector reform) would continue to be supported by IMF and World Bank country programmes.

In view of this agreed division of labour, the Investment Compact approved by the Stability Pact, while recognising that 'a well regulated and supervised financial and banking sector are the *sine qua non* of economic revitalisation' (Stability Pact, 2001, p. 7), identified the task of the Stability Pact structures mainly in the field of legal, tax and administrative frameworks for foreign investment. In this context, special attention was to be devoted to measures designed to fight corruption among public administrators and to avoid illegal practices such as money laundering.

FINANCIAL SECTOR REFORM IN SOUTH-EAST EUROPE AND THE ROLE OF INTERNATIONAL FINANCIAL INSTITUTIONS

The need for financial sector reform in South-East Europe is well known to the major international financial institutions, which have been active in the region in various capacities for many years. The IMF, the World Bank and the EBRD have all been involved in the region during the 1990s and the same is true for the European Commission, which has been dealing with Bulgaria and Romania under its policy for accession countries and with other Western

Balkan countries (the countries of former Yugoslavia, except Slovenia, plus Albania) under the framework of its Stabilisation and Association Agreements. Each institution has held an active policy dialogue with SEE countries according to its specialisation and mandate; joint activities have also been performed and inter-institutional collaboration has been generally applied. What follows is a concise description of the initiative undertaken by the major international organisations and the European Union. The objective is not to provide a full and comprehensive account, but to give an overall impression of the range of issues, instruments and institutions covered by the reform effort.

The IMF has been primarily involved in the process of macroeconomic management and has put in place stabilisation programmes with all six regional countries at an early stage of their transition and has also extended financial support through its various facilities, including a new 'Systemic Transformation Facility', established for a limited period (1993–95), which had lower conditionality than the traditional IMF financing arrangements.[7] At the end of 2000, the IMF had financial assistance programmes in operation or under negotiation within all the six regional countries. In order to carry out the stabilisation policy measures, the IMF normally requires 'prior actions' that involve the establishment of appropriate procedures and institutions needed for a well-functioning market economy. In this endeavour, the IMF has worked closely with the World Bank, whose primary responsibility is assisting members in the field of structural adjustment and reforms. In the financial sector, the IMF and the World Bank, together with bilateral donors, have helped to transform the former monobank system into a two-tier system, with a central bank and a commercial banking system, and to introduce modern payment systems. The IMF has provided extensive technical assistance to regional countries covering a wide range of areas, such as monetary policy operations and instruments; bank restructuring, supervision and regulation; design of deposit insurance and payments system; central bank operation and accounting; development of money, foreign exchange and capital markets.

The World Bank has been and is currently active in all regional countries with a variety of projects including adjustment operations, technical assistance and investment projects. The main objectives of these operations are strengthening the regulatory framework for the financial sector, increasing supervisory capacity, and improving the performance of banks and the quality of banking intermediation. The non-banking financial sector is receiving significantly less attention than the banking system.[8] In all countries, the Bank is linking activities in the financial sector with initiatives in support of private sector development in collaboration with the EBRD. The World Bank is not currently involved in financial sector activities on a regional scale; however, a regional trade credit insurance facility and a regional export support facility were proposed by the World Bank at the Stability Pact Regional Funding Conference in March 2000 in the context of the private sector development initiatives of the EBRD. Although these proposals did not receive specific financial support from participants, the World Bank is still developing the concept for such facilities. Together with the IMF, the World Bank is planning to undertake financial sector assessment in a few SEE countries. These assessments, which are part of a World Bank–IMF institutional collaboration programme, will focus on the sensitivity of financial institutions to macroeconomic shocks, evaluate the development of the financial system, assess the adequacy of legal and institutional infrastructure, assess compliance with international standards, and propose priorities for strengthening the financial sector.

The EBRD has also been active in South-East Europe since its foundation and has supported a number of projects aimed at promoting the development of private companies, particularly small and medium-sized enterprises (SMEs), through a variety of instruments including co-financing with bilateral donors, and direct purchase of equity in SMEs and financial institutions (both banks and non-banks). In the context of the Stability Pact, the EBRD was given a mandate to co-ordinate the international community's efforts to promote economic development and regional integration in South-East Europe through a private sector development strategy. To this end a paper was presented to the March Funding Conference (EBRD, 2000b), which describes ten specific regional initiatives which have been selected through a process of consultation among the international financial institutions as having the most immediate impact. Most of the initiatives are based on existing operations or proven models which can be extended from one country to another. The following projects of the EBRD are relevant for the development of the financial sector:

1. a trade facilitation programme, amounting to €30 million to be carried out with participating banks in the region. The bulk of demand for this facility has been in FYR Macedonia with strong growth expected in Bosnia and Herzegovina;
2. a micro-enterprise bank (MEB) programme, amounting to €14 million which is a significant sum for small loan programmes. MEBs are now established in Bosnia and Herzegovina, Kosovo, and Albania, and are under preparation in Macedonia and Romania. MEB Kosovo has successfully supported the recovery of small businesses and has provided basic banking and payments services; and
3. a small equity funds programme, which has obtained donor support totalling €22 million. The Albanian Reconstruction Equity Fund

(USD 14 million) has expanded its operations into Kosovo (USD 5 million). In addition a similar project is under development to benefit small enterprises in Macedonia.

The European Union and the European Commission are also promoting financial sector reform in the context of the EU strategy of institution building in Eastern Europe. Among the SEE countries that are beneficiaries of Stability Pact initiatives, two, namely Bulgaria and Romania, are included in the list of so-called accession countries which are expected to meet the requirements spelled out by the Copenhagen European Council of 1993.[9] These countries are also eligible for a special type of financial assistance, especially designed to support the pre-accession process. Following the conclusion of the conflict in Kosovo in the summer of 1999, the European Union has developed a strategy for co-operation with the other Western Balkan countries which is centred on the Stabilisation and Association Agreements. In this connection, the European Union has also undertaken to rationalise its own financial assistance activities to these countries. The process has led to the approval, by the EU Council on 5 December 2000, of a new regulation on Community Assistance for Reconstruction, Development and Stability (CARDS), which allocates funds totalling €4.65 billion for the 2000–2006 period to Albania, Bosnia and Herzegovina, Croatia, and Macedonia, as well as to the Federal Republic of Yugoslavia, following the establishment of a democratic Federal government in that country. The CARDS regulation (European Union, 2000) specifically states that: 'EU assistance will aim in particular at developing the institutional, legislative, economic framework in relation to the values and models on which the EU is based and at promoting a market-based economy'; moreover, the regulation indicates that 'particular attention will be devoted to the regional dimension of Community assistance, in order to strengthen regional co-operation and underpin the leading role of the European Union in the context of the Stability Pact'. The European Union is also providing financial support to SEE countries under its Macro Financial Assistance programme. The purpose of this assistance is essentially to finance a current account balance of payments deficit during a period of economic reform and to smooth the cost of transition.[10] The macro financial assistance loans are associated with conditionality, which is similar to that applied by the IMF and may also cover structural aspects such as financial sector reform. Recent macro financial assistance in 1999–2000 has been granted to Macedonia, Bosnia and Herzegovina, and Montenegro and all include financial sector reform conditions.

The European Union is also active in the region through the European Investment Bank (EIB). Although the EIB is primarily financing large infrastructural projects, it is also extending credit to selected development and commercial banks for on-lending to SMEs (the so-called 'global loans'). In this way the EIB is in a position to assist such banks in the improvement of lending and risk-management techniques. The EIB has extended global loans to banks in Albania, Bulgaria and Romania.

THE FINANCIAL SECTOR IN SOUTH-EAST EUROPE

An in-depth evaluation of the impact of the various initiatives undertaken in the region over the past decade by the international community would go beyond the scope of this chapter. There is, however, sufficient information to draw an overall impression of the state of the transition of financial sector in individual countries of South-East Europe.

The best systematic surveys available of the status of the financial sector in South-East Europe have been conducted by the EBRD in its Transition Reports (EBRD 1998, 1999, 2000a) which have analysed in detail the financial system of Eastern Europe in 1998 and updated the relevant statistical information in 1999 and 2000. However, these reports do not include information about the Federal Republic of Yugoslavia (that is, Serbia and Montenegro) and the analysis is based on the experience of transition economies in general without a specific focus on South-East Europe. Moreover, in some cases, the underlying statistics do not go beyond 1997 or 1998. Despite these limitations the picture that comes out is quite clear and can be captured at a glance by looking at the transition indexes elaborated by the EBRD staff and presented in Table 3.1. The table covers the six countries that are considered as beneficiaries of Stability Pact initiatives (Albania, Bosnia and Herzegovina, Bulgaria, Croatia, FYR Macedonia, and Romania); Slovenia is also included for the sake of comparison and as a member of the former Yugoslavia although it is not a beneficiary country.

The indexes show that, despite some differences in the rating of individual countries, with relatively more satisfactory progress in the reform efforts in Croatia and Macedonia, the banking and financial systems of the region remain on average underdeveloped, both in absolute terms and in comparison with other transition economies of Central Europe such as Hungary or Poland, where the ratings in 1999 were well above three for both components of the financial sector. Reform efforts have been concentrated more on the banking sector than on the non-banking sector, which in all countries is relatively lagging behind. The momentum of the reform process, after an initial brisk pace in the 1991–96 period, appears to have faltered since then; in the case of Romania the banking reform process experienced a setback in 1997–98 and the recovery in 1999 was still insufficient to regain the lost improvements. This situation is similar to that experienced by other transition countries in the 1990s, which reflects the legacies of central planning and the heavy reliance on a monobank model typical of that era. However, in South-East Europe such deficiencies have been made more acute by the combination of political instability, regional wars, economic upheavals and financial crises that has plagued the region in the last decade. More detailed information about recent developments in the financial sector in South-East Europe drawn from the EBRD reports, is presented in the Appendix to this chapter.

Table 3.1 *EBRD banking and financial sector reform indexes*

		1991	1993	1996	1997	1998	1999
Albania	B	1.0	1.3	2.0	2.0	2.0	2.0
	F	1.0	1.0	1.7	1.7	1.7	1.7
Bosnia and	B	–	–	–	–	2.0	2.3
Herzegovina	F	–	–	–	–	1.0	1.0
Bulgaria	B	1.0	2.0	2.0	2.7	2.7	2.7
	F	1.0	1.0	2.0	2.0	2.0	2.0
Croatia	B	1.0	2.0	2.7	2.7	2.7	3.0
	F	1.0	1.0	2.0	2.3	2.3	2.3
FYR Macedonia	B	1.0	1.3	3.0	3.0	3.0	3.0
	F	1.0	1.0	1.0	1.0	1.7	1.7
Romania	B	1.0	1.0	3.0	2.7	2.3	2.7
	F	1.0	1.0	2.0	2.0	2.0	2.0
Slovenia*	B	1.0	3.0	3.0	3.0	3.0	3.3
	F	2.0	2.0	2.7	2.7	2.7	2.7

Notes:
* Not a beneficiary of Stability Pact initiatives.
Explanation of abbreviations:
B = EBRD Index of banking sector reform.
F = EBRD Index of reform of non-banking financial institutions.
Definitions of rating scores:
Banking sector reform
1 Little progress beyond establishment of two-tier system.
2 Significant liberalisation of interest rate ceilings.
3 Substantial progress in establishment of bank solvency and of a framework for prudential supervision and regulation; full interest rate liberalisation with little preferential access to cheap refinancing; significant lending to private enterprises and significant presence of private banks.
4 Significant movement of banking laws and regulations towards standards of the Bank for International Settlements; well-functioning banking competition and effective prudential supervision; significant term lending to private enterprises; substantial financial deepening.

4+ Standards and performance norms of advanced industrial economies; full convergence of banking laws and regulations with BIS standards; provision of full set of competitive banking services.

Financial sector reform

1 Little progress.
2 Formation of securities exchanges, market makers and brokers; some trading in government paper and/or securities; rudimentary legal and regulatory framework for the issuance and trading of securities.
3 Substantial issuance of securities by private enterprises; establishment of independent share registries, secure clearance and settlement procedures, and some protection of minority shareholders; emergence of non-bank financial institutions (e.g. investment funds, private insurance and pension funds, leasing companies) and associated regulatory framework.
4 Securities laws and regulations approaching international standards; substantial market liquidity and capitalisation; well-functioning non-bank financial institutions and effective regulation.
4+ Standards and performance norms of advanced industrial economies; full convergence of securities laws and regulations with international standards; fully developed non-bank intermediation.

Sources: EBRD (1998, 1999 and 2000a).

The conclusions of the EBRD reports are confirmed if the periodic IMF reviews of South-East European countries' performances are taken into account. The situation of the financial system is, of course, different from country to country, and it is recognised, not surprisingly, that more progress in the process of consolidation appears to have been made by countries where banking crises have recently erupted, such as in Bulgaria in 1996–97 and in Croatia in 1998. Even in these countries, however, the IMF finds that weaknesses remain and the amount of credit extended to the private sector is still very low. Vulnerabilities are also present in Macedonia and more seriously in Romania, while the performance of financial systems is considered unsatisfactory in Albania and especially in Bosnia and Herzegovina.

Despite the different situations prevailing in each country, common factors have been at play in South-East Europe and are at the root of the structural weakness of financial systems in the region. At the risk of oversimplifying the picture, the following elements appear of significant regional relevance.[11] A major element of weakness is the lack of a true banking culture, which requires that financial resources are allocated on the basis of a thorough assessment of the credit risk involved. Under the old system of central planning, banks were public entities which were de facto obliged to extend credit to public sector enterprises irrespective of their ability to repay. The consequence of the inability to properly assess credit risk is at the root of another major structural weakness of South-East European banks, namely the very high percentage of non-performing assets in their balance sheets, which in many cases would result, if properly valued, in a negative net worth. This phenomenon has not been corrected with the emergence of private enterprises following the process of privatisation. In fact banks have also continued to lend, without a proper assessment of the credit risk, to newly formed companies of insufficient credit standing.

The history of currency and banking crises in the region has created a deep-seated mistrust by the public *vis-à-vis* the banking and financial system as evidenced by the low level of bank deposits and the widespread hoarding of banknotes, preferably of foreign countries. Such lack of confidence has been corrected only marginally following the process of bank privatisation. In several cases, in fact, privatisation has not implied a change of management, as shareholdings have been fragmented and unable to express a new managerial function. Despite strong pressures from all quarters for a modernisation of banking legislation and the introduction of effective banking and financial sector supervision, progress in both areas has been slow and inadequate. While overall banking legislation has been reformed in recent years in most countries, efforts still need to be made to translate general principles into operational provisions and guidelines that would allow banks to monitor and manage their risk exposure effectively. Banking supervision also needs to be strengthened in this actual implementation, as central banks do not appear to have gained so far the autonomy necessary to deal with the prevention and resolution of banking crises. A key element in this regard is a more severe policy regarding the concession and the withdrawal of banking licences.

The level of competition in the South-East European banking systems is generally inadequate. This is to a large extent a legacy of the past system of reliance on one or two state banks, but it has not been significantly modified by the privatisation process or by the opening up of the market to foreign institutions. In fact, in most cases foreign banks operating in the region through local branches limit their business to documentary import–export credit or to financing customers from their own country, and do not engage in lending to local business or in retail banking. It must be stressed, however, that the incentives for foreign banks to acquire local banks are limited, as their poor financial standing and negative image are not reflected adequately in the 'asking price' suggested by the national governments.

Finally, a number of technical deficiencies, different from country to country, hamper the operation of the banking systems in South-East Europe. Among these the most important is the inefficiency of the payment system, still controlled in some countries by a network of payments bureaux run by the state, which makes the flow of payments slow and costly. Another major technical weakness is the inadequacy of the telecommunication system, which does not allow the transfer of information among banks through dedicated and secure channels.

All the above factors have combined in limiting the role that the banking system should play in the process of allocation of resources in the economy and in producing an inadequate supply of banking and financial services to households and enterprises, to savers and investors. Moreover, it is difficult to avoid the impression that the banking system of South-East Europe is a prisoner of a vicious circle. There is little doubt that despite the positive reforms introduced so far through new banking legislation, privatisation and institution building, in its present financial and organisational standing the banking system is unable to consolidate itself in a sustainable way and to support the revival of growth and economic activity in the region. These trends, in turn, are likely to undermine the efforts to address in a comprehensive manner the structural weaknesses of financial systems in South-East Europe.

WHAT ROLE FOR THE STABILITY PACT?

The question of whether the Stability Pact could play any role in promoting a process of financial sector reform in South-East Europe, which could be faster and more comprehensive than the set of separate actions undertaken to date by individual countries, boils down, de facto, to the more general question of whether the conditions exist in South-East Europe for the success of a more ambitious reform strategy to be implemented on a regional scale. In other words, is the present state of the financial sector in South-East Europe the best possible result that could be achieved under the circumstances, or could the outcome have been better? And as far as the future is concerned, is the continuation of the current slow-placed and country-specific approach the only realistic course of action that the international community can endorse and support?

These questions tend to be addressed on the basis of political considerations which can be used to justify both negative and affirmative responses. However, with the experience of ten years of the transition process in Eastern Europe, economic analysis and political economy are providing important elements to answer the questions in a more objective manner. A first element can be derived from the assessment about the controversy between the 'big-bang' and the 'gradualist' approaches to transition. Two papers, by Wyplosz (1999) and by Fischer and Sahay (2000), have reviewed the arguments for and against each approach and analysed the evidence of the performance of transition economies over the last decade; these studies broadly favour an intermediate approach that leans more towards the big bang than towards gradualism. Wyplosz (1999, p. 27) draws the following lesson:

> It has paid to start early and move fast. The first lesson is that Big Bang is highly desirable but impractical, while gradualism is unavoidable but ought to be compressed as much as possible. Clearly the countries that bit the bullet early and hard are those that have done better over the last decade.

Fischer and Sahay (2000, p. 17), in their empirical analysis, reach a similar conclusion:

> The experience accumulated in the past decade, whether viewed informally or with the help of data, charts and regressions, provides support for the view that the most successful transition economies are those who have both stabilised and undertaken comprehensive reforms and that more and faster reform is better than less and slower reform.

It follows from these analyses that gradualism must be redefined to mean not so much a slow, step-by-step process, but rather a comprehensive design to be carried out in a relatively short period of time and in which the various components of the reform are set in an appropriate sequence. Sequencing is thus the second element of the reform process that has to be taken into consideration and it has particular relevance for the financial sector. Here, again, the evidence shows that attempts to bypass the establishment of a sound domestic banking system, via a programme based on privatisation involving the creation or the rehabilitation of the stock market, have not worked. Wyplosz (1999, p. 30) notes that:

> Transition countries might conceivably jump the banking stage and move on to what appears as the next stage, stock market financing. This is unlikely, though, and could even be a dangerous strategy as stock markets may be far too volatile to attract a substantial part of domestic savings. This is why it is urgent to establish a sound banking system.

It is clear, therefore, that banking reform should rank highly in the list of reform priorities. The third element regards the timing of the reform strategy. As clearly explained by Balcerowicz (1994), the authorities should try to exploit the 'window of opportunity' represented by the special combination of political, social and economic conditions which inevitably materialises in the early stages of the transition process and which could facilitate the introduction of a broad range of reform measures. A consistent set of mutually reinforcing policies is likely to speed up the transition process, reducing its social and economic costs. The problem is that the window does not remain open for ever and if the opportunity is not taken, political short-sightedness and vested interests are likely to prevent it being opened again.

What are the implications of all this for South-East Europe? With the return of democracy in the Federal Republic of Yugoslavia, a unique window of opportunity is opening up to tackle financial sector reform with a comprehensive regional strategy to be implemented in a relatively short period of time. The main components of the strategy could be the following:

- speeding up reform of banking and financial sector legislation and regulation;
- launching a massive programme of training in modern banking and financial techniques for employees of financial sector institutions and in supervisory instruments and procedures for central bankers;
- restructuring of banking systems through the financial rehabilitation of viable institutions and the liquidation of structurally weak banks or their acquisition by stronger ones; and
- strengthening competition in the banking system through increased participation of foreign financial institutions to the capital and/or management of local banks or through greater involvement of branches of foreign banks in domestic retail banking.

The formulation and the implementation of this strategy could be discussed within the Stability Pact in the context of an *ad hoc* initiative co-ordinated by Working Table II to promote financial sector reform. The key objectives of the initiative would be to highlight the urgency of a comprehensive reform strategy and to gather support for a multilateral action plan. Working Table II could organise *ad hoc* meetings to discuss the details of the plan and could utilise the institutional framework of the Investment Compact to monitor its implementation. The main actors of the play would be:

- the monetary, financial and regulatory authorities in the region's countries;
- the main international institutions (IMF, World Bank, EBRD) which, together with the European Union, have been involved in financial sector reform projects; and
- the main private commercial banks and financial institutions of the Western world.

It is not the purpose of this chapter to guess what should be the concrete results of such initiative. A few general considerations, however, may be in order.

First, it is essential that the monetary and financial authorities of the region establish regular working relationships to deal with common problems in the financial sector. The institutional framework for these relations could be patterned on models derived from the experience of Western Europe since the end of the Second World War. One model is the European Payments

Union (EPU) established in 1948 to manage the Marshall Plan financial assistance and to provide for a multilateral settlement of intra-European trade transactions. A second model is the Committee of Central Bank Governors in the European Community set up in 1964, which played an extremely important role in fostering monetary and financial co-operation among member states, eventually leading to the establishment of the European Monetary System, the abolition of exchange and capital restrictions and the creation of Economic and Monetary Union.

Second, resources for the recapitalisation of banks would need to come from an appropriate combination of official and private funding. To this end, in future regional funding conferences a certain amount of funds from donors and international organisations (such as the EBRD and the World Bank) should be pledged to facilitate operations of mergers and acquisitions in the financial sector. An example of how to move forward in this field is the activity played by Swedfund, a Swedish state-owned risk capital company, in the rehabilitation of banks in the Baltic countries. The company has been active though the acquisition of equity on the concession of subordinated loans in ailing banks, providing at the same time the know-how to increase their intermediary capacity. Such investments have generally been made jointly with other national or international institutions (such as the EBRD). Ways could be found to associate in such investments and in the related transfer of know-how from private banks of foreign countries. In this context, innovative forms of collaboration with private foreign banks, such as incentive-based management contact, should be devised to cope with problems of personnel training, restructuring of internal risk-management procedures, and strengthening of auditing and accounting functions. The Stability Pact could facilitate the involvement of the private sector in banking sector restructuring by underlining the progress achieved in restoring conditions of peace and democracy in the region, reducing the 'political risk' normally associated with investment in South-East Europe; Working Table II in particular could highlight the strategy under way to rebuild the main infrastructural networks and to create a favourable investment climate though the process of institution building in the legal, tax and administrative fields.

Third, it is necessary that banking systems in the region, in order to be viable in the long run, gain full control of payment flows in domestic and foreign currencies, which is an important source of business and revenue for banks. The experience of countries of former Yugoslavia, such as Slovenia, and Bosnia and Herzegovina, shows how important it is and how long is necessary to abandon the regime of state control over the payment system and how essential this is for improving the efficiency of banking services provided to households and enterprises. In this context it may be considered an opportunity for establishing a regional payment system for retail transactions, patterned along the lines of TARGET, the real-time gross settlement system adopted by the member countries of the European Union. The technology for such a system, including both hardware and software, is also available for non-EU members and its acquisition could be the subject of *ad hoc* financing arrangements involving private and official resources.

CONCLUSION

In concluding the analysis of the projects for financial sector reform in South-East Europe, it is appropriate to place the issue in the general context of the process of economic and financial integration in Europe, *lato sensu.* As the purpose of the Stability Pact is the integration of South-East Europe into EU structures, the pattern established in Western Europe has to be regarded both as a target and as a model. In the preceding sections, several references have been make to the need for SEE countries to adopt a regional approach and to draw any possible lessons from the experience of the EU countries.

There are obvious differences between the process of integration realised by the European Union and the process initiated under the aegis of the Stability Pact. European economic and monetary integration started almost fifty years ago and has reached a status of constitutional and institutional maturity, enshrined in the Maastricht Treaty. The Stability Pact is a one-and-a-half-year-old baby, of still unclear gender: in part, it is a political agreement on a set of principles, the implementation of which depends on the good will of the contracting parties; in part, it is a new international institution with a mandate to fulfil. Still, there are important similarities. Both processes share the same final objectives: creating a framework within which neighbouring countries with different histories, languages, religions and traditions, can entertain mutually rewarding economic relationships in the pursuit of peace and prosperity. Both processes were initiated directly after years of protracted conflicts with the open aim of turning a page of bloody history and beginning a new era of co-operation. Both processes made ample use of what economists call 'constructive ambiguity', deliberately ignoring certain intractable aspects of reality and never spelling out in detail the full implications of the policies advocated. To describe this tactic, Jacques Delors, former President of the EU Commission, used to say that economic integration in Europe 'must proceed with a mask on the face'. Both processes, in line with the methodology developed by Jean Monnet, a father of the modern idea of European Integration, assume that in any situation we can find an issue on which it is possible to reach a significant agreement or to make a substantive progress and that this will act as a catalyst leading on to more agreements and progress in other related areas. In the case of Western

Europe the catalyst was 'coal and steel', from which started the long journey towards the Coal and Steel Community, the Common Market, the European Economic Community and now the Economic and Monetary Union with the euro and the European Central Bank. In the case of the Stability Pact for South-East Europe, the key principles are 'reconstruction and reform' and it has been argued here that a catalytic role could be played by financial sector reform.

It is understandable that the emphasis placed by the Stability Pact on the need for a regional approach may give rise to reservations and misgivings in a region where secessions and partitions have appeared to be the only solution to stop wars and conflicts. Yet, economic efficiency requires that economic and financial systems are shaped and organised consistently with the growing integration of markets at European and global levels. As has been the case of the European Union, trade, monetary and financial integration can make significant progress even in the absence of political unification. Thus the efforts of the Stability Pact to promote integration in South-East Europe with a regional approach should not be greeted with suspicion; after all, no one thought that Jean Monnet wanted to create a 'fourth Reich' in Europe just because he believed that his and other European countries should join Germany in rebuilding the foundations for peaceful co-existence and fruitful economic co-operation.

NOTES

1. The views expressed here are mine and do not represent necessarily the positions of the Bank of Italy or the Stability Pact, with which I am associated.
2. These documents are available on the Stability Pact web site www.stabilitypact.org.
3. The full text of the Investment Compact is available on the web site of the Stability Pact.
4. This is the position outlined in the European Central Bank Press Conference of 13 April 2000 by President Wim Duisenberg. The full text of the transcript is available on the ECB web site www.ecb.int.
5. The text of the Conclusions of the Nice European Council are available on the EU web site www.ue.eu.int.
6. For an analysis of international financial contagion in the 1990s and its policy implications, see IMF (1999).
7. On the role of the International Monetary Fund in the transition process, see IMF (2000).
8. Among the main World Bank projects the following are worth mentioning to give an example of the range of initiatives: in Albania, a Financial Sector Institution Building Technical Assistance Project (USD 6.5 million); in Bosnia and Herzegovina, an Enterprise and Bank Privatisation Project (USD 50 million); in Bulgaria, two Financial and Enterprise Sector Adjustment Loans (totalling USD 200 million); in Croatia, a Bankruptcy Technical Assistance Project (USD 5 million) and a Capital Markets Development Project (USD 9.5 million); in Macedonia and Bulgaria, Financial and Enterprise Sector Adjustment Loans (for USD 50 million and USD 280 million, respectively).
9. The Copenhagen criteria read as follows:

- stability of institutions guaranteeing democracy, the rule of law, human rights and respect for and protection of minorities;
- the existence of a functioning market economy as well as the capacity the cope with competitive pressure and market forces within the European Union; and
- the ability to take on the obligations of membership including adherence to the aims of political, economic and monetary union.

10. There is no general regulation covering macro financial assistance and each operation is authorised by the Council on an *ad hoc* basis.
11. What follows is a personal view of the situation based on my own reading of the reports of the major international financial institutions involved in South-East Europe. I have also benefited from discussions held with members of Working Table II and with Mr Franco Batzella of the Italian Treasury and a former senior official of the World Bank with considerable experience in the region.

REFERENCES

Balcerowicz, L. (1994), 'Common Fallacies in the Debate on the Transition to a Market Economy', *Economic Policy*, 19S, 18–50.

Eichengreen, B. (1999), *Toward a New International Financial Architecture: A Practical Post-Asia Agenda*, Washington, DC: Institute for International Economics.

Emerson, M. (1999), 'A System for Post-War South-East Europe', Working Document No. 131, 3 May, Brussels: Centre for European Policies Studies.

European Bank for Reconstruction and Development (1998), *Transition Report 1998. Financial Sector in Transition*, London: EBRD.

European Bank for Reconstruction and Development (1999), *Transition Report 1999. Ten Years of Transition*, London: EBRD.

European Bank for Reconstruction and Development (2000a), *Transition Report 2000. Employment, Skills and Transition*, London: EBRD.

European Bank for Reconstruction and Development (2000b), 'International Financial Institutions; Regional Private Sector Initiatives in South-Eastern Europe', unpublished paper, London.

European Union (2000), 'Regulation of the Council, No. 2666/2000 of 5 December 2000', *Official Journal of the European Communities*, L. 306/1, 7 December, Brussels.

Fischer, S. and R. Sahay (2000), 'The Transition Economies after Ten Years', IMF Working Paper, 00/30, Washington, DC.

Gros, D. (1999), 'An Economic System for Post-War South-East Europe', Working Document No. 131, 3 May, Brussels: Centre for European Policies Studies.

International Monetary Fund (1999), *World Economic Outlook*, May, Washington, DC.

International Monetary Fund (2000), 'Transition: Experience and Policy Issues', *World Economic Outlook*, October, Washington DC, 84–133.

Saccomanni, F. (2000), 'A New Architecture or New System? A Survey of International Monetary Reform in the 1990s', in P. Savona (ed.), *The Architecture of the International Monetary System*, Boston: Kluwer Academic, pp. 15–41.

Stability Pact, available at http://www.stabilitypact.org.

World Bank (2000), *The Road to Stability and Prosperity in South-Eastern Europe: A Regional Strategy Paper*, March, Washington, DC.

Wyplosz, C. (1999), 'Ten Years of Transformation: Macroeconomic Lessons', paper prepared for the Annual World Bank Conference on Development Economics, 28–30 April, Washington, DC: World Bank.

APPENDIX 3A

Albania

One of the two remaining state banks has been privatised

The sale by the government of the second-largest bank in the country, the National Commercial Bank (NCB) to Kentbank of Turkey, the EBRD and the International Finance Corporation (IFC), was signed in June 2000. Kentbank bought a 60 per cent stake in NCB, with the EBRD and IFC each taking 20 per cent. This leaves only the Savings Bank, the largest bank in the country with by far the widest branch network and deposit base, in state hands. It too is being prepared for privatisation and bids will be invited in early 2001. A government recapitalisation to cover the negative capital of this bank (currently estimated at lek 12–15 billion, about 2–2.5 per cent of GDP) will take place before the privatisation (see Table 3A.1).

Table 3A.1 *Financial institutions in Albania, 1995–1999*

Financial institutions	1995	1996	1997	1998	1999
Number of banks (of which foreign owned)[a]	6 (3)	8 (3)	9 (3)	n/a	n/a
Asset share of state-owned banks (in %)[a]	94.5	93.7	89.9	n/a	n/a
Bad loans (% of total loans)[b]	34.9	40.1	91.3	n/a	n/a
Domestic credit to enterprises (% of GDP)	3.6	3.9	3.8	3.2	3.6
Stock-market capitalisation (% of GDP)	n/a	n/a	n/a	n/a	n/a

Notes

[a] Excludes branches of foreign banks.

[b] Includes loans of banks under forced administration.

Source: EBRD (2000a).

Bank intermediation remains low, despite an easing of credit restrictions

In order to foster competition in the financial sector and improve the supply of credit to enterprises, the central bank has granted licences to several new banks in the past year (including the micro-enterprise bank FEFAD, the Greek-owned InterCommercial Bank and a branch of First Investment Bank) and has eased tight prudential controls by lifting credit ceilings on privately owned banks in November 1999. However, banks remain reluctant to extend credit, preferring instead to buy treasury bills, which currently yield about

9–13 per cent in real terms. The central bank is also working towards establishing internationally accepted accounting standards for banks and is planning to introduce a real-time gross settlement system for payments within two years.

Bosnia and Herzegovina

Bank privatisation is proceeding very slowly …

At the end of 1999, there were 62 banks operating in Bosnia and Herzegovina: 44 in the Federation and 18 (including one postal savings bank) in Republika Srpska: RS. By March 2000, the total number had fallen to 56 (39 in the Federation and 17 in RS), of which six (all in the Federation) were in receivership (see Table 3A.2).

Table 3A.2 *Financial institutions in the Federation, 1995–1998*

Financial institutions	1995	1996	1997	1998
Number of banks (of which foreign owned)	29	41 (5)	52 (9)	53 (9)
Asset share of state-owned banks (in %)	94.7	78.7	83.9	73.9

Source: EBRD (2000a).

Despite the large number of banks, the sector is relatively concentrated, with most assets in a small number of state-owned banks. Many banks are too small and undercapitalised to survive over the medium term and further consolidation in the sector is inevitable. Seventeen banks (ten in the Federation, seven in RS) are mainly or entirely state owned and the privatisation programme for these banks is well behind schedule (see Table 3A.3).

Table 3A.3 *Financial institutions in Republika Srpska, 1995–1998*

Financial institutions	1995	1996	1997	1998
Number of banks (of which foreign owned)	11	12	12	18
Asset share of state-owned banks (in %)	99.4	99.3	99.8	99.9

Source: EBRD (2000a).

New deadlines for their privatisation by the middle of 2001 have now been set in both entities. Banks that fail to meet the deadline will be liquidated, even if they are solvent.

... but closure of the payments bureaux is on track

Reforms to the payments system are proceeding on schedule. By the end of 2000, all payments bureaux are to be closed and their payment functions transferred to commercial banks. Banking agencies in both entities are issuing licences to existing commercial banks for this purpose. By June 2000, 22 banks in the Federation and two banks in RS had received a licence. To assist the process, the central bank has decided to introduce a real-time gross settlement system as a means of settling accounts among commercial banks. An international tender for this system was issued in April 2000 and won by Logica of the United Kingdom.

Access to capital for SMEs remains very limited

Slow progress in both entities in restoring confidence to the banking system has meant that virtually the only sources of finance available to SMEs are from international financial institutions and bilateral donor programmes. However, these programmes are insufficient to meet the demands of the sector, and SMEs face very high real interest rates on commercial bank loans. The recent entry of foreign strategic investors into the banking sector is expected to provide competitive pressure, which may improve borrowing terms for SMEs. Most programme funding is made available to SMEs outside the banking system, using a network of non-governmental organisation. The majority of these are aimed at providing highly subsidised loans to SMEs rather than building sound banking institutions that can sustain SME lending over the medium term. A more commercially oriented approach to programme funding or SMEs could enhance the sustainability of these important efforts.

Bulgaria

Bank privatisation is nearing completion ...

A 98 per cent share of Express Bank has been sold to Société Générale and a 98 per cent stake in HebrosBank was acquired by the Regent Pacific Group in late 1999. The largest bank, Bulbank, was sold in the middle of 2000 to a consortium led by UniCredito with Allianz. The privatisation process for Biochim Bank experienced a setback when it was cancelled after the selection of a bidder. A new procedure will be initiated in the autumn of 2000. Completion of these sales would leave only the State Savings Bank (SSB) in public ownership.

... although bank intermediation remains limited

Although the banking sector is liquid and profitable, bank credit available to the private sector remains very low, at only 12 per cent of GDP at the end of 1999. Banks continue to hold government bonds instead of extending commercial loans. Several steps are being taken to promote prudent credit expansion, including continued bank privatisation, the creation of a central credit registry (improving the information on which credit decisions are based), the training of judges and a new law on land registration and *cadastre*, which would facilitate the use of land as collateral (see Table 3A.4).

Table 3A.4 *Financial institutions in Bulgaria, 1995–1999*

Financial institutions	1995	1996	1997	1998	1999
Number of banks (of which foreign owned)	41 (3)	42 (3)	28 (7)	n/a	n/a
Asset share of state-owned banks (in %)	n/a	82.2	66.0	n/a	n/a
Bad loans (% of total loans)	12.6	14.6	12.9	n/a	n/a
Domestic credit to enterprises (% of GDP)*	21.1	35.6	12.6	12.7	14.6
Stock-market capitalisation (% of GDP)	0.5	0.2	0.0	7.7	6.0

Note: * Credit expansion in 1995 and 1996 was followed by a banking crisis in 1997, greatly reducing the stock of credit to the enterprise sector.

Source: EBRD (2000a).

Regulation of the financial sector has improved ...

Following bank consolidation and a tightening on regulation and supervision since 1997, banking sector soundness has improved substantially. The incidence of violations of major requirements (including capital adequacy, open foreign currency positions, and loan concentrations to individual borrowers) has been reduced significantly. Nevertheless, account standards and disclosure rules for banks still need to be applied more stringently and supervision efforts need to be strengthened. The regulatory and supervisory foundations for securities and the non-banking financial sector are largely in place. The new Law on Public Offerings of Securities became effective in January 2000, bringing the legal framework of Bulgaria's securities markets in line with European Union requirements. Also in line with international practice, the new Law on Insurance defines two-tier insurance supervision, and the insurance industry is now operating under the regulations and supervision of the Insurance Directorate. However, some financial institutions such as finance companies and investment holdings are still unregulated.

... but the securities market remains limited

Although a large number of companies are listed on the Bulgarian Stock Exchange (BSE), overall trade volumes are extremely low and many of the smaller companies have no trades at all. Public information on listed companies needs to be improved to foster market transparency. Some companies have pioneered the bond market in 1999 with small issues.

Croatia

Consolidation of the banking sector continues ...

With the expansion of its powers under the new banking law (effective from December 1998), the central bank has overseen a period of bank consolidation. During the past two years, bankruptcy procedures have been initiated against 11 banks and temporary administrators had been placed in three others. In addition, in early 2000, the central bank placed two small banks, Istarska Banka and Cibalae, under temporary administration collateral (see Table 3A.5). While Cibalae is now undergoing bankruptcy procedures, the state has partially recapitalised Istarska Banka and this has been taking place through mergers and acquisitions. Erste Group of Austria has added to its initial investment in Bjelovarska Banka with recent acquisitions of Trgovačka Banka and Čakovečka Banka. Erste Group is now finalising the merger of these three banks, while Zagrebačka Banka acquired Varaždinska Banka in June 2000. The banking system is now dominated by eight banking groups and they account for more than 75 per cent of total banking assets.

Table 3A.5 *Financial institutions in Croatia, 1995–1999*

Financial institutions	1995	1996	1997	1998	1999
Number of banks (of which foreign owned)	54 (1)	58 (4)	61 (7)	60 (10)	53 (13)
Asset share of state-owned banks (in %)	51.9	36.2	32.6	37.5	39.6
Bad loans (% of total loans)	12.9	11.2	10.1	13.7	23.8
Domestic credit to enterprises (% of GDP)	22.9	21.4	25.3	26.5	21.8

Source: EBRD (2000a).

... and privatisation of rehabilitated banks nears completion

The privatisation of the banks that have been taken into rehabilitation between 1996 and 1998 is almost complete. Following the successful privatisation of Slavonska Banka to Kartner Landes-und Hypothekenbank (KLUH) in 1998, a 66 per cent share in the second-largest bank, Privredna Banka, was sold to Banca Commerciale Italiana for €301 million in late 1999. Splitska Banka (third-largest bank) and Riječka Banka (fourth-largest bank) have been sold to UniCredito Italiano and Bayerische Landesbank, respectively. Remaining banks to be privatised are Dubrovačka Banka and Croatia Banka. The privatisation of these large banks to foreign strategic investors is likely to strengthen the system further. Foreign-owned banks now account for 75 per cent of total bank assets.

Capital markets remain subdued

Capital markets, once buoyed by Pliva and Zagrebačka Banka listings in both domestic and international markets, have subsequently lost momentum. Market capitalisation of the Zagreb Stock Exchange at 13 per cent of GDP in 1999 is among the lowest of the advanced transition countries. It was expected that the market would be given a further boost by the introduction of pension reform. However, the introduction of a private voluntary tier (the 'third' pillar) has been delayed until an independent pension regulator is established.

Macedonia

The state has sold its remaining shares in the largest bank ...

At the end of 1999, the share of total bank capital in the country that was privately owned reached 77 per cent, with five banks 100 per cent privately owned. The full privatisation of the largest bank in the country, Stopanska Banka (SB), was completed in April 2000. The strategic investor is the National Bank of Greece, which now holds approximately two-thirds of the capital of the bank. The EBRD and the IFC have each taken a 10 per cent stake. Prior to privatisation, SB was forced to provision heavily against bad loans, due to its large exposure to loss-making companies. Under the privatisation agreement, the four largest exposures have been removed from its books and replaced by government bonds.

... but consolidation of smaller banks is needed

As of December 1999, there were 23 banks in FYR Macedonia, a large number for a country with a population of 2 million and where financial intermediation is relatively low (see Table 3A.6). The two largest banks (Stopanska Banka and Komercijalna Banka) hold more than half of total assets and two-thirds of total deposits in the banking system. Many of the smaller banks are weak and some are unlikely to be able to meet the new capital requirements, scheduled for April 2001, of DEM 21 million for a full foreign operations licence, or even the lower requirement of DEM 7 million for domestic operations. Some of these banks are exploring merger possibilities.

Table 3A.6 *Financial institutions in Macedonia, 1995–1999*

Financial institutions	1995	1996	1997	1998	1999
Number of banks (of which foreign owned)[a]	6 (3)	22 (5)	22 (5)	24 (6)	23 (5)
Asset share of state-owned banks (in %)[b]	n/a	0.0	0.0	1.4	2.5
Bad loans (% of total loans)[c]	n/a	21.7	21.1	7.8	9.4
Domestic credit to enterprises (% of GDP)	23.1	26.5	27.4	18.1	11.3
Stock-market capitalisation (% of GDP)	n/a	2.3	0.3	0.2	0.2
EBRD index of banking sector reform	3.0	3.0	3.0	3.0	3.0
EBRD index of reform of non-banking financial institutions	1.0	1.0	1.0	1.7	1.7

Notes:
[a] Number and assets of banks exclude branches of foreign banks.
[b] Increase in 1998 is due to the establishment of the Macedonian Bank for Development Promotion.
[c] Includes loans of banks under forced administration.

Source: EBRD (2000a).

New banking law moves legislation towards international standards

A new banking law passed in July 2000 has led to significant changes in legislation. The law brings supervisory standards closer to European Union standards and those recommended by the Basle Committee. In addition, it sets new frameworks for credit approval procedures and for strengthening corporate governance of banks. The new legislation will also allow foreign banks to establish branches and subsidiaries in the country.

Romania

Some progress has been achieved in restructuring the banking sector …
While Bancorex, which accounted for two-thirds of the losses of the banking system, was closed in July 1999, Banca Agricola (BA), the second-largest ailing state-owned bank with large exposure to loss-making enterprises in the agro-sector, was put under special supervision and subjected to a freeze on new lending. The bank has also been recapitalised. However, the privatisation of BA and that of Banca Comerciala Romana, which were planned for 2000, are encountering delays (see Table 3A.7).

Table 3A.7 *Financial institutions in Romania, 1995–1999*

Financial institutions	1995	1996	1997	1998	1999
Number of banks (of which foreign owned)	24 (6)	31 (8)	33 (13)	36 (16)	34 (19)
Asset share of state-owned banks (in %)	84.3	80.9	80.0	75.3	50.3
Bad loans (% of total loans)[a]	37.9	48.0	56.5	67.5	36.6
Domestic credit to enterprises (% of GDP)	n/a	11.5	13.7	15.2	10.5
Stock-market capitalisation (% of GDP)[b]	0.4	0.2	2.0	3.0	3.1

Notes:
[a] Includes overdue loans and interest classified as doubtful and loss-making; data for bad loans for Credit Bank between 1994 and 1996 and Dacia Felix Bank in 1997 are not included.
[b] Includes listings on the Bucharest Stock Exchange and RASDAQ over-the-counter market.

Source: EBRD (2000a).

… but banking restructuring is costly and slow
The closure of Bancorex in July 1999 and the restructuring of BA have helped to improve the financial performance of the banking system. The share of non-performing loans fell by one-half between May and December 1999. However, government support has added USD 1.3 billion (equivalent to 3.8 of GDP) to the domestic debt. With better enforcement of regulations, several private banks have failed but the exit process for these failed banks has been slow. The Romanian Religion's Bank was put under special supervision after it was unable to raise capital in May 2000.

Mutual financial intermediaries (MFIs) are causing financial disruption

In May 2000 the largest investment fund (FNI) collapsed owing to mismanagement and fraudulent practices as well as poor regulatory oversight. The failure of the fund also involved the state-owned Savings Bank (CEC), which was a shareholder in FNI's management company and which had invested in FNI certificates and issued a guarantee for investments in FNI. The collapse of FNI put pressure on the largely unregulated 'popular banks', that is, credit co-operatives without deposit insurance. Banca Populara Romana, the largest credit co-operative, closed its operations in June 2000 after being unable to meet demand for deposit withdrawals. A new emergency ordinance, stipulating that the central bank will be in charge of authorising, regulating and monitoring MFIs, has been in effect since July 2000 and the licensing of new MFIs has been suspended.

4. Governance Structures

Mervyn K. Lewis

INTRODUCTION

The need for good governance has become almost a mantra in analyses of the problems of Central and Eastern European economies. Governance has been used in a number of different contexts, such as 'monetary governance' (the making of monetary policy) and 'economic governance' (ensuring the effective functioning of a market economy). It has also been used for defining the interests of international economic institutions like the Organisation for Economic Co-operation and Development (OECD) and the World Bank in programmes of social and economic development and structural adjustment. Our focus here is upon corporate governance, for the simple reason that it was in this area that the contradictions of the centrally planned economies (that perhaps really weren't) were most marked. Since then many of the old controls over enterprises and firms have been swept away without alternative control mechanisms coming into play. This chapter reviews some of the possible ways in which this vacuum of corporate governance can be filled, but first we examine what is meant by governance.

THE MEANING OF GOVERNANCE

In the prologue to his book *The Mechanisms of Governance*, Oliver Williamson provides two definitions of governance. One, based on the concept of economics, is 'good order and workable arrangements' (Williamson, 1996, p. 11). The other, based on John R. Commons (1932), is 'the means by which *order* is accomplished in a relation in which potential *conflict* threatens to undo or upset opportunities to realise *mutual* gains' (Williamson, 1996, p. 12). These definitions make clear that the concept can be applied to a variety of organisations and institutions. A governance structure can be seen as the institutional framework which brings about these results.

At its broadest, governance – the act of governing – refers to the relationship between the governors and the governed, such as that between the government and the people, and has at its basis the decision-making powers ceded by individuals to those in authority so that the common interests of society can be served. It is thus not limited to economic activities, and can be expressed in a variety of political and social arrangements.

This is the approach to the concept of governance employed by the World Bank and the OECD. For example, World Bank documents have used the concept of governance to 'capture and define the interest of both the World Bank and other international institutions in the political and institutional factors affecting structural adjustment' (Frischtak and Atiyas, 1996). As another example, the Development Assistance Committee of the OECD defined governance from the particular viewpoint of donor institutions as denoting the 'use of political authority and exercise of control in a society in relation to the management of its resources for social and economic development' (OECD, 1993). In this respect, three specific aspects of governance are identified: the form of political regime, the processes by which authority is exercised in the management of a country's economic and social resources, and the capacity of government to formulate and implement policies and discharge its functions.

From the particular perspective of transition economies, however, a more tightly focused set of outcomes has been suggested. Dhonte and Kapur (1997) argue that a secure economic environment is essential to sustained growth in a market economy. This is brought through from the assurance that the return on enterprise and investment will accrue to the entrepreneur and the investor; as such, it is a critical requirement for sustained growth. The provision of such an environment seems particularly important for the development of private initiatives in a market economy, in contrast to government investment (or investment by an enterprise in a command economy) which is less dependent on the certainty of expected returns and where the government is in a better position to influence the outcome. Their suggestion is that such a secure environment requires the existence of effective laws and institutions, including the government, which must ensure that there is freedom of entry into the market, access to relevant information, and the security of contracts.[1] Accordingly, good governance in their view promotes the creation and maintenance of these conditions in a rules-based system. This is the basis of what they term 'economic governance' where 'good' or 'bad' is assessed from the capacity to support the effective functioning of a market economy.

Yet the authors recognise that markets cannot operate effectively without 'reasonable macroeconomic and political stability'. The risk for the private investor is that the business environment, as shaped by government behaviour and policies at a point in time, may be adversely affected by shifts in government policy, resulting in harm to the conduct of business. Some would put the point stronger. Buiter et al. (1997, p. 3) argue that the 'first priority for a government interested in promoting the welfare of its citizens must be macroeconomic control'. Because lack of macroeconomic control is an important cause of poor enterprise performance, provision of macroeconomic stability is a pure public good. And since high inflation is the most obvious manifestation of a lack of macroeconomic control, this places a premium on 'monetary governance'. Krzak and Schubert (1997, p. 28) define monetary governance as 'the combination of the legal framework, the strategy and the operational framework of monetary policymaking in a particular country'. At issue are matters such as central bank independence, monetary policy targeting, the instruments of monetary policy, and the interdependence of monetary and exchange rate policy.

Economic governance and monetary governance, as defined above, can be regarded as establishing the *preconditions* for the workings of a market economy, but will the right set of outcomes emerge? Arguably what the transition economies in Central and South-East Europe most need is a culture of business – what Dittus (1994, p. 11) describes as 'effective management able to restructure firms and adapt them to the new market environment'. He also argues persuasively that the principal failing of the old economies of Central and Eastern Europe was one of corporate control. 'Central planning' as such never existed. Rather, production plans were the result of long and protracted negotiations between the planning agency, the ministries responsible and the state enterprises. But there was a central dilemma: managers and workers in the enterprises had their own objectives and they were the only ones with the necessary information. Thus the failure and ultimate breakdown of the system derived from an inability to solve two problems of corporate control: how to punish poor performance and how to obtain undistorted information. Reward systems for both managers and workers were limited and linked to volume rather than quality variables, while the lack of bankruptcy provisions allowed poorly performing enterprises to continue in operation. At the same time, performance indicators could be manipulated so that plan targets were easy to meet, while horizontal integration across firms and plans made it difficult to assess individual enterprise performance.

When the reform process took place, the control mechanisms of the planning process were removed but the agency problems of insider control remained – asymmetric information, adverse selection and moral hazard

(Revoltella, 1998). Market economies have developed alternative approaches to corporate control, and we turn now to the literature on corporate governance which deals with them.

CORPORATE GOVERNANCE

Any organised society engaged in productive activities needs to establish some conditions or rules relating to business organisation, namely:

1. Conditions for entry and establishment, that is, how and in what form are business enterprises to be formed?
2. Conditions for ownership, that is, who should own firms and under what conditions?
3. Conditions for financing, that is, how should enterprises be financed?
4. Conditions of operation, that is, how are firms organised and run?
5. Conditions for exit and closure, that is, how are business enterprises closed down?

Corporate governance, that is, the institutional arrangements and relationships through which companies and institutions are 'directed and controlled' (Cadbury Committee, 1992), bears most directly upon the fourth aspect, but is obviously shaped by the others. This is as true of a centrally planned economy as it is for a market one. A system in which there is no freedom of entry, monolithic state ownership, finance provided to firms such as those which supply electricity, that is, allocated to meet production targets,[2] and with few provisions for bankruptcy, is one in which insider control by workers and managers seems the likely result. Moreover, changes to one or more of the other provisions may alter how enterprises are run, as occurred in China with the competing ownership of state enterprises at the national, regional/provincial and local levels.

In a market economy, how well firms are run will be influenced by whether foreign participation is allowed or whether companies must be domestically chartered and owned, whether shares are closely held or widely owned, whether and how easily ownership can be transferred, whether banks and other financiers can own shares in companies in which they lend, and whether creditor rights or debtor rights are reflected in insolvency laws.

An important conditioning factor is the nature of ownership. In a private company, the owner and the manager is often the same person, who can be assumed to act in the best interests of the company. In a public company, there is no assurance that this will be the case. Because of the process of delegation inherent in the indirect ownership of productive real assets, there is in many systems a separation between the ownership and the managerial control of assets. This separation resulting from widely-held shares enables the financial risks to be spread over a large group of shareholders when attracting equity capital, and facilitates the hiring of professional managers who have more information and expertise on production and management than the ultimate owners of corporate wealth. But the corollary is that the shareholders who own the company need to ensure that the managers engaged in the day-to-day running of the organisation are marshalling the enterprise's resources for the owners' benefit. The managers might invest too much in projects that require little management effort or engage in activities that increase salaries, power and status. Without some checks and balances on managerial behaviour, there can be no guarantee that the owners' interests will be furthered. Ever since Berle and Means (1933) characterised modern corporations as having a separation of ownership from control, the question of how to align the interests of managers with owners and others who possess a direct financial stake in the corporate entity has been an active issue.[3]

This control problem is normally couched in terms of agency theory: shareholders must ensure that the managers who are their agents are monitored, motivated and disciplined to act to the best advantage of the owners at large. Agency theory sees managers and employees of the company as agents whose interests may diverge from those of the principals. Thus Oliver Hart (1995) argued:

> Corporate governance issues arise in an organisation whenever two conditions are present. First, there is an agency problem, or conflict of interest, involving members of the organisation – these might be owners, managers, workers or consumers. Second, transactions costs are such that this agency problem cannot be dealt with through a contract. (Hart, 1995, p. 678)

Due to this conflict of interest and the inability to solve it by explicit, contingent contracts, a major part of corporate government is concerned with the design of checks and balances on management behaviour. Some of these checks and balances may be internal to the enterprise, for example, the internal audit process, while others are external, for example, the external auditors. Within the latter, a further distinction can be made between formal and informal relations. Informal links cover the relationship between the company and industry and society generally, while the formal relations derive from legal and contractual arrangements. A further distinction can be made between those with a direct interest (namely, shareholders, employees and those with contractual relationships) as opposed to those with an indirect interest (in other words, all of the parties).

If we confine ourselves to those with a direct interest, for obviously they have the strongest incentives to monitor and shape the way the enterprise is run, then we can divide the governance structures into three categories shown in Figure 4.1. The term 'work governance' is used to describe the relationship between management and workers. The description 'contractual governance' covers the links between supplying and procuring firms. The expression 'financial governance' refers more narrowly to the relationships between those supplying capital and finance to the firm and its management.

Figure 4.1 *Corporate governance relationships*

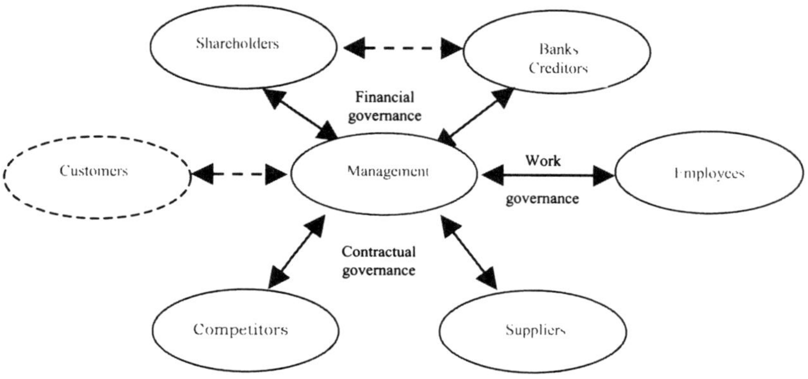

Source: Adapted from Gelauff and den Broeder (1997).

Many writers limit corporate governance to this last category; for example, 'corporate governance deals with the ways in which suppliers of finance to corporations assure themselves of getting a return on their investment' (Shleifer and Vishny, 1997, p. 737). Others narrow down the topic to shareholders alone: 'good corporate governance is the stewardship of an enterprise's assets for the benefit of its owners' (Pardy, 1992, p. 15). Our view is that participants in all three categories have some part at least potentially to play in the mechanisms of governance.

MECHANISMS OF GOVERNANCE

A study by the OECD (1995) suggested that existing systems of corporate governance can be classified into two opposing models: an 'outsider' and an 'insider' model. In the 'outsider' or Anglo-Saxon model, prevalent in the United States, the United Kingdom and many English-speaking countries, the managers are relatively free from control by the board of directors, and instead control mostly relies on the discipline of the capital market and the 'market for corporate control'.

Under the alternative 'insider' model, specific interests are represented on the board of directors, which exerts a strong monitoring and supervisory role *vis-à-vis* management. Such a system recognises more diverse groups of 'stakeholders' or 'constituents' than simply management and shareholders, including workers, banks, non-financial companies with close ties to the corporation, local communities and the central government. Insider systems are also often characterised by concentrated shareholding, and the market for corporate control is weak.

However, the insider model has evolved quite differently in a number of environments. Although described as the European–Japanese model, its exemplification is quite different in, say, Germany from Japan. Italy, France and Spain are different again. Among the Asian countries, Korea is closest to Japan, but has its own distinctive features, while the South-East Asian countries resemble the Latin countries, but are different again, due to the role of the overseas Chinese. This led the present writer (Lewis, 1999) to identify six models of corporate governance: Anglo-Saxon, Germanic, Japanese, Latin, Overseas Chinese and, finally, the Arabic and other Islamic countries, where religion adds an extra dimension to governance structures (Algaoud and Lewis, 1999).

These different models focus upon what is, rather than what could be, and typically reflect a combination of factors rather than a reliance upon one mechanism alone. For these reasons we look at the various ways in which corporate control can be exercised.

While a corporation can be viewed as a nexus of complex relationships among a broad set of participants including shareholders along with others with a direct and indirect interest, the legal position is more straightforward and less encompassing. The statutory framework under which companies in most countries operate rests on a number of common principles which provide for three sets of participants:

1. shareholders, who supply risk capital under conditions of limited liability;
2. directors, who are responsible for the stewardship of the company's resources; and
3. employees, including managers, who conduct the company's operations on a day-to-day basis.

Among small enterprises, this three-way split may be more formal than real, for the same individual or related group may be simultaneously owners, directors and managers. When, however, there is a separation of function the framework provides for a strict two-sequence line of accountability,

shareholders – directors – management

which is designed to prevent shareholders from interfering directly in the management of the company while placing the directors at the heart of corporate governance. It is thus with the directors that we begin.

Board of Directors

Boards are meant to play an important role in corporate governance. Formally, board members are elected by shareholders to look after shareholders' interests. Under the Cadbury Committee's Code of Best Practice, the board of directors should meet regularly, retain full and effective control over the company and monitor the executive management. Then the directors must account for their stewardship to the shareholders in the annual report and in the annual general meeting (AGM). For their part, the shareholders appoint auditors to provide an independent, external check on the directors' financial statements.

In theory, then, the board of directors 'direct' and the managers 'execute' the board's directions. But that is not quite what happens in practice. Usually, the chief executive officer (CEO) and the senior management team are in charge. Candidates for the board are often hand-picked by management and are elected unopposed. Others are co-opted to the board by its existing directors, who were chosen by their predecessors and perpetuate the 'clubbiness' by choosing their successors. Some board members have a direct conflict of interest since the board generally includes a number of executive directors, who are employed by the company itself (in the UK they are in the majority), and the CEO may also be chairman of the board (although not usually in the UK). Boards have as a result often tended to operate on a collegial basis under the aegis of senior management and, under ordinary circumstances, the management is in control, although in a crisis the CEO's power wanes and the board's legal responsibilities define its role and give it the authority to take action.

Shareholders

Shareholders are the owners of the company's assets. Normally, ownership of an asset entails a number of rights: the right to determine how the asset is to be managed; the right to receive the residual income from the asset; and the right to transfer ownership of the asset to others. The last two clearly apply to shareholders, but what of the first? Can shareholders exercise control if the directors fail to protect their interests?

Two factors militate against them doing so. Both are related to the dispersal of ownership needed for risk diversification in large corporations. In return for the privilege under law of limited liability, shareholders' powers are generally restricted. There is the AGM to approve the directors' report and accounts, elect and re-elect the board and vote on such issues as allowed for in company legislation. But, apart from this, shareholders' rights are limited to the right to sell the shares. They have no right to interfere in the management of the company. Awkward questions can be asked at the annual meeting, but the chairman of the board usually holds enough proxy votes to hold off any challenge, although the nuisance value of giving voice to any concerns is often underrated.

The second factor is in many ways more fundamental. An essential requirement for the exercise of effective control is the possession of an adequate flow of information. As outsiders, shareholders face considerable hurdles in obtaining good information. Then there is the free-rider issue. Any one small shareholder investing in the information needed to monitor management will bear all of the costs, whereas the benefits accrue to shareholders as a group, while co-ordination of monitoring efforts is not easy to arrange. Often it is easier for the shareholder to sell the shares, and thus vote with one's feet.

In short, someone with ownership rights in a company can express their disappointment with the company's performance by either getting rid of their shares or in some way expressing their concern. Hirschman (1970) called this the dichotomy between 'exit' and 'voice'. Where there are obstacles to the exercise of voice, the right of exit and transferring ownership to another party becomes not so much the accompaniment but the substitute for the other two components of ownership rights.

Supervisory Board

Not all market systems inhibit shareholders (and others) from directly influencing management. In Germany, for example, the use of 'voice' is encouraged through the accountability arrangements of the *Aufsichtsrat* (supervisory tier). In the Germanic countries (Germany, Austria, Switzerland, the Netherlands), there is a formal separation of executive and supervisory responsibilities. With the Anglo-Saxon one-tier board, managing executives are also represented on the board, and all directors, executives as well as non-executives, are appointed by the controlling shareholders and must answer to the annual meeting. A two-tier board consists of an executive board and a supervisory board. The executive board encompasses the top-level management team, whereas the supervisory board is composed of outside experts, such as bankers, executives from other corporations (for example, interlocking directorships) along with employee-related representatives. There is reliance on the supervisory board for oversight and disciplining of the management as well as for a co-operative conflict resolution between shareholders, managers and employees.

This control function has a broader setting than in Anglo-Saxon countries, for in the Germanic countries, the supervisory boards of large companies are legally bound to incorporate specific forms of employee representation. Under co-determination laws all corporations with at least 500 employees, and all those with more than 2,000 employees must allow employees to elect one-half of the members of the supervisory board. Co-determination rules cover the supervisory board, the functions of which are to control and monitor the management, to appoint and dismiss members of the management board, to fix their salaries, and to approve major decisions of the management board. In 1998, the power to appoint auditors was vested with the supervisory board (OECD, 1998).

How effective is this 'voice'? Obviously, it allows a participatory framework between shareholders, managers and employees under the co-determination principle, but the supervisory board system is also designed for overseeing and constraining management. The OECD argues that 'the degree of monitoring and control by the supervisory board in the German two-tiered board system seems to be very limited in good times, while it may play a more important role when the corporation comes under stress.' (1995, p. 21). Of course, the same is true of Anglo-Saxon boards; they exert more authority in a crisis too. But the boards in Anglo-Saxon countries have not been notably successful in *preventing* crises. Does the German-type system of board structure do better? There is not much evidence on this point. Some (for example, Mayhew and Seabright, 1992) argue that the system encourages worker commitment to the firm and reduces day-to-day interference in management decisions, allowing both to get on with the job. Others (for example, Ball, 1998) consider that the system encourage 'cosiness', with bad strategic decisions internalised rather than subjected to the public gaze as occurs when the 'exit' option is followed.

Market Disciplines

When shareholders utilise the 'exit' option, other control mechanisms come into play. One derives from the capital markets since the firm's share price dictates the terms on which it can raise additional capital either directly by share issue or indirectly from banks, because of the valuation of firm-specific assets used as collateral for borrowings and other fund-raising. Lenders can re-set the terms on which they are prepared to provide funds, and alter covenants into loan agreements to constrain the actions of managers and shareholders. However, this discipline is weakened if the company relies upon internal funding and does not need to go to the equity market or rely extensively upon external funds.

In tandem with these capital market pressures, the managerial labour market can help to align the interests of managers and shareholders when management remuneration is linked to the profitability of the firm (through performance-enhanced bonuses) or the share price value (in the form of stock or stock options).[4] Ownership of shares by management is indeed a significant element in Anglo-Saxon systems of corporate governance. Holdings of shares by managers in the UK and the US are generally higher than elsewhere (Prowse, 1994, p. 45), and use of the stock option for compensation is extensive (Blair, 1995, p. 92). Yet Jensen and Murphy (1990) observe that the amount of CEO wealth really 'at risk' for poor performance is generally a trivial percentage of the CEO's total income. In part this is because public disapproval of high salary awards truncates the upper tail of the earnings distribution. Also, large penalties for poor performance are rare. Indeed, with the increased complexity of stock options, retirement benefits, perquisites, expense accounts, golden handshakes, parachutes, handcuffs, good-byes and coffins, it is doubtful whether anyone really knows to what extent genuine incentive schemes are effective (Ryan, 1993).

Finally, with only limited opportunities for shareholders to influence management directly or through the board of directors, changes in share prices which trigger takeover threats are the main instruments to discipline management. Falling share prices signal the need for managers to improve firm performance, while hostile takeover bids are the ultimate means to replace managers. Protective measures against hostile bids are relatively difficult to implement; for instance, the repurchase of shares by management is tightly regulated. From the viewpoint of the literature on corporate governance, takeovers are attractive because they provide a general control mechanism to keep managers on their toes in all circumstances whereas many of the others operate in some but not all situations.

This, at least, was the theory (Jensen, 1989). In practice, 'in all circumstances' needs to be qualified. The takeover mechanism presumes good information flows, ample disclosure information, strict trading rules and liquid stock markets, but breaks down when shares are closely held. It also may work best when there is the *threat* of takeovers; actual takeovers (especially hostile ones) are expensive and there is only mixed evidence that they improve performance in the target firms, many of which may not exhibit mismanagement (Jenkinson and Mayer, 1993). Yet the threat of takeover can work well only if there exist alternative buyers who would be able to exercise control rights more effectively than the existing owners and are in a position to do so. Otherwise, the agency problem facing the shareholders *vis-à-vis* the existing managers may not be solved but merely be transformed into one *vis-à-vis* the bidder, since the empire building and other motives of the bidding firm need to be investigated.

Financial Institutions

Not all shareholders have an inaudible voice and find it too costly to monitor firm performance. In the US, the UK and elsewhere, institutional investors have become dominant among the class of shareholders. They have been seen as a potential important instrument for improving corporate control. Historically this was apparently the case in the United States before 1914, when banks and institutional investors held sway in the boardroom and CEOs had little real decision-making powers (Hawkins, 1997; Simon, 1998). Recent activism and the increased power base of institutional investors may indicate some reversion towards historical norms (Brancato, 1997). Nevertheless, in the US, institutional investors are discouraged from exercising a 'godfather' role: banks and bankholding companies are restricted in their shareownership, while mutual funds, insurance companies and pension funds have constraints on concentrated shareownership and would face a strong conflict of interest in their portfolio trading.

Banks in Europe and in many Asian countries are in a different position. Indeed, in the case of Germany, it has been argued that the question of employee representation on supervisory boards is something of a red herring (Charkham, 1989, 1995). There can be two-tiered boards without employee representation in the upper tier, while the power of supervisory boards in Germany owes much to the special relational role of banks. In Germany, the *Hausbank* has been seen as a bank that accompanies a firm throughout its life cycle 'from cradle to the grave'. In some cases, the long-term relationship is underpinned by a direct equity interest under the universal banking system (Lewis, 1996). Also, many bank customers keep their shares deposited with banks and allow the banks to exercise voting proxies on their behalf. A further feature is that banks can appoint their representatives to the supervisory boards of companies. Deutsche Bank has been represented on the boards of over one-quarter of all German public corporations, for example. By means of this 'triplet of influences', banks establish close ties with industry and form long-run relationships with firms for borrowings.

Such a system enables banks to collect a large amount of information from the firms with which they have a relationship; they can use this information to allocate credit in an internal capital market; and they have the potential to monitor borrowers' performance, and control their behaviour. These mechanisms should reduce the scope for conflicts of interest to arise between shareholders and creditors, while rendering the firm less vulnerable to premature liquidation. This close and continuous link is in contrast with the position in the US and the UK where the interaction is arm's length and often sporadic. Unless there is the likelihood of a default or a request for an extension of new loans, banks in those countries have little influence over, or concern with, corporate governance.

There are, however, three problems with the German-type system. First, it has usually gone hand in hand with an oligopoly of large banks. Second, the price of banks' access to privileged information has been some softening of the debt claim they hold over the firms in favour of reconstruction and re-organisation rather than closure. Third, in order to provide support to firms with which they have equity links, the banks themselves need to be largely free of debt and balance sheet problems, something which is not true of banks in many transition countries.

Creditors

Even more so than in Germany a well-developed support system operates in Japan in times of serious financial hardship in terms of the main bank system, and assistance to an ailing company involving management support, reorganisation of the business, interest rate 'holidays' and extra finance (Sheard, 1989; Lewis, 1994). This main bank system in turn overlaps with the *keiretsu* type of relationship which has developed between Japanese companies in terms of the six company groups (*kigyo shudan*), in which banks have a leadership role. These groups of companies are connected by interlocking shareholdings, common directorships, a shared corporate logo and supplier–purchaser links. They form broad-ranging alliances which go beyond financing links to embrace marketing, research and development, and the exchange of business information (Gerlach, 1992). But again it is the case that information flows are 'internalised' and financial disclosure is compromised for the sake of ensuring corporate viability.

Nevertheless, the Japanese example brings out the point that a company's creditors have an obvious interest in the enterprise and are a potential source of corporate control. There are two ways in which this can be done. One is by means of cross-shareholdings in order to reinforce business relationships across firms and across business groups. Companies can purchase reciprocal shareholdings and take seats on one another's boards. France is one example of this system of 'financial networks', with one-fifth of shares in such holdings (Morin, 2000). The other is bankruptcy, that is, the enforced transfer of control rights in a firm to the creditors.

Both devices have merits and faults. The system of interlocking stakes enables creditors *qua* shareholders to be recipients of 'inside' information, but also means that they are to a large degree captured by it as well. On the other hand, impending bankruptcy is a wonderful way of concentrating the management's mind and so enforcing control over the debtor.[5] Yet its application also involves large deadweight costs, since the enterprise's value as a 'going' concern will generally be in excess of its liquidation or 'gone' value. Moreover, bankruptcy may do little to improve corporate governance other than serving as a warning to others; creditors will want to monitor the debtor firm's management only in so far as this enhances the monitoring firm's position in the bankruptcy stakes. Also, of course, as an 'outsider' the creditor faces the usual information asymmetry problem.

Auditors

If information really is the key to good corporate governance, then a company's accountants are in a better position than most. For one thing, they are in a privileged position to acquire information and they are appointed by the shareholders to provide an external and objective verification of the financial statements. That, at least, is what should happen, but ignores the ambiguous situation in which auditors are placed. While shareholders in principle appoint the auditors, they do not select them. The accounting firm is chosen and hired by the firm, paid by the firm and, more controversially, owes its prime allegiance to the firm unless this obligation is explicitly overridden. One such instance is in the case of banks, where auditors must in some instances report directly to the regulator should anything untoward present itself. But this provision is a rarity, and generally the accounting firm is in a subservient position, with its rights to outsiders ill-defined and unclear.

What does this leave? There is one situation in which the agency problem and information asymmetries are largely absent. Also, there is one control mechanism which is more universal than that of takeover or the threat of takeover.

Private Ownership

In many countries, the dominant shareholder is the founding individual or family. This is the case in Switzerland where there are many family-owned businesses, in Italy which has privately-controlled conglomerates, and across South-East Asia where ethnic Chinese business groups dominate the ownership of corporate wealth (Lewis, 1999). Private companies solve the information problem by internalising it and using it very selectively. For them, the Berle and Means 'divorce' of ownership from control does not apply.

Does this make for good corporate governance? The answer is yes and no. Control of information can be a very powerful business tool, and disclosing it only to those who one knows implicitly can be trusted to use it to the benefit of the group has been at the root of the success of the Overseas Chinese for generations. It is also often forgotten that the same ingredients of family ownership and control of cross-border information flows lay at the heart of the British trading groups which played such a prominent role in Empire trade. The strength of the family business groups is not about trust alone: families also have ways of punishing and controlling errant members, not open to outsiders.

Against these factors must be recorded some obvious difficulties: the problem of ensuring succession; the tendency for the old generation to cling to power; the desire to diversity risk (Goodhart, 1994). When there are other non-controlling shareholders, the stage is set for a conflict of interest whereby the controlling shareholders can make decisions which are inimical to the interests of the others. For this reason, many countries restrict the voting rights of individual shareholders to a specified limit. Yet such a restriction may not always be to the benefit of shareholders. On the one hand, it may reduce 'transparency' by encouraging elaborate pyramiding as a way of minority shareholders retaining control. On the other hand, there may also be advantages in having large shareholders to control management.

Product Markets

Competition in product markets entails one of the most powerful influences on corporate governance, forcing management of companies to maximise the value of the firm irrespective of the system of corporate governance which is followed. Let us go back to the Berle and Means (1933) study which really began the literature on corporate governance. Paul Samuelson (1997) argues that Berle and Means's description of corporate governance in 1929 and 1930 was an accurate one, but it is no longer so. Management back in those years, and in the early post-war years, did have considerable autonomy – as did unions – because of the oligopoly power enjoyed by the Fortune 500 corporations. That oligopoly position has now been competed away, in part by foreign competition but mainly as a result of changes in transport and technology that have allowed small independents to erode the market power of the larger firms. Greater competition has in turn forced the changes in financial, contractual and work governance/practices. Corporate takeovers, downscaling, removal of lifetime tenure for workers and management, the emasculation of trade unions, mergers, split-ups, the short tenure of CEOs, and performance-related remuneration schemes are all, in Samuelson's view, endogenous to the new competitive environment.

In the US, this process has taken decades to operate – witness the US automobile industry where it took twenty or thirty years for foreign competition to be recognised in the boardroom (Herzel, 1992). But, from the perspective of transition economies, the process can be speeded up by appropriate industry policies. There are five main tools to influence industrial structure in the transition economies (Dittus, 1994; Mayhew and Seabright, 1992). One is the break-up of existing large enterprises. A second is the entry of foreign firms. The third is the encouragement of foreign competition. A fourth is the growth of new firms. The final policy is the instituting of a properly functioning exit mechanism in the form of bankruptcy proceedings. In this view, entry, competition and exit – generating a natural selection process – provide, if not quite a necessary ingredient, then certainly a basic underpinning to methods of corporate governance.

CONCLUSION

'Governance' has been used in the context of a number of social and economic issues in Central and East European economies, including corporate governance which is the topic of this chapter. Corporate governance structures ensure 'good order and workable arrangements' in corporate life, although they are usually used more narrowly in terms of financial governance. Given the potential principal/agent conflict between the suppliers of capital and the management of the firm, governance structures ensure that corporations are managed for the benefit of the owners, as residual claimants of the ownership rights after other suppliers of funds have been paid.

This agency problem was not absent under central planning. Indeed, it can be argued that the combination of insider control, bad information and the manipulation of plan targets to suit workers and management was *the* central failing of the old order. Now many of the old problems have re-emerged in the new environment, for the traditional control devices, however ineffective, have been dismantled, leaving a vacuum in corporate governance.

When we consider the alternative control mechanisms employed in market economies, it is apparent that this void is not easy to fill. Albert Hirschman (1970), in his well-known dichotomy, depicted the corporate control choices open to shareholders as 'voice', that is, directly influencing management, or 'exit', that is, disposing of poorly performing shares. In the US and the UK, the small shareholder is said to use 'exit', leaving takeovers as the ultimate discipline over management. In Germany and Japan, 'voice' is said to be the tool, with banks and other companies as shareholders exercising accountability via a complex of links. Neither view offers much comfort to transition economies which lack the capital markets needed for the 'exit' option to operate, and in terms of 'voice' have a shortage of banks with the experience and financial strength to play 'godfathers' to the corporate sector.

In any case, it is probably unwise for countries to try to home in on a particular model of corporate governance, for a number of reasons. First, different systems are suited to different circumstances. For example, Germany and Japan benefited from bank-based governance in their post-war reconstruction phases, but are moving towards a more market-oriented one now. Second, any system rests on a business ethos and national culture, as well as a set of formal rules and regulations. Formal rules include contract, corporate, securities, antitrust, employment, environmental protection, tax and intellectual property law which create the setting in which economic interactions take place, but social norms, cultural traditions, a respect for the law and an ethos of managerial initiative and entrepreneurship also shape the functioning of companies. These aspects are less easy to transplant. Third, no system of corporate governance relies upon one mechanism alone. Threat of takeover may be the ultimate discipline over management in the Anglo-Saxon system, but it is not the only one; shareholder activism, managerial incentives, pressure from bankers and other creditors all have a part to play. A number of suggestions have been made from time to time to improve other mechanisms, such as making directors and auditors more independent, and these are worthy of consideration.

An interesting question is to what extent countries can mix and match in governance mechanisms, importing the best features of other countries' corporate control arrangements. The supervisory board system is one obvious candidate. Whether it can be grafted on to other systems is a moot point. Control through supervisory boards depends on the existence and retention of a stable ownership structure which deflects hostile takeover moves, giving management time to get its own house in order. Such an insider system is to a large degree self-monitoring, in that it relies on a network in which companies own, monitor and control one another. It is possible for companies to break out from this network, as is occurring in Japan and Germany today. But it is not possible to break in unless there is a set of reciprocal cross-shareholdings. Thus it is relatively easy to shift from an insider to an outsider regime, but difficult to go the other way. Consequently, the nature of corporate ownership rights established and the initial route down which the country has embarked conditions the extent to which it can pick and choose among governance structures.

Finally, we have argued that product market competition provides the most enduring and effective force for good governance. These competitive pressures upon governance come from two sources. One is from individual business establishments that are easier to set up than joint-stock companies. As these enterprises are individual proprietor or family controlled, they are more fleet of foot and are not plagued by the agency problems to which public corporations are subject – at least for the first generation. The other controlling mechanism upon governance comes from a Darwinian selection process due to competitive pressures in input and product markets which forces management to maximise the value of the firm irrespective of formal rules and processes of corporate control. However, the natural selection process can be painfully slow. Competition policy thus moves to centre-stage in encouraging the break-up of large ex-state enterprises, the entry of foreign firms, foreign trade, the growth of new firms and properly working bankruptcy procedures. The entry and exit of firms, not just shareholders, is also vital for corporate governance.

NOTES

1. Bulgaria provides an excellent example of the nature of the legal framework required, having introduced new constitutional law, company law, contract law and competition law, while incorporating rights to real property, intellectual property, foreign investment, and provisions for bankruptcy, along with a new courts system, see Gray and Ianachkov (1992).
2. The expression belongs to Dornbusch and Giavazzi (1999). Dittus (1994) argues that the banking system was effectively part of the budgetary process, and whether enterprises were financed from budget grants or by bank loans was almost immaterial. According to Goodhart (1994) the banks' role was that of 'a somewhat mechanical scorekeeper'.
3. Berle and Means (1933) portrayed a US economy, in 1929 and 1930, that was dominated by the 200 largest non-financial corporations. In a few of these, control was in the hands of a single individual or family, but most of the companies (65 per cent by number, 80 per cent by total assets) were in non-ownership or management control.
4. The varieties of remuneration systems, and their incentive and disincentive effects, are examined by Prendergast (1999).
5. 'Depend upon it, Sir' said the venerable Dr Johnson, 'when a man knows he is to be hanged in a fortnight it concentrates his mind wonderfully' (Boswell's *Life of Johnson*, vol. 1, p. 167, 19 September 1777).

REFERENCES

Algaoud, L.M. and M.K. Lewis (1999), 'Corporate governance in Islamic banking: the case of Bahrain', *International Journal of Business Studies*, **7** (1), 56–86.

Ball, R. (1998), 'Daimler-Benz AG – evaluation of corporate governance from a code law "stakeholder" towards a common law "shareholder value" system', Bradley Centre Working Paper Series, University of Rochester, Rochester, NY.

Berle, A. and G. Means (1933), *The Modern Corporation and Private Property*, New York: Macmillan.
Blair, M.M. (1995), *Ownership and Control: Rethinking Corporate Governance for the Twenty-first Century*, Washington, DC: Brookings Institution.
Brancato, C.K. (1997), *Institutional Investors and Corporate Governance: Best Practices for Increasing Corporate Value*, Chicago: Irwin.
Buiter, W., R. Largo and N. Stern (1997), 'Enterprise performance and macroeconomic control', *Banca Nazionale del Lavoro Quarterly Review*, **50** (200), 1–22.
Cadbury Committee Report (1992), *The Financial Aspects of Corporate Governance*, London: Gee & Co.
Charkham, J. (1989), 'Corporate governance and the market for control of companies', *Bank of England Panel Paper*, (25), London.
Charkham, J. (1995), *Keeping Good Company*, Oxford: Oxford University Press.
Commons, J.R. (1932), 'The problem of correlating law, economics and ethics', *Wisconsin Law Review*, **8**, 3–26.
Dhonte, P. and I. Kapur (1997), 'Towards a market economy: structures of governance', IMF Working Paper, WPS 97/11, International Monetary Fund, Washington, DC.
Dittus, P. (1994), 'Corporate governance in Central Europe: the role of banks', *BIS Economic Papers*, (42), BIS: Basle.
Dornbusch, R. and F. Giavazzi (1999), 'Hard currency and sound credit: a financial agenda for Central Europe', available at http://www.stern.nyu.edu/nroubini/asia
Frischtak, L. and I. Atiyas (eds) (1996), *Governance, Leadership, and Communication*, Washington, DC: World Bank.
Gelauff, G.M.M. and C. den Broeder (1997), 'Governance of stakeholder relationships. The German and Dutch Experience', SUERF Studies, No. 1, Amsterdam: Société Universitaire Européenne de Recherches Financières.
Gerlach, M.L. (1992), *Alliance Capitalism*, Berkeley: University of California Press.
Goodhart, C.A.E. (1994), 'Banks and the control of corporations', *Economic Notes by Monte dei Paschi di Siena*, **23** (1), 1–18.
Gray, C.W. and P. Ianachkov (1992), 'Bulgaria's evolving legal framework for private sector development', Policy Research Working Paper, WPS 906, World Bank, Washington, DC.
Hart, O. (1995), 'Corporate governance: some theory and implications', *Economic Journal*, **105** (430), 678–89.
Hawkins, J.A. (1997), 'Why investors push for strong corporate boards', *McKinsey Quarterly*, **3**, 144–8.
Herzel, L. (1992), 'Corporate governance', in P. Newman, M. Milgate, J. Eatwell (eds), *New Palgrave Dictionary of Money and Finance*, Vol. 1, London: Macmillan, pp. 472–5.
Hirschman, A.O. (1970), *Exit, Voice and Loyalty*, Cambridge, MA: Harvard University Press.
Jenkinson, T. and C. Mayer (1993), *Hostile Takeovers*, London: McGraw-Hill.
Jensen, M.C. (1989), 'Eclipse of the public corporation', *Harvard Business Review*, **67**, September–October, 61–74.
Jensen, M.C. and K.J. Murphy (1990), 'Performance pay and top-management incentives', *Journal of Political Economy*, **98** (2), 225–64.
Kzrak, M. and A. Schubert (1997), 'The present state of monetary governance in Central and Eastern Europe', *Focus on Transition*, **1**, 28–56.

Lewis, M.K. (1994), 'The Japanese financial system after liberalization', *Review of Policy Issues*, **1** (1), 3–31.

Lewis, M.K. (1996), 'Banking, securities and commerce in Europe: where do the universal banks stand now?' in *Universal Banking*, Seoul: Korean Institute of Finance, 183–233.

Lewis, M.K. (1999), 'Corporate governance and corporate financing in different cultures', in Ž. Šević, (ed.), *Banking Reform in South East European Transitional Economies*, Sofia and London: University of Greenwich Business School, Balkan Centre for Public Policy and Related Studies, Humanities Research Centre, pp. 33–66.

Mayhew, K. and P. Seabright (1992), 'Incentives and the management of enterprises in economic transition: capital markets are not enough', *Oxford Review of Economic Policy*, **8** (1), 106–29.

Morin, F. (2000), 'A transformation in the French model of shareholding and management', *Economy and Society*, **29** (1), 36–53.

Organisation for Economic Co-operation and Development (OECD) (1993), 'Development Assistance Committee', *DAC Orientations on Participatory Development and Good Governance*, Paris, December.

Organisation for Economic Co-operation and Development (OECD) (1995), 'Financial markets and corporate governance', *Financial Market Trends*, **62**, 13–35.

Organisation for Economic Co-operation and Development (OECD) (1998), 'Corporate governance reform in Germany', *Financial Market Trends*, **71**, 21–5.

Pardy, R. (1992), 'Institutional reform in emerging securities markets', Policy Research Working Paper, WPS 907, Washington, DC: World Bank.

Prendergast, C. (1999), 'The provision of incentives to firms', *Journal of Economic Literature*, **37** (1), 7–63.

Prowse, S. (1994), 'Corporate governance in an international perspective: a survey of corporate governance mechanisms among large firms in the United States, the United Kingdom, Japan and Germany', *BIS Economic Papers*, **41**, May.

Revoltella, D. (1998), 'Financing firms in East European countries: an asymmetric information and agency costs approach', *SUERF Studies*, No. 3, Amsterdam: Société Universitaire Européenne de Recerches Financières.

Ryan, L. (1993), 'Corporate governance', *Irish Banking Review*, Winter, 9–17.

Samuelson, P. (1997), 'Where do the European and American models differ?', *Temi di discussione*, **320**, Banca D'Italia, November.

Sheard, P. (1989), 'The main bank system and corporate monitoring and control in Japan', *Journal of Economic Behaviour and Organization*, **11**, 399–422.

Shleifer, A. and R.W. Vishny (1997), 'A survey of corporate governance', *Journal of Finance*, **52** (2), 737–83.

Simon, M.C. (1998), 'The rise and fall of bank control in the United States: 1890–1939', *American Economic Review*, **88** (5), 1077–93.

Williamson, O.E. (1996), *The Mechanisms of Governance*, New York: Oxford University Press.

5. Central Bank Reform in South-East Europe: Recent Developments and Prospects

Željko Šević[1]

INTRODUCTION

The central bank is at the core of the whole banking system; it is a central institution of the monetary system and an executive body for the implementation of monetary policy. The central bank as an institution is characterised by:

1. its exclusive right to issue money and/or make coins;[2]
2. being an entity regulated by public law;
3. its concentration of monetary reserves (money, foreign exchange, gold and other precious metals);
4. a legally defined and strictly limited authority;
5. the centralisation of transfer payments and its role as state banker; and
6. a central position in the pyramid of the banking system, with a duty to support the stability of the financial system (Šević, 1996a, p. 6).

The activities of a central bank may be derived from these characteristics. The central bank is in charge of:

1. the issuing and annulling of banknotes and coins;
2. foreign reserve management;
3. state banking;
4. acting as a lender of last resort under some systems;
5. supervision of banks, and other financial institutions under some financial system architecture, and
6. foreign exchange control (Šević, 1996b, pp. 1–2).

Some of these functions had already been performed by the State Bank in the former socialist financial system, but in a different capacity and with different rules regulating its position. The main determinant for the development of a new position for the central bank is its *independence*, which as we have just seen, has been more or less achieved, at least *de jure*.

The following tasks are usually set, by law, before the central bank:

1. the protection of the internal and external value of the domestic currency;
2. the provision of the soundness of the financial system;
3. the maintenance of balanced economic growth and development; and
4. the development of financial markets and the overseeing of money markets (Šević, 1996a, pp. 6–7).

In performing these tasks, the central bank uses a number of instruments of monetary and financial policy. Some of these are the sole responsibility of the central bank, while others may be employed only through the co-ordinated action of the central bank and the government (Šević, 1996c). Another problem is that these tasks are often in conflict. It is very difficult, if not impossible, to maintain price stability and spur economic growth. Usually, laws on central banking stick to the main function of *maintaining price stability* (monetary stability), ignoring other tasks. However, the legislators in Albania have prioritised the bank's targets. The National Bank of Albania's main duty is to achieve and maintain price stability, and then, if possible, to promote and support the development of a market-based foreign exchange system, the internal financial market and the payments system, and to foster monetary and credit conditions conducive to the orderly, balanced and sustained economic development of the country (Art. 3, Law No. 8269 on the Bank of Albania).

This chapter analyses changes in the legal and institutional framework for central banking in South-East European transitional economies, and the extent to which these changes contribute to the efficiency of the financial and banking system. The main features of the State Bank structure are considered, followed by an analysis of legal regulations on central banking. Finally we shall look at the complexities of monetary policy in these transitional economies and conclude by outlining future developments.

A POINT OF DEPARTURE: THE CLASSICAL SOCIALIST STATE BANK

In the communist financial system the central bank, called the *State Bank*, was at the same time a central bank (albeit with very limited functions compared to its

Western counterparts) and was also involved in regular commercial banking activities. As a part of the central plan, it was in charge of channelling credits to enterprises according to the plan set by the Central Planning Commission.

Although we believe that economic policy in the traditional sense[3] hardly existed in the communist system, it should be said that the central plan had two quasi-instruments: (i) a physical plan, and (ii) a cash plan. The central bank, that is, the State Bank, was the core of the system, and in charge of the system in which other banks might be considered as its affiliates. The entire system was fully state owned, so in some ways a *common denominator* for all its elements was the state budget which, it was noted, even appropriated deposits from the state savings banks.

However, in the late 1980s the centrally planned economies (CPEs) began the process of separation of the State Bank functions, together with the establishment of a two-tier banking system. From that time, the State Bank retained its classical central banking functions, while commercial banking activities that were previously part of the State Bank structure were transferred to newly created entities. However, the process of change has not been straightforward. Democratisation and the introduction of free-market oriented economic relations were followed by rising nationalism and a desire for national independence, which led further to the dissolution of all the federations that had existed under Communism: the Soviet Union, the former Yugoslavia and Czechoslovakia. Those federations broke up into a number of new independent states, which at the time of independence inherited a two-tier banking system, but not a central bank.[4] These newly independent states had to develop a central bank, while states with a long tradition of central banking needed to reformulate the organisation and tasks of the old socialist State Bank.

Usually, the republican head office of the former federal State Bank (the National Bank of Yugoslavia in the case of the former Yugoslavia) became the new central bank, and newly independent countries at first adhered to the former federal regulations on central banking. However, a new law on central banking was among the first laws to be passed through parliament after the declaration of independence. In this chapter, we argue that for a few Balkan countries (for example, Bulgaria and Romania) the introduction of a two-tier banking system and the incorporation of the central bank was not in fact new, because they already had a central bank operating before the introduction of the communist system. In Balkan countries that were independent in the nineteenth century, the central banks date back to the second half of that century, such as in Bulgaria and Serbia where central banks were established in 1879 and 1884 (1883, *de jure*)[5], respectively. At the same time, central bank was created in Romania (Kent, 1966).

For Bulgaria and Romania, the creation of a central bank has been seen as the restoration of the former central bank and they are proud of their central bank history. Countries in Central Europe that emerged after the dissolution of the Austria-Hungarian (*K-und-K*) monarchy and Imperial Russia (Czechoslovakia, Poland, Hungary, the Baltic states) created their central banks after the end of the First World War and were particularly active in the Bank for International Settlements (BIS) in the 1920s and 1930s. It can be seen, for instance, that there was close co-operation among central banks of the Kingdom of Yugoslavia, Czechoslovakia and Poland on various matters of common interest.[6]

It is important to analyse the development of central bank independence from the government. While most Central and East European (CEE) countries opted to copy the status of the German Bundesbank, South-East European transitional economies took into consideration the German experience, but attempted to create a different structure. Hungary, for instance, adopted almost all of Germany's central banking structures (for instance, the central bank is not in charge of banking supervision), while the others opted for a 'monolith' central bank that monitors the banking system, rather than merely providing liquidity. However, each and every one of those central banks had its own specific institutional rules to which it is necessary to refer in institutional research.

PERILS OF MODERN CENTRAL BANKING IN THE BALKANS

The crucial question about a modern central bank is whether it should have one or multiple tasks. Answering this question requires a thorough observation of monetary policy implementation and the set of instruments which are available to the central bank in fulfilling its task(s). Some of these are more administrative in their nature, while others are more market oriented. What is the practical trade-off among them, and in what way can the central bank achieve its targets? It is also necessary to consider the relationship between the government and the central bank, because government fiscal policy can diminish or sometimes cancel the positive results of central bank monetary policy measures, as we have witnessed in many developing countries, especially in Africa.

The institutional transition of the central bank occurred first in all of these countries, as the initial step of banking reform. But, after the creation of a central banking framework, it was necessary to create a proper central banking context. The central bank represents the first tier in either a two-tier or three-tier banking system.[7] Financial reform begins with the central bank and ends when the central bank is operating successfully. The central bank has an important function in the development of both the banking sector and financial markets, and their *ex post* supervision, affecting further development.

In Bulgaria and Romania, the central banks re-emerged from the former State Bank (which kept its old name – National Bank – even under Communism) through the separation of a monobank into a central banking entity and a number of commercial banks. The former Yugoslavia had a quite different experience, since a two-tier banking system had been established in 1964/65 and, ever since, the National Bank of Yugoslavia has been charged with the implementation of monetary policy as the central monetary authority. But, even with this more established practical experience, Yugoslav banking was not notably successful, due to the presence of the same systematic problems suffered by both the classical, socialist financial system and the Yugoslav socialist, self-management financial system. Allocative inefficiency, bad-loan procedures (or a lack of such procedures), negligence, and non-performing services, were characteristics of the system. These problems were reflected in the central banking system as well.

In Balkan countries other than the former Yugoslav republics, the 'State Bank' was relieved of its commercial duties but remained fairly close to the government, acting as its fiscal agent, by granting credit to the government when the latter had budget imbalances. Of course, such behaviour seriously brings into question the ability of the central bank to conduct monetary policy properly, as will be demonstrated later. If the central bank is a (quasi-) governmental agency, the banking supervision function is changed. Its top priority changes from protecting depositors to protecting governmental interests, acting as a sort of governmental tax-controlling agency. In this situation the central bank will prefer to impose high rates of non interest-bearing compulsory reserves on banks, since these can provide a cheap source of revenue to the government. This is just one of the problems that can occur when the government and central bank are too close, or when the central bank is fully dependent on the government. Nevertheless, almost all Balkan economies (including market ones, that is, Greece and Turkey), at a certain stage of economic development, implemented a policy of excessive compulsory reserves. Compulsory reserves are preferred monetary policy instruments, as they are of an administrative nature, and consequently easy to administer and the results can be readily quantified. Compulsory reserves also have some fiscal consequences and there is usually no need for monetary and fiscal policy co-ordination when compulsory reserves are used.

In the former socialist countries in the late 1980s, the State Bank retained control over the central bank. Only in the early 1990s (almost five years later) was the legal independence of the central bank established. Central European countries, the Baltic states and the Balkan republics opted for a legal solution that gives independence to the central bank, enabling it to perform its functions adequately. In all these countries, laws relating to the central bank stipulate the full independence of the bank from the government.[8] Accordingly, the government has no right to submit instructions or orders to the bank, although the central bank is obliged to have regular consultations with the government.[9] The central bank is expected to support the economic policy of the government, but without compromising its main task. It is at this point that transitional countries differ. The central bank can be de facto close to the government, because of the very strong position of the ruling party (Albania, Bulgaria, Croatia, Yugoslavia), while in other countries the central bank is perceived as similar to the civil service, that is, as a professional body (Macedonia, Slovenia). In order to facilitate co-operation, the government has the right to appoint its own representatives to attend the bank's board meetings, but these representatives have no voting rights on the board. The bank has the right to express its position towards any proposal submitted to the government if the proposal concerns the bank's formal competencies.

In all of these countries, the governor of the bank can express the bank's opinion in his or her capacity as adviser to the government. Some limits are also set on the amount that government deficits can be financed by the bank. In some of the Balkan countries the central bank cannot extend credit to the government (Bosnia), while in all other countries credit is allowed but within statutory limits.[10] In the Federal Republic of Yugoslavia, the legislation is very generous. The National Bank of Yugoslavia can approve short-term credit to the Federation and/or federal units to cover the current deficit caused by imbalances between current tax income and expenditures. Such credit can be approved to the amount of 100 per cent of a planned budget revenue, but cannot exceed 15 per cent of the planned growth of the monetary base. All credits of this type must be repaid by the end of the current fiscal year.[11] Although similar arrangements are permitted in other countries, the Yugoslav solution is unduly liberal: it gives the central bank the legal backing to monetise the public deficit to some extent; and also it is explicitly stipulated that interest rates on this type of credit can be lower than the current discount interest rate fixed by the National Bank.[12]

The bank has achieved not only organisational independence, but also financial and staff independence from the government. In all of these countries, the governor (or president) of the bank is appointed by the President of the Republic or, alternatively, by parliament. Unlike government ministers, a board member of the bank must not be a member of parliament. In addition to this, a board member must not occupy any position within the government, or in commerce, or perform any other public duty. For instance, in Yugoslavia the highest body is the Council of the National Bank of Yugoslavia (NBY), which has seven members, comprising the governor and six members who are appointed by the Federal parliament. Three members are proposed by the Federal government, and three by the governor. The mandate of the governor and the Council members is five years, when they may be reappointed. The law stipulates explicitly that the members of the Council must have special knowledge of monetary, credit and foreign exchange systems.[13] Laws in other countries also require special knowledge and experience for appointment to the central bank board.[14]

The second most senior person in the bank is the deputy governor, who is appointed by the Federal parliament, on the recommendation of the governor and with prior NBY Council support.[15] The next most senior staff are the vice-governors, of which there are currently five. They are appointed by the NBY Council after being nominated by the governor.[16] Other senior bank officials, such as director-generals, the secretary-general, their deputies and assistants are appointed solely by the governor. The National Bank of Yugoslavia is an institution with more than 10,000 employees. A similar concept has been adopted by all of the other former Yugoslav republics. Indeed, the appointment procedure and other requirements are so similar, that the laws might have been formulated in concert. Similar solutions have been adopted in other South-East European transitional economies. In Albania for instance, the management of the Bank of Albania consists of the Supervisory Council and the governor and two deputy governors. The governor and his/her deputies are *ex officio* members of the Supervisory Council. The President of Albania is authorised to appoint the governor, following nomination by the prime minister. Deputy governors, nominated by the governor, are appointed by the Supervisory Council. This creates a curious situation, since deputy governors will later be members of the Council, and as such will be in a position to decide upon their own eventual demotion from the post.

At the National Bank of the Republic of Macedonia, the management function is exercised legally though two bodies: the Council and the governor. As in Yugoslavia and other former Yugoslav republics, the governor is appointed by parliament, following nomination by the President of the Republic. The deputy governor and vice-governor(s) are also appointed by parliament, but are nominated by the governor. The same procedure is envisaged for the appointment of most senior officials in the Bank of Slovenia, the National Bank of Croatia and the National Bank of Romania. All these countries include a collective management body (the Council) and the governor. They are appointed for a relatively long period, from five to seven years. One of the reasons for these lengthy appointments was to make central bankers independent of political cycles, as they do not change when general elections take place in the country. However, in countries with a strong politicisation of the public sphere, the provision for lengthy tenure in office did not bring stability, and a rapid turnover in high positions prevailed.

Within this new institutional framework, former socialist economies made the first steps towards successful and efficient central banking. Leaving behind the concept of a monobank also limited the opportunities for the excessive credit creation. The introduction of specific regulations in these countries opened up the possibility of responsibility and social accountability. Central banks had clearly defined tasks and duties, as well as an appropriate set of instruments to accomplish these duties. The link with government, which had been so strong before the monobank concept was abandoned, was substantially weakened after only three to five years. The internal organisational structure of a bank was based upon the Western blueprint, especially the German experience. New departments/divisions were organised in order to meet the new requirements. Legal regulations in South-East European transitional economies clearly established a relationship of responsibility and accountability between the central bank and parliament. As the most widely democratically elected body in the country, parliament would resume the overall responsibility for the state of the nation. Therefore, parliament would be in a position to oversee the activities of the central bank up to the highest levels, as proposed by many economists and political scientists (Šević, 1996b, pp. 52–3; Berman and McNamara, 1999). The bank is required to report to parliament at least once a year (usually twice, every six months), and parliaments can ask for special reports at any time. The central bank can be invited to comment on crucial issues of economic policy and policy proposals put forward by the government, in an advisory capacity.

In the transitional phase, the relationship between the government and the central bank must be redefined. The central bank is not a servant of the government and is not required to supply the government with credit when required. The central bank performs the function of a banker to the government, and is not merely its creditor. The central bank in all countries fulfils the function of banker, agent, and adviser to the government. It administers the accounts of the government. In some countries, this duty can be extended to all the other levels of government and government-related institutions. In the majority of cases when deficits occur, the central bank assists the government, technically and as an adviser. In keeping the government's accounts, the central bank accepts its deposits of cash, cheques and drafts, and undertakes the collection of cheques and drafts drawn on other banks. On the other hand, the bank supplies the government with the cash required (for example, for the payment of salaries and wages), and also debits its accounts with the amount of payment instruments drawn by the government and presented for payment by other customers.

The central bank operates as a governmental banker for several reasons. First, it is more convenient and economical for a government to centralise its operation, keeping its accounts with the central bank. Second, such arrangements are also preferred because of the (supposedly) close relations between monetary and fiscal authorities. Also, it should be kept in mind that the government is, usually, the largest receiver of revenue and invariably is the biggest borrower. Government expenditure also plays an important role in the entire economic life of a country. Balkan transitional economies without exception established some form of a development bank or fund, and the central bank was released from its development role. This is a particularly important achievement in the republics of the former Yugoslavia, where the central bank (or more precisely, from 1974, the *system of central banks*) was in charge of supporting the development of targeted branches of the real economy, especially agriculture. With the creation of a development bank and/or fund, the development role of the central bank began to diminish, but is still present to some extent. The law forbids direct credit to the government, but different arrangements can be made with a chosen few commercial banks which will channel money to the final users, according to government policy. Formally this is not considered to be public borrowing, but it does assist the government to achieve some of its development targets. The problem arises when the final users are not economically viable; the credits will be declared bad debts, and will be recorded in the balance sheet of commercial banks. Then, through different rescue plans, public money will be used to support troubled banks and monetisation will occur indirectly. The so-called quasi-fiscal deficit (deficit for which the public sector is *indirectly* accountable) is a very difficult problem in all Balkan transitional economies, especially in the republics of the former Yugoslavia, but the extent to which economies are exposed to this phenomenon differs.

The central bank is primarily responsible for influencing monetary conditions in the economy and for assessing the overall conduct of monetary policy. It is believed that the centralisation of government accounts with the central bank at least gives the central bank better opportunities for judging the general financial situation at any given time, especially after disturbances in the financial markets.[17] The central bank also acts as an adviser to the government and co-operates closely in defining the global national economic policy. The central bank in Balkan economies is also entrusted with the management of public debt. In particular, it handles new issues of governmental bonds. As a rule, the central bank sells these securities in a primary market, or sells them on the secondary money market, acting as an agent. It is also likely that the central bank will keep the registry of securities issued by the government, and act as a foreign exchange control agent (for example, Yugoslavia).

A unique and important issue in the relationship between the government and the central bank is the financing of the government by the central bank. As we have already seen, legislation strictly limits this ability, because direct credit to the government can spur inflation. These legal restrictions faced by the central bank in financing budget deficits incurred by the government are justified not only in terms of avoiding large monetary stimuli, but also in terms of social efficiency. It can be argued that the government should be largely, if not completely, prevented from using central bank credit rather than taxing or borrowing from the private sector. Taxes make the cost of government expenditure more explicit to the public, which in turn contributes to a more optimal allocation of a nation's limited resources, while inefficiencies in the tax collection system are more likely to be reduced if central bank credit is limited.

Likewise, borrowing from the private sector rather than from the central bank makes the cost of borrowing more apparent, because the government has to pay a market-determined interest rate, while the interest charge is reflected in current government expenditure in the annual budget. Thus the pressures to curb governmental expenditures are stronger.

The central bank in post-socialist economies, without exception, performs the function of a government, that is state, banker. On the other hand, effective legal constraints prevent excessive central bank finance being available to the government, which might endanger the entire implementation of monetary policy. These ties can be stronger (the best examples being Moldova and Belarus) or weaker (all the other CEE countries). Almost without exception, in all these countries governmental accounts are kept with the central bank. Also, the central bank is entrusted, as an agent, with a duty to service public debt or to manage foreign exchange reserves for the government, as well as to monitor repayment of foreign debts, and so on.[18]

The central bank also acts now as a lender of last resort, that is, as a bank of banks (*bankers' bank*). This is a completely new function for a central bank in most of the South-East European transitional economies, because there was no requirement for such an activity by the central monetary authority within a monobank system. Historically, only repurchase arrangements were used by the existing central banks between the two world wars. In the socialist period, credit was approved directly according to need and, since the whole financial system was owned by the state, the State Bank was not supposed to *rescue itself*. The institution of lender of last resort is created to protect the system itself, because the central bank should not be interested in a particular bank's salvation. Before the request for this instrument is lodged, a bank should try to obtain finance in the market, from other banks, or from some other source (Šević, 1996a). In a sound banking system the banks keep some *compulsory reserves* with the central bank, which will act as their first source of liquidity, if necessary.

Banks are legally required to keep in their portfolio easily transferable (*marketable*) securities and other reserves which can be realised in the case of liquidity problems. However, if a country adopts a monetary (currency) board arrangement there are limits to the use of marketable securities in portfolio creation (Bosnia and Herzegovina, and Bulgaria). If these marketable securities held in the bank's portfolio and bank reserves are not sufficient to meet matured obligations, the bank tries to provide the necessary finance through the inter-bank or money markets. If all these attempts cannot provide enough money, the bank approaches the central bank. The lender-of-last-resort credits are *short term*, because their aim is to provide instant liquidity and bank stabilisation, and cannot be used for the growth of a bank's credit potential. Although practice in some Balkan economies (Croatia and Yugoslavia, primarily) has proved different, this instrument is based on a higher interest rate than for regular credits, compulsory collateral and the control of a bank's status. Higher interest rates are introduced in order to force banks to address themselves first to the interbank or money market. Collateral gives security to the central bank, so that it does not support banks which are insolvent. If credit is granted to an insolvent bank, this would only postpone imminent bankruptcy.

There are two dominant theories of lender of last resort in the banking literature. The first, European or *convenience* theory, argues that the central bank has to save a bank in order to prevent systemic failure and structural imbalances. The second, the American or *necessity* theory, is a bit narrower, and argues that the central bank has to provide positive assets and liquidity to the struggling bank, while the salvage of insolvent subjects is left to the Treasury.[19] The broader European approach is seen by the Americans as the result of tradition and political opportunism.[20] The central bank acts as a lender of last resort only in order to maintain public confidence and to prevent runs on banks. This activity is very important in a banking system where soundness is not yet achieved, and where there is some threat of systemic failure. In practice, the central bank tends to support large banks, while smaller banks are usually left to find a solution on their own. But even this rule has exceptions for political reasons. Since a bank-based financial system is of the exclusive type in South-East European transitional economies, they consequently apply convenience theory. Banks can use credits of last resort, which are somewhat more expensive than other sources, but are available under all regular conditions. That is, when the bank faces liquidity problems and there are no doubts as to its solvency. But, a well-known lender-of-last-resort function can raise the question of moral hazard and adverse selection (Goodhart, 1989), and practice in Balkan economies has shown that central banks are very protective when it comes to closing large banks. Also, some central banks perceive their function as protecting the domestic banking sector from foreign competition.

An often forgotten role of the central bank is its particular responsibility for the performance of the whole financial system. For a long time this function was overlooked in the shadows of monetary policy duties. However, the monetary policy functions of the central bank are of utmost macroeconomic importance. In the West, with deregulation and innovation it became obvious that monetary targeting would be much more complicated, and therefore the central bank must pay close attention to the system's institutional features.[21] After deregulation, preventive supervision becomes even more important. Such supervision includes keeping a close watch on liquidity, solvency, deposit guarantee, administrative and accountancy matters, internal control and risk exposures.[22] The central bank requires banks to achieve certain financial ratios and controls their achievements using these rules. In CEE countries there is an increasing number of newly created institutions and this requirement is very important.

These transitional countries decided to implement the Basle Committee requirements of an 8 per cent capital ratio, but in the first years of transition the tolerated ratio was below 8 per cent. At present all Balkan transitional economies without exception strictly enforce Basle requirements. However, all these activities are still not enough to provide good banking supervision. The central bank still has a lack of qualified staff able to engage in supervision. Banking laws reflect the significant concern, or even obsession, with banking supervision. Some of the penalties prescribed in central bank law are for prudential supervisors who fail to fulfil their duties. As the commercial banks offer better pay packages, young and middle-aged staff tend to leave the central bank and move out into the private banking sector. This is a trend present in all transitional economies, and is not unique to South-East European transitional economies. Although European post-socialist countries have improved their overall economic performance, banking sector reform and changes in supervisory practices have been delayed.

INSTITUTIONAL PREREQUISITES OF MONETARY POLICY IMPLEMENTATION

Maintaining price (monetary) stability is the main task of the central bank. The central bank manages monetary policy affecting the yields in the financial markets. Consequently, monetary policy influences the behaviour of the commercial banks significantly, as has been shown in a number of research studies.[23] The setting and choice of monetary instruments and *measures*, especially in underdeveloped financial systems, affects the banks' behaviour even more directly. For instance, compulsory reserves, which have been abandoned in developed countries,[24] are widely used instruments in transitional and developing economies.[25] We cannot neglect this important issue, even though it is not directly connected with the institutional development of the banking sector in a transitional economy.

Theoretically, monetary policy can be defined as a series of actions taken by a central bank in order to affect monetary and other financial conditions in pursuit of the broader objective of price stability (Šević, 1996a, pp. 91–2). But there is no unique definition for the target of monetary policy. Most countries would stress monetary or price stability, while others would choose growth and development, or the sustainable growth of real output, high employment and price stability.[26] So the central bank in one country may have one objective for monetary policy, while others may have multiple objectives. In South-East European transitional economies, central banks have *de lege ferenda* only one objective – price stability. All other eventual tasks are subordinated to this one main task.

It is widely disputed which task is more important, and whether this dispersion of tasks endangers the monetary policy implementation process, because the central bank can be required to pursue often contradictory objectives. Therefore, for a transitional economy probably the best solution is a single objective so that the central bank has a clear definition of the task to be performed. Subsequently, with financial system advancement, the concept of multiple objectives can be introduced, because the central bank will be more experienced in defining and implementing monetary policies. The legislators in South-East European transitional economies have followed this approach, stipulating that the main duty of the central bank will be to preserve internal and foreign monetary stability.[27] In performing monetary policy the central bank should affect the financial markets, that is, their yields. In this manner, monetary policy is transmitted from the instruments of monetary policy to the financial markets and from the financial markets to the rest of the economy. An economy in transition opens a series of new questions and problems, from the instability of money demand to the underdevelopment of sensitive financial markets. These countries also inherited a *monetary overhang*, which they are required to cope with. In some countries this monetary overhang was reduced by high inflation, or *hyperinflation*, while in others it was reduced by sound economic financial policies.

The central bank has its objective, but the way in which this will be achieved has to be defined more precisely. The central bank must, therefore, target something more immediate and feasible than price stability, for example:

1. the volume of money supply;
2. the prices at which gold or foreign currency are convertible into domestic currency;[28]
3. interest rate variables, such as the minimal market rate or real interest rate; and
4. other variables, such as the balance of payments or GDP.

The problem with all these targets, however, is that they require precise measurement and a good information set. For instance, real interest rates can be measured properly only if the price expectations of the public are known,[29] GDP can be measured only with a significant time-lag, and so on. The stability of the structural parameters which underlie monetary policy and their volatility defines what can be used as an intermediate target. A monetary target can be some of the monetary aggregates (M0, M1, M2). However, every country is free to define these monetary aggregates according to its approach and needs.[30] This is reasonable since money does not mean only the notes and coins in circulation, but also the liquid deposits, or 'near money', which can also be considered as money. The countries focused upon opted to target the growth of monetary aggregates, apparently M2. It seems that the structure of the monetary aggregate M2 responds best to the needs of the central bank and its ability for macroeconomic action, as it encompasses most of the monetary holdings of a still too strong state-owned or state-related sector (education, public services, and so on).

As a result of an information problem and expectations of higher volatility, a transitional economy may decide to bind its national currency to a foreign currency, establishing a monetary board. By definition there is no need for intermediate target(s) in this regime, because the quantity of national currency issued will depend directly on the quantity of foreign currency which the monetary (currency board) has at its disposal.[31] Usually, the choice of target currency is mainly a political question. It is important to take into account the possible magnitude of financial and/or real shocks in the economy when deciding on the intermediate target (Buch, 1995, p. 5). Interest rates can be targeted better in the case of financial shocks (the disturbances affecting money demand), but not in the case of real shocks, where there is discrepancy between interest rates and nominal spending.

The central bank, in order to act, asks for structural parameters to be stable, that is, the income velocity of money should be reasonably stable. But again, as practice in South-East European transitional economies has shown, the velocity of money is very high, a significant volume of money is outside legally controlled channels, engaged in the 'black' or grey' economy. In a transitional economy, with the ending of administrative restrictions, a one-time shift in velocity may occur (Khan and Sundararajan, 1992, pp. 68–72). Hardening the budget constraint should lead to an increased elasticity of demand for money from the corporate sector. Both of these events require adjustments of monetary targets to the shifts in money demand. This is a problem that affects not only the central bank, as the measurement of velocity is a problematic issue. First, during the initial stages of transition the private sector is not fully reflected in official statistics, and second, the transitional environment can lead to an overestimation of true velocity (Buch, 1995, p. 7).

In order to achieve its objectives in conducting monetary policy, the central bank has a set of monetary instruments at its disposal. The instruments are usually grouped in two distinctive classes: direct and indirect monetary instruments. Direct instruments of monetary policy are: (i) interest rate controls and (ii) credit controls, while indirect instruments of monetary policy are: (i) *reserve requirements*; (ii) open market operations; and (iii) central bank lending. Interest rate controls may take different forms, such as controlling lending rates and/or deposit and savings rates by using regulations, or using a set of administered refinance rates and spreads for the banks. Another direct monetary instrument is credit ceilings, also known as selective credit control, where credit is limited to certain sectors of the economy. This control can be positive (by setting an upper limit for the credit) or negative (by setting a lower limit for selected credits). While positive credit ceilings have prudential considerations, negative credit ceilings aim to support the sectors which are considered to require it. It is possible to introduce a ceiling which is applied to the total credits granted by the commercial banking sector. Since this measure is linear, each bank faces the same level of restriction. Also, it is possible to introduce progressive taxation for exceeding the target, thereby giving the banks the choice between reducing their credit growth, or paying a penalty (tax) (Hilbers, 1993a, p. 4). Competitive banks will choose to pass the limit and pay tax, because they will earn a profit anyway. The concept of credit ceilings, called *net credit ceilings*, is characteristic of the French and Dutch experiences. In this case, the central bank recognises the difference between the extension of credit using long-term papers (effect of securitisation) and crediting by current accounts and their influence on inflation (Hilbers, 1989, pp. 27–39).

There are a few requirements that must be met in order to have effective direct monetary instruments. According to Hilbers, a legal framework must exist, that is, the central bank has to have the right to impose credit ceilings and interest rate control; the central bank must have the right to impose sanctions; banks must have a duty to report their credit volume to the central bank and the reporting system must be appropriate, with a relatively short time-lag (Hilbers, 1993b, pp. 5–6). However, direct monetary instruments alone also have some disadvantages. They are not market based, so direct control hampers the market's efficiency of resource allocation. They can also affect competition in the banking sector, severely influencing the small banks or new entrants, and provide an incentive for disintermediation. The use of these instruments can be avoided by borrowing from foreign investors, borrowing outside of the banking sector, and imposing credit constraints on sectoral changes in business policy (Hilbers, 1993b). Long and extensive application of direct, administratively based instruments of monetary policy may affect market structure and force disintermediation which severely affects the whole financial system. But the introduction and long-term use of indirect alternatives can produce a loss of monetary control and, historically, authorities were forced to introduce direct monetary instruments again for a period.[32]

In transitional economies the central bank usually opts for direct monetary instruments, because they are easier to implement, and the evaluation of results is straightforward. This problem has also faced South-East European transitional economies. Their financial markets are still not structurally developed enough, and/or underperforming, so direct monetary instruments are preferable and often the only possibility. In a situation in which negative macroeconomic conditions (primarily high inflation) are present, these measures are more likely to be effective, because financial flows will be directed from official channels to unofficial ones. When the central bank has incomplete knowledge and experience of the financial market (Hanke et al., 1993, p. 37), it is likely that it will opt for direct instruments. Also, there are some legal limitations as well. The Central Bank of Bosnia and Herzegovina is by law forbidden to perform open-market operations, so only direct monetary instruments are to be used. The social image of a central bank is still not developed, so it cannot rely on *moral suasion*, and policy should be as direct as possible without much explanation. In this way, although interest rate controls can disturb market forces, they are able to limit monetary expansion. It should also be noted that banks still report using the old systems of procedures. Therefore, at the beginning of the transition process, substantial use of direct monetary instruments can be expected.

Indirect instruments of monetary policy themselves require some important economic and social preconditions before they can be introduced successfully. These are:

1. there should not be excess reserves, or these should be very limited;
2. interest rates as a target of indirect instruments must fluctuate;
3. credit demand must be sufficiently interest sensitive;
4. there should be a competitive character to and smooth functioning of the financial market;
5. the financial system should be sound; and
6. a satisfactory level of indirect monetary programming skills should be in place.

The problem is that these *cumulative* conditions can be met only in market economies, while market-oriented, post-socialist economies face many imbalances. A high level of excess reserves can be a significant problem for monetary policy implementation, because in a transitional economy the banks are likely to hold excess reserves, especially in a situation where the real sector of economy is in the early stage of transformation and privatisation has not delivered any significant structural change or increased efficiency. It has also been noted that the small banks are interested in granting credit to larger ones, in order to reduce risk emerging in the real sector. Interest rate and credit demand sensitivity will increase with the development of the financial and banking system. It is of particular importance to develop financial markets, especially the money market.

In a well-functioning banking system and money market, the central bank is in a position to influence the banks' marginal cost of funds, to steer money market rates, and indirectly supply, and to price bank credit (Leite and Sundararajan, 1990). Credit insensitivity in a transitional economy is the remnant of the former practice known as a *soft-budget constraint* (Kornai, 1986). Under this constraint, enterprises do not respond properly to credit variables, simply because they expect governmental subsidies or an eventual bailout from bankruptcy by the government.

New emerging markets may also be the subject of *colluding deals* of a few players, which will prevent the establishment of market interest rates, and create problems for central bank intervention. This situation will create excess liquidity as well. Authorities must take into account the market structure, and influence market segmentation in order to have the new instruments successfully accepted. There is mutual interaction between indirect instruments and the market because they influence each other's development.

Minimum reserve requirements imposed on the commercial banks are still the most preferred monetary instrument in South-East Europe, and these are set very high. According to reports, commercial banks still have high levels of excessive reserves, which is partly due to inefficient payment systems. Although commercial banks will become increasingly independent, they still rely heavily on support from the central banks, that is, refinancing. And it seems that the central banks still subsidise lending, although the total amount has been reduced (Buch, 1995, pp. 37–8). Undoubtedly all these changes require a significantly redesigned financial system.[33]

CONCLUSION

This chapter discussed central banking issues in a transitional economy, with particular attention to South-East European transitional economies (Albania, Bulgaria, Bosnia and Herzegovina, Croatia, Macedonia, Romania, Slovenia and Yugoslavia). The central bank as such did not exist in the former communist system. The socialist 'State Bank' was an entity which performed both central banking and commercial banking duties. The first step in financial sector reform was the separation of these two duties and the creation of a two-tier banking system. Quite soon the central bank resumed only its *original* central banking duties. The new institutional framework stressed the independence of a central bank and limited credit grants to the government. *De jure*, it is (almost) impossible to *monetise* the governmental debt. The central bank can only make some advances to the government, but these must be repaid by the end of the fiscal year, in most of the observed countries.

The central bank's internal structure differs, but not significantly, among these countries, and it is obvious that a blueprint was the German Bundesbank. The laws have strengthened the relationship between the central bank and parliament as the highest democratically elected body in the country. The central bank is accountable to parliament, but also has to sustain the global economic policy pursued by the government. However, if there is any discord with the government, the central bank and government enter into a reconciliation process. In the case of an open dispute which cannot be solved, parliament acts as a conciliator, according to the usual customs of Continental European legal tradition. It is also concluded that the current institutional framework allows the central bank to pursue active monetary policies. It has been pointed out that a central bank in a transitional economy tries to develop the same set of instruments as the central bank in developed market economies. However, at the beginning of the transition process, the set of *available* instruments is narrower. Due to the imbalances facing transitional economies, such as macroeconomic instability, the administrative approach to monetary policy has to be applied. The most compelling reason for using administrative control is to compensate for the structural problems in the financial markets.

In countries that have a limited market for government and other securities (and all South-East European countries belong to this group), the central bank cannot readily utilise open-market operations efficiently and effectively to control the monetary base. The absence of a viable money market means fewer traditional tools of central bank credit and reserve requirements must serve this purpose. The concentration of bank activity in a few institutions facilitates the imposition of lending limits. Practice has also shown the other advantages of the administrative approach, that is, direct monetary instruments, which provide a way of dealing with inflationary pressures. In periods of high and variable inflation, notions of normal or desirable levels of interest rates have no real meaning. The central bank usually adopts *total lending targets* as the appropriate measure for regulating monetary policy (Šević and Šević, 1998). However, administrative methods limit the growth and development of the financial system, and practice has shown that they lose their impact over time, as financial institutions look for ways to avoid restrictions. Theory, when arguing in favour of administrative measures, offers the opinion that they provide a superior method for stimulating balanced economic growth. But it is rather difficult to find empirical studies which would support these theoretical claims. The evidence does not demonstrate that the use of credit ceilings makes the monetary policy more effective, especially when the banking system participants have strong beliefs in the availability of *lender of last resort* facilities.

Practice has suggested that the extensive use of administrative measures supports the creation of a parallel black market, as well as the rent-seeking behaviour of the central bank officials. In such a case, despite temporary results in monetary policy, in the long term, administrative measures can make most of the economy inert (long-term existence of unrestructured and semi-restructured sectors), force private entities to be involved in seeking ways to evade the restrictions and protect inefficient state-owned sectors which have enjoyed government support, despite their economic non-viability. This is the main reason why we have argued for the almost immediate implementation of indirect monetary instruments. It is now apparent that in the near future, the central bank must develop its *moral suasion* function, that is, increase its credibility not only in financial markets but also within the general public. In this way, the overall influence of a central bank can be increased and the conduct of monetary policy can become more sophisticated. The central bank bears responsibility not only for monetary policy implementation, but also for the soundness of the entire financial system. While performing the latter duty, the central bank must not discriminate between banks on the grounds of ownership form, that is, it must establish equal access to its facilities to all the licensed or chartered banks. In South-East European transitional economies, the state-owned banks and recently fully or partly privatised banks dominate the system. Increasing competition should very soon lead to narrowing margins and reduced lending rates. However, the domestic banks argue that they need governmental protection from foreign competition. In our view, an open entry for the foreign banks has had very positive results on market structure, market competition and the overall performance of the banking sector, as we have previously demonstrated.

Sound relations between the central bank and banking sector are necessary for the successful conduct of monetary policy, and for providing a sound financial system in the country. Until now, a number of positive moves have been made, but there is still a long way to go. As has been noted, transitional economies are finding that banking reform is a never-ending process.[34] As a result of this, the financial system must be permanently subjected to upgrading, eliminating weak points and introducing new, improved (well-performing) instruments and participants. The central bank is there to regulate, supervise and, when necessary, act as a moderator.

NOTES

1. The author would like to extend his gratitude to the central banks of all South-East European transitional economies (Bank of Albania, National Bank of Bulgaria, Central Bank of Bosnia and Herzegovina, National Bank of Croatia, National Bank of the Republic of Macedonia, National Bank of Romania, Bank of Slovenia and National Bank of Yugoslavia) for making available their national legislation regarding central banking and the banking system, recent annual and monthly reports and in-house analytical materials. Many colleagues working in those institutions commented on some parts of this work and the author acknowledges their support which improved the overall quality of this chapter. However, all eventual errors are the sole responsibility of an author, and opinions expressed in this chapter cannot in any way be associated with the mentioned institutions.
2. In some countries coins can be issued by the Treasury, as a so-called 'state issue'. History has shown that following considerable social upheaval, such as a revolution, the first issue of the national currency was usually made by the Ministry of Finance (Treasury).
3. Understood as the use of a set of instruments required to achieve desired results within a given framework.

4. This was not the case for the former Yugoslavia, because in 1974 it introduced a *united monetary system* which consisted of the National Bank of Yugoslavia and the system of National Banks of the Republics and Autonomous Provinces. Although the National Bank of Yugoslavia was responsible for monetary policy, members of the system often acted more or less independently, especially after 1988. With the dissolution of the Federation, republican national banks simply resumed their old functions, adding the issuing of national currency.
5. See more in Šević (1996d).
6. For the co-operation of central banks see Flandreau (1997).
7. In a two-tier banking system, the first tier is reserved for the central bank, while the second tier comprises commercial (universal) banks. In a three-tier banking system (as proposed by Corbet and Mayer, 1991) the first tier is the central bank, the second tier is reserved for state-owned commercial banks, while the third tier comprises new, private commercial banks, which are not encumbered with a communist past.
8. See, for instance: Arts 9–14, Law on the Czech National Bank; Art. 1, Law on the National Bank of Yugoslavia, 1993 (The National Bank of Yugoslavia is autonomous ...); Art. 1/3, Law No. 8269 on the Bank of Albania; Art. 2/3, Law on the National Bank of Croatia; Art. 2, Law on the Bank of Slovenia; Art. 3, Law on the National Bank of the Republic of Macedonia; Art. 44, Law on the National Bank of Bulgaria; Art. 3, Law of Bosnia and Herzegovina on the Central Bank of Bosnia and Herzegovina. (Within the limits of its authority established by this Law, the central bank shall be entirely independent from the Federation of Bosnia and Herzegovina, Republika Srpska, any public agency and any other authority in the pursuit of its objective and the performance of its tasks. Except as otherwise specified by law, the central bank shall take no instructions from any other person. The independence of the central bank shall be respected and no person shall seek improperly to influence any member of a decision-making body of the central bank in the discharge of his duties towards the central bank, or interfere in the activities of the central bank.) It is not known why the Law on the National Bank of Romania has no explicit provisions concerning the independence of the National Bank of Romania. However, it is stated that in pursuit of its main objective, the National Bank of Romania will be required to state its point of view on public authority rulings concerning monetary policy, banking and foreign exchange operations, as well as public debt, which shows that the Romanian National Bank may have the necessary instruments to pursue its prime objective independently.
9. The National Bank of Yugoslavia collaborates with the Federal government in setting the main aims of economic policy, and within its remit supports the fulfilment of these aims. (Art. 23, Law on the National Bank of Yugoslavia, 1993); see also: Art. 3/1, Law on the National Bank of Romania (The National Bank of Romania co-operates with central and local public authorities in order to attain its goals); Art. 64, Law on the Bank of Slovenia (the Bank of Slovenia and the Ministry of Finance of the Republic are obliged to exchange data and information important for the monetary and the banking system to function properly); Art. 2/2, Law on the National Bank of Croatia (the National Bank of Croatia shall by its activity support the economic policy measures of the Republic of Croatia whereby this support shall not endanger the currency stability and the general settlement of liquidity of payments in the country and abroad); Art. 3, Law on the Bulgarian National Bank. (In the formulation of the general outlines of the monetary and credit policy, the Bulgarian National Bank and the Council of Ministers shall inform each other of their intentions and actions.) In other countries similar provisions, which have roots in the Bundesbank Law, are not stipulated. The full independence of the central bank is of paramount importance to the legislator, so any kind of relationship with the government is *de jure* prevented.
10. See: Art. 30, Law on the Bank of Albania (limit of 5 per cent of average annual governmental revenues in last three years); Art. 58/2, Law on the National Bank of Croatia (5 per cent of the budget for a current year); Art. 61/4, Law on the Bank of Slovenia (5 per cent of the annual budget, but not more than 20 per cent of the total anticipated budget deficit); Art. 46/1, Law on the National Bank of the Republic of Macedonia (5 per cent of the budget for a current year); Art. 29/4, Law on the National Bank of Romania (7 per cent of the budget for the previous year, but not more than double the National Bank's own capital); the central banks of Bosnia and Herzegovina and Bulgaria *stricto lege* cannot extend any credit to the government.

11. See Art. 34/1–3, Law on the National Bank of Yugoslavia, 1993.
12. As an exception to Art. 32/3 of this law, on credits approved by the National Bank of Yugoslavia in accordance with the first paragraph of this article, the interest rate can be lower than the discount rate (Art. 34/4, Law on the National Bank of Yugoslavia, 1993).
13. See Art. 12/3, Law on the National Bank of Yugoslavia, 1993.
14. Art. 13/1, Law on the Bank of Slovenia (The independent experts – members of the governing board shall ...); Art. 66/1, Law on the National Bank of Croatia (... and at the most eight members to be appointed from among independent experts); Art. 44/3, Law on the Bank of Albania (Candidates for membership on the Supervisory Council must be citizens of the Republic of Albania, they must be persons of recognised integrity, and (a) be well educated in economics or jurisprudence; (b) have professional experience in monetary and banking matters; (c) hold postgraduate professional qualifications; (d) have not less than five years' experience in public administration or in financial and banking institutions ...); Art. 111/3 (Only persons of the highest integrity and with outstanding qualifications in economics, finance and banking ... shall be elected/appointed as members of the managing board) and so on.
15. See Art. 18/3, Law on the National Bank of Yugoslavia, 1993.
16. See further: Šević (1996d, pp. 12–15).
17. Although we stress that these close connections can be useful for a central bank as a source of information they can also be dangerous for monetary policy efficiency (see Schieber, 1994).
18. In the case of Yugoslavia.
19. See Todd (1988).
20. Todd (1988, p. 3).
21. See Šević (1999).
22. See Art. 15, Second Banking Directive COM 89/646.
23. See, for instance, the seminal work of Morrison (1966).
24. See, for instance, Sellon and Weiner (1997).
25. *Compulsory (obligatory) reserves* weaken the credit ability of banks, and therefore affect the creation of money by the banks, keeping monetary aggregates under firm control. However, it works this directly only in an underdeveloped monetary system.
26. 'The objectives of U.S. monetary policy are high employment, stable prices (no inflation), and growth in output on a sustainable basis. These ultimate goals, as they are often described, are not directly under control of the Federal Reserve' (see FRB of San Francisco, 1987, p. 6).
27. Only in Moldova does the law stipulate explicitly (among others) that is the duty of the National Bank of Moldova to provide loans to the state. (see Art. 4,. Law of the Republic of Moldova on the State National Bank of Moldova (National Bank of Moldova), 1991).
28. Although in some countries foreign exchange determination is left in the hands of the government. For instance, Yugoslavia (see Arts 39 and 40, Law on the National Bank of Yugoslavia, 1993).
29. The interest rate is a main target of the Bank of Finland, but the whole institutional framework supports this choice (see Aaltonen et al., 1994, esp. p. 41).
30. See cross-country comparison in Šević (1996a, pp. 106–9).
31. For example, Estonia accepted the option of a currency board. Estonia's Law on Security for the Estonian Kroon (1992), directly links the exchange rate of the kroon to the German mark. The Estonian Central Bank is forbidden to devalue the kroon. However, devaluation may take place, but only if the law is changed, and this can be done only by parliament itself. This is the first time in financial history that the authorisation for the devaluation of a national currency has been granted to a parliament.
32. For instance, the British and French experience in the early 1970s.
33. Monetary policy in the new conditions should comprise the following elements: (1) quick decontrol of interest rates; (2) maintenance of net direct ceilings for large state-owned banks until budget constraints have been hardened; (3) unification of reserve requirements and, possibly, payment of interest on reserves; (4) elimination of preferential central bank refinancing rates and special lending programmes; (5) granting or refinancing credit on the basis of solvency and/or provision of collateral; and (6) promotion of the development of the interbank money market, and of the securitisation of financial claims (Buch, 1995, p. 21).

34. *Financial Times* (1996, p. III).

BIBLIOGRAPHY

Aaltonen, A., E. Aurikko and J. Kontulainen (1994), *Monetary Policy in Finland*, Bank of Finland, Helsinki.

Abel, I. and J.P. Bonin (1990), 'Two Approaches to the Transformation in Eastern Europe: The Big Bang Versus Slow but Steady', *Acta Oeconomica*, **43** (3–4), 213–30.

Abel, I. and J.P. Bonin (1992), 'Capital Markets in Eastern Europe: The Financial Black Hole', *Connecticut Journal of International Law*, **8** (1), 1–17.

Berman, S. and K.R. McNamara (1999), 'Bank on Democracy', *Foreign Affairs*, **78** (2), 2–8.

Bernanke, B. (1983), 'Non-Monetary Effects of the Financial Crisis in the Propagation of the Great Depression', *American Economic Review*, **73**, 257–76.

Bernanke, B. and F. Mishkin (1992), *Central Bank Behavior and the Strategy of Monetary Policy: Observations from Six Industrialized Countries*, NBER Reprint No. 1784, National Bureau of Economic Research, Cambridge.

Blanchard, O.J., R. Dornbusch, P. Krugman, R. Layard and L. Summers (1990), *Reform in Eastern Europe: Report of the Wider World Economy Group*, WIDER, Helsinki.

Blanchard, O., R. Dornbusch, P. Krugman, R. Layard and L. Summers (1991), *Reform in Eastern Europe*, MIT Press, Cambridge, MA.

Bosworth, B.P. and G. Ofer (1995), *Reforming Planned Economies in an Integrating World Economy*, Brookings Institution, Washington, DC.

Brainard, L.J. (1990), 'Reform in Eastern Europe: Creating a Capital Market', in R. O'Brien and S. Hewin (eds) (1990), *Finance and International Economy 4*, The AMEX Bank Review Prize Essays in Memory of Robert Marjolin, Oxford University Press for the AMEX Bank Review, London, 6–22.

Buch, C.M. (1995), 'Monetary Policy and the Transformation of the Banking System in Eastern Europe', Kiel Working Paper No. 676, Kiel Institute of World Economics, Kiel, February.

Calvo, G.A. and J.A. Frenkel (1991), 'From Centrally Planned to Market Economy', *IMF Staff Papers*, **38** (2), 268–99.

Caprio, G., D. Folkerts-Landau and T.D. Lane (eds) (1994), *Building Sound Finance in Emerging Market Economies*, International Monetary Fund and the World Bank, Washington, DC.

Clague, C. and G. Rausser (eds) (1992), *The Emergence of Market Economies in Eastern Europe*, Basil Blackwell, Cambridge.

Colombatto, E. (1992), 'The Integration of the East and Option for the West', *Journal des Economistes et des Etudes Humaines*, **3** (2/3), 273–88.

Colombatto, E. and J.R. Macey (1996), 'A Public Choice Model of International Economic Cooperation and the Decline of the Nation State', *Cardozo Law Review*, **18** (3), 925–56.

Commission of the European Communities (1995), *White Paper: Preparation of the Associated Countries of Central and Eastern Europe for Integration into the Internal Market of the Union*, COM(95) 163 final/2 of 10 May.

Commission of the European Communities (1996), *The Impact of the Development of the Countries of Central and Eastern Europe on the Community Territory*, Office for Official Publication of the European Communities, Luxembourg.

Corbet, J. and C. Mayer (1990), 'Financial Reform in Eastern Europe: Progress with the Wrong Model', CEPR Discussion Paper, No. 603, Centre for Economic Policy Research, London.

Corbet, J. and C. Mayer (1991), 'Financial Reform in Eastern Europe: Progress with the Wrong Model', *Oxford Review of Economic Policy*, **7** (4), 57–75.

Coricelli, F. and A. Thorne (1992), 'Creating Financial Markets in Economies in Transition', mimeo, World Bank, Washington, DC.

Cukierman, A. (1994), 'Central Bank Independence and Monetary Control', *Economic Journal*, **104** (427), 1437–48.

Debs, R.A., H. Shapiro and C. Taylor (eds) (1991), *Financing Eastern Europe: A Study Group Report*, The Group of Thirty, Washington, DC.

EBRD, *Transitional Report*, various issues, 1994–1999, European Bank for Reconstruction and Development, London.

FDIC (1997), *History of the Eighties: Lessons for the Future*, Federal Deposit Insurance Corporation, Washington, DC (two volumes).

Federal Reserve Bank (FRB) of San Francisco (1987), *Monetary Policy in the United States*, Federal Reserve Bank of San Francisco, San Francisco.

Financial Times (1996), 'Czech Finance and Investment', in *Financial Times Supplement*, Friday, 26 April, p. III.

Fischer, S. and A. Gelb (1990), 'Issues in Socialist Economy Reform', mimeo, World Bank, Washington, DC.

Fischer, S. and A. Gelb (1991), 'The Process of Socialist Economic Transformation', *Journal of Economic Perspectives*, Fall, 91–105.

Flandreau, M. (1997), 'Central Bank Cooperation in Historical Perspective: A Sceptical View', *Economic History Review*, **50** (4), 735–63.

Goodhart, C.A.E. (1989), *Money, Information and Uncertainty*, Macmillan, London.

Goodhart, C.A.E. (1994), 'What Should Central Banks Do? What Should Be Their Macroeconomic Objectives and Operations?', *Economic Journal*, **104** (427), 1424–36.

Goodhart, C.A.E. (1995), *The Central Bank and the Financial System*, Macmillan, Basingstoke.

Goodman, L.S. (1982), 'On the Interaction between Bank Risk and Lender of Last Resort', Federal Reserve Bank of New York Research Paper No. 8224.

Gros, D. and A. Steinherr (1995), *Winds of Change: Economic Transition in Central and Eastern Europe*, Longman, London.

Hanke, S.H., L. Jonung and K. Schuler (1993), *Russian Currency and Finance: A Currency Board Approach to Reform*, Routledge, London.

Hilbers, P.L.C. (1989), 'The Monetary Cash Reserves Arrangement', *The Netherlands Bank Quarterly Review*, **2**, 27–39.

Hilbers, P. (1993a), 'Monetary Instruments and their Use During the Transition from a Centrally Planned to a Market Economy', IMF Working Paper No. 93-87, International Monetary Fund, Washington, DC.

Hilbers, P.L.C. (1993b), 'The Use of Monetary Instruments During the Transition from a Centrally Planned to a Market Economy', Domestic Research Department Series, No. 73, De Nederlandsche Bank, Amsterdam.

Hinds, M. (1990a), *Issues in the Introduction of Market Forces in Eastern European Economies*, World Bank, Washington, DC.

Hinds, M. (1990b), 'Issues in the Introduction of Market Forces in Eastern European Socialist Economies', Internal Discussion Paper, Report No. IDP-0057, World Bank, Washington, DC.

Kent, R.P. (1966), *Money and Banking*, Holt, Reinhart and Winston, New York.

Khan, M.S. and V. Sundararajan (1992), 'Financial Sector Reform and Monetary Policy', in V.A. Jafarey (ed.), *Structural Adjustment and Macroeconomic Policy Issues*, International Monetary Fund, Washington, DC., pp. 58–79.

Kornai, J. (1986), 'Soft Budget Constraint', *Kyklos*, **39** (1), 3–30.

Kornai, J. (1990), *The Road to the Free Economy*, W.W. Norton, New York.

Kornai, J. (1993), 'The Evolution of Financial Discipline under the Post-Socialist System', *Kyklos*, **46** (3), 315–36.

Leite, S. and V. Sundararajan (1990), 'Issues in Interest Rate Management and Liberalization', IMF Staff Papers, **37**, pp. 735–52.

Mayer, C. and X. Vives (eds) (1993), *Capital Markets and Financial Intermediation*, Cambridge University Press for the Centre for Economic Policy Research, Cambridge.

Morrison, G.R. (1966), *Liquidity Preferences of Commercial Banks*, University of Chicago Press, Chicago.

Saunders, A. and I. Walter (1994), *Universal Banking in the United States: What Could We Gain? What Could We Lose?*, Oxford University Press, Oxford.

Schieber, H. (1994), 'The Central Bank as Fiscal Agent for the Government', mimeo, University of Chicago Law School, Chicago.

Sellon, G.H., Jr. and S.F. Weiner (1997), 'Monetary Policy Without Reserve Requirements: Case Studies and Options for the United Studies', *Federal Reserve Bank of Kansas City Economic Review*, Second Quarter, **82** (2), 5–30.

Šević, Ž. (1996a), *Centralna banka: Položaj – organizacija – funkcije* [Central Bank: Position – Organisation – Functions ...], Čigoja štampa, Belgrade.

Šević, Ž. (1996b), 'Notes on the Contemporary Management of a Central Bank', mimeo, Department of Economics and Management, University of Dundee, Dundee.

Šević, Ž. (1996c), 'Odnos izmedju centralne banke i izvršne vlasti' [Relationship between the Central Bank and Executive Power], *Jugoslovensko bankarstvo*, **26** (1–2), 29–36.

Šević, Ž. (1996d), 'Centralna monetarna vlast u Srbiji, odnosno Jusoslaviji: Istorijska Perspektiva' [Central Monetary Authority in Serbia, that is, Yugoslavia: A Historical Perspective], *Finansije*, **51** (5–6), 459–80.

Šević, Ž. (1997a), 'Yugoslav Path to Privatisation: Why It So Differs and What Is To Be Done with the Financial System?', in: B. Sloan, E. Zavadskas and A. Kaklauskas (eds), *Property Valuation and Investment in Central and Eastern Europe During the Transition to Free Market Economy*, Technika, Vilnius, pp. 114–23.

Šević, Ž. (1997b), 'Law and Economics of (Economic) Policy Reform', in Ž. Šević and G. Wright (eds), *Transition in Central and Eastern Europe*, YASF, Belgrade,Vol. I, pp. 152–72.

Šević, Ž. (1999), *Restructuring Banks in Central and Eastern European Countries as a Part of Macroeconomic Changes Towards Market Oriented Economies*, Belgrade: Balkan Center for Public Policy and Related Studies and Čigoja Štampa.

Šević, Ž. (2002), 'An Institutional Choice: Bank-based vs. Market-based Financial System', *Commentaries in Law and Accountancy*, forthcoming.

Šević, Ž. and A. Šević (1998), Monetary Policy in a Transitional Economy: Some Open Questions and Experience, *Economic Systems*, **22**(3), pp. 299–304

Sundararajan, V. (1990), 'Financial Sector Reform and Central Banking in Centrally Planned Economies', IMF Working Paper WP/90/120, International Monetary Fund, Washington, DC.

Thakor, A.V. (1996), 'The Design of Financial Systems: An Overview', *Journal of Banking & Finance*, **20**, 917–48.

Tietmeyer, H. (1994), *Role and Instruments of Monetary Policy*, Kiel Institute of World Economics, Kiel.

Todd, W.F. (1988), 'Lessons of the Past and Prospects for the Future in Lender of Last Resort Theory', Federal Reserve Bank of Cleveland Working Paper No. 8805, FRB of Cleveland, Cleveland.

Udell, G.F. and P. Wachtel (1995), 'Financial System Design for Formerly Planned Economies: Defining the Issues', *Financial Markets, Institutions, and Instruments*, **4** (2), 1–60.

van Wijnbergen, S. (1994), 'On the Role of Banks in Enterprise Restructuring: The Polish Example', CEPR Discussion Paper No. 898, Centre for Economic Policy Research, London.

Zecchini, S. (1991), 'Economic Reform and Western Assistance', in P. Marer and S. Zecchini (eds), *Transition to Market Economy*, Vol. I, OECD, Paris, pp. 256–69.

Zecchini, S. (ed.) (1997), *Lessons from the Economic Transition: Central and Eastern Europe in the 1990s*, Kluwer, Dordrecht.

6. Currency Boards and Currency Arrangements in Transition Economies

Mervyn K. Lewis

INTRODUCTION

When should a country adopt a currency board system, and when should it dispense with one? Both economic theory and policy practice offer a relatively clear set of answers to the first question, and the experience of Bulgaria – considered elsewhere in this volume – illustrates one of the reasons. Countries have resorted to currency board arrangements when other methods of controlling inflation have failed, and in all cases the results are striking: the currency board has served to bring inflation speedily under control. In Bulgaria's case, inflation fell from 2,040 per cent per annum in the first quarter of 1997 to 1 per cent per annum in 1998!

However, the second question – if and when to leave – is more difficult to answer. Of course, not all countries may wish to exit a system described by Dornbusch and Giavazzi (1999) as 'not a luxury, but a first best strategy to avoid crises exposure ... [and] a strong mechanism for economic development' (p. 25). Yet countries which adopt a currency board invariably do depart from the system, and the results are not always inauspicious,[1] for example, Singapore and Malaysia. In 1960, 38 countries had a currency board system. Currently, there are nine in operation. Djibouti (1949), Brunei (1967), East Caribbean (1968) and Hong Kong SAR (1986) are the oldest; the other five are creations of the 1990s (see Table 6.1).

This chapter examines the characteristics of a currency board in order to identify those features which would prompt a country to exit from it. Currency boards are often described as modern-day equivalents of specie systems, such as the gold standard (Hanke and Schuler, 1992; IMF, 1997; Kopcke, 1999) and we shall use this analogy to explore the similarities and

Table 6.1 *Features of existing currency boards*[1]

Economy	Year began	Reserve currency	Reserve assets	Minimum cover	Actual cover[2]	Deposits in foreign currency[2]
Argentina	1991	US dollar	⅔ foreign assets and gold; ⅓ Argentina's government bond denominated in USD	100% of base money	139% of base money 27% of M2	53%
Brunei-Darussalam	1967	Singapore dollar	Liquid foreign assets and securities	70% of the central bank's current liabilities	About 80% of the central bank's demand liabilities	n/a
Bosnia	1997	DEM/Euro	DEM assets, except for ½ of the central bank's capital	100% of the central bank's monetary liabilities	100% of base money 66% of M2	86%
Bulgaria	1997	Euro	Foreign assets and gold	100% of base money plus some excess coverage	105% of base money 84% of M2	56%
Djibouti	1949	US dollar	Foreign assets	100% of circulating currency	125% of base money 22.5% of M2	n/a
Estonia	1992	DEM/Euro	Foreign assets and gold	100% of base money, excluding the central bank's certificates	145% of base money 41% of M2	41%
Hong Kong, China	1983	US dollar	Foreign assets	105% of currency	109% of base money 7% of M2	44%
Lithuania	1994	US dollar	Foreign assets and gold	100% of base money and the central bank's liquid liabilities	105% of base money 63% of M2	61%
ECCB[3]	1968	US dollar	Foreign assets and gold	60% of base money	82–99% of base money 12–20% of deposits	n/a

Notes: 1 Excluding Bermuda (since 1915), Cayman Islands (since 1972), Falkland Islands (since 1899), Faroe Islands (since 1940), Gibraltar (since 1927).
2 For 1998.
3 Eastern Caribbean Central Bank: comprising Antigua and Bermuda, Dominica, Grenada, St Kitts and Nevis, St Lucia, St Vincent and the Grenadines.

Sources: Ghosh, Gulde and Wolf (1998), Kopcke (1999).

differences between currency board arrangements and the classical gold standard. Based on this analysis, we then outline a variant to conventional currency board arrangements which addresses one of the principal difficulties of a currency board system, along with other alternatives. Finally, the chapter considers the role that currency boards might play in the evolving world monetary system.

CURRENCY BOARDS AND GOLD COMPARED

A currency board[2] is often defined as an arrangement which fixes the exchange rate of the currency board country to that of an anchor currency. That in fact is not quite the case. Strictly speaking, the currency board does not peg the exchange rate but instead determines and maintains the parity at which notes (and coin) issued by it exchange for the currency of the reserve currency. The fixed exchange rate follows from and is a consequence of this arrangement, as we now explain.

There are many different types of currency board, but in its purest form it is an institution which issues currency fully (that is, at least 100 per cent) backed by the reserves of foreign assets – there is no fiduciary issue – and which stands ready to redeem the domestic currency on demand at a fixed price in terms of the foreign currency (or currencies). Its sole purpose is to issue or buy back currency as and when the public demand it. The board's staff thus undertake two functions: exchanging notes and coin for the reserve currency, and investing its assets in high-grade securities denominated in the reserve currency.

Although in principle the currency board is required to convert on demand all offers to it of domestic or reserve currency, two features of the workings of currency board systems serve to circumscribe this function. First, most of the foreign exchange business is normally carried out by the banks. In some cases, as in Hong Kong, the currency board deals only with banks. There may be other restrictions such as minimum transaction amounts or commissions charged for every transaction. Such requirements are probably unnecessary; most people will choose to exchange currency through the banks much as they would do in the absence of the board. The result is that the currency board can effectively confine itself to accepting and paying the reserve currency by cheque or electronic transfer, leaving the job of supplying reserve currency to the commercial banks.

However, and this is the second feature, the currency board does not back bank deposits. The guarantee of automatic convertibility and the 100 per cent reserve-currency backing condition does not extend to bank deposits or other financial assets. In order to shift wealth from local currency bank deposits into the foreign reserve currency, the individual must initially convert the bank deposit into domestic currency and then present the local currency to the currency board for conversion into the foreign currency.

In practice, most entities will not use this indirect route but will convert their bank deposits directly into foreign currency. When doing so, they rely in the first place upon banks maintaining the convertibility of bank deposits into domestic currency and thus the reserve currency. In the second place, transactors rely on the competitiveness of the interbank currency market to ensure that the exchange rates at which bank deposits trade for foreign exchange will be broadly in line with the rates offered by the currency board. Restrictions on who has access to the currency board, in what amounts and for what charges, loosen the link between market exchange rates and the official parity, introducing an element of floating exchange rates into the system, although only within a very narrow range. Thus the exchange rate at which bank deposits trade for foreign exchange will deviate within relatively small arbitration points from the currency board's defined parity.

There are obvious parallels here with the operation of the gold standard, to which a currency board link is often compared. A gold standard requires that all paper and deposit money be interconvertible with gold at a fixed mint parity. This convertibility combined with the free trade in gold provided one mechanism by which foreign payments could take place. For example, it was always open for an entity in England needing to make a payment in dollars to take sterling notes to the Bank of England for conversion into gold bars at the official gold parity, ship the gold to New York, exchange the gold for dollars at the Federal Reserve Bank, and then arrange payment of the debt. Most international transactions were not made in this way but were made instead through the foreign exchange markets. In order to buy dollar goods, English people had to persuade someone to exchange sterling for dollars. Americans buying British goods had to persuade someone to change dollars for sterling. Either the total purchases of the two groups must balance, or members of one group had to be willing to accumulate the currency of the other, with the exchange rate adjusting to help bring this about – much the same as occurs at present. The difference from now was that exchange rates fluctuated only within strict limits – the gold export and import points – reflecting the existence of the indirect, roundabout payments mechanism described above, in much the same way as interconvertibility via the board puts strict limits upon market exchange rates under a currency board system. In both cases, of course, the existence of the roundabout conversion mechanism – and confidence in its retention – encourages arbitrageurs to take positions which largely obviate the need for actual conversions to take place.

Other points of similarity exist between currency board systems and gold-backed currencies. All are ramifications of the two fundamental features they share, namely parity and full and automatic convertibility. Nevertheless, it may be useful to examine the parallels as a way of assessing the strengths and weaknesses of the currency board *vis-à-vis* other exchange rate arrangements.

Money Creation

Under a currency board, monetary policy is literally 'outsourced', in the words of Dornbusch and Giavazzi (1999), and money creation is put on automatic pilot. With the domestic currency convertible at a fixed price in terms of a reserve currency, the currency issuing authority has no control over the quantity in circulation which is consequently determined by the demand to hold it. Due to the 100 per cent reserve requirement, the board's role in determining the supply of reserves is entirely passive, acting as a sort of warehouse, storing reserves in the form of foreign currency securities and issuing notes and coin in their place. It is the central bank of the reserve-currency country that determines the supply of reserves. But it does so for the whole currency area, including the currency board country. The only way for the board to acquire new reserves is to obtain currency from the reserve-currency country, which in turn means that residents in the country must run a balance of payments surplus.

At the simplest, the only source of money creation is from international reserves, in line with the classical specie-flow theory or the monetary theory of the balance of payments. The starting-point is to assume that only currency board notes and bank deposits serve as money (M) in the currency board country, which is expressed as a multiple of the monetary base (B)

$$M = m\,B \tag{6.1}$$

where $m = 1 + d/d + r$ is the usual money multiplier. The money base is synonymous with the balance sheet of the currency board, comprising currency board notes (N) held by the public and the banks, backed by foreign reserves (R),

$$B = N_P + N_B = R. \tag{6.2}$$

The currency board's reserve holding are directly related to the balance of payments via the balance of payments identity

$$\Delta R = X - Z + K \tag{6.3}$$

where $(X - Z)$ is the current account surplus and K is the net private capital inflow, the sum of which add to the official acquisition of foreign exchange.

Overall, we have

$$\Delta M = m(X - Z + K) \tag{6.4}$$

with the money supply moving in line with the balance of payments position, the degree of proportionality depending on constancy of the bank reserve–deposit ratio (r) and the public's currency to deposit ratio (d). Proportionality is also governed by the extent to which reserve backing falls below 100 per cent, allowing fiduciary issues of domestic currency and introducing what has become known as a 'modified currency board system' (Hanke and Schuler, 1994). In this aspect there is also a close parallel with fiduciary issues under the gold standard.

Financial Stability

Holding 100 per cent backing[3] for the domestic currency represents a resource cost. While reserves can be invested in interest-bearing financial assets, some part must be maintained in liquid form, and the portfolio as a whole presumably earns less than having the funds invested in capital projects or imported capital equipment. One solution is to lower the official backing, and allow fiduciary issues of base money. Such a decision may erode confidence in the authorities' commitment to the arrangement, while removing one of the currency board's principal features – the inability of the monetary authorities to finance a budget deficit by money creation.

The alternative – which is what happened under the gold standard – is to allow the growth of unbacked, private issues of fiduciary money in the form of deposits for which banks themselves hold domestic or foreign currency reserves as backing. If the banks can function effectively with reserves that are some fraction of their outstanding liabilities, so that the quantity of money is much larger than the stocks of international reserves, society gets its monetary services at a lower cost while individuals benefit from the explicit or implicit interest (services) which banks pay on deposits. It was a feature of the gold standard that this economising process occurred over time without design, undertaken by banks and other institutions engaging in financial intermediation which involves maturity transformation and able successfully to issue call liabilities considered as 'good as gold'. While the whole superstructure of claims was still ultimately tied to gold by the redemption of bank liabilities and central banks' reserves of gold and gold-based assets, the indirect linkage meant that there could be no certainty that a country's money supply would always rise and fall automatically in line with gold movements as was expected under the 'rules of the game'. Further, the pyramiding of an increasing quantity of debt money on a limited quantity of gold created the potential for instability in times of crisis when the threat of gold conversions loomed.

Under gold there was usually some leeway for the authorities to come to the aid of banks when gold conversions threatened their solvency. Under a currency board system this support may not be possible. Currency boards, in their pure form, cannot extend credit to the government, the banking system, or anyone else. This is because a currency board can act as lender of last resort only to the extent that it has, or can draw upon, external reserves in excess of those needed to back the monetary base. Its capacity to support the commercial banking system is therefore bounded to a degree that a conventional central bank is not, and this limited ability for the currency board to act as lender of last resort means that the banking system must be sufficiently robust so as to function without the backing of central bank credit extensions. All of this means that the cast-iron guarantee of the convertibility of domestic currency into the reserve currency is obtained at the expense of the convertibility of commercial bank deposits into domestic notes and coin.

A further corollary is that more of the burden of adjustment is thrown upon the banking system and, by implication, the economy as a whole. Establishment of a currency board may represent an unequivocal commitment by the government concerned, but it is not an entirely convincing one since the law creating the board can always be reversed. In a crisis, with the monetary base contracting and an expectation of a devaluation in the offing, interest rates must rise to levels which demonstrate that the authorities remain committed to the peg. This reliance on interest rates to equilibrate financial markets forces banks, for their part, to assume a larger share of the burden of adjustment, either by borrowing reserves from abroad or by contracting their own balance sheets in line with the contraction of liquidity. That contraction then shifts the burden onto product and labour markets. This is the deflationary spectre which accompanies a gold standard type rule. For currency boards to deliver their promise of credibility and monetary stability, they must be seen as durable commitments. But for the peg to be seen as durable, so must the banking system, while wages and prices need to be flexible enough to weather any currency market volatility.

Price Stability

A currency board can limit the rate of inflation in an economy, but cannot guarantee a low rate of inflation or the absence of significant price movements, as the experience of gold shows. When the price of a currency is fixed against an asset or commodity, the price level is determined by the relative price of the chosen anchor against goods and services in general. That relativity in turn is governed by the respective productivity movements. Linking to gold provided countries with a remarkable degree of long-run price stability (prices of consumer goods in Britain in absolute terms in 1931 were at virtually the same level as they were 110 years before in 1821) yet there were substantial periods of both secular rising and falling prices when productivity in the gold industry differed substantially from that of other industries.

Similarly, the fixing of exchange rates under external stabilisation is not in itself sufficient for price stability. It merely fixes relative price relations between the countries which are pegged and allows for only one monetary policy across the linked systems; there is a direct link between the macroeconomic behaviour of the domestic economy and that of the country to which it is pegged which precludes the taking of independent, national policies for internal stabilisation of prices. By opting for external stabilisation, a country forgoes its monetary autonomy and effectively delegates to the major country the responsibility for its inflation performance. Obviously that policy could be inflationary, and this would be imported by the fixed peg. Yet, marked inflation rate differentials can arise even when a country anchors itself to a low-inflation country, because of significant differences in productivity growth rates.

The reason is that the tendency to absolute (or relative) price equality applies only to tradable goods and services; competition will ensure that there cannot be large and persistent price discrepancies, at least in the longer run, for goods and services of the same quality which are readily transportable. Commodities, readily transportable manufacturing goods, and those services carried 'on the wire' are obvious examples. When scaled in terms of a common currency, prices for such internationally traded goods tend to be much the same in all competitive markets. It is this mechanism which produces long-run inflation convergence for countries adhering to a fixed exchange rate peg.

But suppose that one country has a high rate of productivity in its internationally traded goods sector. The country concerned will be able to pay its workers larger wage increases than elsewhere while remaining competitive on world markets. Most likely, wages growth will not be confined to the traded sector and will flow on to wages in the non-traded industries (predominantly services). If productivity in the non-traded services sector is growing more slowly than in other parts of the economy, prices will increase more rapidly for non-traded than for traded goods and services. This is because the wage increases are similar, but productivity growth is different.

In each country the inflation rate is a mixture of inflation in the traded and non-traded sectors. Inflation in traded goods will tend to equality, implying no loss in competitiveness, but the high-productivity country will have more rapid inflation in the non-traded goods sectors and a higher inflation rate overall. The greater the gap in productivity the greater will be the inflation gap between the countries. Japan had a higher inflation rate than the United States under Bretton Woods. For much the same reasons, Hong Kong inflation has been much higher than in the United States, despite Hong Kong having tied its currency to the US dollar since 1983 using a currency board scheme. In fact, the rate of inflation in Hong Kong from 1983 to the mid-1990s was, on average, more than double that in the United States (Kopcke, 1999). While there are special reasons why Hong Kong chose to revert to its colonial-type currency board, the experience is nevertheless instructive for other small countries in showing that a fixed exchange rate link as under a currency board can conflict with price stability.

Exchange Rate Stability

A currency board system imparts considerable stability to the nominal exchange rate expressed in terms of the reserve currency. But, it does not necessarily stabilise either the real exchange rate or the trade-weighted exchange rate (in nominal or real terms). The former requires sufficient flexibility of wages and prices to bring about conformity of inflation rates. The latter requires that the exchange rates of other countries, which have trade and financial links with the currency board country, move in line with that of the reserve currency. Otherwise, any change in the relationship between those countries' exchange rates *vis-à-vis* that of the reserve-currency country might alter the currency board country's competitiveness relative to that of those other countries.

Hong Kong after the onset of the Asian currency crisis in 1997 illustrates the point. Following the floating and large depreciation of the Thai baht in July 1997, there were large falls in the currencies of Korea, Malaysia, Indonesia and the Philippines. Singapore and Taiwan allowed their currencies to float down. Other currencies such as the Japanese yen, the Australian and New Zealand dollars and the Indian rupee also fell. But the Hong Kong currency board system held firm and the Hong Kong dollar retained its fixed link with the US dollar, albeit by deploying some unconventional measures such as intervention by the Hong Kong authorities in the equity and land market, and 'borrowing' the People's Republic of China's (PRC) massive reserves as potential backing for its own holdings.

Nevertheless, Hong Kong's 'success' came at a price. Table 6.2 shows over the period from June 1997 to March 1998 movements of the bilateral exchange rates *vis-à-vis* the US dollar and the Japanese yen, along with trade-weighted exchange rates in both nominal and real terms, for a number of countries in the Asia-Pacific region. Hong Kong's bilateral rate with the US dollar obviously did not change. Yet the Hong Kong dollar appreciated by nearly 13 per cent against the yen and by 12 per cent against its trading partners in nominal terms and 14 per cent in real terms. Australia's experience was almost the direct opposite of Hong Kong's.

Table 6.2 *Bilateral and trade-weighted exchange rate movements, June 1997 to March 1998*

	Bilateral exchange rate *vis-à-vis*		Trade-weighted exchange rate	
	US dollar	Japanese yen	Nominal terms	Real terms
Japan	–11.5	–	5.3	2.1
PR China	–0.2	12.7	11.3	7.3
Hong Kong SAR[1]	–	12.9	12.1	14.3
Korea	–39.0	–31.0	–30.6	–26.4
Singapore	–11.9	–0.5	6.2	4.7
Taiwan POC[2]	–14.1	–3.0	–4.4	–7.6
Indonesia	–73.9	–70.6	–70.3	–61.9
Malaysia	–32.3	–23.5	–23.5	–22.4
Thailand	–37.5	–29.4	–29.8	–25.4
India	–9.5	2.2	0.9	3.7
Australia	–11.1	0.4	3.6	1.3
New Zealand	–16.8	–6.0	–6.9	–7.2

Notes:
1. SAR = Special Administrative Region.
2. POC = Province of China.

Source: IMF, *World Economic Outlook*, May 1998.

Whereas the Hong Kong dollar remained unchanged in terms of the US dollar but appreciated in real trade-weighted terms, the Australian dollar remained largely constant on a real trade-weighted basis but depreciated *vis-à-vis* the US dollar (a fact which grabbed all the headlines). In Australia the exchange rate did its job: larger exports to Europe and the United States made up for much of the falling exports to Asia, largely insulating the economy from the effects of the crisis. Singapore and Taiwan also remained largely unscathed.

With a similar depreciation blocked in Hong Kong by the currency board system, something else had to give in order for Hong Kong to restore its competitiveness. What ensued was a classic gold standard-type deflation of nominal prices across the board – retail prices, wages and asset values. The decline of land and property prices was particularly severe. Prime retail rentals in Hong Kong Central (the financial district) fell by 40 per cent between June 1997 and December 1998. Capital values for prime space fell by 53 per cent. Values in the Wanchai and Causeway Bay sub-market of Hong Kong fell by 70 per cent over this period. To some extent, these falls reflected the malaise of commercial property markets in Asia as a whole (Browne et al., 1998; Bentick and Lewis, 1999). Yet, prime retail rentals in Singapore fell by 25 per cent and capital values for prime retail space fell by 23 per cent over the same period, very much less than the declines that took place in Hong Kong. Many factors may account for this differential movement (for example, the handover to the PRC), but one element surely was the need for Hong Kong to maintain some comparability with competing locations for service activities in an environment in which nominal price movements were left as the principal mode of adjustment.

ALTERNATIVE ARRANGEMENTS

This section examines alternative arrangements. The first to be considered is a modified currency board system. The other possibility discussed is the exit mechanism from a currency board, along with the different exchange rate systems on offer.

A Modified Currency Board

A number of modified currency boards have developed in recent years with the aim of addressing some of the difficulties identified in the previous section while retaining features which resemble a conventional currency board. Thus Argentina, for example, allows for a minimum foreign currency reserve of 66.66 per cent, not 100 per cent as would be required for an orthodox arrangement. Other countries have grafted boards on to existing central banks, which have retained some of their old powers, but are constrained by currency board-type rules governing the exchange rate and reserve banking.

These modifications have been prompted to a large degree by concerns about the fragility of the local banking system in the face of a speculative attack. Bank collapses have occurred in some currency board countries (Hong Kong in 1986, Estonia 1992 and 1994, Argentina and Lithuania in 1995) and, although these were handled without abandoning or suspending the operation of the board, in some cases the 'rules of the game' were honoured more in the letter than in the spirit of the law. In other cases where currency boards have come under speculative attack, unusual forms of intervention were required (such as the open-market operations by the Hong Kong authorities in the stock market in 1998 and 1999, and the special discount window of the Hong Kong Monetary Authority introduced in September 1998).[4]

None of the modifications have tackled the problem of swings in competitiveness, although the choice of the anchor currency has generated much soul-searching. One of the major considerations shaping the choice of the anchor is the degree of diversification of trade. The greater is the diversification, the greater the problem in selecting any particular currency, given that fixing to one of the major currencies will imply substantial fluctuations relative to the others. For near European countries the obvious candidates are the US dollar and the euro. Foreign exchange market considerations and 'globalisation' of trade and finance favour the US dollar, whereas actual (or potential) trade links might support a euro link. The fact that Lithuania opted for the US dollar and Bulgaria for a DEM/euro peg shows that there is no natural choice, and both countries remain exposed to variations in competitiveness resulting from cross-Atlantic exchange rate swings.

Anna Schwartz (1993) has argued that the choice of an anchor currency, and the potential loss of competitiveness, is a more complicated one now, with the preponderance of floating between the major currency blocs, than it was for the currency board-type systems which operated under the gold standard. In a sense this is correct. For two countries tied to fixed gold parities, the bilateral exchange rate was effectively bounded by the gold points, and gold parities for all countries meant fixed exchange rates all round, so removing the cause of the problem for currency boards under the current conditions of generalised floating.

But gold was not the only anchor – there was also silver. The long period of falling prices from the 1870s to the late 1890s led many to clamour for a return to silver in order to escape from the 'cross of gold'. The process of deflation produced considerable hardship among debtors because nominal interest rates did not fall as rapidly as did commodity prices so that real interest rates increased. (This behaviour has been the case in most periods of deflation.) The deflationary trend affected all nations with a gold standard, but was especially severe in the USA because it started with the inflated prices of the Civil War years, and from 1865 to 1879 when gold convertibility was resumed, price deflation averaged 6.5 per cent per annum.

In these circumstances, leading economists such as F.Y. Edgeworth, Irving Fisher, Alfred Marshall, N.G. Pierson, and Léon Walras all came out against gold, most favouring a return to bimetallism, the system which had operated for centuries until it was superseded by the near-universal adoption of gold in the last quarter of the nineteenth century (Friedman, 1990). A bimetallic monetary standard is one in which the unit of account has a fixed legal parity in terms of either of two commodities – say, gold and silver – and a debtor has the choice of which one to use to value the payments media with which the debts are settled. Because of the changing composition of the money stock in circulation, as one commodity takes over the monetary functions of the other, the effect of monetary shocks upon the price level is dampened. In particular, if the major shocks arise from variations in the gold market, then a bimetallic standard produces a more stable price level than gold alone (Dowd, 1996).

A move from gold to bimetallism would likely have provided some stability to the price level in the face of fluctuations in the relative price of the anchor. However, greater stability still could be achieved if prices were tied to a basket of gold and silver rather than to fixed amounts of either metal, and this was the basis of Marshall's (1887) proposed alternative of symmetallism. Under symmetallism, the monetary unit would be defined in terms of gold and silver rather than gold or silver, as under bimetallism. One can imagine, say, one ounce of gold and fifteen ounces of silver combined in one bar. Broadening the base to the two metals would lessen the impact of demand and supply variations affecting one metal alone, and thus lead to a less variable price level. In effect, the idea is that shocks to the relative prices of each metal will cancel each other out to some extent in the impact upon the relative price of the basket as a whole, leading to a more stable price level than would result from either one of the two metals or a bimetallic system. By the same reasoning using a basket of three or more metals would presumably generate more price stability still. In this respect, symmetallism is a forerunner of commodity reserve proposals in which a group of commodities would be chosen to be representative of prices in general (Lewis and Mizen, 2000).

Edgeworth (1895) considered that symmetallism had one major disadvantage. Unlike bimetallism, in which the money price of gold and silver is fixed, the relative price of gold and silver in terms of monetary units would fluctuate freely in world and domestic markets, as symmetallism might be introduced independently by countries without international agreement on a common bundle of gold and silver. If countries defined their currencies in terms of different amounts of gold and silver, the exchange rates between them would not be fixed and would need to vary. Fluctuating exchange rates were clearly out of phase with the times, which favoured the stable exchange rates provided by the use of one metal.

Nevertheless, in the generalised floating world of our times, where large swings in exchange rates have become the norm, Edgeworth's objection carries less force. Although the existing currency boards have confined themselves to one currency, in principle a board could use two, or a basket of, currencies as a base. Many countries already peg their currencies to a trade-weighted basket, and the dual currency board system simply carries this concept through in a more rigid form. It would imply that reserves would need to be kept in both currencies, but many currency board countries do so already by holding gold alongside the reserve currency. Some simplicity of operation would admittedly be lost, yet a basket system – especially of two currencies – is not much more complex than a system based on a single foreign currency, while a good choice of the basket would avoid much of the variation in competitiveness that can arise when the currency is fixed to one particular currency – witness the case of Hong Kong, noted above.

The Exit Option

Currency boards are not for all countries. Those attracted to the arrangement can be grouped into three categories: small open economies with limited expertise of central banking and nascent financial markets; countries that wish to ally themselves with a broader trade or currency area; and countries seeking to enhance the credibility of disinflationary policies by means of external stabilisation. Although the three categories are not mutually exclusive, most of the recent adherents fall into the third grouping, whereas the ex-colonies which previously made up the membership were of the other types.

This distinction as to the nature of countries which opt for currency board arrangements is relevant because, while some currency boards have been long-standing, most countries eventually dispense with the system. Obviously, the departure should take place only when the factors that motivated entry in the first place have been resolved. Perhaps the degree of development of indigenous institutions and markets will provide an appropriate exit point, as was the case with Malaysia and Singapore in the 1960s, and Ireland in the 1970s. Or, perhaps an exit may be prompted by a belief that domestic policies are strong enough to maintain market credibility in their own right. In other cases, the decision may have little to do with economics. Instead, severing the currency board link and other such colonial trappings may be a signal of political independence, as reflected in Honohan's (1997) evocative description of a currency board issuing 'a local (*slave*) currency at a fixed rate of exchange against a foreign (*master*) currency' (p. 39 – our emphasis).

A number of reasons can be suggested as to why countries may come to consider that a currency board has outlived its usefulness. One is the sheer lack of flexibility, particularly the inability to deal with monetary and price disturbances, other than by what Roubini (1998) calls 'cheating', that is, departing from the mechanical operation of the currency board by various subterfuges. Then, again, the currency board link itself may be the source of disturbance if it erodes competitiveness of the local currency. As Kopcke

(1999) notes, many of the factors governing the choice of reserve currency are the same as those for ascertaining whether an optimal currency area exists.

The longer a currency board is in operation the longer it is exposed to the occurrence of asymmetric shocks between the two countries while the absence of other adjustment mechanisms available for 'metropolitan' regions such as fiscal transfers and labour market migration will become more apparent. An inflexible commitment to parity deprives the country of one tool for mitigating the effects of exchange rate misalignments.

Another factor is the limited nature of the fiscal discipline under a currency board arrangement. A currency board of the traditional sort is entirely passive; all it does is convert notes and coins either into or out of the reserve currency as the public and the banks demand. It has no other money-creating capacity, and thus cannot finance government deficits by issuing more money. But budget deficits *per se* are not prevented, so long as they are financed from borrowings and not from money creation (that is, seigniorage). If fiscal deficits are the problem, then a currency board goes only part way to solving the problem. The real solution has to involve reforms to expenditure programmes and taxation. When this is done, the currency board is to some extent redundant as a device for fiscal discipline, although it may have provided the initial spur to begin the reform process.

A final factor is that the currency board itself seems likely to condition institutional developments in the currency board country. In choosing to maintain a currency board link to another currency, the country concerned connects itself not only to the monetary policy of the reserve-currency country, but also to the markets and institutions of that country. As can be seen from Table 6.1, foreign currency deposits represent a substantial share of bank deposits in the currency board countries – ranging from 40 to 86 per cent. Clearly, many currency boards owe their existence to a lack of confidence in the local currency. At the same time, the currency boards obviously do not solve this problem of lack of confidence.

In some cases this currency substitution is a deliberate strategy – the country is endeavouring to join and gain the benefits of the wider currency area, such as the EU11, and wants transactors to become accustomed to the other currency. Yet not all of those countries aspiring to European Union (EU) membership have chosen this route. Table 6.3 sets out the currency regimes of the ten countries that are candidates for EU membership. Of these, three have opted for a currency board approach (two with the euro, one with the US dollar). One has a fixed peg, two have crawling pegs, and four have adopted managed floats. There is obviously no single route to salvation!

It remains an open question whether a currency board can provide a route to EU monetary integration. According to the EU framework, the process of monetary integration of applicant countries will take place in three stages.

Applicants first join the European Union, then participate in the exchange rate mechanism (ERM II) and finally adopt the euro. There are no formal constraints on exchange rate regimes before EU accession, although exchange rate policy should be conducive to an orderly integration into EU and economic and monetary union (EMU) and be embedded, in a consistent manner, into a stability-oriented overall policy framework. Upon EU accession, applicant countries have to treat their exchange rate policies as a matter of common concern, and are expected to join ERM II based on a fixed (but adjustable) peg to the euro.[5] Crawling pegs and exchange rate links to anchor currencies other than the euro have to be phased out. Equally, floating regimes must be ended. But currency boards do not appear to fit in with this framework either, since they do not allow the applicant countries to provide evidence of their central banking skills and prowess at monetary management – airlines do not allow pilots to rely on the auto pilot controls alone when coming in to land.

Table 6.3 *Exchange rate regimes of EU candidate countries in Central and Eastern Europe, as of 14 November 1999*

Country	Exchange rate regime
Bulgaria	Euro peg under a currency board (BGL 1.95583 = €1)
Czech Republic	Managed float (euro reference currency)
Estonia	DEM/euro peg under a currency board (EEK 15.6466 = €1)
Hungary	Crawling peg versus basket (70% euro, 30% US dollar) Fluctuation band: ± 2.25% Automatic monthly devaluation: 0.4%
Latvia	SDR peg (LVL 0.7997 = SDR 1) Fluctuation band: ± 1%
Lithuania	US dollar peg under a currency board (LTL 4 = USD1)
Poland	Crawling peg versus basket (55% euro, 45% US dollar) Fluctuation band: ± 15% Automatic monthly devaluation: 0.3%
Romania	Managed float (US dollar and euro reference currencies)
Slovakia	Managed float (euro reference currency)
Slovenia	Managed float (euro reference currency)

Note: SDR = special drawing right.

Source: *Focus on Transition* 2/99, Oesterreichische Nationalbank.

But how viable are the alternatives to currency boards? Economic theory offers a continuum of exchange rate systems, ranging from monetary union at one limit through currency boards, multilateral pegs, unilateral pegs, basket pegs, adjustable pegs, crawling pegs, target zones, managed floating to freely floating exchange rates at the other limit. But, now that capital controls and many supports have been lifted, the viability of many of these middle paths between the two limits has been sharply reduced, and this is reflected in actual practice among IMF member countries. Table 6.4 shows there has been a marked shift in exchange rate arrangements over the years. In 1999, 25 per cent of countries had independently floating exchange rates (compared with only 8 per cent in 1982). Also, a further 30 per cent of countries had a managed float (although this classification embraces a wide degree of different practices, for example, Singapore's and Thailand's managed floating regimes differ from that of China). While the use of currency boards has revived, in general the use of fixed rates has declined – in 1999, 34 per cent of countries were on some form of fixed rate as compared with 60 per cent of countries in 1986.

Table 6.4 *Exchange rate arrangements of national currencies, 1986–1999*

	1986	1989	1991	1993[a]	1995[a]	1997[b]	1999[b]
Fixed to:							
US dollar	32	32	23	23	23	21	20
French franc	14	14	14	14	14	15	15
Other single currencies	5	5	4	13	8	9	12
SDR	10	7	6	4	3	2	4
Currency basket	30	35	33	27	20	20	13
Target zones:							
EMS	8	9	10	9	10	12	13
Other currency	5	4	4	4	4	4	4
Controlled flexibility	27	26	32	25	38	47	56
Independently floating	19	20	29	48	59	51	48
Total[c]	150	152	155	167	179	181	185

Notes: SDR = special drawing right; EMS = European monetary system.
[a] 1st quarter.
[b] 2nd quarter.
[c] Classification not always available for some currencies. The method of classifying exchange rate arrangements changed in 1999. Information for 1999 inserted on old basis.

Sources: International Monetary Fund, *Annual Report* (various issues).

Reasons for the declining use of the fixed exchange rate option are not difficult to find. A number of writers have spoken of the 'incompatible triangle' or 'conflict triangle' (fixed rates, independent monetary policy, and freedom of capital movements) or the 'inconsistent quartet' (free trade, free capital movements, national policy autonomy and fixed exchange rates). The point made is a simple one: it is not possible to combine all of the three or four 'desirables' in one system, and successful implementation of policy involves some trade-offs. Floating rates obviously negate the objective of having an assured fixity of rates even if they turn out to be relatively stable. At the other extreme, a rigidly fixed rate involves the loss of national monetary sovereignty. Choosing a crawling or adjustable peg involves trading off all three or four. During the interwar years, for example, when countries went off gold and its required sacrifice of monetary autonomy, fixed exchange rates were sacrificed, and there was some compromise to free trade and capital movements. Architects of the Bretton Woods system envisaged that official controls over capital flows would reconcile the inconsistency, and were consequently prepared to compromise on freedom of capital flows. The IMF promoted stability of exchange rates by lending out resources ('drawings') to help countries ride out minor fluctuations in the demand and supply of foreign exchange, while permitting orderly changes in parity to correct a 'fundamental disequilibrium'. Much the same compromises were built into ERM I. In both cases, the policy dilemmas posed by the 'inconsistent quartet' became all too apparent when restrictions on capital flows were lifted and members sought to move to greater fixity of exchange rates.

The basic problem of a fixed exchange rate peg is that however much a country may declare its willingness to sacrifice monetary independence, and put up with the interest rates and the real exchange rate misalignments generated by the anchor-currency country's policies, markets will remain sceptical and be prepared to put the commitment to the test. When that occurs, the cost of defending the parity is greatly increased since interest rates must then cover the market's expected rate of realignment, turning an unpleasant trade-off involving for a time somewhat-higher-than-desired interest rates into one that has undesirable and possibly politically unacceptable outcomes (Artis and Lewis, 1993). Currency boards offer a more credible commitment, although the problem does not go away. The example of Hong Kong, noted earlier, makes clear that even the most impregnable position can come under attack (Kasa, 1999). The reserves may be there and in abundance, but will the authorities be willing to put them on the line and defend the fixed parity at all costs? Only a monetary union, and the complete surrender of monetary sovereignty, then remains along the fixed rate path as the ultimate radical solution to the policy dilemma of the inconsistent quartet.

These, at least, are the conclusions suggested by the experience of those countries at the centre of the ERM I and Asian currency crises. Cooper (1999) argues that the choices may be even more circumscribed for the small economies with poorly developed capital markets. He contends that two prescriptions given to developing countries – greater exchange rate flexibility and freer capital movements – may themselves be incompatible or, at least, contradictory. For the countries concerned, some form of restriction on freedom of capital movements may be needed to flank floating exchange rates. The theoretical reason for this is that in the absence of a guarantee of convertibility into something else (for example, a commodity or foreign currency) acting as a nominal anchor, the exchange rate is thus 'indeterminate', in the works of Kareken and Wallace (1981), being nothing more than the barter price between one nominal variable (for example, fiat money) and another. The practical reason is that because of this indeterminacy, demand-side currency substitution may take place, and the development of the local capital market may never occur.

FUTURE DIRECTIONS

Cooper's point about the workability of floating rates for small economies in a way turns us around full circle. We noted earlier that dissatisfaction with the operation of the gold standard led Marshall and some others to propose symmetallism, an idea that we suggested could be usefully modified for a currency board. Much the same dissatisfaction led a later generation of economists, most notably Keynes, in his Tract, and Knut Wicksell, to a quite different and at that time much more radical proposal in the form of a system of managed money, that is, an inconvertible paper money standard.

A paper (fiat) money system is what we have today. But it is vastly different from the one Keynes had in mind.

> There are probably no countries, other than Great Britain and the United States, which would be justified in attempting to set up an independent standard. Their wisest course would be to base their currencies either on sterling or on dollars by means of an exchange standard, fixing their exchanges in terms of one or the other. (Keynes, 1923, p. 205)

A universal system of floating exchange rates was clearly beyond his contemplation. It was also beyond the conception of Lord Robbins. As late at 1971, Lord Robbins urged:

> Rather than let their exchanges fluctuate freely in terms of all other currencies, the authorities of many centres would take steps, as they did in 1931 and again in 1949, to attach themselves at fixed rates to one of the larger currencies. The idea

> of a world in which the exchange rates of every sovereign state are perpetually free to fluctuate in terms of the exchange rates of every other, is purely fanciful. It is perfectly realistic to conceive of floating rates between large blocs, the sterling area and the dollar area, for instance. It is not realistic to think of floating rates all round. (Robbins, 1971, p. 143)

He went on to explain (in the introduction): 'The real dispute concerns, not the practicability or the prudence of floating rates here and there or now and then, but rather whether all rates should be free everywhere and all the time' (Robbins, 1971, p. 21).

Yet, however fanciful and unrealistic, floating rates all round, everywhere and all the time, is essentially what has transpired for the major currencies (US dollar, euro, Japanese yen, GB pound, Swiss franc, Canadian dollar, Australian dollar and so on). It seems unlikely that this position will change. What remains to be settled is the status of the minor currencies. Economic theory has addressed the question of an optimal currency area, but not that of its minimum viable size. If the non-major currencies are to adopt the Keynes–Robbins solution and attach themselves to one of the larger currencies, then monetary union is the only assured way of doing so. That is undoubtedly what will eventuate in the European time zone. For the others, the next most credible commitment comes from a currency board arrangement. For some the choice of the anchor currency is natural (for example, Mexico and the US dollar)[6]. For many others, a dual or basket currency board system, as advocated here, may be the answer, if only because it waters down Honohan's master – slave currency connotation and distances the arrangement from the past association of currency boards with colonial status.

NOTES

1. The description belongs to Walters and Hanke (1992) who contend that the financial experience of countries which departed from currency board systems 'has not been auspicious' (p. 560).
2. In addition to the references cited above, other recent studies of currency board systems include Bennett (1994), Humpage and McIntire (1995), Pautola and Backé (1998), Enoch and Gulde (1998) and Gulde (1999).
3. In practice, many currency boards which specify a minimum 100 per cent backing of reserve currency maintain the backing at more than 100 per cent (see Table 6.1). One reason is to allow for fluctuations in the value of foreign currency assets such as bonds and marketable securities, another is to provide confidence in case of financial crisis.
4. As no market supply of HK dollars exists outside Hong Kong, speculators wishing to sell HK dollars have to borrow them first, then convert them into foreign currency, forcing interest rates up. In October 1997, following Taiwan's devaluation, short-selling pushed up rates to 280 per cent per annum on settlement day (23 October). Access to the special discount window now effectively expands HK dollar liquidity beyond the HK dollars in circulation, theoretically up to the full amount of Hong Kong's foreign exchange reserves,

reducing the extent to which rates will be pushed up in future crises (East Asia Analytical Unit, 1999).

5. The ERM II governs exchange rate relations between the euro area and those EU member states which have not yet introduced the single currency. It is based on fixed but adjustable central parity rates of the participating currencies *vis-à-vis* the euro. In order to avoid significant misalignments, realignments will be conducted in a timely fashion. There will be a standard fluctuation band of ± 15 per cent around the central rates of participating currencies, but formally agreed (as well as informally accorded) narrower bands will also be possible.
6. The pros and cons of a US dollar-based currency board for Mexico are examined by Humpage (1995).

REFERENCES

Artis, M.J. and M.K. Lewis (1993), 'Après le déluge: monetary and exchange-rate policy in Britain and Europe', *Oxford Review of Economic Policy*, **9** (3), 36–61.

Bennett, A.G.G. (1994), 'Currency boards: issues and experiences', Paper on Policy Analysis and Assessment, PPAA/94/18, International Monetary Fund, Washington, DC.

Bentick, B.L. and M.K. Lewis (1999), 'Real estate speculation as a source of banking and currency instability: lessons from the Asian crisis', *The Third International Stockholm Seminar on Risk Behaviour and Risk Management*, 14–16 June, Stockholm, **1**, 15–28.

Brown, L.E., R. Hellerstein and J.S. Little (1998), 'Inflation, asset markets and economic stabilisation: lessons from Asia', *New England Economic Review*, September/October, 3–32.

Cooper, R.N. (1999), *Rethinking the International Monetary System*, Boston, MA: Federal Reserve Bank of Boston.

Dornbusch, R. and F. Giavazzi (1999), 'Hard currency and sound credit: a financial agenda for Central Europe', available at http://www.stern.nyu.edu/nroubini/asia.

Dowd, K. (1996), *Competition and Finance. A Reinterpretation of Financial and Monetary Economics*, London: Macmillan.

East Asia Analytical Unit (1999), *Asia's Financial Markets. Capitalising on Reform*, Canberra: Department of Foreign Affairs and Trade.

Edgeworth, F.Y. (1895), 'Thoughts on monetary reform', *Economic Journal*, **5**, 434–51.

Enoch, C. and A.-M. Gulde (1998), 'Are currency boards a cure for all monetary problems?' *Finance and Development*, **35** (4), 40–3.

Friedman, M. (1990), 'Bimetallism revisited', *Journal of Economic Perspectives*, **4** (4), 85–104.

Ghosh, A.R., A.-M. Gulde and H.C. Wolf (1998), 'Currency boards: the ultimate fix?', IMF Working Paper WP/98/8, Washington, January.

Gulde, A.-M. (1999), 'The role of the currency board in Bulgaria's stabilization', *Finance and Development*, **36** (3), 36–9.

Hanke, S.H. and K. Schuler (1992), 'Currency boards for Eastern Europe', Geld and Wahrung Working Papers 23, Frankfurt-am-Main, Johann Wolfgang Goethe-Universität.

Hanke, S.H. and K. Schuler (1994), *Currency Boards for Developing Countries: A Handbook,* San Francisco: International Centre for Economic Growth.

Honohan, P. (1997), 'Currency board or central bank? Lessons from the Irish pound's link with sterling, 1928–79', *Banca Nazionale del Lavoro Quarterly Review*, **50** (200), March, 39–67.
Humpage, O.F. (1995), 'A Mexican currency board?', Economic Commentary, Federal Reserve Bank of Cleveland, 15 March.
Humpage, O.F. and J.M. McIntire (1995), 'An introduction to currency boards', *Economic Review*, **31** (2), 2–11.
International Monetary Fund (IMF) (1997), 'Currency board arrangements more widely used', *IMF Survey,* 24 February, 54–7.
Kareken, J. and N. Wallace (1981), 'On the indeterminacy of equilibrium exchange rates', *Quarterly Journal of Economics*, May, 207–22.
Kasa, K. (1999), 'Why attack a currency board?', Federal Reserve Bank of San Francisco Economic Letter No. 99–36, Pacific Basin Notes, 26 November.
Keynes, J.M. (1923), *A Tract on Monetary Reform*, London: Macmillan.
Kopcke, R.W. (1999), 'Currency boards: once and future monetary regimes', *New England Economic Review*, May/June, 21–37.
Lewis, M.K. and P.D. Mizen (2000), *Monetary Economics*, Oxford: Oxford University Press.
Marshall, A. (1887), 'Remedies for fluctuations of general prices', reprinted in A.C. Pigon (ed.) (1925), *Memorials of Alfred Marshall*, London: Macmillan.
Pautola, N. and P. Backé (1998), 'Currency boards in Central and Eastern Europe: past experience and future perspectives', *Focus on Transition*, **1**, 72–113.
Robbins, Lord (1971), *Money, Trade and International Relations*, London: Macmillan.
Roubini, N. (1998), 'The case against currency boards: debunking 10 myths about the benefits of currency boards, http://www.stern.nyu.edu/~nroubini/asia/CurrencyBoardsRoubini.html.
Schwartz, A.J. (1993), 'Currency boards: their past, present and possible future role', *Carnegie-Rochester Conference Series on Public Policy*, **39**, December, 147–87.
Walters, A.A. and S.H. Hanke (1992), 'Currency boards', in P. Newman, M. Milgate and J. Eatwell (eds), *The New Palgrave Dictionary of Money and Finance*, Vol. 1, London: Macmillan, 558–61.

7. Comparative Models of Banking Reform

Djordje Djukić

INTRODUCTION

The efficiency of completed reform of the banking sector of transition countries must be measured by its long-term impact on the structure of these countries' bank balance sheets. For the South-East European (SEE) countries, this requires the removal of inherent weaknesses that have produced a high share of non-performing loans (NPLs), as defined under international standards, in the SEE countries' bank balance sheets. On-site inspection may then be used to monitor the loan portfolios of those banks previously defined as technically insolvent, but since rehabilitated (usually with a large infusion of capital from a government budget). Where on-site inspection finds 'rehabilitated' banks that have again accumulated large amounts of NPLs, this provides clear evidence that important structural weaknesses in the banking sector have not been addressed. For example:

- a lack of profit-oriented owners (due to an interest by shareholders in access to cheap credit, rather than dividends);
- an unhealthy asset/liability structure in the balance sheets of the largest banks;
- the complete reliance by the largest banks on a central bank as a source of protracted liquidity support;
- asset/liability maturity mismatches and, accordingly, interest rate and/or exchange rate exposures;
- a lack of responsibility and penalties for bad management practices (leading to poor credit assessment and fraud);
- the lagging behind world standards in the use of modern information technology; and
- the absence of appropriate internal controls.

The presence of these weaknesses requires us to reconsider the appropriate method of bank restructuring and rehabilitation for each of the SEE countries.

In this chapter a comparative analysis of two possible methods for restructuring the banking sector in transition economies will be given – centralised and decentralised. A critical analysis of these methods is based, among other things, on the effects of their application to a group of transition countries in Central Europe during the 1990s – the Czech Republic, Hungary and Poland. Each of these countries is now a candidate for entering the European Union. In the conclusion, recommendations will be given regarding the selection of the optimal model for bank restructuring and rehabilitation in the SEE countries that are just beginning to implement banking sector reform.

MODEL BASED ON THE CENTRALISED APPROACH TO RESTRUCTURING OF THE BANKING SECTOR

A comparison between centralised and decentralised approaches to banking sector restructuring and rehabilitation is given in Table 7.1. A centralised approach to banking sector restructuring and rehabilitation implies that a state entity takes all, or most, NPLs from bank balance sheets. Interest-bearing assets are then substituted for these loans, most often in the form of long-term government bonds. This carve-out technique is a type usually classified as part of the set of 'stock solutions'. The other two 'stock solutions' comprise capital injection by the private or public sectors and liquidation (Sheng 1996).

By cleaning bank balance sheets under a rehabilitation regime, the state becomes, in most cases, the banks' biggest shareholder. For all that, the final aim of the state is not to acquire these shares on a permanent basis. Rather, it intends to sell them in the capital market after rehabilitation of the targeted bank group has been accomplished. This is to cover, as much as is possible, fiscal expenses arising from the implementation of the bank rehabilitation programme.

There are different versions of the centralised approach but, in practice, two are most common in developed and emerging-market countries. Following the eruption of the banking crisis in South-East Asia and Japan, at the end of the 1990s, the predominant approach is for an asset management corporation (AMC) to be established by the state. The AMC has its own balance sheet, and it buys NPLs and other bad assets from the banks.[1] In such a way one large 'bad bank' is created for the entire banking sector.

Table 7.1 *A comparison of centralised and decentralised approaches to banking sector restructuring*

Centralised approach	Decentralised approach
The state entity takes over NPLs (completely or for the most part) from the banks' balance sheets and replaces them, usually, with long-term government bonds	The obligation of every bank in the rehabilitation regime is to take responsibility for the NPL payments that are located on its balance sheet
Through its recapitalisation of the banks with government bonds under the rehabilitation regime, the state (in most cases) becomes the banks' largest shareholder	
Efficient application presumes that the state entity removes large government-style resources practices, and is responsible for the adequate provision of professional staff	Successful application presumes the creation of workout units in banks which take care of NPL payments, using the advantages the banks possess with respect to information on their debtors and other specialised knowledge
	Locates the responsibility for bad loans with the banks' management
The burden of bank restructuring and rehabilitation falls mainly on the state (taxpayers)	The burden for taking on bank restructuring and rehabilitation is, in order: existing bank shareholders, bank depositors, the state (taxpayers)

Source: Author's.

Economies of scale have become prominent in negotiations on achieving a restructuring agreement. This is because of two common features of banking crises (Hawkins and Turner 1999): (a) a large numbers of banks are in difficulty (undercapitalisation and insolvency); and (b) the level of homogeneity in the bad assets purchased is relatively high. The latter factor reflects the fact that many bad assets are loans for real estate, which have became problematic due to drastic decreases in real estate prices. Consequently, the AMC can consolidate properties from different banks and, by possible purchase of complementary properties, achieve returns on collateral better than would be the case without such a consolidation.

In order that the above method is efficient in practice, it is necessary that the AMC operate in a very transparent and objective manner. An additional positive incentive is available when a legislated closing date is prescribed for the AMC, up to which it is required to hold assets before it sells them. When making decisions on assets sales the AMC is faced with two risks: (a) market risk (the price decreasing when assets are sold); and (b) a risk that assets can be repurchased at a huge discount by a loan beneficiary. This latter risk is only present if legislation does not prescribe a suitable date prior to which this type of transaction cannot be concluded.

The essence of the other method of the centralised approach is that during bank crises the state entity should not take over all NPLs from distressed banks. Part of the NPLs' restructuring is left to these banks, including small NPLs (for example, the case of Sweden). It is claimed that:

> It is desirable for the bank to maintain some experience with work-out procedures; this was one reason why in Sweden small NPLs were generally left with the bank. It is also unfair to the better managed banks if the distressed banks end up with no NPLs. In the Swedish case the authorities aimed to leave the problem banks with a ratio of bad loans to assets similar to that of the other banks. (Hawkins and Turner 1999, pp. 67–8)

The experience of transition countries that have opted for a centralised approach to resolving the problems of accrued NPLs unambiguously indicates that newly created, state-run, special-purpose entities (agency, national bank and so on) are hardly substitutes for commercial banks in this regard. The Czech Republic example illustrates this point in the 'best' way. At the beginning of the 1990s the newly founded, state-owned Consolidation Bank (Konsolidačni Banka), under Consolidation Program I, took over the resolution of the stock problem of NPLs while the banks were recapitalised by government bonds. However, it was only during the 1990s that one of the state's three attempts to implement bank recapitalisation through privatisation was successful. The centralised approach to bank restructuring and consolidation in the Czech Republic failed at the beginning of the 1990s. This was because, among other things, after the first bank recapitalisation the substituting of contaminated assets with government bonds did not prevent a further accrual of non-performing assets. An open banking crisis could not be avoided in 1995, and particularly in 1996, because Czech banks could collect hardly any collateral from their debtors.[2]

The launching of Consolidation Programme II followed, under which seven banks were recapitalised through existing shareholders or new investors, while the central bank and government had recourse to creating a special financing unit. That unit is under the administration of the Consolidation Bank, which is again derived from the banks which, under the regime of rehabilitation, took over NPLs and their repayments.

The second wave of bank rehabilitation in the mid-1990s in the Czech Republic did not interrupt the trends in banking towards mass default in the payment of debt principal and interest charges by debtors. What is more, the share of NPLs in the total credits of the Czech banking sector achieved a 29.4 per cent growth rate in the first quarter of 1999. This was due to bank credit policy, under which little attention has been given to protection from credit risk.

Since banks built up huge portfolios of credit, backed with little or no collateral, a strong recession resulted in few of the collateralised assets having more than a fraction of their book value. Consequently, banks in the Czech Republic were forced to post major losses in 1998, an event that showed few signs of abating in 1999. The problem was made all the more acute because banks, through their investments, held large portfolios in the industrial sector, and were forced to continue lending even when firms had stopped paying. In 1998, this led to loans classified as being between substandard and loss making comprising just over 27 per cent of all outstanding credits. This, in spite of the state bailout of the country's main savings bank (Češka sporitelna) in which the government assumed Kc 10.5 billion in bad debt from its books at a 40 per cent discount. Besides this, the state subscribed to a Kc 5.5 billion subordinated debt issue in order to enable this bank to meet the central bank's capital requirement.[3]

As of early 2000, because of its problematic application of a centralised model of bank rehabilitation, the Czech Republic was again required to clean up the balance sheets of large banks before offering them for sale to foreign and local investors. For example, in August 1999 the Ministry of Finance disclosed its intention for the Consolidation Bank (the state factoring bank), to buy Kc 23.1 billion (USD 674.6 million) in NPLs from Komercni Banka for Kc 13.6 billion.[4] (Komercni Banka had the second-largest amount of paid-in capital of any Czech bank at the end of May 1999.) A discount of 41.13 per cent should be sufficient to keep Komercni Banka's capital adequacy ratio above the legal minimum.

The case of the Czech Republic shows that transition countries can apply the centralised approach of bank restructuring several times (a method of trial and error). However, this is only if the state has resources available to it through privatisation and/or from current budgetary revenues, a low inflation rate has been achieved, and the value of the national currency has been stabilised. On the other hand, in transition economies, the state entities for bank restructuring may be ineffective if the state cannot recapitalise banks (which are in the process of being rehabilitated) by using an inflow of resources into the budget from state enterprise privatisation (enterprise selling). In short, because of a chronic budgetary deficit and absence of significant budgetary income from privatisation, the state entity for bank restructuring and rehabilitation cannot get the necessary funds from the state. A typical example of this is the Federal Republic (FR) of Yugoslavia (the Republic of Serbia accounts for about 95 per cent of FR Yugoslavia's GDP). In FR Yugoslavia, enterprises with social, and not state, ownership are privatising. This is mainly through the application of an insider privatisation model. Under this model, shares are distributed to employees, and priority is given to the employees in buying enterprise shares, an approach which is not obligatory, and which reduces the funds raised via the privatisation process.

Efficient application of a centralised approach implies that during a programme of restructuring and rehabilitation, the state entity has at its disposal not only extremely large budgetary resources but also professional staff (in both number and profile). This means that it must offer attractive wages to employees, wages similar to those of leading banks. In addition, it should be able to engage periodically in the market, whenever necessary, local and foreign consultants, particularly those who are dealing with debt restructuring of enterprises, to appraise debt values and to prepare them for auction. In developed industrial countries this is not a problem. Examples are the Resolution Trust Corporation in the United States, which is essentially the liquidation arm of the Federal Deposit Insurance Corporation (FDIC), and the *Treuhandanstalt* in Germany.

In transition countries, a lack of professional staff for banking operations often necessitates delays in reform for an indeterminate time; that is, until state entities employ enough professional staff who can deal with NPL restructuring. This includes the packaging of NPLs into homogeneous groups and selling these packages to parties such as private companies for enterprise debt trading. This automatically makes the centralised approach less efficient even when the problem of providing local and foreign resources for the supporting programme on bank restructuring does not exist, and when there is a political willingness to carry out the adopted programme consistently. In some SEE countries, where there is a combined application of the centralised and decentralised approaches, the lack of staff in state entities has led to the development of a bank rehabilitation methodology with the assistance of foreign advisers. This increases pressure on the management of the banks to perform the rehabilitation process. Consequently, bank management has been permitted to take an active role in operational decision making in the banks, while the state entity has largely restricted itself to providing governance and control.[5]

MODEL BASED ON THE DECENTRALISED APPROACH TO RESTRUCTURING OF THE BANKING SECTOR

The decentralised approach to banking sector restructuring and rehabilitation implies that NPLs are part of the bookkeeping of banks that are undergoing rehabilitation. Additionally, it implies that debt recovery is the obligation of these banks. This essentially pro-market approach provides an opportunity for taking into account all of the specific features that exist in bank–enterprise–debtor relationships and, consequently, greatly facilitates the financial restructuring of debtor enterprises.

A comparative analysis of 1990s' experiences in the application of the centralised and decentralised approaches to the restructuring and rehabilitation of the banking sector in a group of advanced transition economies (Poland, the Czech Republic and Hungary), shows the following:

- successful bank restructuring and consolidation cannot be based on use of only one method, instead requiring a combination of both decentralised and centralised methods; and
- a decentralised approach should dominate in the restructuring and rehabilitation of the targeted group of banks – implicitly this suggests the obligation of each bank in the group to deal with bad loan payments located in its balance sheet (Montes-Negret and Papi 1997; Ábel and Szakadát 1997; Dziobek and Pazarbasioglu 1997; Buch and Heinrich 1997).

Why, almost uniformly in modern literature, has preference been given to a decentralised solution for NPLs? First, banks have more information on the customers to whom they approved loans, and employ personnel with a highly specialised knowledge on the actual and potential performances of debtor enterprises from certain branches of business. This enables them to monitor enterprises more effectively during implementation of a restructuring programme.

Second, by leaving the largest part of NPLs on the banks' books, the decentralised approach locates the responsibility for bad placements with the bank management which made the poor decisions that led the bank into insolvency. Through this, the compulsion mechanism is for banks to take over the responsibility for decisions, to refer to policy on enterprise credit provision, and to draw appropriate lessons from the evaluation of credit applications, credit security instruments and credit monitoring. On the other hand, with a centralised approach the problem of monitoring and control of the very state entities that take over the resolution of the existing stock of NPLs has been imposed. For all that, in the course of transferring NPLs to the state entity, part of the information on debtors that banks hold is lost. This by itself provides opportunities for bad management practices, active participation in fraudulent activities on the credit market, and for these activities to go unpunished.

Third, restructuring of enterprises is speeded up, because the decentralised approach includes, implicitly, the parallel development of the bank and enterprise restructuring processes. The success of an applied approach in resolving the problems of NPLs is measured by its contribution to the restructuring of debtor enterprises (state or socially owned). And, through this, to resolving 'flow' problems (that is, the prevention of the renewed accrual of NPLs).

As the Polish experience showed at the beginning of the 1990s, a decentralised approach to bank restructuring may largely prevent banks from having future stock problems. This is through a decentralised restructuring forcing banks to improve their credit assessment and risk-control systems. Besides, the Polish programme strengthened the incentives of banks to restructure NPLs by effectively changing the priority of claims. Thus, the problem of requiring several attempts at recapitalisation of the banks from budgetary resources, and (as a result of the clean-up of previous NPLs) the extremely high costs of establishing a sound banking system were avoided. In that sense the Polish programme of bank restructuring has been more successful than that in Hungary:

> The Polish experience seems to show that pursuing debt workouts and forcing banks to have proper loan-loss provisions, a high capital-asset ratio, strong governance and ultimate privatisation in a competitive banking environment can do much to prevent banks from having future stock problems. (Montes-Negret and Papi 1997, p. 23)

The World Bank recommendations (which were given to authorities in Hungary in late 1993) specify that banks should receive limited funds for recapitalisation at the beginning of their consolidation programme. Indeed, it is recommended that technically insolvent banks should only be recapitalised to provide a capital adequacy ratio (CAR) of zero per cent (while ensuring a positive cash flow).

As Balassa has commented: 'The World Bank experts insisted on recapitalisation to no more than zero per cent, because they thought that this would exert pressure on the banks to speed up their internal restructuring' (1996, p. 45). The available resources for recapitalisation (domestic and foreign) certainly determine the time interval in which the minimum CAR level of 8 per cent prescribed by the Basle Committee must be achieved.

In order for the application of a decentralised approach to bank restructuring and rehabilitation to be successful, the role of the special 'workout' department in the compulsory programme for banks undergoing rehabilitation, must be precisely stated. The workout department should be treated as a 'house-bank' department, which requires that it has an autonomous accounting system, and that it has no right to perform new operations in which the most qualified personnel are engaged on a bilateral basis to reorganise borrowers' debts. These operations, in any case, could not be performed by employees of a bank that has participated in granting credits that will be unpayable. With a view to the efficiency of the workout department, the person in charge of its work must be appointed as a new member of the bank's managing board.

It is important to determine how those employed in workout departments will sacrifice mortgage in favour of ownership rights (debt–equity swap). This may be calculated using cash flows in the name of sold shares, with discount, or based on ownership rights realised according to a mortgage. Inefficient work by the judiciary in SEE countries (that is, a long judicial procedure with mortgage sales by a mortgagee) has to date made debt–equity swaps more attractive for banks. However, if by amendments to the law on rights and liabilities on the basis of mortgages the procedure of selling pledged assets becomes simplified, the attractiveness of a debt–equity swap in debt reorganisation for banks will be reduced significantly.

Application of the decentralised approach to bank restructuring and rehabilitation implies that the burden of restructuring will be shared by:

- the banks' shareholders, by writing off indicated and potential losses to the debit of existing shareholders' capital;
- the depositors, mainly corporate customers whose deposits at sight were the main source of generating the unpayable loans by applying the net principle; and
- the state (taxpayers).

As bank shareholders will be the first to shoulder the burden of restructuring and rehabilitation, a transformation of ownership in the bank will be initiated, necessitating a write-off of shareholders' capital. One method suggested is to effect a shareholder capital write-off for all loan beneficiaries who are at the same time shareholders, no matter how these loans have been classified after on-site control. That is, regardless of whether the shareholders' loans have been classified as performing or non-performing.

A second possible method is to effect a shareholder capital write-off according to the credit-risk rating of shareholders' borrowings. For example, loans may be divided into credit-risk categories A, B, C, D and E according to their probability of non-payment. A ranking of A indicates a minimal risk of non-payment. Loans with the highest risk of non-payment are rated under category E. Shareholders whose loans have been classified according to risk into groups A and B, would have no shareholder capital write-off against their loans. Shareholders with loans ranked under category C would suffer a capital write-off of 50 per cent against their loans. Finally, shareholders who are beneficiaries of loans classified into groups D and E would suffer a full shareholder-capital write-off against their bad loans. We are of the opinion that this second method of shareholder capital write-off is more acceptable, because it preserves a sound core of shareholders for banks in rehabilitation.

Application of the net principle to depositors rules out the possibility of those bank customers being penalised, who, on average, had a higher balance of deposits *vis-à-vis* the balance of credits. There is no other practicable solution for the state except by the use of long-term treasury bonds with a maturity date of ten or more years. The length of the term in each country depends directly on fiscal capacity (projected rate of economic growth and public income payment), and on the servicing of commitments due to foreign and domestic creditors.

Treasury bonds would bear interest at variable rates, where interest would be calculated quarterly starting from the interest rate on treasury bills with a maturity date within 90 days. The payment of interest would be made at the end of the fiscal year. This method of establishing and paying interest to banks was applied by the state in Hungary in the early 1990s.

Measures relating to the restructuring of debt enterprises, taken by banks undergoing rehabilitation include:

- rescheduling of enterprise obligations which are due to the banks, with longer maturity, moratoria on principal and more favourable interest rates;
- enabling enterprises to settle their obligations to banks at a discount;
- the replacement of NPLs by enterprise shares, with the worst enterprises aiming to sell these shares in a period specified by the banks' restructuring and rehabilitation programme; and
- the write-off of debts from bad debtors when it is estimated that they cannot be repaid.

The decentralised approach enables the successful completion of a bank's rehabilitation and consolidation process without great reliance on resources from the budget and/or large support by the central bank through credits for liquidity. Nevertheless, at the very beginning of the programme's implementation the state should make it clear that there will be no protection of debtor enterprises and banks. Such an action changes the expectations and attitude of managers in enterprises and banks.

An empirical analysis of 24 countries that have implemented a programme of bank restructuring (based on alternative methods), shows that best-practice policy minimises reliance on a central bank as a source of protracted liquidity support (Dziobek and Pazarbasioglu 1997).

There is no requirement under the decentralised approach to isolate within banks the debts of large public or state enterprises whose restructuring is very complex and, due to the number of employed, very delicate from both social and political viewpoints. NPLs associated with these enterprises may be removed from the bank balance sheets where they were generated, and transferred to the newly created state entity that will take responsibility for them. This requires a temporary engagement of special budgetary resources. On the other hand, it provides for full transparency of the whole bank restructuring and rehabilitation programme, and its faster adoption by the important political structures in the country.[6]

To fully realise the advantages of a decentralised approach to bank restructuring and rehabilitation, it is necessary to provide strong incentives to banks to achieve a much higher percentage of NPL repayments at the beginning of the programme's implementation. In order to motivate those employed in workout units of banks undergoing rehabilitation, it is envisaged that in addition to fixed wages, a bonus will be paid (that is, payment of a specified percentage of repaid NPLs).

If there is no provision of incentives for banks, there is a risk of decentralised approaches to bank restructuring and rehabilitation being more expensive for taxpayers. This is due to the increased likelihood that managers of debtor enterprises will attempt to bribe those employed in workout units. By offering a fee to those in charge of restructuring a given loan, debtor enterprise managers hope to bring about a 100 per cent debt write-off. Even worse, such an approach may fail to put pressure on banks to improve their functioning and on enterprises to undergo restructuring. This is a common characteristic of centralised approaches to bank restructuring and rehabilitation.

The weaknesses of a decentralised model may become more noticeable if there is a high tolerance of poor payment of NPLs by banks' workout units. This may result from a lack of application of penalty measures to banks and their management if they have not fulfilled specified performance criteria – the prescribed CAR. This by itself encourages moral hazard on the credit market because of a bank's belief that bad loans will eventually be transferred to a state institution.

Because the workers employed in a state entity responsible for implementing a programme of bank restructuring are poorly motivated, the possibilities for the emergence and spread of bribery are much greater, and the satisfactory resolution of NPLs will probably be slower. Easy write-offs of NPLs by those employed in the state entity may become a widespread phenomenon if the practice of receiving bribes from managers of debtor enterprises becomes commonplace. Besides, certain lobby groups can more easily apply pressure to obtain a general write-off of the debts of enterprises from certain sectors, when NPLs are transferred from banks to the balance sheet of a state entity. Thus, the risk that the work of a state entity will become politicised and subject to new state interference is extremely high.

With regard to the view of international financial institutions, it is significant that the International Monetary Fund explicitly mentioned the following criteria for instrument choice when implementing a programme of bank restructuring (IMF, 1997):

- efficiency regarding expenditures;
- simplicity in application;
- an equal loss distribution over banks to minimise the burden on the public sector;
- promotion of good governance (an impetus for creating responsible owners and healthy management) which by itself should reduce moral hazard; and
- consistency with non-inflationary macroeconomic policy.

The point in question here is where, ideally, the chosen instruments should be aimed. With regard to the characteristics of a decentralised approach to bank restructuring, which we have already emphasised, it may be concluded that if a decentralised approach is subsequently applied it may satisfy almost all the mentioned criteria. The only exception is that its application does not allow a simple comparison with the centralised approach, under which NPLs are replaced in the balance sheets of banks under the rehabilitation regime, most often by long-term government bonds.

CONCLUSION

Essential banking sector reforms in transition countries that suffer from numerous structural weaknesses cannot be based on a unique solution. A comparative analysis of international experiences in the application of centralised and decentralised approaches to bank restructuring and rehabilitation indicates that, for transition economies in South-East Europe, the best combination is one that favours a decentralised approach. This is because the decentralised approach not only resolves the problem of the existing stock of NPLs efficiently, but also prevents the new accrual of bad debt, thus resulting in the lowest cost to taxpayers.

Application of a decentralised approach to restructuring and rehabilitation of a targeted group of insolvent banks would initiate:

- changes in ownership structure through share capital write-offs against the largest debtors;
- changes in management and thus restructuring of operations;
- improvements to techniques for credit assessment and pricing, ensuring adequate accountability and disclosure; and
- review of the branch network structure and organisation, which should result in the reduction of operating costs and so on.

Without internal restructuring and balance sheets without bad debts in large banks, banking sector consolidation is not possible on a sound basis and foreign partners will have no interest in investing capital in these large banks.

As a rule, a centralised approach to banking sector restructuring and rehabilitation is applied to NPLs of large public enterprises held with local banks and expressed in national currency, as well as to foreign currency loans guaranteed by the state. NPLs that have been granted to enterprises that employ a large number of workers, and whose restructuring is not possible without budgetary funds, must be transferred from the bank to a state entity. This, by itself, requires radical parliamentary debate.

NOTES

1. In Thailand NPLs are found in the books of financial companies, while the restructuring agency is in charge of organising auctions to sell these loans or the real estate that serves as collateral.
2. At the end of 1996, the share of non-performing loans in total loans for the Czech Republic amounted to more than 37 per cent, while in Hungary and Poland this share was less than 20 per cent (Buch and Heinrich 1997, p. 15).
3. *Country Finance*, Economist Intelligence Unit 01/07/1999; *Country Briefing*, Economist Intelligence Unit 06/01/2000.
4. *Business Eastern Europe*, Economist Intelligence Unit 11/08/1999; *Country Finance*, Economist Intelligence Unit 01/07/1999.
5. The Law on the State Agency for Deposit Insurance and Bank Rehabilitation (DASB) was adopted in Croatia in 1994. However, until April 1996 professional staff to perform DASB operations had not been employed, in spite of pressure from World Bank representatives (Lovegrove 1998). On the other hand, the Slovenian Agency has, within a few months, employed professionals who could join in operational decision making in banks that are in the rehabilitation regime. This is thanks to a government decision to offer those so employed salaries that are equivalent to those in the banks.

6. In the case of Poland, for the restructuring of large state enterprises according to the programme from 1993, a governmental 'resolution' agency, the 'Industrial Development Agency', has been formed.

BIBLIOGRAPHY

Ábel, I. and L. Szakadát (1997), 'Bank Restructuring in Hungary', May (mimeo).

Ambrus-Lakatos, L. and M.E. Schaffer (1996), *Banking Sector Development in Central and Eastern Europe*, London: Centre for Economic Policy Research.

Balassa, B. (1996), *Restructuring and Recent Situation of the Hungarian Banking Sector*, Workshop Studies, December, Budapest: National Bank of Hungary.

Blommestein, T. (1997), 'Transformation of the Banking Sector in Central and Eastern Europe – Policy Assessment and Next Steps', in *The New Banking Landscape in Central and Eastern Europe*, Paris: OECD, pp. 17–63.

Bonin, J., K. Mizsei, I. Székely and P. Wachtel (1998), *Banking in Transition Economies*, Cheltenham, UK and Lyme, NH, USA: Edward Elgar.

Buch, C.M. and R.P. Heinrich (1997), 'The End of the Czech Miracle? Currency Crisis Reveals Need for Institutional Reforms', Kiel Discussion Papers No. 301, **5** (2), Kiel: Institute for World Economics.

Caprio, G. (1998), 'Banking Crises – Expensive Lessons from Recent Financial Crises', Policy Research Working Paper No. 1979, Washington, DC: World Bank.

Djukić, Dj. (1998), 'Banking Sector Restructuring in Yugoslavia', *Economic and Financial Review*, **5** (2), 79–96.

Dress, B. and C. Pazarbasioglu (1998), 'The Nordic Banking Crises – Pitfalls in Financial Liberalisation?', IMF Occasional Paper No. 161, Washington, DC: International Monetary Fund.

Dziobek, C. and C. Pazarbasioglu (1997), 'Lessons and Elements of Best Practice', in W.E. Alexander, J.M. Davis, L.P. Ebrill and C.-J. Lindgren (eds), *Systemic Bank Restructuring and Macroeconomic Policy*, Washington, DC: International Monetary Fund, pp. 75–143.

Gray, C.W. and A. Holle (1996), 'Bank-led Restructuring in Poland – An Empirical Look at the Bank Conciliation Process', Policy Research Working Paper No. 1650, Washington, DC: World Bank.

Hawkins, J. and P. Turner (1999), 'Bank restructuring in practice: an overview', in *Bank restructuring in practice*, BIS Policy Papers, No. 6, August, pp. 6–105.

International Monetary Fund (IMF) (1997), *Annual Report*, Washington, DC: International Monetary Fund.

Latter, T. (1997), *Causes and Management of Banking Crises*, Handbooks in Central Banking No. 12, London: Bank of England, Centre for Central Banking Studies.

Lovegrove, A. (1998), *Bank Rehabilitation in Croatia*, Leatherhead: Glendale Consulting Limited.

Montes-Negret, F. and L. Papi (1997), 'The Polish Experience with Bank and Enterprise Restructuring', Policy Research Working Paper No. 1705, Washington, DC: World Bank.

Organisation for Economic Co-operation and Development (OECD) (1997a), *Economic Survey: Hungary*, Paris: OECD.

Organisation for Economic Co-operation and Development (OECD) (1997b), *Economic Survey: Slovenia*, Paris: OECD.

Sheng, A. (1996), *Bank Restructuring – Lessons from the 1980s*, Washington, DC: World Bank.
Simoneti, M. and S. Kawalec (eds) (1995), *Bank Rehabilitation and Enterprise Restructuring*, Ljubljana: Central & Eastern European Privatisation Network.
Štiblar, F. (1997), 'Bank Restructuring in Slovenia', in *The New Banking Landscape in Central and Eastern Europe*, Paris: OECD, pp. 295–365.
World Bank (1996), *World Development Report*, Washington, DC: World Bank.

8. Banking Reform in South-East European Countries in the Light of the Central European Experience

Sonya Dilova-Kirkowa and Andy W. Mullineux

INTRODUCTION

It is almost a decade since the transition to a market economy in the former socialist countries began, and there are marked disparities in progress with economic reform in general, and financial sector restructuring in particular.

Financial sector restructuring is an extremely important component of the transition to a market economy. This has been highlighted by the crisis in the South-East Asian emerging market economies in the late 1990s. A stable financial sector is a necessary condition for macroeconomic stability and monetary (and inflation) control. An efficient financial sector ensures that capital is allocated on a continuous basis to enterprises that make the best use of it (as long as they continue to do so) and withdrawn (using effective bankruptcy procedures, where necessary) from inefficient users. Once the centrally planned allocation of capital is abandoned, a new financial infrastructure must be put in place. The more efficiently this is done, the greater the benefits derived from abandoning central planning.

The countries under study in this chapter (Albania, Bulgaria, Croatia, the Czech Republic, Hungary, Poland, Romania and Slovenia) began the 1990s with very different economic conditions, banking systems at different stages of reform, and a wide variation in their bad-debt inheritances. As the chapter demonstrates, their approaches to financial sector restructuring have varied considerably and so has the progress they have made with it to date.

We argue that the South-East European (SEE) transition economies differ from the Central and East European (CEE) countries in their levels of financial development and in the extent of banking reform. The SEE economies, often considered as 'late reformers', also appear to be lagging behind the CEE countries in their level of financial development. This is perhaps a result of their persistent macroeconomic disturbances, half-hearted resolution of non-performing loan problems and the sheer scope of unregulated activities, which increase the costs of intermediation and contract enforcement.

In this chapter, measures of financial sector development are presented and the importance of banks in financial intermediation is highlighted. The relationship between financial development and economic growth is investigated using the financial ratios proposed by King and Levine (1993). Progress towards resolution of the bank bad-debt problem is then assessed, along with the role of banks in the evolving corporate governance system. The performance of banks and progress with banking privatisation and its implications for corporate governance *inter alia* are then assessed. Lessons for SEE late reformers are then drawn from the experiences of the Czech Republic, Hungary and Poland.

FINANCIAL DEVELOPMENT IN SELECTED TRANSITION ECONOMIES

Studies focused on the relationships between progress with banking sector development and economic growth (King and Levine, 1993, p. 719; Levine 1997, p. 688) have indicated that financial development can positively affect subsequent economic growth. This contrasts with the opposite view that financial development follows economic growth. In addition, Levine (1997, p. 690) argues that higher growth is experienced by countries that start with less-fragmented banking systems.

There are some recent studies on economic growth in CEE economies which support the impact of financial liberalisation (Buch, 1996, p. 51) and financial system development (Sutela, 1997, p. 4) on economic performance. Despite the growing evidence of a positive influence of financial development on economic growth, there has been less convincing work on the channels through which the financial sector influences developments in the real economy (EBRD, 1995, p. 99).

Indicators for Financial Development

In this chapter, we have adopted King and Levine's (1993) approach to measuring financial development. King and Levine conducted a regression analysis based on financial data from 80 countries over 30 years, aiming to establish a relationship between four financial indicators and four growth indicators: real per capita GDP growth, the rate of physical capital accumulation, the ratio of domestic investment to GDP and a residual on physical capital accumulation (1993, p. 723). They concluded, among other things, that financial development could influence subsequent long-term economic growth. We calculated similar financial ratios for eight transition countries to provide a comparative assessment of this early financial development. The selection of the countries included in the study depended on the availability of appropriate comparative data and was thus limited to those countries included in the IMF's *International Financial Statistics*. Results are depicted in Table 8.1.

There appear to be marked differences in financial development (measured by *LLY*, that is, M2/GDP) in the eight countries, which included three CEE countries (Poland, Hungary and the Czech Republic) and five SEE countries (Albania, Bulgaria, Croatia, Romania and Slovenia). The low level of financial depth may reflect substantial price instability, a high degree of uncertainty over asset yields and currency substitution, which was witnessed in Argentina and Bulgaria before the introduction of currency board arrangements in 1990 and 1997, respectively. The *LLY* ratio is high in some of the countries with less-sustained economic growth (for example, Bulgaria), but it could be argued that this ratio may indicate that the government was mainly benefiting from increasing financial depth (EBRD, 1999, p. 94). Hence, the low level of financial depth registered in Poland should be taken in conjunction with other economic indicators in characterising the overall progress in economic reforms in this country. The high score for the Czech Republic is equally suspicious, given the relative lack of financial sector restructuring that has since become evident.

In contrast, there seems to be strong evidence for a direct impact of banking reforms on the increase of private sector credit (EBRD, 1999, p. 94). The results from calculating the *PRIVY* ratio (see Table 8.1) suggest that the late reformers tend to have a low share of private sector credit to GDP. This is perhaps a result of the slow pace of privatisation. At the same time, a low share of private sector credit to total domestic credit (*PRIVATE* ratio) could indicate that other means of financing the private sector apart from banking credit have been developed. This may stem from the lack of interest of commercial banks in supplying the small-scale loans frequently demanded by small- and medium-sized enterprises (SMEs). For instance, the number of individual entrepreneurs, used as proxy for the number of SMEs in Poland, was growing rapidly from 813,000 at the end of 1989 to 2.09 million at the end of 1997 (OECD, 1998, p. 47). The low level of reliance on bank credit by private companies in Poland encouraged 'parabanking', that is, a form of financing firms independently from banks (Jerschina, 1995, p. 62).[1]

Table 8.1 *Financial development in selected transition economies (end of period, in per cent), 1993–1998**

	1993	1994	1995	1996	1997	1998
			LLY			
Czech Rep.	69.57	73.10	80.50	75.40	71.22	68.35
Hungary	49.57	45.55	42.33	38.14	47.36	45.42
Poland	35.90	36.74	36.48	37.63	39.73	21.29
Albania	–	37.67	47.82	55.00	58.59	53.68
Bulgaria	77.56	77.95	64.92	71.15	33.62	26.81
Croatia	25.68	19.76	24.83	34.09	42.23	40.77
Slovenia	64.96	33.76	36.54	39.23	42.48	45.20
Romania	22.32	21.39	25.10	27.97	24.88	27.32
			BANK			
Czech Rep.	86.77	89.63	93.56	93.99	93.57	94.97
Hungary	54.52	54.73	58.77	57.82	69.91	75.26
Poland	70.38	71.97	82.95	84.51	86.01	88.53
Albania	–	57.14	71.00	73.59	57.28	66.47
Bulgaria	85.05	83.34	81.11	74.53	75.32	73.70
Croatia	98.23	98.96	98.74	99.14	99.91	98.60
Slovenia	93.79	93.80	94.14	97.14	97.2	98.67
Romania	70.52	70.73	68.40	78.55	87.62	85.93
			PRIVATE			
Czech Rep.	68.34	76.02	72.21	75.06	83.14	79.82
Hungary	41.53	40.81	45.33	39.24	33.78	35.22
Poland	30.04	30.54	37.09	44.29	48.86	53.86
Albania	–	7.62	9.77	8.64	7.22	6.96
Bulgaria	2.79	3.64	29.21	30.94	41.89	64.67
Croatia	46.87	58.16	63.63	64.89	81.73	84.20
Slovenia	65.72	72.19	75.14	80.21	79.84	81.95
Romania	–	–	–	39.80	44.07	53.21
			PRIVY			
Czech Rep.	50.75	59.48	59.44	57.38	66.37	59.43
Hungary	28.11	26.11	22.46	19.10	20.99	19.42
Poland	12.21	11.96	12.83	15.87	18.09	20.81
Albania	–	3.83	3.72	3.88	3.84	3.33
Bulgaria	3.71	3.76	21.30	5.57	12.58	12.15
Croatia	47.32	28.55	30.83	29.19	38.22	40.21
Slovenia	22.05	23.05	27.45	28.83	28.55	32.66
Romania	–	–	–	11.55	8.47	12.75

Note:* The table is based on the methodology proposed by Robert King and Ross Levine (1993, p. 721), where *LLY* measures financial depth M2/GDP; *BANK* ratio of deposit money in banks to deposit money bank domestic assets and central bank domestic assets; *PRIVATE* is a ratio of claims on the non-financial private sector to total domestic credits and *PRIVY* is a share of claims on non-financial sector to GDP.

Sources: IFS (September 1999); PlanEcon (June 1998); EBRD (1999).

Overall, the ten-year period of transition to a market-based financial system reduced the dominance of central bank credit creation in relation to the expansion of credit distributed by commercial banks (see the *BANK* ratio in Table 8.1). However, this indicator provides little evidence on the quality of banking credit allocated. One might assume that late reformers would tend to have a higher share of non-performing loans to total loans. This is illustrated in the next section, and supports Schaffer's (1998, p. 92) argument that banking systems in 'late reformers' are primarily responsible for the continued existence of soft-budget constraints.[2]

It is important to recognise that substantial progress has been made by the countries under study in this chapter towards developing efficient financial intermediaries, albeit at different speeds. The instability of financial institutions stems from internal factors (for example, quality of institutions, enforcement of regulation, monitoring and transparency) and external factors (for example, enterprise restructuring, privatisation and macroeconomic stability). The selected financial indicators do not give the whole picture of the future growth prospects of these countries. Other aspects of financial development, related to savings and investment also need to be considered.

Savings and Investment

The transition to a 'market economy' entails considerable economic restructuring, which in turn requires substantial investment to raise productivity and ensure competitiveness. The abandonment of the centrally planned system fundamentally changed investment allocation and sources of its funding. A previous dependence on corporate savings channelled through the state budget was replaced by a reliance on household savings, which in turn were affected by high inflation rates (EBRD, 1996, p. 78). This is particularly evident for SEE economies. They have not yet managed to recover their pre-transition ratios of savings to GDP, which amounted to about 30 per cent in 1990 (EBRD, 1996, p. 79).

During the transition period of almost ten years, savings have been the main source of investment in the economy. There has been a close correlation between the increase of savings and investment as shares of GDP. This is evident in all countries included in the study (see Table 8.2). The increase in savings and investment is more modest in the SEE countries compared to the three CEE countries, yet the late reformers appear to be more prone to 'economic reversals' due to outside shocks and unsustainable economic performance (EBRD, 1999, p. 66).

Table 8.2 *Savings and investment in selected transition economies,1993–1998*

	1993	1994	1995	1996	1997	1998
Domestic savings/GDP[a]						
Czech Rep.	28.37	28.00	29.63	28.52	28.39	30.71
Hungary	11.75	15.72	21.89	25.69	12.84	14.89
Poland	16.53	16.90	18.48	17.38	17.04	–
Bulgaria	7.69	8.94	14.09	11.55	16.02	13.13
Slovenia	20.43	23.12	21.74	22.40	22.49	–
Romania	23.96	22.73	18.68	17.51	4.70	9.19
Investment/GDP[b]						
Czech Rep.	26.85	30.13	34.06	35.53	33.88	32.16
Hungary	19.96	22.19	24.08	26.78	17.51	20.56
Poland	15.55	15.86	18.29	20.17	22.11	–
Bulgaria	15.38	9.51	15.68	8.46	10.47	14.14
Slovenia	19.34	20.94	23.38	23.38	23.67	–
Romania	28.93	24.80	24.27	25.98	21.85	17.67
Current account/GDP						
Czech Rep.	1.49	–1.95	–2.70	–7.61	–6.16	–1.09
Hungary	–11.00	–9.77	–5.73	–3.77	–2.17	–4.85
Poland	–6.73	1.03	0.72	–2.43	–4.24	–4.54
Albania	1.21	–7.92	–0.47	–3.99	–11.96	–2.20
Bulgaria	–10.10	–0.33	–0.20	0.16	4.37	–0.75
Croatia	5.56	5.67	–7.72	–5.83	–12.02	–7.10
Slovenia	1.51	4.17	–0.12	0.21	0.20	–0.02
Romania	–4.67	–1.51	–5.02	–7.34	–6.13	–7.65
Government budget deficit/GDP						
Czech Rep.	0.10	0.91	0.53	–0.12	–0.96	–1.64
Hungary	–5.72	–7.12	–6.39	–3.11	–4.54	–6.20
Poland	–3.10	–2.29	–2.01	–2.16	–1.39	0.21
Albania	–14.40	–12.40	–10.30	–12.10	–12.6	–10.4
Bulgaria	–12.10	–4.66	–5.25	–15.41	1.97	0.67
Croatia	–0.8	0.62	–0.73	–0.13	–0.98	0.91
Slovenia	0.37	–0.27	–0.29	0.06	–1.49	–0.81
Romania	–0.47	–2.51	–2.96	–4.04	–1.27	–0.93

Notes:
The data are for end of the period and expressed as percentages.
Note that data on domestic savings and investment are not available for Albania and Croatia.
[a] Domestic savings = Gross investment + Exports – Imports.
[b] Gross investment = Gross fixed capital formation + Change in inventories.
Minus means deficit.

Sources: IFS (September 1999); PlanEcon (June 1999); EBRD (1999).

It appears that the Czech Republic, Hungary and Poland experienced smaller declines in gross investment than the five SEE transition economies (see Table 8.2). It was suggested by some researchers that countries which opted for a rapid liberalisation were less likely to experience a sharp decline in their gross investment than those opting for a more prolonged liberalisation process (EBRD, 1995, pp. 69–70). Following this reasoning, one could conclude that CEE countries are in the first category, while SEE countries are in the second group. Perhaps as a result of not only liberalisation, but also other factors, such as credibility and consistency in government policies, the net resource transfer to/from abroad differs across CEE countries, and is strongly influenced by confidence in the domestic economy.

Figure 8.1 *Average share of savings, investment and FDI to GDP in eight transition economies (in per cent, end of period), 1992–1998*

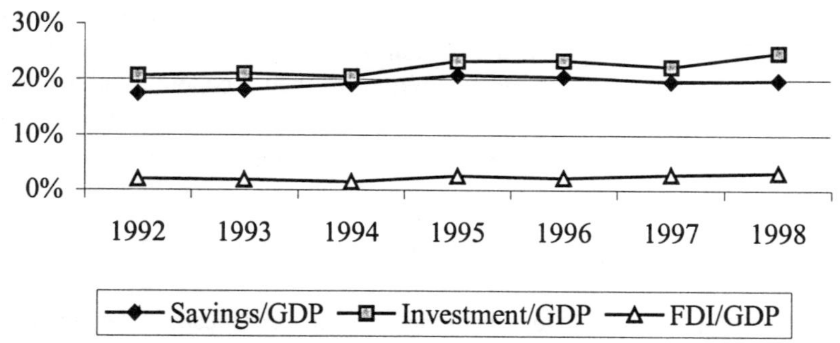

Sources: IFS (September 1999) and EBRD (1999, p. 7).

Another source of financing for domestic investment is capital inflows, measured here as the share of foreign direct investment (FDI) to GDP. On average, it appears that the FDI inflows are insufficient to finance a large proportion of investment demand in the selected transition economies (see Figure 8.1). Accordingly, the results plotted in Figure 8.1 seem to suggest that the main source of investment financing in transition economies is likely to be domestic savings. However, the amount of savings channelled by banks to finance the enterprise sector accounted for only 6 per cent, in contrast to internal funds (for example, retained earnings), which amounted to 60 per cent of total investment funds (EBRD, 1999, p. 137). The absence of other sophisticated financial intermediaries at that time emphasised the importance of achieving efficient and adequate lending by banks.

It is worth noting that, at the end of 1998, all the countries under study had negative current account balances which, in conjunction with government deficits, created a 'twin deficits' situation (see Table 8.2). In the case of the CEE countries, this might simply be a result of economic recovery, as seems to have been the case in Poland in 1998. In the SEE countries the 'twin deficits' could be a warning indicator of future problems. The current account deficit observed in late reformers could have been caused by three factors: (i) increased investment activity; (ii) a decline of domestic savings and rising consumption, and (iii) fiscal imbalances; or some combination of these (EBRD, 1998, p. 59). Foreign borrowing could for a time offset the increase in the current account deficit, but it is unlikely to be sustained. FDI inflows would have been much more beneficial.

In a well-functioning financial system, banks play an important role in collecting savings and allocating funds for investment activities. In a number of SEE countries, however, persistent financial upheavals generated inflation and a consequent depreciation in the value of domestic savings. It had been hoped that FDI and capital market development would underpin investment demand. The experience of the CEE countries suggests that access to foreign capital markets allowed more flexibility in their economic adjustment. However, Bulgaria, and other late reformers, proved to be examples of how vulnerable transition economies could be to economic reversals.

ROLE OF BANKS IN TRANSITION ECONOMIES

The development of efficient banking intermediaries cannot be achieved without proper treatment of inherited non-performing loans (and the consequent bank–enterprise relationships), as well as newly emerging bad loans. Resolving the banks' loan problems and enterprise restructuring are interrelated. Moral hazard problems and poorly regulated institutional arrangements will persist so long as the restructuring is postponed.

Non-performing Loans

The liberalisation policies introduced at the outset of economic reforms and the resulting 'disorganisation' of economic networks undermined the financial strength of enterprises and their ability to service their loans (Rutland, 1996, p. 23). Banks faced massive challenges. Even where non-performing loans (NPLs) inherited from the past were wiped out by inflation (as in Poland), new NPLs resulted from 'bad' lending (by inexperienced loan officers in a highly uncertain environment) during the transition. This increased the pressure on both banks and enterprises. Some of the immediate causes of the new NPLs were: 'lax' banking supervision (by inexperienced supervisors) and regulation (which was in the process of being reformed); delayed enterprise restructuring and bankruptcy laws; and the unexpected depth of the transition recession. It was later recognised that other factors were also responsible, including: distressed lending resulting from the banks' expectation of a bailout; the banks' short-term policy orientation and a fear that some clients could cause a bank run (Buch, 1996, p. 131); 'creditor passivity' or forbearance (for example, the rolling over of debt in default); and trade-off deals between borrowers and lenders in response to government policies (Mitchell, 1993 and 1998).

Although the reasons for the re-emergence of NPLs in the transition period may differ across countries, it seems important to distinguish between various approaches to the cleaning of banks' portfolios. Overall, transition economies tend to adopt either a centralised or a decentralised approach to tackle NPLs. The former requires government to play an active role in banking recapitalisation and the removal of bad loans from bank balance sheets. The latter requires the banks to agree a financial restructuring plan with enterprises prior to receiving government assistance. In Poland such restructuring agreements were required before permission to privatise was granted. It is reasonable to expect that government interference in NPL resolution might increase moral hazard problems among banks and enterprises. On the other hand, recapitalisation and restructuring can be more quickly executed. The centralised approach was applied in Hungary, the Czech Republic, Albania, Bulgaria and Romania. It yielded different results in these countries in terms of improving the quality of the financial institutions and alleviating the NPL burden (see Figure 8.2).

It appears that Albania, Bulgaria and Romania have a lower quality of financial institutions and a relatively higher level of NPLs than the Czech Republic and Hungary in 1998. The latter, however, achieved this at a very high cost of recapitalisation, amounting to about USD10 billion (Borish et al., 1995, pp. 16–17). Nevertheless, the success of the Czech recapitalisation programme is dubious. Although it managed to reduce the level of NPLs in 1998 compared to 1994, the share of NPLs in total loans remains relatively high, perhaps due to the persistence of cross-shareholdings and the insider credit allocation that has resulted from them.

In contrast, countries which adopted a decentralised approach to NPL resolution (Poland, Croatia and Slovenia) seem to have addressed their bad-debt problems more effectively. In 1998, however, Croatia experienced a banking crisis resulting in closure of two banks and government bailout amounting to USD1billion. This increased the share of NPLs to total loans from 9.8 per cent in 1997 to 14.6 per cent in 1998 (EBRD, 1999). In contrast, Poland is an exceptional example of the positive results yielded by applying debt-for-equity swaps as an instrument for debt conversion and for developing bad-debt 'workout' units within banks responsible for designing loan restructuring schemes for individual borrowers. Some researchers, however, have reservations about the ability of debt-for-equity swaps to resolve banking solvency problems, mainly because the quality of equity reflects the quality of converted debt (Buch, 1996, p. 139).

Figure 8.2 *Institutional index and non-performing loans in 1998 (end of period)*

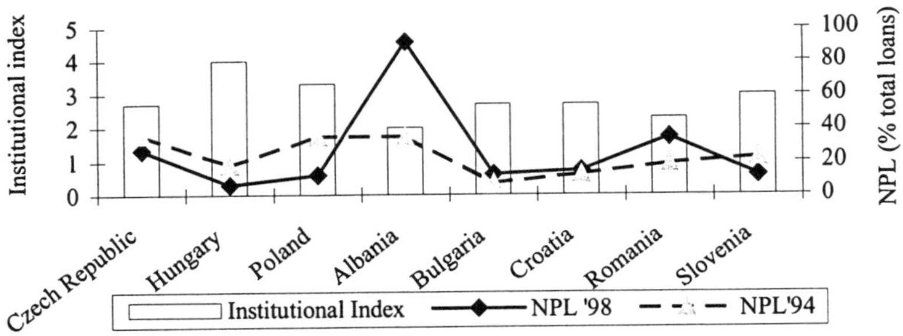

Note: Data on NPL share of total loans for Albania in 1994 are for 1995 and in 1998 are for 1997.

Source: EBRD (1999).

It is not unreasonable to assume that countries like Poland, which actively involved banks in restructuring enterprises' debt, made significant progress in both resolving the NPL problem and improving banking practices. Countries like Bulgaria and the Czech Republic, which applied a centralised approach to non-performing loans, cast banks in a passive role. They seem to have suffered from moral hazard problems and slow restructuring as a result of their prompt intervention to recapitalise banks to underpin their solvency.

From the enterprises' standpoint, recapitalisation programmes yielded positive results if they were implemented in conjunction with restructuring prior to the transformation of ownership (as in Poland, and unlike the Czech Republic). Prolonged and belated measures to tackle unserviced credits encouraged distortions, such as development of informal rules and relationships among economic agents, which we refer to as 'networks' (Mullineux and Dilova-Kirkowa, 1999, pp. 187–8). Networks were used to help reduce the adjustment costs caused by the dismantling of historic economic relations.

This assessment of the recapitalisation programmes emphasises two issues: the importance of banks in enterprise restructuring, and the allied corporate governance issues, to which we turn next; and a recognition that the development of the main institutional pillars of economic reform, such as ownership and laws, takes time and needs attention from the beginning of the transition process. The absence of an appropriate institutional infrastructure encourages temporary institutional solutions, such as networks, which suffer from considerable drawbacks and cause distortions if allowed to persist.

Corporate Governance

Corporate governance issues centre on principal–agent problems, the role of shareholders, the structure and function of the management boards of companies (Mayer, 1997, p. 2), and legal protection of investors and concentration of ownership (Shleifer and Vishny, 1996, p. 5). In developed economies, according to the 'Anglo-Saxon perspective', effective corporate governance of financial firms involves maximising the return to shareholders (Shleifer and Vishny, 1996, p. 2). In transition economies, attention is focused on issues of privatisation, the development of competition, properly functioning bankruptcy procedures (Dittus, 1994, p. 9), and bank involvement in enterprise restructuring (Anderson et al., 1996, p. 8), as well as on the general topic of monitoring and control of managerial behaviour (World Bank, 1996, p. 52).

Ownership and control are fundamentals of corporate governance structure. From the standpoint of the state-owned sector, corporate governance was normally based on a debt relationship and 'outsider' type of control.[3] Debt holding was encouraged by the absence of developed capital markets at the inception of economic reforms and of programmes of banking recapitalisation. This left banks responsible for controlling enterprise management. Deficiencies emerged on both the ownership and control sides. This undermined the quality of corporate governance as a whole.

By holding debt contracts, banks were left with little room for manoeuvre due to their inability to alter conciliation agreements and initiate bankruptcy and the sale of pledged collateral.[4] At the same time, bank control of enterprises was undermined by insider control,[5] which distorted information, prevented transparency and enjoyed political support. Some researchers, therefore, suggested that investment funds were required to serve as the mechanism for corporate governance in transition (Dittus and Prowse, 1996, p. 59), but others considered them inadequate (Aoki, 1995, p. 13). Yet other studies questioned whether an emphasis should be given on depoliticisation rather than corporate governance (Boyko et al., 1996, p. 83).[6]

It appears that conflicts of interest resulting from the sharing of control rights between insiders and outsiders were aggravated by ownership problems caused by the privatisation of large state-owned enterprises through mass distribution of shares; which predominated in SEE transition economies and the Czech Republic. As a result, the ownership structure that evolved tended to be concentrated, with a mixture of state and private property; which David Stark referred to as 'recombinant property' (1995, p. 74 and 1997, p. 48). It resulted in a 'decentralised organisation of assets and centralised management of liabilities' (Stark, 1997, p. 48). The unclear ownership structure undoubtedly contributed to an increase in transaction costs, asset stripping, and poor corporate governance.

Figure 8.3 *Corporate governance index and the unofficial economy**

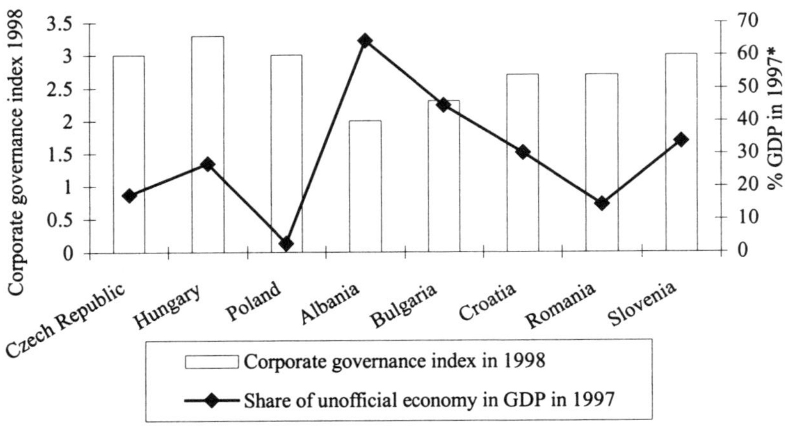

Note: * The share of unofficial economy is measured as a proxy of electricity consumption to GDP.

Sources: EBRD (1998, p. 26; 1999, pp. 184–268) and internal staff calculations.

Problems of delineating property rights and exercising control in transition economies were further aggravated by weak contract enforcement. The latter was often promulgated by mafia or other informal institutional arrangements existing outside the underdeveloped law (Benham and Benham, 1997, p. 44). Figure 8.3 suggests that the quality of the corporate governance is poor in countries where informal institutions prevail.

Accordingly, some researchers argue that the prevalence of the kinds of vested interests associated with the 'oligarchs' in Russia, or private benefits exploited by cross-shareholding between banks, investment funds and enterprises in the Czech Republic, could undermine corporate governance (EBRD, 1999, p. 119). At the same time, institutions designed to address corporate governance problems, such as stock markets, the law, and the 'ethos of managerial professionalism', take time to develop (Stiglitz, 1999, p. 12). Thus, a possible means of improving corporate governance in the short term is to shorten the agency chain (Stiglitz, 1999, p. 13).[7]

It appears that state-owned banks (and presumably banks set up by enterprises) were not appropriate vehicles for corporate governance (Dittus and Prowse, 1996, p. 44). Banks faced an intractable challenge to adjust from their previously assigned role as 'cashiers' and their current responsibilities as 'partners' (Mullineux and Belka, 1996, p. 91).[8] This may be a result of delayed enforcement of bankruptcy law or the slow pace of banking reforms and inadequate training of staff. But the underlying problem was that property rights lacked clear demarcations and often overlapped (that is, 'fuzzy property'), thus causing distortions (Verdery, 1997, p. 104).

It was logical to expect that banks would play a key role in forcing enterprise restructuring, but the opposition from enterprise management (that is, insiders) was underestimated. Privatisation did little to improve the underlying problems of ownership. On the contrary, it muddled the control of assets and substantially legitimised the control of insiders, particularly in countries which implemented mass privatisation programmes prior to restructuring. Moreover, a lack of clearly delineated property rights fostered mismanagement, increased transaction costs and paved the way for various forms of informal rules to manage contract enforcement. As has been observed, countries with a high share of unofficial economic activity to GDP tend to have a lower quality of governance and less enterprise restructuring. It was not surprising, therefore, that the development of networks, as a temporary institutional solution of corporate governance problems, became deeply embedded in such economies and that resistance to changes often undermined economic policy initiatives.

BANKING PERFORMANCE

Given the potential lack of competitiveness and the inefficiency of the banking systems identified in the previous sections, it is not unreasonable to assume that the costs of financial intermediation, particularly in SEE economies, might increase over time. This could be a result of the high interest spreads in transition economies studied, as it is clearly depicted in Table 8.3.

Table 8.3 *Interest spreads in selected transition economies (in per cent, end of period), 1992-1998*

	1992	1993	1994	1995	1996	1997	1998
Czech Rep.	–	7.04	6.05	5.84	5.75	5.49	4.73
Hungary	8.70	9.70	7.10	6.50	5.10	3.30	4.50
Poland	1.20	1.30	–0.60	6.70	6.10	5.60	6.30
Albania	2.10	2.30	3.90	4.40	7.20	14.50	18.50
Bulgaria	11.68	17.18	21.44	23.04	48.80	129.00	9.86
Croatia	499.28	1064.30	16.39	14.71	16.93	11.17	11.13
Romania	21.20	43.09	12.30	16.10	14.70	21.50	15.70
Slovenia	42.09	15.57	10.77	7.98	7.52	6.83	5.55

Sources: IFS (September 1999) and EBRD (1999).

Interest spreads are significantly higher in the SEE economies than in the three CEE countries. This is perhaps a result of the higher inflation rates in the SEE countries (see Table 8.4). At the same time, SEE countries vary in their levels of interest spreads. For instance, Bulgaria failed to address properly its NPL problems via a banking recapitalisation programme and enforcement of stringent banking regulation. Consequently, the financial crisis in 1996 triggered both an increase in the inflation rate and wider interest spreads. While similar problems were experienced by other SEE countries at the outset of their banking reforms, it was not anticipated that features of financial repression[9] would resurface later in transition in some of them.

In addition, high interest spreads in selected transition economies could indicate a lack of competition in the banking sector. This is perhaps to do with complete banking privatisation in SEE economies and the substantially concentrated banking sector. The latter implies that some of the remaining state-owned banks extract monopoly rents by maintaining high interest spreads.

Post-privatisation benefits from transforming state ownership of banks in a transition economy can be expected to take time to develop. At the same time, the degree of vested interests in the economy, which could be measured by the level of unofficial economic activity and development of informal mechanisms for asset allocation, may pose further obstacles to banking performance in these countries.

Table 8.4 *Average interest spreads and annual inflation rate in selected countries from Central and South-East Europe (in per cent, end of period), 1992–1998**

	1992	1993	1994	1995	1996	1997	1998
Central Eastern Europe							
Inflation	25.70	26.20	20.33	21.70	17.43	13.90	12.27
Spreads	4.95	6.01	4.18	6.35	5.65	4.80	5.18
South-East Europe							
Inflation	278.34	393.0	74.84	23.50	37.58	256.18	23.16
Spreads	115.27	228.65	12.96	13.25	19.03	36.60	12.15

Note: *Annual inflation rate is measured by CPI annual percentage change with the exception of Croatia where the inflation rate is measured by retail prices annual percentage change.

Sources: EBRD (1999) and IFS (September 1999).

One could plausibly conclude that the financial performance of banks was altered by the existing institutional weaknesses in ownership structures and law enforcement. In regard to ownership, state-owned banks dominated the market for banking services as a result of government bailout programmes, political support and relationships with the non-financial state-owned sector. One way to change the status quo is to allow freer entry for foreign banks. In Poland, such policy measures are yielding positive results.[10] In regard to the law enforcement, particularly in compliance with prudential standards, many problems are yet to be addressed. This is perhaps a result of the inability to separate banking problems from the wider context of economic reforms, which have not been completed.

LESSONS FOR SOME LATE REFORMERS IN SOUTH- EAST EUROPE

It appears that the monobanking system left a different legacy, in terms of non-performing loans, concentration of banking assets and quality of financial institutions, in each of the countries studied here. Banking reforms have aimed to address these problems, but their impact seems to have been limited by specific institutional and political changes in the formerly centrally planned economies, both before and after the economic transformation. As a result, the development of financial intermediaries has proved to be a long and costly process. This was not anticipated at the inception of economic reforms.

Following the collapse of the centrally planned system, Bulgaria and other 'late reformers' from South-East Europe adopted their own distinct paths of development. The slow pace of their banking reforms, compared to those in Poland, Hungary and the Czech Republic, is notable. The lack of sufficient evidence on sustainable economic development in the countries under study makes it impossible to draw any firm conclusions about the possible relationship between financial development and economic growth. Nevertheless, there is strong evidence that banks are increasingly playing a pivotal role in credit allocation. This may sustain economic growth in these countries in the long run. But in the short run, it appears that in countries like Bulgaria, which had high inflation rates during the transition, the development of a large number of financial intermediaries, particularly banks, did not eliminate financial shortcomings.

The SEE transition economies, which delayed their financial reforms, appear to be lagging behind the CEE countries in their level of financial development. In the Czech Republic, however, one could argue that despite financial restructuring, the country failed to achieve adequate financial development. At the other end of the scale, the Polish banking sector recovered quickly despite delays in commercial and labour laws. Law enforcement seemed pivotal for economic restructuring and benefited from the economic possibilities created by marketisation, enabling it to underpin economic growth. Financial development in the countries studied seems to be consistent with the argument that in opting for a decentralised banking system after practising monobanking for a long time, it was essential for transition economies to restructure their banking systems prior to their privatisation.

The current problems in some transition economies are likely to be the result of specific approaches to tackling non-performing loans at an early stage of banking reforms. The study suggests that countries which assigned a passive role to banks seem to be prone to moral hazard and further accumulation of non-performing loans. In contrast, Poland actively engaged banks in loan restructuring and seems to be better off as a result in the medium term, despite an initial preparatory delay.

It is reasonable to argue that Bulgaria and other 'late reformers' should consider as paramount for their financial development the achievement of macroeconomic stability. At the same time, the credibility of financial institutions should no longer be questionable. Financial stability would itself enhance growth by stimulating domestic savings. The latter should be the primary source of domestic investment funding since capital inflows from abroad can be very volatile, as the Asian crisis in the late 1990s has shown. Indeed macro and financial stability go hand in hand.

It appears that state-owned banks in Bulgaria and other 'late reformers' failed to adopt a proper corporate governance structure because of their heavy NPL burden, political interference and unresolved ownership structure. The main policy measures used to tackle these problems were, respectively, recapitalisation, depoliticisation and privatisation. In reality, they were often only partially implemented, thus creating opportunities for moral hazard, political lobbying and informal networks.

In line with the progress made in financial development and the restructuring of banks in transition economies, SEE transition economies had poor performance indicators when compared to Poland, Hungary and the Czech Republic. In particular, high intermediation costs could be a result of the high level of inflation rates and costs of recapitalisation. Although there is little evidence on the impact of banking privatisation on corporate governance in the economies studied, it is reasonable to assume that a reduction of intermediation costs would result from banking privatisation and enhanced competition.

While there was no question about the importance of bank credit allocation in the transition, although the private sector needs to become the main recipient, there are a number of questions relating to law enforcement, delineation of property rights and banking regulation. A number of the problems encountered in the transition were evident throughout 1993–98, such as: banks appear to be drawn to risky investments, thus increasing the threat of non-performing loans; a lack of enforcement mechanisms for banking regulation; concentrated banking; and problems of moral hazard and mismanagement were aggravated by repeated bailouts. Many countries only addressed these problems following financial upheavals. It is worrying that the transformation of bank ownership is still not completed in the SEE countries, thus creating a vicious circle: a lack of incentives creates a lack of action, which encourages moral hazard, embezzlements and illegal operations, while the system remains improperly regulated because of corruption and a lack of effective courts and moral norms.

We anticipate that if late reformers, such as Bulgaria, accelerated privatisation on all fronts and over a short period of time, they are likely to demonstrate resilience. The banking system would benefit most because the market for collateral would finally get off the ground at the expense of the distribution of credit via informal networks. As a result, proper market incentives created among domestic entrepreneurs would break the vicious circle. It is unlikely, however, that privatisation of state-owned banks in countries with incomplete transformation of ownership in the real sector alone would be able to resolve the underlying banking problems. Banking privatisation, initiated after a successful resolution of bad-debt problems, could, with the aid of well-functioning banking laws, assist in the restructuring of the real sector by fostering competition between banks and thereby raising the quality of banking while cutting off inefficient enterprises from credit. The experience of economic reform in transition economies suggests that expectations often fail to match the realities, but the South-East Asian financial crisis of the late 1990s has highlighted the importance of banking sector restructuring to the transition processes.

NOTES

1. This refers to companies that specialise in financing firms independently from banks. Although these companies maintained 1 per cent interest per day compared to 30–40 per cent interest per annum charged by banks, they were a preferable source of financing enterprises due to their flexibility in credit arrangements.
2. 'Soft budget constraints' are defined by Janos Kornai (1992, p. 140) as a state subsidy subject to bargaining. Mark Schaffer referred to 'soft budget constraints' as *ex post* bailouts of loss-making firms resulting from paternalistic preference (1998, p. 85).
3. The term 'insiders' refers to incumbent managers, often in collusion with workers, who act to protect their controlling rights, thus opposing any attempt to change the ownership status quo and lacking incentives to restructure firms. Any involvement of investors via capital markets or direct acquisition via privatisation can impose outside controls. The latter may vary according to the ownership structure, thus affecting decision making on restructuring issues (EBRD, 1997, p. 76 and Anderson et al., 1996, p. 17).
4. Conciliation refers to out-of-court arrangements between banks and their indebted enterprises aiming to prevent a recurrence of non-performing loans (Borish et al., 1995, p. 46).
5. *Supra* note 3.
6. Depoliticisation is a recognition that the political influence over the economic activity often contributes to economic inefficiency (Boyko et al., 1996, p. 10).
7. Stiglitz refers to 'agency chains' such as those existing in developed economies, in which 'workers are agents for managers who are agents for shareholders such as mutual funds whose shares are held by pension funds which act as agents for their beneficiaries such as workers' (1999, p. 12).
8. Banks are considered as 'cashiers' when they provide loanable financial resources, often on request. This was mainly observed at the beginning of banking reforms. By piling out equity stakes as of end 1992, banks became concerned about the financial state of state-owned enterprises and began acting in a more prudent manner, being referred to as partners (Mullineux and Belka, 1996, p. 91).
9. The idea of financial repression is elaborated in the McKinnon–Shaw model, which emphasised distortions caused by financial prices (Fry, 1988, p. 13).
10. By the end of 1999, two-thirds of the Polish banking sector was controlled by foreign investors (EIU, 1999, p. 19). Foreign investors contributed to know-how transfer and the development of new products and services in acquired banks, for instance WBK Zachodni and Pekao (Dzierwa and Czepliewicz, 1999, p. 3). In many ways, the Polish government is the main beneficiary of banking privatisation in terms of revenues amounting to USD 1.5 billion resulting from the sale of majority stakes in two banks in 1999. Nevertheless, there is an increasing political opposition to allowing a substantial number of Polish banks to be placed under foreign control (Dzierwa and Czepliewicz, 1999, p. 2).

REFERENCES

Anderson, R.W., E. Berglof and K. Mizsei (eds) (1996), *Banking Sector Development in Central and Eastern Europe*, Forum Report of the Economic Policy Initiative, No. 1, Warsaw: Institute for EastWest Studies.

Aoki, M. (1995), 'Introduction', in M. Aoki and H. Kim (eds), *Corporate Governance in Transition Economies: Insider Control and the Role of Banks*, Economic Development Institute, Washington, DC: World Bank, pp. i–xiv.

Benham, A. and L. Benham (1997), 'Property Rights in Transition Economies: A Commentary on What Economists Know', in J.M. Nelson, C. Tilly and L. Walker (eds), *Transforming Post-Communist Political Economies*, Washington, DC: National Academy Press, pp. 35–60.

Borish, M.S., M.F. Long and M. Noel (1995), 'Restructuring Banks and Enterprises: Recent Lessons from Transition Countries', Discussion Paper No. 279, Washington, DC: World Bank.

Boyko, M., A. Shleifer and R. Vishny (1996), *Privatizing Russia*, Cambridge, MA: MIT Press.

Buch, C.M. (1996), *Creating Efficient Banking Systems: Theory and Evidence from Eastern Europe*, Tübingen: Kiel Institute of World Economics, Kiel Studies, No. 277, J.C.B. Mohr.

Dittus, P. (1994), 'Corporate Governance in Central Europe: The Role of Banks', Bank for International Settlements, Economic Paper No. 42, Basle: BIS.

Dittus, P. and S. Prowse (1996), 'Corporate Control in Central Europe and Russia. Should Banks Own Shares?', in R. Frydman, C. Gray and A. Rapaczynski (eds), *Corporate Governance in Central Europe and Russia*, Vol. 1, Budapest: Central European University, pp. 20–67.

Dzierwa, J. and M. Czepliewicz (1999), *Polish Banks*, Global Equity Research, London: Salomon Smith Barney.

EBRD (1995), *Transition Report 1995*, London: European Bank for Reconstruction and Development.

EBRD (1996), *Transition Report 1996*, London: European Bank for Reconstruction and Development.

EBRD (1997), *Transition Report 1997*, London: European Bank for Reconstruction and Development.

EBRD (1998), *Transition Report 1998*, London: European Bank for Reconstruction and Development.

EBRD (1999), *Transition Report 1999*, London: European Bank for Reconstruction and Development.

Economist Intelligence Unit (EIU)(1999), *Poland*, Country Report, 4th Quarter, London: EIU.

Fry, M.J. (1988), *Money, Interest and Banking in Economic Development*, Baltimore, MD: Johns Hopkins University Press.

International Financial Statistics (IFS) (1999), *International Monetary Fund*, Washington, DC.

Jerschina, J. (1995), 'The Banking Services Market in Poland: Consolidation and Privatisation of Banks', in E. Miklaszewska (ed.), *Competitive Banking in Central and Eastern Europe*, Krakow: Jagiellonian University, 47–66.

King, R. and R. Levine (1993), 'Finance and Growth: Schumpeter Might be Right', *Quarterly Journal of Economics*, **108** (3), August, 717–37.

Kornai, J. (1992), *The Socialist System – The Political Economy of Communism*, Oxford: Clarendon Press.
Levine, R. (1997), 'Financial Development and Economic Growth: Views and Agenda', *Journal of Economic Literature*, **35**, 688–726.
Mayer, C. (1997), 'Financial Systems and Corporate Governance: A Review of International Evidence', paper presented at the 15th International Seminar on the New Institutional Economics 'Financial Institutions in Transition: Banks and Financial Markets' 6–7 June, Wallerfangen, Germany.
Mitchell, J. (1993), 'Creditor Passivity and Bankruptcy: Implications for Economic Reform', in C. Mayer and X. Vives (eds), *Capital Markets and Financial Intermediation*, Cambridge: Cambridge University Press, pp. 197–224.
Mitchell, J. (1998), 'The Problems of Bad Debts: Cleaning Banks' Balance Sheets in Economies of Transition', Discussion Paper No. 1977, London: Centre for Economic Policy Research.
Mullineux, A.W. and M. Belka (1996), 'Hardening Micro Budget Constraints: Bank Behaviour and Corporate Governance in Poland', in A.W. Mullineux (ed.), *Financial Reform in Central and Eastern Europe*, Commack: Nova Science Publishers Inc., pp. 75–99.
Mullineux, A.W. and S. Dilova-Kirkowa (1999), 'Privatisation and Financial Sector Restructuring in the Czech Republic, Poland and Russia: Lessons for Bulgaria and Other Late Reformers', in Ž. Šević (ed.), *Banking Reform in South East European Transition Economies*, London and Sofia: University of Greenwich Business School, Balkan Center for Public Policy and Related Studies and Humanitarian Research Centre, pp. 187–8.
Organisation for Economic Co-operation and Development (OECD) (1998), *Economic Survey: Poland*, June, Paris: OECD.
Rutland, P. (1996), 'Bankers Bullish About Central and Eastern Europe', *Transition*, 17 May, 22–4.
Schaffer, M. (1998), 'Do Firms in Transition Economies Have Soft Budget Constraints? A Reconsideration of Concepts and Evidence', *Journal of Comparative Economics*, **26** (1), 80–103.
Shleifer, A. and R. Vishny (1997), 'A Survey of Corporate Governance', *Journal of Finance*, **52**, June, 737–84.
Stark, D. (1995), 'Not by Design: The Myth of Designer Capitalism in Eastern Europe', in J. Hausner, B. Jessop and K. Nielsen (eds), *Strategic Choice and Path-Dependency in Post-Socialism Institutional Dynamics in the Transformation Process*, Aldershot, UK and Brookfield, USA: Edward Elgar, pp. 67–83.
Stark, D. (1997), 'Recombinant Property in East European Capitalism', in G. Grabher and Stark D. (eds), *Restructuring Networks in Post-Socialism: Legacies, Linkages and Localities*, Oxford: Oxford University Press, pp. 35–69.
Stiglitz, J. (1999), 'Whiter Reform?', Keynote address, Annual Bank Conference on Development Economics, World Bank, Washington, DC, 28–30 April.
Sutela, P. (1997), 'The Strategic Role of Banks in Financing Russian Economic Growth', first draft, paper presented at 29th National Convention of the American Association for the Advancement of Slavic Studies in Seattle and later published in *Post-Soviet Geography and Economics*, 1998, **39** (2), 96–124.
Verdery, K. (1997), 'Fuzzy Property: Rights, Power and Identity in Transylvania's Decollectivisation', in J.M. Nelson, C. Tilly and L. Walker (eds), *Transforming Post-Communist Political Economies*, Washington, DC: National Academy Press, pp. 102–17.

World Bank (1996), *World Development Report 1996: From Plan to Market*, Washington, DC: World Bank.

PART TWO

Country Studies

9. Banking Reform in Albania

Fiqiri Baholli and Amika Stavri

INTRODUCTION

After nearly fifty years of political isolation and economic stagnation, Albania is now undergoing a rapid transformation. During the period from the mid-1940s to late 1990, Albania maintained a rigid system of central planning and state economic control, accompanied by self-imposed isolation from the international community. All forms of private economic activity were totally destroyed.

During most of this period Albania ran large external current account deficits financed initially by external assistance, then by drawing on reserves and then using short-term borrowing from foreign banks. Clearly, this economic approach could not last and, in 1990, the system began to seriously unravel. Production in key economic sectors, such as agriculture, and in key export industries (chromium, oil and electricity) declined sharply.

In 1991, the old economic and political regime collapsed, causing major social unrest and disruptions in public administration. Real GDP dropped drastically while, by mid-1992, inflation had risen to monthly rates of 10–15 per cent. The election of a new democratic government in 1992 set in motion a series of much-needed and far-reaching changes.

The old centralised regime in Albania has been replaced by a modern free-market economy based on private initiative. The road has been hard, because Albania has started anew, but it has already accomplished much: an aggressive fight against inflation, a decrease in the budget deficit through spending restraint, the introduction of a market-based tax structure and, with the support of the international community, the refinancing of its outstanding debt and the financing its current account deficit without adding new debt.

Albania is a small, open economy, where changes in the banking sector, in recent years, have been directed towards creating an independent central bank and a market-oriented banking system. The Bank of Albania has played a major role in establishing monetary stability in the country.

SEQUENCE OF BANKING REFORM

The structure of the banking system in Albania at the end of 1991 was typical of a centrally planned economy. It comprised four state-owned institutions, with the State Bank of Albania performing both central bank and commercial bank functions.

A two-tier banking system was introduced following the passage of new central bank and commercial banking laws in April 1992, creating, for the first time in Albania, a separate and independent central bank with full power over monetary policy and three commercial banks. The reforms focused initially on the separation of central and commercial banking activities and the creation of a modern financial system out of the remains of the former monobank. In turn, this has led to a new approach to interest rates, full external convertibility for the lek (the Albanian currency) and a market-determined floating exchange rate. The full-scale dismantling of domestic controls and exchange and trade liberalisation accompanied these sweeping initiatives. The government's 1992–93 programme has been financially supported by the International Monetary Fund (IMF), the World Bank, the European Community, and by major countries.

Banking System Reform

Banking system reform is concentrated in:

- avoiding the intervention of the state in the banking system 'affairs', so that this system is developed pursuant to the principles of market economics. The privatisation or liquidation of the state-owned banks is considered as a very important step in achieving this target; and
- creating an appropriate legal framework that allows banks to perform their activities on the basis of commercial principles. In order to achieve this, the right legal and political support (with respect to bankruptcy, collateral and other related issues), a sound regulatory framework, the right supervisory capacities and infrastructure, and financial basis (payments, accounting, auditing) are required.

Privatisation of Banks

Although credit creation activity has been very low over the last two years, the phenomenon of not paying back loans is still evident. Credit evaluation and discipline in the state-owned banks were at very low levels. The only way out of this situation was considered to be a non-extension of credit on the part of the state-owned banks to the economy in 1998 and 1999.

The first step in implementing the banks' privatisation programme was the closing of the Rural Commercial Bank in December 1997 and the establishment of a Loan Collection Agency.

In 1998 steps were taken towards the privatisation of the other two state-owned banks. The Ministry of Finance has appointed a foreign administrator to the National Commercial Bank who is in charge of controlling and preparing the bank for privatisation. During 1999 an international tender was declared and the buyers of this bank were three foreign institutions.

With regard to the Savings Bank, a management contract was signed with the board of directors of the bank. The ultimate aim of this contract, whose implementation will be supervised by a foreign bank, is to prepare the bank for privatisation. Representatives of the foreign bank will serve on the board of directors of the Savings Bank. It was anticipated that the privatisation of the Savings Bank should start by the end of 1999, but the only thing completed during 1999 was the approval in parliament of the Law for Privatisation of the Savings Bank. Nevertheless, the Bank of Albania acknowledges that the steps taken with respect to the privatisation of both banks have been very slow and requires that this process be accelerated and finished as soon as possible.

Banks' Regulatory Framework

Improvements of the banking laws in 1996, 1997 and 1998 have followed the first laws adopted in 1992. The Bank of Albania has taken measures to improve the rules and regulations of the financial system, starting with the review of the Law on the Banking System in the Republic of Albania. This was in order to provide for the appropriate capitalisation of banks and for rules regarding entry to and exit from the banking system.

The minimum amount of regulatory capital increased from lek 200 million in 1996 to lek 350 million in 1997 and further to lek 700 million in April 1998 (approximately USD 5 million at the January 2000 exchange rate). The requirements for granting licences have been strengthened and additional information is now required with respect to the business plan and qualification of the administrators. All banks licensed to perform banking activity in Albania are required to comply with the new criteria defined under this regulation.

The Bank of Albania has increased the capital adequacy ratio to 12 per cent. Although positive measures have been taken for the creation of a legal and regulatory framework and the regulations of banking supervision are in general in compliance with international standards, there are still problems in the implementation of these regulations.

In the course of 1998, the legal and regulatory framework, on the basis of which the banking system functions in Albania, recorded a number of qualitative developments. First, the sanctioning of the independence of the Bank of Albania by the constitution, approved in November 1998, which lays down, under Article 161, the main functions of the Bank of Albania: (a) the exclusive right to issue and circulate the domestic currency; (b) the right to implement the monetary policy of the Albanian state independently; and (c) the right to maintain and manage the foreign exchange reserve of the Republic of Albania. Second, the new banking law of the Republic of Albania clearly defines: the respective sanctions for those who undertake banking activities or collect deposits from the public without being licensed; banking supervision rules, administrative measures and sanctions; and definitions of concepts such as 'bank', 'banking activity', 'receivership' and 'liquidation of a bank'.

This part of legislation review was compiled by taking into consideration the Basic Principles of Banking Supervision of the Basle Committee:

- *Exercise of banking activity* The new law clearly defines the procedures for undertaking banking activities and gives the Bank of Albania full rights to license or supervise these activities. The law provides for a group of criteria that are related to factors such as the reputation, main objectives, transparency, and intellectual and professional capacity of the administrators of the bank. Pursuant to the new law the Bank of Albania is responsible for defining all the licensing elements and procedures to be met by the applicant banks.
- *Banking activity* The list of permissible banking activities is sufficient to cover all the banking activities currently performed by all the banks in the Republic of Albania and this enables a useful and secure banking business to function. Nevertheless the Bank of Albania has the power to authorise the development of other activities that are, or can become, common banking activities in international markets.
- *Required capital and supervisions regulations* The new law gives the Bank of Albania full power to stipulate that the banks maintain capital reserves and a minimum amount of paid-up capital, to be adjusted by the bank from time to time.
- *Administrative structure and responsibility* Different sanctions and administrative measures are available to be applied to different types of violation and to prevent illegal activities.

- *Receivership and liquidation* The law gives the Bank of Albania the right to nominate a receiver who would take over control of the bank. The receiver is empowered to adopt or recommend appropriate measures to restore the bank to a sound financial position.

With regard to the regulatory aspect, in 1998 the Bank of Albania reviewed all the rules and regulations relating to the management of its activity and that of the banking system. Notwithstanding the above-mentioned achievements, the main challenges for 1999 are related to the parliamentary approval of a category of laws, including those relating to banking in the Civil Code, the 'Law On the Prevention of Money Laundering', 'Collateral Law', and so on.

The Bank of Albania has been assisted technically by foreign sources in the area of banking supervision. The manual relating to the supervision of the commercial banks is prepared and used by the banks' inspectors. Although progress has been made there is still much room for improvement.

Financial Infrastructure

The authorities have plans to establish a credit information agency, whose function is to maintain basic information concerning the reliability of clients applying for a loan. The establishment of this office will help to improve credit-risk management and facilitate mediation procedures in Albania.

The payments system is another element of the modern banking system (this is explained in a separate section). There have been many important developments in the areas of accounting and auditing. In 1998, the Council of Ministers approved the New Accounting Law, which is in compliance with international accounting standards and which all banks are required to implement. In addition, there have been many modifications to the forms that the banks prepare for the Bank of Albania in accordance with the New Accounting Law and its regulations.

Other Financial Markets

Tirana Stock Exchange, established in May 1996, continues to function in a limited way by trading treasury bills in the secondary market. These are traded by only a few banks, and measures should be taken to develop this market further. The Tirana Stock Exchange is still far from being an important financial institution for the country's economy and finance. Indeed, it is barely functioning and the review of its regulatory and legal framework is one of the priorities of short-term economic and financial development in Albania. For this reason some amendments to the Securities Law were proposed in 2000.

The current experiences of some programmes that have experimented with loanable funds in the rural areas have proved that these funds may be transferred into credit co-operatives. This holds true especially for those areas where incomes are so high that they can generate credit demand. Therefore, provision of the legal framework is imperative for the establishment of this kind of financial institution.

STRUCTURE OF THE BANKING SYSTEM

All banks in the Republic of Albania (except the Arab–Albanian Islamic Bank, which does not accept term deposits or perform lending operations) provide all types of bank services. (See Table 9.1.)

Table 9.1 *Banking system in Albania, end of 1998*

Banks	Ownership	Branches
Central bank		
Bank of Albania (BoA)	State owned	5
State banks		
National Commercial Bank of Albania (NCBA)	State owned	10
Savings Bank of Albania (SBA)	State owned	24
Joint-venture and other private banks		
Italian–Albanian Bank	(NCBA–Banca di Roma, Italy)	1
Arab–Albanian Islamic Bank	(NCBA–Arab Islamic Bank, Bahrain)	1
Dardania Bank	Foreign Private Bank	1
National Bank of Greece	Foreign Private Bank	1
Tirana Bank	Foreign Private Bank	3
Alpha Credit Bank	Foreign Private Bank	1
International Commercial Bank	Foreign Private Bank	1
American Bank of Albania	Foreign Private Bank	1
FEFAD Bank	Foreign Private Bank	2
First Investment Bank	Foreign Private Bank	1

Source: Bank of Albania.

The financial sector reforms on which the Bank of Albania has embarked (in concert with the government), aim at increasing the central bank's efficiency as a monetary authority, the development of a number of commercial banks capable of performing basic banking services, an appropriate regulatory framework and the creation of an efficient payments system. The services offered by the banking system are shown in Table 9.2.

Table 9.2 *Banking products in Albania*

Banking products	Wholesale banking	Retail banking
Current accounts	√	√
Term deposits	√	√
Money transfers	√	√
Loans	√	√
Bankcards and related services	√	√
Cheques	√	√
Certificates of deposit	√	√

Source: Bank of Albania.

The National Commercial Bank of Albania (NCBA) has a branch network consisting of ten branches throughout Albania, and it accepts all types of deposits by enterprises, private institutions, private companies and Albanian individuals and foreigners. It finished formal privatisation procedures during the first half of 2000.

The Savings Bank of Albania has 24 branches throughout Albania and its domestic network is the largest among all Albanian banks. Currently it holds the largest part of household deposits. Its lending portfolio has many non-performing loans. The year 2000 should be the decisive year for its privatisation.

The Bank of Albania has recognised the crucial role of foreign capital and technology in the modernisation of the banking system. The establishment in late 1992 of the first joint-venture bank in the Italian–Albanian Bank is an important step forward in this regard. Its shareholders are NCBA, the Banca di Roma and the European Bank for Reconstruction and Development (EBRD). The Italian–Albanian Bank provides full banking services. Dardania Bank was the first private bank to be licensed by the end of 1993. The Arab–Albanian Islamic Bank is a joint-venture bank. Its shareholders are NCBA and foreign Islamic banks and individuals. Tirana Bank was established in Tirana by its principal shareholder, the Bank of Piraeus in Greece. Created in 1916 and privatised in 1991, this bank has improved its indices and efficiency considerably. Tirana Bank, established on 12 September 1996, is the first foreign private bank. It acts as a universal bank according to its paid-up capital.

The National Bank of Greece, Tirana, licensed in 1996, is the first branch of a foreign bank in Albania. In 1997, the Bank of Albania licensed the International Commercial Bank, which is a foreign private bank established in Tirana by Malaysian investors. During 1998 four other private foreign banks were licensed: Alpha Credit Bank in Tirana; American Bank of Albania; FEFAD Bank; and First Investment Bank, Tirana. In 1999 one other private foreign bank, InterCommercial Bank, was granted a licence with capital from the Commercial Bank of Greece.

Some statutory ratios, ratios of assets and liabilities' items versus totals, and savings of citizens in Albania are shown in Tables 9.3, 9.4 and 9.5.

Table 9.3 *Statutory ratios in Albania, 1994–1998*

	1994	1995	1996	1997	1998
Capital adequacy	24.6	16.5	9.7	5.5	–1.8
Capital/total liabilities	3.6	5.1	3.4	7.1	1.2
Coeff. of investments in fixed assets (as a % of bank capital)	11.6	21.2	54.4	44.4	208.6

Source: Bank of Albania.

Table 9.4 *Balance sheet ratios and share of treasury bills in Albania, end of June 1999*

Banks	A	B	C	D	E
National Commercial Bank	8.0	67.2	38.1	11.6	0.8
Savings Bank of Albania	0.3	101.2	11.5	64.6	96.4
Italian–Albanian Bank	11.3	73.7	34.8	7.8	0.5
Arab–Albanian Islamic Bank	66.0	37.4	0.0	0.0	0.0
Dardania Bank	8.0	17.2	4.4	100.0	0.0
Tirana Bank	10.8	76.2	17.4	14.7	1.1
National Bank of Greece	10.1	82.9	0.0	0.0	0.3
Internat. Commercial Bank	37.7	80.2	37.6	0.0	0.0
Alpha Credit Bank	13.5	62.3	19.4	0.0	0.5
American Bank of Albania	11.5	89.3	4.0	0.0	0.2
FEFAD Bank	23.8	42.0	47.6	2.5	0.2
First Investment Bank	95.5	1.1	0.0	0.0	0.0

Notes:
A = Capital/total liabilities.
B = Total deposits/total liabilities.
C = Total loans/total assets.
D = Bad loans/total loans.
E = Market share of treasury bills.

Source: Bank of Albania.

Table 9.5 *Savings of citizens in Albania, 1994–1998 (in Albanian leks)*

Deposits	1994	1995	1996	1997	1998
1.Total deposits in national currency	19,081	28,964	29,454	71,102	115,35 5
Current account	822	1,305	2,179	627	641
Giro account	–	–	–	–	–
Other demand Deposits	–	–	–	–	–
Short term	–	–	–	–	–
Long term	18,259	27,659	27,275	70,475	114,71 4
2.Total Forex deposits	3,941	7,438	10,152	16,789	19,510
Short term	1,879	1,705	2,342	2,714	3,370
Long term	2,062	5,733	7,810	14,075	16,140
3.GDP (in billions)	170,385	224,746	279,802	338,912	460,83
Lek/USD exchange rate (annual average)	94.7	92.8	104.5	148.9	150.6
1/3 (in per cent)	11.2	12.9	10.5	21.0	25.0
2/3 (in per cent)	2.31	3.30	3.36	4.95	4.23

Source: Bank of Albania.

Albania is following a freely floating foreign exchange regime. Foreign exchange bureaux play a very big role both in supporting the banking system and in competition. These offices are regulated by Bank of Albania rules and, following the changes in the banking law in early 1998, there have been many improvements in the respective regulations.

By the end of June 1999, 16 foreign exchange bureaux, under the supervision of the Bank of Albania, had been licensed. Under the new regulations governing the financial activities of non-bank institutions, some of the bureaux are now involved in money transfer activities.

CENTRAL BANK REFORM

Since mid-1992, the Bank of Albania has made significant progress in assuming the functions of a central bank. A stable macroeconomic environment in the course of the last two years bears testimony to the bank's successful monetary policy.

The law governing the Central Bank of Albania has been revised twice, in 1996 and late 1997, with the main aim of ensuring the bank's independence. The major areas of improvement in this regard include: jurisdiction, organisation and management, objectives, government financing, exchange rate policy and accountability.

Within the limits of its authority as established by the law, the Bank of Albania is entirely independent from any other authority in the pursuit of its objectives and the performance of its tasks. The independence of the bank is paramount, and no one can improperly influence any member of its decision-making body in the discharge of his or her duties or interfere in the bank's activities.

The principal objective of the Bank of Albania is to achieve and maintain price stability. The bank's policies are largely consistent with this objective and the bank promotes and supports the development of a market-based foreign exchange system, an internal financial market and the payments system, and fosters monetary and credit conditions conducive to the orderly, balanced and sustained economic development of the country.

The other objectives of the bank, which are subordinate to its primary objective, are to foster the liquidity, solvency and proper functioning of a stable market-based banking system.

In this context the basic tasks of the Bank of Albania are:

- the formulation, adoption and execution of monetary policy in Albania that is consistent with its primary objective;
- the formulation, adoption and execution of exchange arrangements and exchange rate policy;
- the licensing or revoking and supervision of banks that engage in banking business in order to secure banking system stability;
- holding and managing its official foreign reserves;
- acting as banker and adviser to, and as fiscal agent of, the government of the Republic of Albania; and
- promoting the smooth operation of payments systems.

Any other objective or duty is subordinate to the achievement of its principal objective.

The Bank of Albania controls inflation by controlling an intermediate target – broad money or M3. In Albania, control of the money supply relies upon the use of direct and indirect monetary policy instruments. (See Figure 9.1.)

Apart from abiding by credit ceilings (which have now been removed), commercial banks are obliged to hold required reserves at the Bank of Albania, which relate to the size of funds or specific categories of liabilities that they possess. The reserve requirement ratio is currently 10 per cent of bank deposits. At the present phase of development, the arguments for the imposition of reserve requirements on banks are: to partially back up their deposit liabilities to the general public; to mop up excess liquidity of the banking system; to function as a source of revenue for the central bank; and to set the stage for the Bank of Albania to shift from direct to indirect monetary policy instruments. Consequently, reserve requirements will become an active instrument of monetary policy only after the removal of the credit ceilings and the full reliance upon indirect instruments of monetary management.

Figure 9.1 *M2 and M3 growth in Albania, December 1994 to October 1999*

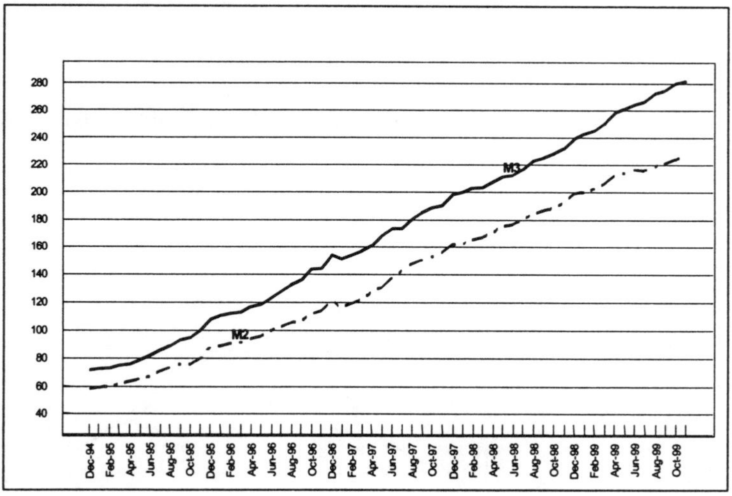

Source: Bank of Albania.

The discount window is another indirect instrument of monetary policy, which enables the individual banks to obtain marginal financing from the central bank. Because of high excess liquidity in the banking system in 1994, the Bank of Albania has encouraged the development of the interbank market, which also provides it with a refinancing facility.

In order to expedite the transition of monetary policy towards the use of indirect instruments, in 1995 the Bank of Albania introduced a liquidity management framework. The principal objective of liquidity management is to avoid an excessive increase in the base money supply in the economy in the presence of credit ceilings. The bank has made good progress in monitoring base money developments and implementing the techniques for forecasting base money. The main instrument for controlling the monetary base and banks' excess reserves is the Bank of Albania's government credit. A yearly limit for the financing of the government budget deficit by the bank is set consistently with the imposed excess reserve targets.

Taking into account the actual economic environment and the lack of developed financial markets, the Bank of Albania has relied on administratively determined interest rates. The interest rates that state-owned commercial banks charge on deposits were determined in terms of a band until 1994, after which extreme values were binding on the banks and more recently rates were set at a minimum level. At first, lending interest rates were set at a maximum level, but in 1993, with the aim of increasing the flexibility of this variable, the Bank of Albania liberalised commercial banks' lending rates. Short-term deposit rates (three-, six-, and 12-month maturities) are given in Figure 9.2.

Figure 9.2 *Short-term deposit interest rates in Albania, July 1992 to June 1999*

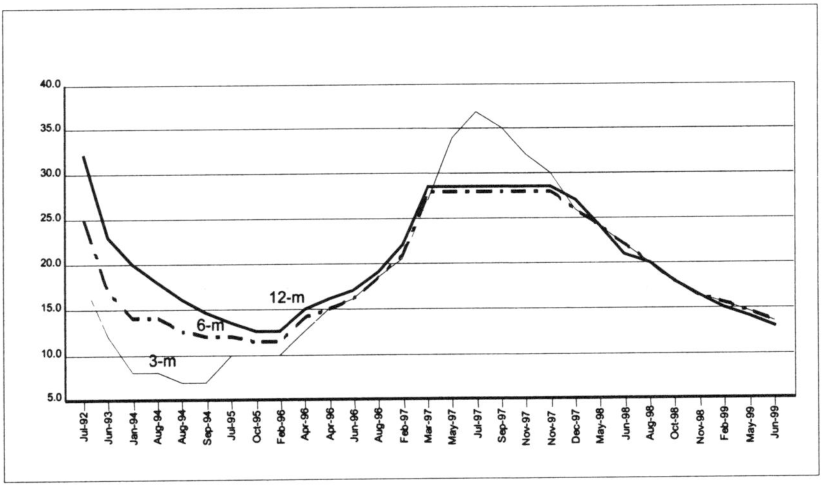

Source: Bank of Albania.

In July 1992 the Bank of Albania moved from a fixed to a flexible exchange rate regime, which excludes the necessity of interventions in the foreign exchange market. The regime was adopted in order to adjust the external imbalances of the economy. This move was prompted by the lack of sufficient foreign exchange reserves at that time. Also, as domestic demand pressures increased, domestic production was not sufficient and imports of goods have increased. The flexible exchange rate regime has proved successful in so far as the lek exchange rate has not generated any major shocks on the economy, but has been fairly stable.

During 1994 treasury bills were introduced by the Ministry of Finance to finance government deficits. The auctions for treasury bills are organised by the Bank of Albania. The introduction of treasury bills also allowed the bank to start influencing the banks' liquidity by way of open-market operations, while sales to the non-bank public help to limit the government's recourse to bank financing. Since then, treasury bill activity has been developed not only in the primary market, but also in the secondary market. With the development of the treasury bill market, bank intervention in the primary market is expected to become the main indirect monetary instrument.

The Bank of Albania has brought interest rates to positive real levels and intends to shift gradually from administered to market-determined rates. The bank recently further liberalised the exchange rate system, releasing it from any restrictions for current transactions. The exchange rate of the lek is freely determined in the domestic interbank market, which competes with an active dealer and bureau market. The exchange rate has been appreciating since early 1993. The domestically financed fiscal deficit was reduced drastically from 44 per cent of GDP in 1991 to about 8 per cent during 1994–95 and was projected to be below 5.5 per cent for 1999. By the end of 1995 the annual inflation rate slowed down to 6 per cent from 15.8 per cent in 1994 and 240 per cent in 1992. At the end of 1999, for the first time, the annual inflation rate was –1 per cent.

The Bank of Albania represents the Republic of Albania in all its banking relationships and activities with foreign states, banks and institutions. On such terms and conditions (agreed with the minister of finance) it acts as fiscal agent for the account of the government of the Republic of Albania. Through the banking system it fulfils the function of the treasury for the state budget, accepts deposits from the government and makes payments within the limits of such deposits.

The Bank of Albania is exclusively responsible for the licensing and supervision of all banks in the Republic of Albania. To that end, the bank issues such rules and regulations as are necessary to ensure the soundness of the banking system in accordance with, and to implement, the law, and also to control any office of the bank, banking books and accounts, documents of banks and those people who are engaged in licensed banking activities. It obtains such information under such forms as it may prescribe.

The Bank of Albania monitors international payments resulting from foreign trade, non-trade transactions and engagements of other Albanian banks, under contract with foreign states, banks and companies. It is authorised to open accounts on its books for, and to accept deposits from, licensed banks under such terms and conditions as it may prescribe.

The discounting and rediscounting operations of the Bank of Albania are restricted to banks that hold an account with it, and to the following securities:

- bills of exchange and promissory notes drawn or made for commercial, industrial, or agricultural purposes, bearing two or more approved signatures of which at least one is that of a licensed depository bank. Bills of exchange will mature within 182 days from the date of their acquisition by the Bank of Albania;
- securities issued by specific state organs and other securities publicly issued or guaranteed by the state, forming part of a public issue and maturing within one year of the date of their presentation to the Bank of Albania; and
- securities issued by the Bank of Albania.

Payments System in Albania

Since 1992, the Bank of Albania has considered the development in the payments system as an important area of work. Although it did not inherit any interbank payments system from former communist times, it has put much effort into creating the fundamentals of such a system.

According to the Law on the Bank of Albania, one of the basic tasks of the bank is to promote the smooth functioning of the payments system in Albania. It has the right to issue regulations in order to ensure the normal functioning of the payments system. It also offers clearing and settlement services to the banks, whereby all customers, as well as interbank, payments are processed. The Bank of Albania maintains accounts in domestic currency – the lek (which does not actually pay any interest) – for all the commercial banks operating in Albania. These accounts are unified and also include obligatory reserves. Banks are allowed to mobilise up to 5 per cent of the required reserve for effecting payments, but the weekly average account balance should at least equal the minimum required reserve.

An interbank payment order is not executed if a bank does not have sufficient funds in its account. Overdrafts are not allowed and no intraday credits are used. Banks can create the necessary liquidity mainly through the interbank market or by making use of central bank facilities. To monitor and control the daily liquidity of the markets, the Bank of Albania uses a variety of instruments such as repo (repurchase agreements) and reverse repo, open-market operations, classic interbank operations and so on. All monetary operations performed by the Bank of Albania are settled through the interbank payments system in the accounts of the banks.

Figure 9.3 *The payments system in Albania*

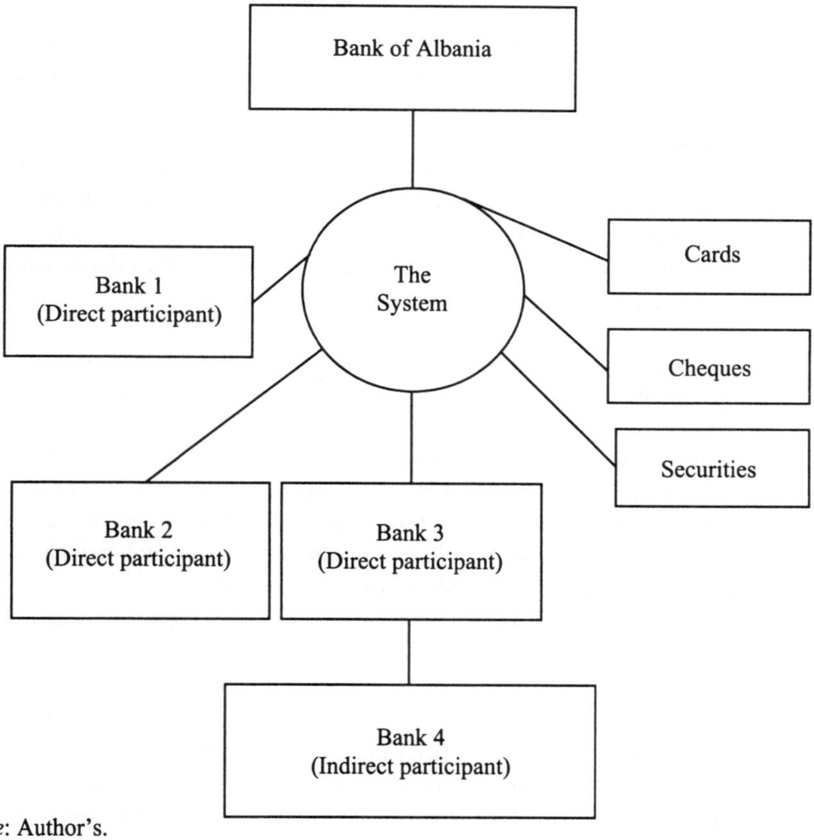

Source: Author's.

Although the current system (see Figure 9.3) represents a big change from the past payments system, it still presents many problems and inefficiencies:

- The system does not contain and offer to the banks and the Bank of Albania measures for credit, liquidity and, furthermore, systemic risk management, control or minimisation.

- The communication infrastructure in the Bank of Albania is based on the physical transport of documents and their manual processing. It is not possible for banks to have real-time account information.
- The system is not able to process rapidly and securely the payments that derive from the active participation of banks in financial and interbank markets (which are time-critical payments and timely information on their completion is crucial for effective liquidity management by the banks).
- The existing payment instruments are all paper based and are transported physically; it takes a long time for such payments to be processed and executed, increasing the risk of their use for the customers and the banks themselves.
- The state-owned banks have a low level of automatisation. Because these banks perform about 90 per cent of the volume of all payments in the banking system, it is inevitable that their inefficiency will affect the rest of the system. Even the advanced technology and infrastructure used by the private banks cannot offset this inefficiency.

However, during this period the Bank of Albania has defined its strategy for payments system reform. The main objective of the bank is to transform the payments system into a modern, efficient and reliable one, able to support the developments in the whole Albanian economy. The payments system in Albania will be similar to that in other European countries. According to the strategy, it will comprise a real-time gross settlement (RTGS) system – in the Bank of Albania – to handle high-value payments and private clearing institutions to handle small-value customer payments.

The reasons for the implementation of the RTGS system and the expected benefits are as follows:

- RTGS will provide the banks with flexibility, speed and security in processing orders, by offering real-time interbank communication, immediate execution of orders, real-time access to balances, and the possibility of prioritising and changing priorities and so on, which will therefore impact on the volume and value of transactions passing through it.
- The implementation of RTGS in the Bank of Albania must be considered a qualitative step in the efficiency of the banking system, because it will bring to it liquidity and credit-risk reduction and minimisation.
- RTGS will provide the necessary support for future projects regarding the introduction of new payment instruments in the domestic market.

The introduction of credit cards, automated clearing of cheques and so on, can be initiated only after RTGS has been implemented; this would ensure completion and final settlement of transactions of the separate clearing centres on the Bank of Albania's books.

- From the monetary policy point of view, the RTGS system would provide the support for and would guarantee the success of monetary policy interventions by the Bank of Albania.
- RTGS would create the basis for further implementation of the DVP (delivery vs payment) principle for the securities market, linking the CSD (central securities depository) and RTGS systems. This would have a big impact on the development and activity of these markets.

In a European perspective, RTGS will create one of the necessary conditions for integrating the system with the European payments system – TARGET.

FINANCIAL RESTRUCTURING OF THE BANKING SYSTEM AND INDIVIDUAL BANKS

The Albanian financial system did not manage to consolidate in the course of the 1990s although the authorities occasionally attempted to establish a regulatory and supervisory base for the participants. It should be pointed out that while the banking system (as a part of this sector) continuously changed both its regulatory base and performance, the rest of this sector, that is, financial intermediaries and subsidiaries such as pension funds, stock exchanges, broker houses and, to a certain extent, insurance companies, are still not established. This diminishes the role of the financial market significantly.

It is obvious that the progress of this system had to endure the ups and downs imposed by the economy in the transition period. But it is important that the lessons of the financial collapse in 1997 have been, and are being, taken into consideration more and more by the Bank of Albania, in its attempts to improve the legal and regulatory framework.

Albania has made considerable progress in stabilising its economy, reducing inflation, strengthening its external position and laying down the necessary conditions to speed up the transformation to a market economy with substantially improved living conditions for its citizens.

Building on this initial achievement, in 1993 a comprehensive medium-term programme of macroeconomic and structural adjustment stretching through to 1996 was adopted. The basic elements of this programme were aimed at reducing the government's role in production and employment and its interference in pricing and resource allocation. At the same time, it was aimed at establishing the proper legal and administrative framework that would encourage both private initiative and foreign direct investment.

The current state of the national banking sector and main experiences from, and obstacles to, banking reform have shown that financial sector reforms in Albania need to involve the following three sets of measures:

1. The state presence needs to be removed from the business of banking in order to foster sound banking in accordance with commercial principles (this entails privatisation or liquidation of the existing state banks).
2. There needs to be adequate regulatory and infrastructural support to ensure that the private banks (including the newly privatised banks, the existing private banks, and potential new entrants into the system) will be able to conduct banking activities in accordance with commercial principles. This includes adequate legal, judicial and political support, the need for credit discipline, sound regulations, adequate supervisory capacity and basic financial infrastructure.
3. The state banks should not be forced into quasi-fiscal activities including purchasing treasury bills at below-market rates and extending loans to public agencies.

As a first step in the implementation of the bank privatisation programme as mentioned above, the government closed the Rural Commercial Bank, the smallest of the three state banks and one that had little hope of being privatised. The government has also established a Loan Collection Agency (LCA). The LCA will be responsible for the collection of the bad-loan portfolio of the state banks. The presence of the LCA should impose some credit discipline by providing an institutional means to pursue bad debtors. In addition, the Bank of Albania and the government have severely restricted lending by the other two state-owned banks in order to minimise losses and are taking steps to prepare them for privatisation. (In early 1998, the Bank of Albania adopted a rule that only those whose bank loan arrears for more than 30 days do not exceed 20 per cent of the loan portfolio can continue lending.)

CONCLUSION: LESSONS AND THEIR RELEVANCE

In conclusion, the banking system is currently undergoing a wide-ranging reform process. A series of measures have been taken for the privatisation and liquidation of banks. Further implementation of reforms is imperative to ensure the establishment of a sound and efficient financial system. Legal and juridictional procedures should be strengthened in order to support the credit system and the enforcement of financial contracts.

Prior to 1996, attempts to restructure the banks in order to establish a functional banking system showed that state management with political criteria was not effective and failure was inevitable.

Reducing the presence and role of the state in the banks will encourage the prosperity of the private banks, thus enabling them to be transformed into credit resources for reliable clients. Although credit extended by the private banks is currently at very low levels, that extended to the private sector by the private banks has increased continuously.

From a central bank viewpoint – taking into consideration the central bank reforms and improvements – the success (limitation) in exercising its functions, especially implementation of monetary policy, is dependent on the reforms in the financial system (banking system).

The delay in the privatisation process has placed the banking system on an unequal (unbalanced) footing. The new banks have created their own credit portfolios and activities, generating profit, even though their market share is small. In addition, the delay postpones the improvement of banking infrastructure, consolidation of network and selection of activities.

Successful bank restructuring implies a comprehensive approach, addressing not only the immediate stock and flow problems of weak and insolvent banks but also correcting shortcomings in the accounting, legal and regulatory framework while improving supervision and compliance. Structural factors that stand in the way of efficient financial intermediation, such as exceedingly high reserve or liquidity requirements, interest rate controls, and distortions in the tax system (such as tax exemptions for state banks), may need to be removed.

Removing non-performing loans from bank balance sheets and transferring them to a separate loan recovery agency is an effective way of addressing the banks' stock problem. This action immediately improves bank balance sheets and it helps banks to focus attention on their core business. It does not, however, solve the banks' cash-flow problems.

BIBLIOGRAPHY

Albanian Banking Legislation, 'Law on the Bank of Albania', December 1997, 'Law on the Banking System of the Republic of Albania', July 1998.

Bank of Albania (1999), *Annual Report '98*, Tirana: Bank of Albania.

Bank of Albania, *Buletini Ekonomik* [Economic Bulletin], Tirana: Bank of Albania, various issues.

World Bank (1998), *Albania Beyond the Crisis – A Strategy for Recovery and Growth*, Washington, DC: World Bank.

10. Banking Reform in Bosnia and Herzegovina

Jean Tesche[1]

INTRODUCTION

Bosnia and Herzegovina was recognised as an independent state by the European Commission (EC) on 6 April 1992. This followed a referendum on independence, held between 29 February and 1 March 1992, in which more than 60 per cent voted and the overwhelming majority voted for independence. The referendum, however, was boycotted by the majority of Bosnian Serbs. The first contested elections in December 1990 had been won by the three main ethnically based parties: the SDA (Party of Democratic Action) for the Bosniaks (Bosnian Muslims), the SDS (Serb Democratic Party) for the Serbs and the HDZ (Croatian Democratic Union) for the Croats. Representation in the parliament was: 41 per cent Bosnian Muslim, 35 per cent Serb and 20 per cent Croat, which reflected the ethnic makeup of the major groups in Bosnia and Herzegovina. War began shortly after the referendum, and ended only when the Dayton Peace Accords were agreed to in Dayton on 21 November 1995, and signed formally in Paris on 24 December 1995.

The Dayton Peace Accords are critical to understanding the political, economic and monetary arrangements in Bosnia and Herzegovina (hereafter: BiH). They contain the constitution and deal with the military aspects of the peace, the role of the international community and that of neighbouring states, borders (with Brcko left for later arbitration), elections, refugees and displaced persons, public corporations and international policing. The Accords set up two entities: the Federation of BiH (created by the Washington Agreement to end the Croat–Muslim war in 1994 and divided into Cantons) and Republika Srpska (RS or Serb Republic). The boundaries were based on the situation in the autumn of 1995, with the Serb army occupying most of the north and east of the country, with the capital in Pale (moved to Banja Luka in early 1998), and the Federation of BiH (or Federation) divided between the parts occupied by the Bosnian army:

Sarajevo, Bihać, Zenica, Tuzla and East Mostar, among others, and the part occupied by the Bosnian Croat army (HVO – Croatian Defence Council) based in West Mostar and including much of Herzegovina.

Article 3 of the constitution states that the institutions of BiH (the state level) are responsible for: foreign policy, foreign trade and customs policies, monetary policy, international obligations, immigration, refugee return, criminal law enforcement, common and international communications, regulation of inter-entity and international transport and air traffic control. The entities have any powers and functions not explicitly given to the higher level. They are able to have parallel relations with neighbouring states that are consistent with the sovereignty of BiH and to assist the state to honour international obligations and provide a safe and secure environment. The presidency may facilitate inter-entity co-ordination in other areas if neither entity objects. Parliament is made up of two chambers, the House of Peoples and the House of Representatives, both with two-thirds representation from the Federation and one-third from the RS. The three-person presidency is made up of one representative from each of the three main ethnic groups. One is designated as the chair, and that position rotates among the three every eight months.

The two entities have separate armies, police, fiscal systems (with the exception of customs policy) and social policies. The entities finance the state budget: two-thirds from the Federation and one-third from the RS. The joint institutions of the state include a council of ministers, the parliament and the central bank. Until the new currency was introduced in June 1998, there were three separate currencies and payment systems. The RS used the Yugoslav dinar and its payment bureau was linked with Belgrade's payment system. The National Bank of BiH (NBBH) was controlled by the Bosniaks and introduced the Bosnian dinar at the end of 1993. The Croat areas used the Croatian kuna, and both parts of the Federation had their own payment bureaux, built from the former Yugoslav SDK (Payment System Administration).

Annex 10 of the Dayton Accords set up the Office of the High Representative to assist in implementation of the Accords. The high representative has been given progressively more authority over time. Although he is empowered to impose laws or replace politicians who block implementation, it is as a last resort. The high commissioner imposed new BiH-wide licence plates, with no distinction as to place of issue, the design of the new currency and the flag, as well as removing the RS president in 1999 and a number of local officials in both entities as well.

Four years after the signing of Dayton, it is clear that there are many shortcomings. However, the Peace Accords did succeed in ending the war. Although the areas of co-operation among the three groups have increased greatly, the same three political parties that won the election in 1990 are still in control, except in the RS, where a coalition which does not include the SDS is in power. All three groups have obstructed reform at different times.

The post-war economic recovery in BiH has been impressive, although mostly based on international assistance. GDP growth was nearly 50 per cent in 1996 and 40 per cent in 1997 in the Federation, and 25 per cent and 42 per cent in the RS for the same years (see Table 10.1). However, the combined GDP of the two entities in 1995 was only 24 per cent of that in the Republic of BiH in 1991 (World Bank, 1997, p. 4). In 1998 and 1999 growth has stayed above 10 per cent in both entities. Inflation has remained low in the Federation following the introduction of the Bosnian dinar in the Bosniak part after near hyperinflation in 1992 and 1993. In the RS, inflation dropped after the switch from the 'new' Yugoslav dinar in late 1998. Recovery started later in the RS, because international assistance was only made available when the new government elected in autumn 1997 was willing to implement Dayton. Unemployment is still very high in both entities. It is difficult to get a good measure of unemployment because of the extensive grey economy. Counting both unemployed and people on waiting lists at their former, mostly non-functioning, enterprises, both entities may have levels of about 50 per cent (World Bank Resident Mission, 1998 and USAID – First Quarter, 1999). Privatisation is only now starting, nearly five years after the war.

Table 10.1 *GDP of Bosnia and Herzegovina (in KM bn; KM 1 = DEM 1), 1995–1999*

	Federation BiH		RS		BiH	
	GDP	Growth %	GDP KM bn	Growth %	GDP	Growth %
1995	1.962	–	0.911	–	2.873	–
1996	3.049	46	1.140	25	4.189	46
1997	4.189	39	1.619	42	5.808	39
1998	5.133	20	1.837	14	6.970	20
1999	5.883	8	2.102	14	7.935	14

Sources: World Bank Resident Mission (1998, p. 7), CBBH (2000, p. 9), USAID 1999–Second Quarter (1999, p. 9).

Banking reform has started and the new central bank, acting as a currency board, has successfully brought in the new currency, the convertible mark (*konvertibilna marka* or KM), which is pegged 1:1 with the German mark

(DEM). This was after the high representative imposed a currency design, since the three groups could not agree. However, the banking system remains quite weak and undercapitalised. Financial reform suffers from the same problems as in other areas in BiH, the unwillingness of the main parties to co-operate. On the whole, they remain uninterested in serious economic reform.

SEQUENCE OF BANKING REFORM

Article 7 of the BiH Constitution (Annex 4 of the Dayton Peace Accords) sets up the structure of the central bank. The central banks that functioned during the war are gradually being closed down. The NBBH liquidation is nearly complete. The NBRS has been abolished in principle, with the Banking Agency of the RS (BA–RS) assuming some of its responsibilities temporarily. It has not yet started formal liquidation. All payment bureaux are scheduled for closure, at least in their current form, by the end of 2000.

In December 1996, the NBBH made the Bosnian dinar convertible for current account transactions. The Croat area used the Croatian kuna, which was also convertible for current account purposes. In the RS, the NBRS had no monetary authority since the Yugoslav dinar was used as the currency until late 1998. It is not convertible. The Federation Banking Agency (FBA) is responsible for bank licensing and supervision. In the RS, the NBRS was responsible until the BA–RS was set up in mid-1998. The central bank does not regulate commercial banks, however, a co-ordination and banking supervision committee made up of the central bank and the entity banking agencies meets regularly. They deal with all issues affecting the banking sector and encourage the harmonisation of banking legislation.

From the date of formal ratification of the Constitution of BiH in early 1996, the central bank has been the sole agency responsible for monetary policy and the issuing of currency. The governing board, with a foreign governor appointed by the International Monetary Fund (IMF) and three vice-governors, was in place by December 1996 and the 'Law on the Central Bank' was adopted in June 1997. The bank began operations in the main Sarajevo office in August 1997, and in the branches in Mostar, Pale and Banja Luka in 1998. It is to function as a currency board for its first six years.

The Federation Banking Agency started functioning in 1997, after the enabling legislation was passed in 1996. The Banking Agency of the RS has been in place from mid-1998. In the Federation the legislation to privatise banks was passed in early 1998; the RS started later, but is moving more quickly. The 11 largest banks, with nearly 90 per cent of total assets, are state owned, so privatisation will have a larger impact than in the Federation. Payment bureau reform began at the end of 1998. By the end of 1999, the

Federation had passed legislation setting up deposit insurance, which is still under consideration in the RS.

In 1996 there were 42 banks in the Federation and 11 in the RS. By mid-1999, the number had increased to 55 in the Federation and 17 plus one postal savings institution in the RS (see Table 10.2). The number is decreasing in the Federation, to 44 by the end of 1999, due to the new capital regulations and bankruptcy being enforced. In 1999, the FBA revoked two licences, and there have been five mergers. Four banks did not meet capital requirements. A total of 11 banks are under provisional administration (FBA, 1999). So far in the RS, only one bank has had its licence revoked due to insufficient capital. However, mergers and liquidations are expected this year as privatisation and the new capital requirements take effect, as happened in the Federation.

Table 10.2 *Banking system in Bosnia and Herzegovina, 1996–1999*

	FBiH mid-1996	FBiH end-1999	RS mid-1996	RS end-1999
Number of banks	42	44	11	18
Of which:				
Majority private	27	34	3	7
Majority public	15	10	8	11

Sources: World Bank (1997, p. 54), FBA (1999, p. 6).

STRUCTURE OF THE BANKING SYSTEM

In 1996 there were 53 banks licensed in BiH. Most were small; average assets were DEM 162 million. Probably 90 per cent of the assets of the old banks were non-performing (World Bank, 1997; Tomas, 1999). After write-offs, the average assets would be DEM 21 million with negative capital for the largest banks.

The total stock of assets in mid-1996 was DEM 8.23 million. If 90 per cent were non-performing, then the total stock of assets would be only DEM 1.1 billion. Total capital would be a negative DEM 6.9 billion. Most bank income is from fees, and there is little long-term lending. Most banks have less than 20–30 active loans, most of which are short-term, trade-related financing. The 23 non-private banks had 95 per cent of total assets. The largest six had 79 per cent of the total. In 1996, 76 per cent of nominal asset values were in banks in the Federation (World Bank, 1997). There are few other financial institutions besides banks.

In 1996, 30 of the 53 banks had a majority private shareholding (of which most were in the Federation, see Table 10.2). There were 23 majority non-private (of which: 15 in the Federation and eight in the RS). Some of the small banks were created from socially owned banks, such as the spin-offs from Privredna Bank, and were founded during the war to handle transfers. In the Federation, the 27 private banks had DEM 384 million in assets. In the RS, the three private banks had DEM 28 million in assets, or 5 per cent of nominal assets, 40 per cent after write-offs (World Bank, 1997). By the end of 1999, 34 out of 44 banks had majority private ownership, and seven out of 18 in the RS.

Total assets of the banking system in BiH have increased slightly since the end of 1997 (Table 10.3). These figures differ from those published by the entity banking agencies, since those include frozen foreign currency assets that are not recoverable and some on-lending that cannot be considered active assets. The bulk of bank assets are claims on enterprises with a very small, but increasing, amount (non-existent in the RS in 1997) of lending to the private sector.

Table 10.3 *Assets and demand deposits in the banking system of Bosnia and Herzegovina (in KM m.), 1997–1999*

	Federation			RS		
	1997	1998	Sept. 1999	1997	1998	Sept. 1999
Assets	2,474	2,553	2,697	603	1,036	1,020
Of which:						
Foreign	447	416	517	63	127	79
Claims on:						
Enterprises	1,630	1,649	1,587	538	898	899
Private sector	134	257	246	–	3	4
Demand deposits						
Of which:						
Domestic	235	224	299	24	76	118
Foreign	372	438	403	69	192	52
Capital	716	920	864	234	290	355

Source: CBBH (2000, pp. 100, 106).

Domestic deposits are increasing, but are still below foreign deposits. Total bank capital is increasing, but is still quite low at less than KM 1 billion in the Federation and about KM 300 million in the RS.

Bosnia and Herzegovina took responsibility for about 13 per cent of the former Yugoslavia's external debt. They concluded re-negotiations of debt servicing with the London and Paris Clubs in 1998 and 1999. Current foreign debt is over DEM 3 billion, down from 4 billion in 1997 (USAID–Third Quarter, 1999).

The Federation has one Investment Bank. The government created it to manage World Bank funds to lend to enterprises. It is not yet clear whether it will remain an investment bank, or become a commercial bank, but in either case it is to be privatised by the end of 2000. In the RS, the Development Bank is combined with the payment bureau. It is currently being split and will be privatised. The current plan is to split the payment operations to form a clearing house run first by the government, and then by the banks themselves. Then the statistical and accounting functions, as well as the Treasury, would be separated.

Lending rates vary by area. The lowest rates in the Federation are in Mostar, and the highest in Tuzla. In general, rates are higher in the RS. Short-term rates range between 6 and 60 per cent annually (with one bank in the RS reporting over 1,000 per cent in 1998). Table 10.4 shows rates in December 1998 and September 1999. Effective rates are difficult to determine both because there is little non trade-related lending, and since some of the higher rates listed are for non-performing loans. Interest rates on deposits also differ greatly: from 1 to 20 per cent, with one RS bank reporting over 1,000 per cent in 1998.

Table 10.4 *Bank loans and deposit rates in Bosnia and Herzegovina (in KM), 31 December 1998 and 30 September 1999*

	Bank lending rates Short term (%)		Bank deposit rates Demand deposits (%)	
	31–12–1998	30–9–1999	31–12–1998	30–9–1999
Federation	6.0–60.0	6.0–50.0	1.0–20.0	1.0–20.0
RS	8.0–1323.6	8.0–60.0	1.0–1022.6	1.0–7.0

Sources: CBBH (1998, pp. 85, 87, 90); (1999, pp. 114, 116, 118).

CENTRAL BANK REFORM

Article 7 of the Constitution of BiH (Annex 4 of the Dayton Peace Accords, signed on 24 December 1995 in Paris) sets out the framework for the central bank. For six years from the signing of the Constitution, the central bank is to be run by a four-person governing board, each with a six-year term. The governor is to be appointed by the IMF and must not be a citizen of BiH (the first governor was French, and the current one is from New Zealand). The other three members consist of two from the Federation, one Croat and one Bosniak, who share one vote, and one from the RS. The central bank may not extend credit by creating money during the first six years. Parliament may give it that authority after six years.

The monetary situation since 1997 is shown in Table 10.5. Both M1 and M2 have grown as the foreign exchange entering the country has increased. Foreign assets have increased somewhat, but foreign liabilities are about the same.

Table 10.5 *Money supply and foreign assets and liabilities in Bosnia and Herzegovina (in KM m.), 1997–1999*

	M1	M2	Foreign assets	Foreign liabilities
September 1997	216	971		
December 1997	252	1,178	1,158	1,514
March 1998	235	1,166	1,046	1,669
June 1998	202	1,140	994	1,640
September 1998	247	1,321	1,087	1,579
December 1998	310	1,547	1,171	1,606
March 1999	332	1,510	1,163	1,524
June 1999	378	1,608	1,269	1,555
September 1999	542	1,726	1,407	1,588

Sources: CBBH (1998, p. 85); (1999, p. 92).

Payment bureau reform is a major issue facing both entities. The current systems are not compatible with a market economy. The three bureaux are the offspring of the Yugoslav SDK system, in which they had a monopoly on all domestic payment transactions over DEM 100. A bank cannot even transfer moneys between two of its own accounts, it must be done by the payment bureau. The bureaux serve as a clearing house for banks and handle tax collection and distribution of revenues and government accounting and statistics. All businesses are required to deposit most cash with the payment bureaux at the close of each business day. Previous international efforts had attempted to unite the two Federation bureaux and facilitate transfers between entity bureaux. There was agreement at the Madrid Peace Implementation

Council meeting of December 1998 that the three payment bureaux should be phased out by the end of 2000.

FINANCIAL RESTRUCTURING OF THE BANKING SYSTEM AND INDIVIDUAL BANKS

The Federation set up the Federation Banking Agency (FBA) in June 1996, and it began functioning in 1997. In 1998 two laws were passed to set up bank privatisation: in October, the 'Law on the Privatisation of Banks' to regulate banks with more than 50 per cent social ownership and in April, the 'Law on Opening Balance Sheets of Enterprises and Banks'. These banks were to begin privatisation or liquidation by preparing opening balance sheets within six months, or by April 1999. Of the 15 original candidates which had assets greater than liabilities, seven had declared themselves to be self-privatised, but are currently being verified by the FBA. Eight are awaiting approval. When the FBA establishes that a bank is solvent, the bank then has to present a preliminary privatisation programme, and the Federation government and the FBA have 90 days to approve the programme. Banks are allowed to sell existing shares or issue new shares. Anyone with a banking licence is eligible to buy banks for sale, including foreigners.

In October 1998, the 'Law on Banks' was published in the Federation. Of the 55 banks at that time, the number had dropped to 44 by the end of 1999. Eleven are under conservatorship, of which three have been declared bankrupt and are to be liquidated, four had their licences revoked in January 2000, and three are to be liquidated in February 2000. In addition, five banks have merged, and eight more will have their licences removed. The FBA has so far taken 38 actions and allocated 13 penalties for non-compliance.

In the RS, the Banking Agency was set up and staffed by June 1998, based on the law that took effect in March 1998. Before that, the NBRS supervised banks. The state-owned banks are generally larger than the relatively inactive private banks, even after adjustments for frozen foreign currency deposits (about 85 per cent of total assets) are made. There is one postal savings bank. One of the large state-owned banks is the Development Bank, which is currently still combined with the payment bureau, but is in the process of being separated. The RS started privatisation later than the Federation, but is moving faster. All 11 state banks are to be privatised. One had claimed to have been self-privatised, but the BA–RS ruled that it was still state owned. One bank licence was revoked in December 1999. The Law on Opening Balance Sheets and on the Privatisation of Banks came into effect in July 1998. Balance sheets were to be submitted by the end of May 1999. By the end of 1999, there were 17 licensed banks and one postal savings bank. The

Banking Law was passed in July 1999, and 15 regulations similar to the Federation regulations had been issued by the end of December 1999. There have been two recent requests for new licences. There is, however, still very little lending by banks. None have the capital capacity to lend to large enterprises. There are also some International Financial Corporation (IFC), USAID, World Bank and other programmes lending to small and medium enterprises.

In the Federation, the minimum level of capital was set at DEM 5 million to be reached by 23 April 1999. It is planned to increase this to DEM 7.5 million in 2000. The 1996 Banking Law in the RS required the equivalent of USD 1.5 million capital. The new banking law of July 1999 raised this to KM 5 million effective from January 2000. On 5 October 1999, the Law on Deposit Insurance came into effect in the Federation. Deposit insurance is not yet available, but the maximum amount of insurance is to be KM 5,000. Probably fewer than ten banks will meet the requirements. Premiums are to be 0.05 per cent of eligible, or possibly total, deposits. In the RS, the Banking Agency is responsible for insurance. Legislation is in process, but has not yet been passed.

In the Federation, the FBA has developed regulations on internal and external control and audit, but they are not fully implemented as yet. There are two professional banking organisations in the Federation, of which one existed before the war and one is more recent. The RS also has a bankers' association.

CURRENT STATE OF THE NATIONAL BANKING SECTOR

Foreign banks have so far played a minor role in BiH. They face the same legal requirements as local banks, but both the general economic situation and informal resistance to foreign investment have limited their role. By the beginning of 2000, there were two foreign-owned banks in the Federation, one Turkish and the other Malaysian. Two Austrian banks began operating in BiH in the first part of 2000. One purchased shares in an existing bank, and the other, Volksbanken, has been granted a licence. It was to have started operations in July 2000. In the RS, one bank has foreign ownership, and there has been some interest shown by two groups of foreign investors, but no actual commitments have yet been made.

Progress has been made in setting up the basis for a sound financial system in BiH. However, the political problems have made progress more difficult than it needed to be. In the RS, the Banking Agency director was replaced last year. In both entities, there are questions about the ability to ensure independent operations of the banking agencies.

CONCLUSION: LESSONS AND THEIR RELEVANCE

Bosnia and Herzegovina faces three separate development problems: rebuilding after a devastating war, creating a new country and moving from a socialist to a market-oriented economy. In the last four years, it has sometimes seemed that the move to markets was the last priority, if indeed it was desirable to the leadership at all.

One of the major successes since the war has been the creation of the new central bank and the introduction of a new currency. This was done almost entirely by foreigners. The structure was laid out by the Dayton Peace Accords, the governor is a foreigner, and the high representative imposed a currency design when the entities could not agree. The banking sectors of both entities are still very weak. There is little lending and existing banks lack the capital to lend to large enterprises. The Yugoslav-era payment bureaux deprive banks of full control over their funds. Although business people recognise the need for change, the leaders of both entities are very reluctant to change the existing system.

Overall, then, although there has been substantial progress in banking reform in BiH, it is difficult to enact banking reform from the outside. If the political will is absent, progress will be slow. It may be that it would have been better to dictate the new system from the beginning, although without some local commitment, it is not clear that such a method would have worked better. Perhaps the slow combination of persuasion and experience is the only way to move a country forward in the absence of real consensus.

NOTE

1. I would like to thank George Mullinax, Greg Tabor and Dale Wilson for their assistance. The views expressed in this chapter are my own and not necessarily those of the US Treasury Department.

BIBLIOGRAPHY

Central Bank of Bosnia and Herzegovina (CBBH) (1998), *Bulletin*, No. 4, January–December, Sarajevo: Central Bank of Bosnia.

Central Bank of Bosnia and Herzegovina (CBBH) (1999), *Bulletin*, No. 3, January–September, Sarajevo: Central Bank of Bosnia.

Central Bank of Bosnia and Herzegovina (CBBH) (2000), *Bulletin*, No. 2, January–June, Sarajevo: Central Bank of Bosnia.
Federal Banking Agency (FBA) of the Federation of Bosnia and Herzegovina (1999), *Information on the Banking System of the Federation of Bosnia and Herzegovina as of 09/30/99*, Sarajevo: FBA.
Federal Office of Statistics (1999), *Statistical Yearbook Federation of Bosnia and Herzegovina 1999*, Sarajevo: Federal Statistical Office.
Federal Office of Statistics (2000), *Statistical Data on Economic and Other Trends, January Year IV*, Sarajevo: Federal Statistical Office.
Lampe, J.R. and J. Tesche (1999), 'Staying the Course: Challenges of Financial Reform in Bosnia and Herzegovina', in Ž. Šević (ed.), *Banking Reform in South East European Transitional Economies*, Sofia and London: University of Greenwich Business School, Balkan Centre for Public Policy and Related Studies and Humanities Research Center, pp. 153–62.
Tomaš, R. (1999), 'Bank Restructuring and Privatisation in Republika Srpska', in Ž. Šević (ed.), *Banking Reform in South East European Transitional Economies, op. cit.*, pp. 163–72.
US Agency for International Development, Economic Restructuring Office (1999), *BiH Economic Updates, 1999*: First Quarter, 4 April, Second Quarter, 12 July, Third Quarter, 15 October, Sarajevo: US Agency for International Development.
US Department of State (1995), *The Dayton Peace Accords: General Framework Agreement for Peace in Bosnia and Herzegovina*, Vienna: Office of Public Communication, Bureau of Public Affairs, December.
World Bank (1997), *Bosnia and Herzegovina, From Recovery to Sustainable Growth*, World Bank Country Study, May, Washington, DC: World Bank.
World Bank Resident Mission (1998), *Economic Brief for Bosnia and Herzegovina*, Sarajevo, 17 July.

11. The Banking System in Bulgaria

Guglielmo Maria Caporale, Kalin Hristov, Jeffrey B. Miller, Nickolay Nenovsky and Boris Petrov

INTRODUCTION

During the ten years since the fall of the Berlin Wall and the beginning of the economic reforms in Bulgaria there have been two periods of sharp economic decline and high inflation. The first period of economic disruption was in the early 1990s as the transformation to a market economy began. The second was a severe financial crisis in 1996–97. The banking system played a central role in both of these events.

The first event coincided with rapid changes in banking institutions as Bulgaria moved swiftly to transform the old monobanking system that existed under central planning into a two-tier banking system designed to support a market economy. While new banking institutions were created quickly, fashioning well-functioning financial institutions proved to be a more formidable task.

During the early transition period the money supply grew rapidly. Many newly formed commercial banks were poorly capitalised and the level of bad loans on their books expanded dramatically. Attempts by the government to manage these problems by recapitalising the banks largely failed. Since the banks were recapitalised by substituting government debt for bad loans on bank balance sheets, government debt increased dramatically. Bank balance sheets did not improve as commercial banks continued to make additional bad loans. With so much credit pouring into state enterprises, there was little incentive to restructure and the real sector of the economy also suffered.

Weaknesses in both government and bank balance sheets led to the financial crisis of 1996–97. The lev depreciated from 0.078 lev/USD in March 1996 to more than 2.7 lev/USD in February 1997, an increase to 34 times its original level.[1] Several banks, holding about one-third of bank assets, folded. The crisis ended when the International Monetary Fund (IMF) provided additional support and a currency board was established in July 1997.

This crisis and the establishment of the currency board were a turning point for the banking system. Under a currency board system the central bank has no discretion to conduct monetary policy. The growth rate of the money supply has decreased significantly and commercial bank balance sheets have improved. The flow of easy credit to the real sector has ceased. Indeed, since the establishment of the currency board, it has been very difficult for firms to get any credit. An important remaining question is whether the banking system can be reformed so that it becomes a reliable intermediary between savers and investors.

ECONOMIC DEVELOPMENTS IN THE 1990s

While the period of transition has been difficult for the countries in Eastern Europe, the macroeconomic performance of the Bulgarian economy has been among the weakest (see Table 11.1). After a sharp decline in output at the beginning of the transition the economy began to grow slowly in 1994. In 1996 and 1997 Bulgaria output fell once more as the financial crisis deepened. After the currency board was established in July 1997 the economy began to grow again. Initial projections for 1999 were optimistic, but the war in Kosovo created additional problems. Preliminary forecasts for 1999 show GDP increasing by 2.5 per cent. This is only the fourth year in the 1990s when output grew, and output is still far below the level achieved at the end of 1995.

The 'big bang' of freeing prices occurred in Bulgaria in February 1991. The reform process started in earnest after the elections of October 1991, when a new coalition government, including the Union of Democratic Forces (UDF), was created. Although the fundamental objective was the same as in the other countries of Central and Eastern Europe, namely ensuring a successful transition to a market economy, Bulgaria has encountered particularly severe problems.

The implementation of the reforms led at first to significant falls in output, both at the aggregate and at the sector level. In 1994 a recovery started, but it was interrupted by the 1996 crisis. It is often argued that this originated from the banking sector. It is clear, however, that the problems were more fundamental. The poor performance of the economy as a whole resulted in high levels of indebtedness of private firms. Non-profitable enterprises obtained substantial loans from the newly created banks and were then unable to repay those loans. This raised doubts about the solvency of the banking sector, undermined the confidence of investors, and eventually led to a number of bankruptcies. The question arises whether banking supervision by the authorities was adequate. The drop in economic activity did not have very high costs in terms of unemployment, but inflation sky-rocketed, and the lev depreciated sharply.

Table 11.1 *Basic economic indicators of Bulgaria, 1991–1999*

	1991	1992	1993	1994	1995	1996	1997	1998	1999
Inflation, based on: CPI[a] (%)	473.9	79.6	63.2	121.9	33.1	310.8	578.4	1.0	6.2
GDP growth	−11.7	−7.3	−1.5	1.8	2.1	−10.9	−6.9	3.5	2.4
Base interest rate[a]	54.0	41.0	52.0	72.0	34.0	180.0	6.7	5.1	4.46
Budget balance[b]	−5.3	−5.4	−11.4	−5.8	−5.7	−10.5	−3.1	1.1	−0.98
Current account[b]	−1.0	−4.2	−10.4	−0.3	−0.2	0.9	4.2	−2.0	−5.2
Trade balance (USD)	−32.0	−212.4	−885.4	−16.9	121.0	187.6	368.8	−315.6	−1064

Notes:
[a] End of period.
[b] Per cent of GDP.

Sources: Bulgarian National Bank (BNB), National Statistical Institute (NSI).

Inflation has remained a serious problem until recently. When prices were freed in February 1991 they jumped sharply and inflation for the year was 473.9 per cent. It then came down but remained at high levels. In the spring of 1994 the nominal value of the lev fell significantly and inflation surged again. Inflation declined to 33 per cent in 1995, but the onset of the financial crisis in 1996 caused it to rise dramatically, reaching 240 per cent per month in February 1997. Since then inflation has fallen continuously. Under the currency board inflation was 1 per cent in 1998 and 6.2 per cent in 1999.

Bulgaria is a small country. Total GDP in 1998 was DEM 21.6 billion (USD 12.3 billion). The foreign trade sector is important. In 1998 exports were USD 4.2 billion or approximately 35 per cent of GDP. Before the transition began Bulgaria was heavily dependent on trade with the CMEA (Council for Mutual Economic Assistance) countries, especially the Soviet Union. Over time, trade with the former Soviet Union has declined and trade with the European Union (EU) has increased. In 1998 more than half of Bulgaria's exports went to the EU, less than 5 per cent to the former Soviet Union.

Foreign investment in Bulgaria has been very low. Total foreign investment for the 1992–98 period was only USD 1.8 billion or about USD 225 per person.[2] There were several contributing factors. Bulgaria borrowed large sums in international markets during the 1980s. Unable to meet debt-service requirements, Bulgaria declared a moratorium on debt repayments in 1991. The moratorium was lifted in 1994 when negotiations with the London Club were concluded. Other factors that discouraged foreign investors were the high levels of political and economic instability. Since 1991 there have been five governments (and two provisional governments). Along with these political changes there have been many changes in the laws governing business activity.

Since the currency board was established the internal economic and political climate has improved, but the international climate has deteriorated. The financial crisis in Russia has reduced international investor interest in the region. The events in Kosovo have reinforced the perception that the Balkans is a high-risk unstable region. As a result, foreign investment has remained at low levels.

After the establishment of the currency board in 1997, earlier indications were that Bulgaria was at last on a course for a relatively rapid transition to a market economy. In 1998 the economic situation improved with GDP growing by more than 3 per cent and inflation being low. Public finances also appeared sound with a budget surplus of slightly more than 1 per cent of GDP. Growth, though, was mainly driven by domestic demand, while the current account moved from a surplus to a deficit. This deterioration in the external balance continued because of geo-political factors. The Kosovo crisis disrupted Bulgaria's export routes and reduced confidence in its economic prospects. In 1998 exports to the EU represented 50 per cent of total exports, and 15 per cent of them passed through Yugoslavia. It is estimated that re-routing trade to bypass Serbia will increase transportation costs by up to 30 per cent. Furthermore the greater perceived risk deterred foreign investors. A planned eurobond issue of USD 200 million was temporarily shelved, due to anticipated lack of demand.

Foreign direct investments (FDIs) fell from USD 504.8 million in 1997 to USD 363.9 million in 1998 as the privatisation programme slowed. Under the currency board arrangement it is crucial to offset the current account deficit with a capital account surplus, otherwise there will be further contraction of the money supply. Since the stock of foreign debt is already very high, obtaining further foreign loans has not been easy. As foreign investment can be an important vehicle for the transfer of technology, the slow trickle of foreign investment has slowed this transfer and reduced the availability of funds for privatisation.

Growth slowed somewhat in 1999; considering the problems in Kosovo this was a reasonably positive outcome. The most serious problem facing the economy is the increasing trade deficit, which rose from USD 315 million in 1998 to USD 1.064 billion in 1999. The increase in the current account deficit is smaller since there has been an improvement in the balance of services.

THE STRUCTURE OF THE BANKING SYSTEM

First Stage: The Centrally Planned Economy and the Monobank (Until 1980)

Under the centrally planned economy the Bulgarian banking system can be characterised as a state-operated monobank. The central bank combined issue and credit functions, and implemented the 'cash and credit plan' which formed part of the general economic plan. The Bulgarian National Bank (BNB) was under the direct control of the government. Besides the BNB there were only two other banking institutions, each with strictly limited functions. The State Savings Bank (SSB), established in 1951, was the only financial institution permitted to hold the accounts of private individuals. The Bulgarian Foreign Trade Bank, created in 1964, handled all foreign exchange operations.

Second Stage: Reform Efforts within the Monobank (1981–1989)

This structure remained in place until the early 1980s when the first commercial banks were formed within the state-owned one-tier banking system. In 1981 the first commercial bank, Mineralbank, was created in Bulgaria with the specific purpose of financing projects in the energy sector and the extraction industry and participating in the establishment of both domestic and foreign joint ventures.

In 1987 eight commercial banks were formed, each restricted to lending in a particular sector of the economy. These banks were: Electronica CB, Biochim CB, Autotechnica CB, Agricultural and Co-operative Bank, Construction Bank, Transport Bank and Economic Bank. The banks' shareholders were enterprises from their respective sectors of the economy. The activities of these banks were restricted to servicing their shareholders, that is, enterprises in the specific sector. The creation of sector-specific banks did not alter the monobank structure of the Bulgarian banking system since these banks were not allowed to accept deposits from or provide bank services to individuals. The liabilities of these quasi-banks included accounts of sector-specific enterprises, credits extended by the BNB and their own capital. In practice, the BNB provided funds to sector-specific commercial banks, which in turn loaned these funds to enterprises in their sector of the economy.

Third Stage: The Two-tier Banking System (After 1990)

At the end of 1989, large-scale restructuring of the Bulgarian financial and banking system began. This reflected the need to shift to a modern two-tier banking system typical of a market economy. The sector-specific banks were transformed into classical commercial banks, accepting deposits from individuals. These banks were separate legal entities, making loans to households and all sectors of the economy. The existing 59 branches of the BNB were transformed into autonomous commercial banks. The Post Bank was recreated. By early 1991 the banking system comprised the BNB, the SSB and 69 commercial banks organised as autonomous joint-stock companies (see Table 11.2).

Table 11.2 *Development of the banking system in Bulgaria, 1990–1999*

	1990	1991	1992	1993	1994	1995	1996	1997	1998	1999
No. of banks	70	53	56	37	42	44	45*	34	34	35
No. of privately owned banks	1	3	6	10	18	22	23	28	29	29
Foreign banks	0	0	0	0	2	4	7	9	10	19
Market share (assets) of largest banks (%)	n/a	77.8	74.8	81.6	78.5	74.9	67	75.4	70.4	70.2
No. of banks		6	8	13	13	7	7	7	7	7

Note: * Banks in liquidation are included.

Sources: BNB Annual Reports.

With the adoption of the Law on the Bulgarian National Bank in June 1991 the roles, objectives and functions of the BNB and the commercial banks were redefined. The new law granted the BNB substantial independence from the government and set its objectives and functions typical of modern central banks.

In 1992 the Bank Consolidation Company (BCC) was formed for the purpose of consolidating, restructuring and privatising state-owned commercial banks. The BCC was not equipped with the appropriate staff and financial resources needed to achieve its ambitious goals, especially in the area of privatisation, however, it did assist in the consolidation of several banking groups. These included the creation of United Bulgarian Bank from the merger of 22 smaller banks, and Expressbank, which represented the consolidation of 12 smaller banks.

In March of the same year the Law on Banks and Credit Activity was adopted. This law established the regulatory framework for the activities of banking institutions. Under this law, commercial banks were granted either a restricted or a full licence. Banks with a restricted licence were allowed to operate only within the national boundaries. Banks with a full licence were permitted to operate both domestically and internationally.

The BNB adopted a liberal licensing policy. By the end of 1992, there were 59 commercial banks. The large number of commercial banks and the low capitalisation levels in many banks generated banking sector consolidation. The initial stage of consolidation took place through the BCC. The first consolidated bank, United Bulgarian Bank (UBB), was formed at the end of 1992. The second wave of consolidation took place in 1993, during this period Expressbank and Hebrosbank were established. The last wave of the process of consolidation ended in 1995 with the takeover of Sofiabank by Biochim Commercial Bank.

Parallel with this initiative, the BNB pursued a policy of promoting consolidation of private commercial banks by raising minimum capital requirements. This policy did not result in the consolidation of private banks as these banks were guided by group interests and it was difficult to find common ground for consolidation.

After the process of consolidation was completed, the Bulgarian banking sector continued to be dominated by state-owned banks. This was a major reason for the severe financial crisis of 1996. During the period leading up to the crisis, commercial banks were used by the government to provide implicit subsidies in the form of credits to loss-making state-owned enterprises. Bank balance sheets were weakened further as the BNB continued to provide additional resources to the commercial banks through refinancing. Private banks also expanded their lending to many newly incorporated private companies. Quite often these loans violated the regulatory framework which was designed to maintain bank solvency by restricting the size of loans and limit loans to bank officers.

In a survey conducted in May and June 1997, Koford and Tchoegl (1999) investigated banking practices in Bulgaria. They found numerous problems. Bankers often lacked sufficient training and internal controls on bank lending decisions were weak. While banks were required to collateralise their loans, the system did not work well. Poor communication among bankers and inadequate data sources made it more difficult to identify poor credit risks. The courts were also ineffective in convicting borrowers when fraudulent behaviour led to loan defaults.

The severe bank crisis of 1996 was a logical outcome of the failure of banks to adhere to basic principles of sound commercial banking practice. During the crisis, conservators were appointed for 17 banks and bankruptcy proceedings were initiated. These 17 banks accounted for one-third of overall banking system assets.

Table 11.3 *Financial sector aggregates in Bulgaria (per cent), 1991–1999*

	1991	1992	1993	1994	1995	1996	1997	1998	1999
Reserve money/GDP	19.5	18.7	15.2	12.5	13.3	8.4	7.0	8.9	11.9
M3/GDP	57.0	60.8	63.3	63.0	61.2	44.4	24.9	28.2	32.3
M1/GDP	15.1	14.0	13.1	10.9	10.2	7.4	6.5	10.4	13.2
M2/GDP	55.0	61.2	62.0	61.6	59.8	42.8	23.7	26.8	30.4
Deposits in foreign currency/total deposits	38.9	31.2	22.4	33.5	30.1	42.0	64.3	56.7	66.5
Domestic credit/GDP	93.6	100.9	106.9	107.9	68.8	60.5	28.7	20.8	18.6
Claims on govt/GDP	25.9	32.0	42.9	57.6	31.9	25.9	11.3	4.3	0.7
Claims on private enterprises/GDP	5.5	5.6	3.5	2.4	18.5	18.4	10.2	9.6	12.2
Claims on household/GDP	n/a	n/a	n/a	n/a	0.6	0.3	0.3	1.7	2.3

Sources: BNB, NSI.

The introduction of the currency board in mid-1997 brought about radical changes in the structure of the banking system as can be seen from the figures in Table 11.3. The currency board arrangement eliminated an extremely distorted incentive system for the commercial banks. It also focused attention on the need to integrate the national banking system into the international financial system, a prerequisite for the stability of the monetary regime. A major step towards this goal was the restructuring of commercial banks through privatisation of state-owned banks and encouraging the entry of foreign banks.

In the period before 1995, a policy of restricting the presence of foreign banks had been pursued. There was concern that domestic banks would be incapable of competing with large international banks. In 1994, five years after the launch of banking sector reform, two foreign banks started operations in Bulgaria (Xios and ING Bank). In 1995 two more foreign banks, BNP-Dresdner Bank and Ionian Bank opened branches. By the end of 1999 more than half of the 35 banks operating in the country were foreign banks or banks with foreign stakes.[3]

THE BULGARIAN NATIONAL BANK

Brief History of the BNB

In January 1999 the BNB celebrated its 120th anniversary.[4] The first governor of the BNB, appointed in 1897, was an official in the Ministry of Finance in Russia. Initially the BNB had no power to issue banknotes, and it struggled financially. National coins of other countries were the principal medium of exchange in Bulgaria. The BNB failed in its attempt to issue gold-backed banknotes in 1885. In these early years the lack of sufficient gold reserves made it difficult for Bulgaria to adhere strictly to the gold standard.

The First World War brought on pressures to finance war expenditures by issuing fiat money. After the war, Bulgaria struggled with attempts to return to the gold standard and in the early 1930s faced a crisis when there was massive flight from the currency. This flight forced a moratorium on foreign debt payments.[5]

During the Second World War the BNB again financed government wartime expenditures. After the war there was high inflation and commodity shortages. In 1947 the financial system in Bulgaria was reorganised to become part of the centrally planned economy. The BNB became a 'monobank' with branches throughout the country.

After the creation of a two-tier banking system in 1989, the Law on the Bulgarian National Bank (1991) and the Law on Banks and Credit Activity (1992) were passed. These laws defined the role of the BNB. The BNB was charged with carrying out monetary policy and regulating the commercial banking system. During the period leading up to the financial crisis in 1996, important weaknesses were revealed. Two problems stand out. The law provided for an independent central bank, but the BNB was not able to resist political pressures. Second, while the BNB regulated the banking system, many difficulties arose when the BNB tried to close insolvent banks.

At the beginning of the transition the hard currency reserves of the BNB were small. A floating exchange system was adopted, but there was extensive intervention by the BNB on the foreign exchange market. Between February 1991 and the beginning of the financial crisis in 1996 the nominal level of the lev depreciated slowly. The one exception to reasonable stability was in 1994 when the nominal exchange depreciated by about 50 per cent. This was due to the very high inflation rates, and the real exchange appreciated during most of this period.

The BNB had several instruments to control the supply of credit. In the early 1990s the most important instrument was a credit ceiling. After the market for government securities markets developed, credit ceilings were abandoned and the BNB tried to control the level of bank reserves using open-market operations.

Political pressures led to a rapidly growing money supply. The pressure or monetary growth operated through two main channels. The government needed to finance large fiscal deficits. Second, public concern that closing state enterprises would lead to layoffs, created pressure to support these enterprises with bank loans. The BNB supported this process by refinancing the commercial banks.[6]

Supervision and regulation of the commercial banks was also problematic for the BNB. The BNB had the legal right to license banks, however, it did not have the power to liquidate banks when they became insolvent. In the early 1990s the BNB had difficulty forcing banks to close as the banks appealed the BNB's decisions in the courts.

In response to the financial crisis of 1996–99, the IMF pressured Bulgaria to establish a currency board. The establishment of the currency board created dramatic changes in the financial system. The new Law on the Bulgarian National Bank (1997), which established the currency board, fixed the nominal exchange rate and limited the discretion of the BNB to alter the money supply.

The establishment of the currency board reduced the growth rates of the money supply. Before the currency crisis in 1996, the money supply grew at a compound annual rate of 64 per cent. In 1996 and 1997 the money supply exploded, but in the two years after the establishment of the currency board in July 1997, the money supply was growing at 15 per cent per annum.

The regulatory power of the BNB was also expanded under the 1997 laws. The BNB can now revoke a banking licence and close a bank. Neither the bank nor the courts can really contest this decision. The BNB used these new powers to place 17 banks, holding 25 per cent of banking system assets, in receivership (OECD, 1999, p. 33).

Payment Systems and Clearing Facilities

The evolution of the settlement system in Bulgaria passed through several stages. At the beginning of the transition to a market economy, the BNB and the commercial banks established a joint-stock company, Bankservice AD. The year 1992 saw the establishment of a banking integrated system for electronic transfers (BISERA). In essence this is an interbank settlement system functioning on the DTGS (designated time gross settlement) principle. The date for effectively settling payments is T+1. All interbank payments in levs within the national banking system are cleared through the BISERA system. The number of payments has grown rapidly (see Table 11.4) and the system has operated smoothly even in extreme situations like the 1996 banking crisis.

Table 11.4 *Payments in Bulgaria handled by BISERA (in thousand lev), 1993–1999*

	1993	1994	1995	1996	1997	1998	1999
BISERA (total)	4,059	8,610	10,282	10,324	10,176	13,226	16,248
Credit transfers	3,537	7,609	9,112	9,136	8,783	10,509	13,779
Direct debits	522	1,002	1,168	1,175	1,093	1,275	1,211
Card payments	n/a	n/a	n/a	11.62	298.37	154	67*
Cheques	n/a	n/a	0.75	1.15	0.35	86	68
Letters of credit	n/a	n/a	0.99	1.09	0.47	195	n/a

Note::* Data are not comparable because of a change in the accounting methodology.

Source: Bankservice Ltd.

In spite of the changes in the monetary system in mid-1997 the need for more efficient and safer liquidity management became apparent. Evidence of this need was the sizeable overhang of excess reserves maintained by commercial banks with the BNB. For this reason the BNB initiated a project to design a real time gross settlement system, BISERA 4, which is due to commence operations before the end of 2000. The new system will make it possible for commercial banks to reduce their reserve positions.

BANKING SUPERVISION, ACCOUNTING AND DEPOSIT INSURANCE

Banking Supervision

With the adoption of the Law on the Bulgarian National Bank in 1991 the central bank was given responsibility as the supervisor of commercial banks, brokerage financial houses and exchange bureaux. Major BNB supervisory powers included granting of licences for conducting banking operations, adopting regulations, and carrying out both off-site and on-site audits. In the case of violations the BNB was granted the power to appoint conservators and ultimately, to revoke licences. The new laws passed in 1997 brought the Bulgarian law into closer conformity with EU legislation and gave the BNB better control of the regulatory process.

Under a currency board arrangement there are strict limitations on refinancing. This has necessitated the adoption of stricter supervisory requirements for commercial banks. To strengthen confidence much higher minimum capital adequacy, liquidity and asset classification requirements were set. The general capital adequacy ratio was gradually raised from 8 per cent in 1997 to 10 per cent and ultimately to 12 per cent. Open foreign currency positions of banks were also altered. The commercial banks are not required to hold a percentage of their foreign currency assets in the reserve currency (euro). The ceiling for the other foreign currency assets is 25 per cent of their equity.

Accounting

Until mid-1995 there was no uniform standard of accounts for the banking system. Commercial banks, the SSB and Bulbank (former Foreign Trade Bank) applied three different accounting systems. It was not until June 1995 that uniform accounting standards for the whole banking system were adopted. Although this was a serious step forward, a number of weaknesses in their practical implementation remained.

Weaknesses reflected the disparity between national and international standards, for example, under the law effective in 1995 government securities were recorded in commercial bank portfolios at their face value even though the market value of these assets was less than half that value. This disparity concealed the actual state of bank assets. This proved to be a time bomb. The financial position of the banks at the time of the crisis was much weaker than had generally been understood.

In 1997, following the crisis, accounting legislation was modified so that it complies fully with international accounting standards and EU directives.

Deposit Insurance

Although the public may have implicitly believed there was some form of deposit insurance, there was no formal insurance arrangement during the early 1990s. At the end of 1995 the Managing Board of the BNB adopted a regulation for banks to contribute to a special insurance fund managed by the BNB. When the 1996 banking crisis stormed through the banking system, the resources of this fund proved insufficient.

A law protecting deposits at insolvent commercial banks was quickly passed in May 1996. Although the government budget situation did not allow for further increases in domestic debt, the law was passed to avoid public discontent. The new law covered 100 per cent of deposit losses of individuals and 50 per cent of deposit losses of legal entities. Under this law the government issued government securities denominated in national and foreign currencies to solvent banks which took over insolvent banks and committed to repay deposits of the failed banks.

In 1997 when the currency board was introduced, the Law on Bank Deposit Insurance was passed. A special deposit insurance fund in levs and foreign currency was established. Commercial banks make mandatory annual premium contributions of 0.5 per cent of their deposit base on 31 December, 1995 per cent of deposits up to 2,000 levs are guaranteed. Eighty per cent of deposits from 2,000 to 5,000 levs are guaranteed. The law also mandates that the insurance agency exercise restricted supervisory powers over the commercial banks.

FINANCIAL SYSTEM RESTRUCTURING

In addition to the institutional restructuring that was a necessary part of the movement to a market economy, the Bulgarian banking system also had to manage a legacy of bad debts that was carried over from the communist period. These were 'loans' made to state enterprises during the communist period under a system where the expectations about repayment were very different. Once these loans became accounting entries on the balance sheets of newly formed commercial banks, they took on a different meaning.

While some of the debts were effectively wiped out during the high inflation of the early 1990s, many of the loans were denominated in foreign currency. These were loans from foreign banks to the government and then recorded internally as foreign currency loans from the BNB to state enterprises. The inflation, instead of reducing the burden on state enterprises, actually increased it.

The bad-debt problem was exacerbated by new loans that state-owned banks made to state enterprises and by private bank loans to private firms. These conditions led to an environment where 'until 1996, commercial credit was expanded to the non-financial sector in Bulgaria to a degree that was unprecedented relative to any other European transition economy' (OECD, 1999, p. 32). This flow of credit was finally reduced after the financial crisis and the establishment of the currency board.

Origins of the Bad-debt Problems

Attempts at banking system restructuring date back to the period of central planning. The BNB exercised financial control over enterprises through its numerous branches. During this period BNB credit policy was entirely directed at execution of the credit and cash plan. Enterprises in the centrally planned economy had no funds of their own and were entirely dependent on credits. This made them 'hostages' to the government's credit policy and unprofitable because of the artificially maintained low prices. *De facto* these enterprises were placed under soft-budget constraints. In this setting, by the end of 1986, enterprises had accumulated a huge investment credit overhang. At the beginning of 1987 the first rehabilitation effort began. The government undertook to reschedule, until 1990, overdue investment credits of the industrial enterprises accumulated since 1986 and to service accrued interest. The same operation was applied with respect to agricultural organisations, but their credits were rescheduled until the end of 1992. The result was that the burden of non-performing credits was assumed by the government through the BNB and Bulbank which processed the expanding foreign debt.

Programmes to Manage the Bad-debt Problems

The issue of bank rehabilitation was on the agenda again in 1990 when the newly transformed autonomous commercial banks inherited these bad debts. The problem was even more acute for the commercial banks due to their low capitalisation. Measures moved along two lines. First, through the Bank Consolidation Corporation (established in 1992), steps were taken to consolidate the commercial banks into several banking groups (see above). Consolidation created a higher concentration of assets in state-owned banks and the number of private banks grew rapidly, especially during the 1993–95 period. Thus the attempt to create an internationally competitive banking system comprising a small number of large-scale banks failed.

A second approach to the bad-debt problems was the adoption of a sequence of statutory instruments which provided for the conversion of the bad debt into long-term government bonds denominated in levs and US dollars (so-called ZUNK bonds). The government for its part assumed responsibility for the management of commercial bank debt. These programmes were always limited in scope since the government was not prepared to take on such large additional indebtedness

The financial restructuring scheme had several major weaknesses. To be successful, it was important that the programme be perceived as a single unique event. Otherwise there would be a moral hazard problem. If banks believed that they would be bailed out again, there was an incentive for them to recreate the problem by making additional bad loans. Unfortunately the problem was recreated, as Table 11.5 illustrates.

Table 11.5 *Credit portfolio of Bulgarian commercial banks, 1993–1999 (in per cent)*

	1993	1994	1995	1996*
Standard	7.61	17.69	25.91	43.67
Doubtful group A	82.75	66.88	54.55	33.89
Doubtful group B	2.19	3.46	4.18	10.67
Loss	7.45	11.97	15.35	11.77
Provisions available	7.18	23.58	23.74	105.42

	1997*	1998*	1999*
Standard	58.2	69.0	73.3
Watch	8.6	10.0	9.3
Substandard	5.9	5.6	2.2
Doubtful	4.7	1.7	3.3
Loss	22.7	13.6	12.0

Note: * Banks in liquidation are excluded.

Source: BNB.

In addition the government, which acquired the bad-debt claims, did not create an efficient operating structure to administer and collect the accumulated claims. This problem was dealt with in 1999 when a specialised agency for collecting government claims was established.

In March 1996, in a desperate attempt to recapitalise several state-owned commercial banks, a new operation was launched. The Ministry of Finance paid Bulbank USD 200 million for ZUNK bonds with a face value of USD 400 million. The securities were then distributed by the BCC as capital contributions to the banks under BCC control.

In parallel with the bank rehabilitation operation the government undertook a number of measures for the rehabilitation of real sector enterprises in the second half of 1996. Loss-making and insolvent enterprises were either restructured or liquidated. All enterprises undergoing restructuring were prevented from receiving new credits from commercial banks. This put an end to the long practice of quasi-subsidising enterprises. The operation had a favourable effect on commercial bank balance sheets and prepared the ground for the next stage of the rehabilitation of commercial bank portfolios.

In 1997, immediately before the introduction of the currency board, the government launched a new operation for the recapitalisation of Biochim CB. The operation involved the buyback from Biochim CB of ZUNK bonds (which were selling at values much less than face value) with a face value of USD 50 million. The government then issued 18-month government securities that were purchased by Bulbank.

CURRENT STATE OF THE FINANCIAL SECTOR

The situation in the financial sector of the Bulgarian economy changed radically in 1997 with the creation of the currency board, the isolation of failing state enterprises and new efforts to privatise the banking system. The first stage of the voucher privatisation auctions were also completed in 1997. Given that citizens now had shares in nearly one thousand former state enterprises, there was pressure to create a stock exchange. More attention was also focused on developing better pension arrangements and improving the laws regulating insurance companies.

Currency Board

The creation of a currency board with a fixed exchange rate of one lev to the German mark, was established on 1 July 1997. The new institutional arrangements proved extremely successful, and a new three-year stand-by arrangement (lasting until the year 2001) was negotiated with the IMF in mid-1998. On 1 January 1999 the German mark was replaced by the euro as the currency against which the exchange rate was fixed (without any change in nominal valuation versus the German mark).

During the economic crisis of 1996 and 1997 neither monetary nor fiscal policy had proved to be effective. The BNB was constantly bailing out banks on the verge of bankruptcy, and the fiscal authorities had to cope with an increasingly heavy burden of servicing the debt. By 1996 government interest payments on this debt were 17 per cent of GDP. The banks are no longer being refinanced by the BNB in the event of a liquidity crisis. However the

BNB still has access to IMF funding for the possible extension of a loan to the Ministry of Finance, and still has a banking department with a limited refinancing facility which can be used in an emergency (systemic risk). Finally it was decided that the government should hold the majority of its surplus accounts with the BNB (rather than commercial banks). This reduces the volatility of the monetary base when IMF tranches are received or foreign debt payments are made.[7]

Since the introduction of the currency board, money supply growth has been linked to balance of payments movements and inflation has dropped sharply, reflecting the revised expectations of agents. It was debated at the time whether an exchange rate of one lev to the German mark was optimal, some economists arguing that a further devaluation would be beneficial in terms of competitiveness, others expressing concern about the possibility of stronger inflationary pressures. In fact, after initially being higher than forecast, inflation has been reduced to acceptable levels.

Progress has been considerable under the currency board. In the first two years its reserves doubled, and there have been clear benefits in terms of macroeconomic stability and transparency of economic policy. In particular, the achievements on the fiscal consolidation front have been impressive, with sizeable reductions in interest payments, budget deficits were very small in 1998 and 1999 (see Table 11.6).

Table 11.6 *Budget deficit and debt ratios in Bulgaria (per cent of GDP), 1991–1999*

	1991	1992	1993	1994	1995	1996	1997	1998	1999
Budget deficit/ GDP	–5.3	–5.4	–10.9	–5.8	–5.7	–10.5	–3.1	–1.1	–0.98
Domestic debt/GDP	n/a	n/a	n/a	n/a	n/a	60	26	14	13
Foreign debt/ GDP	n/a	n/a	n/a	n/a	n/a	91	81	72	71
Total debt/GDP	n/a	n/a	n/a	n/a	n/a	152	107	87	84

Sources: BNB Annual Reports.

Bank Privatisation

Under the currency board, the Issue Department of the BNB is allowed to hold only foreign (but not domestic) assets and is committed to buying and selling foreign or domestic currency at the fixed exchange rate. As a result the BNB is no longer able to control the money supply and the supply of domestic currency is now determined by demand at the existing exchange rate, with foreign currency reserves always being sufficient to sustain it. The implication for the fiscal authorities is that the deficit can be financed only through external borrowing or the sale of state assets. This obviously entails more fiscal discipline and a strengthening in the fiscal position.

Another area where there has been substantial change in the last two years is the privatisation of the banking system, largely to foreign interests. Rather than seeing foreign banks as unfair competition, the entry of foreign banks is now seen as a way to increase training, bringing in more expertise and improving the overall functioning of the commercial banking system. Prior to 1996 bank privatisation was supposed to be undertaken under the direction of the BCC, but this method was perceived to be subject to political influence rather than a means of enhancing competitiveness in the economy; for this reason the BCC did not pursue any concrete measures to accelerate the process. The year 1997 marked a turning point because it was then that the first privatisation deal was concluded. Most of the shares of UBB, the third largest bank, were sold to the Oppenheimer Group and the EBRD. In 1998 four state-owned banks were prepared for privatisation. One of them, Bulgarian Post Bank, was sold in the last quarter of 1998 to a consortium led by American Insurance Group. In 1999 two other big state-owned banks, Expressbank-Varna and Hebrosbank-Plovdiv, were purchased by Société Générale and the Regent Pacific Group, respectively. Bulbank and Biochim CB are due to be privatised in 2000.[8]

The government's programme envisages the privatisation process in the banking sector to be completed by mid-2001 with the sale of the SSB. The comparatively long preparation period for the privatisation of the SSB is driven by the necessity to restructure the SSB from a purely savings bank into a commercial bank.

The Growth of Non-bank Financial Institutions

Since mid-1997 non-bank financial institutions have expanded their operations, but they are still relatively small and do not pose serious competition to the banks.

Before the financial crisis, activity on the stock exchanges was extremely small and the exchanges closed during the crisis. Following the mass privatisation programme of 1996–97, the equity markets expanded. Unlike the Czechs, who deliberately attempted to minimise supervision of the equity markets, the Bulgarian authorities established three important institutions to regulate the market. The Bulgarian Stock Exchange–Sofia (BSE–Sofia) was organised as a semi-private institution to facilitate trading in shares, mostly from the mass privatisation programme. A Central Depository Institution

(CD) was established to register transfers and shareholding in privatised companies. The Securities and Stock Exchange Commission (SSEC) was created as the regulatory body to oversee the operations of the securities market.

In spite of efforts to create a well-regulated securities market, serious problems remain. BSE–Sofia suffers from very low trading levels, and as a result, there is little price integrity. Potential investors are likely to be discouraged in such an environment.

Insurance companies and pension funds are relatively small at present, but they will become increasingly important in the future. In 1998 the insurance sector underwent a fundamental restructuring. The Insurance Supervision Directorate undertook licensing of insurance companies in accordance with new amendments to the Law on Insurance. A number of insurance companies could not meet the new capitalisation requirements, and the new requirements regarding the origin of capital, and legitimacy of the activity of major shareholders. As a result the sector has been significantly restructured.[9]

At present, 16 general insurance companies and six life insurance companies are in operation. The sector is highly concentrated with three companies dominating the industry. Total revenues from insurance premiums were 1.27 per cent of GDP in 1997 and 1.18 per cent of GDP in 1998.

Private pension plans are not very important. Voluntary pension funds emerged first in early 1994. These funds began operations without any specific regulation or legal basis. At the beginning of 1999 there were 30 (all private) registered pension funds in Bulgaria, but only 12 were actually in operation. It is estimated that pension funds have attracted about 200,000–250,000 people, or about 6–8 per cent of the total number of employed people. In July 1999 the Law on Supplementary Pension Insurance (LSPI) was passed. Pension funds must now be licenced by the State Agency of Insurance Supervision (SAIS) – a new body established under the LSPI. This agency will supervise the activity of pension funds and pension companies.

CONCLUSION

The economic transition of the 1990s has been very difficult for Bulgaria. The movement to a two-tier banking system was swift, but this organisational change masked many operational difficulties. The system looked like a two-tier banking system, but this was really a façade. The banking system did not function like a Western capitalist financial system. The banks were a conduit for financing government deficits and providing quasi-subsidies to state enterprises and private firms.

This intermediate phase came to an end with the financial crisis in 1996. The establishment of the currency board changed everything. It limited the discretion of government policy makers and helped created hard-budget constraints for state enterprises. The era of large government deficits and quasi-subsidies ended.

There is still much to be done. Banks still do not function well as intermediaries. Credit, even for worthwhile business ventures, is scarce. Despite the fact that there is greater macroeconomic stability under the currency board, the business environment is still very risky. Bank officials need more training and more experience in evaluating credit risks. It is hoped that by bringing in more foreign banks this problem can be solved.

While serious challenges remain, the establishment of the currency board and the concurrent changes in the commercial banks form an important positive change of direction. If these changes can support further restructuring of enterprises and the growth of new businesses, the prospects for future economic growth will be much brighter.

NOTES

1. Because of the dramatic nominal depreciation in the lev in 1996–97, it was re-denominated in July 1999. One new lev is equal to 1000 old levs. To maintain consistency, all values in the chapter are stated in new levs.
2. Total foreign investment for 1999 is expected to be USD 600–700 million or about USD 72–84 per person. Total foreign investment includes privatisation, capital market, green field and reinvestment (Agency for Foreign Investment).
3. At the end of 1999, 48.3 per cent of banking system assets are concentrated in state-owned commercial banks, 41.1 per cent in foreign banks and the remaining 10.6 per cent in private Bulgarian banks.
4. The description of the early history of the Bulgarian National Bank is drawn from Avramov et al. (1999).
5. See also Nenovsky and Petrov (1999).
6. See Christov (1997) for an analysis of the independence question. He argues that while the laws were designed to support independence, in practice the BNB was not able to resist the political pressure.
7. See OECD (1999), Nenovsky and Hristov (1998) and Miller (1999) for more details on the currency board arrangement.
8. At the time of writing (May 2000), there were three bidders for Biochim, all from the local banking community. The expectation was that the bank would be sold by the end of June. Three Western European investors have expressed interest in purchasing Bulbank. Completion of the sale is expected by the end of 2000.
9. An important motivation for the new law was a desire to put pressure on mafia groups that were masquerading as insurance companies.

BIBLIOGRAPHY

Avramov, R., V. Dimitrov, L. Dimova, B. Petrov, H. Yanovski, and G. Vandalova (1999), *Bulgarian National Bank 1879–1999*, Sofia: Bulgarian National Bank.

Bulgarian National Bank, *Annual Report*, 1990–1998, Sofia: Bulgarian National Bank.

Bulgarian National Bank (1996a), 'Monetary Policy in the Transition', Conference, Borovetz, Bulgaria, 25–27 April.

Bulgarian National Bank (1996b), 'Banking System Restructuring: A Step Toward Integration with the European Union', Conference 26–28 June, Sofia: Bulgarian National Bank.

Christov, L. (1997), 'A Role for an Independent Central Bank in Transition? The Case of Bulgaria', in Derek Jones and Jeffrey B. Miller (eds), *The Bulgarian Economy: Lesson from Reform during Early Transition*, Aldershot: Ashgate, pp. 129–60.

European Bank for Reconstruction and Development (EBRD) (1998), *Transition Report*, London: EBRD .

European Bank for Reconstruction and Development (EBRD) (1999), *Bulgaria Country Profile*, London: EBRD.

Gros, D. and A. Steinherr (1995), *Winds of Change – Economic Transition in Central and Eastern Europe*, London: Longman.

Hilfe, *Daily Brief*, various issues.

Koford, K. and A. Tchoegl (1999), 'Problems of Bank Lending in Bulgaria: Information Asymmetry and Institutional Learning', *Moct-Most*, **9**, 123–51.

Koparanova, M. (ed.) (1997), *Emerging Capital Markets in a Transitional Environment*, Sofia, Anko Ltd.

Miller, J. (1993), *The Bulgarian Banking System*, Sofia: Bulgarian National Bank.

Miller, J. (1999), 'The Currency Board in Bulgaria: The First Two Years', Bulgarian National Bank Discussion Paper, DP/11/99, Sofia: Bulgarian National Bank.

Miller, J. and S. Petranov (1995), *Banking in the Bulgarian Economy*, Sofia: Bulgarian National Bank.

Nenovsky, N. and K. Hristov (1998), 'Financial Repression and Credit Rationing under Currency Board Arrangement for Bulgaria', Bulgarian National Bank Discussion Paper, DP/2/98, Sofia: Bulgarian National Bank.

Nenovsky, N. and B. Petrov (1999), 'Monetary Sector Modelling in Bulgaria, 1913–1945', Bulgarian National Bank Discussion Paper, DP/5/99, Sofia: Bulgarian National Bank.

Organisation for Economic Cooperation and Development (OECD) (1997), *Economic Survey of Bulgaria, 1997*, Paris: OECD.

Organisation for Economic Cooperation and Development (OECD) (1999), *Economic Survey of Bulgaria, 1999*, Paris: OECD.

Oxford Analytica, *East Europe Daily Brief*, various issues.

Yotzov, V., N. Nenovsky, I. Petrova, K. Hristov and B. Petrov (1998), 'The First Year of the Currency Board in Bulgaria', Bulgarian National Bank Discussion Paper DP/1/99, Sofia: Bulgarian National Bank.

12. Reforming the Banking System in Croatia and its Broader Macroeconomic Environment

Radmila Jovančević

INTRODUCTION

The Croatian economy is burdened with numerous problems. In 1998, GDP reached 84 per cent of its 1990 level. After a sudden decrease of GDP in the 1990–93 period, the Croatian economy had an average increase of 6.3 per cent annually from 1994 to 1997. In 1998 GDP growth amounted to only 2.3 per cent, while a negative growth rate of –1 per cent occurred in 1999. The 1998 industrial production level amounted to only 64 per cent of the 1990 level, and in 1999 was 2 per cent lower than in the previous year.

Foreign trade shows an exceptionally high increase in imports, whereas exports have remained stagnant (USD 4.3 billion annually). This sector of the economy accounts for about one-fifth of the aggregate demand for domestic goods and services. The coverage of exports by imports (merely 53 per cent in 1998) has resulted in a huge foreign trade deficit amounting to more than USD 4 billion annually in the 1995–98 period, and USD 1.6 billion in the first half of 1999.

Part of the trade deficit is covered by a surplus in services: the main credit earner was tourism (travel). The foreign currency inflows from the export of services in tourism amounted to USD 2.7 billion in 1998, or 68.8 per cent of the total receipts from services in 1998. Tourism results were poorer in 1999 due to the negative consequences of the Kosovo crisis. Revenue from other services over the past two years has been falling slowly (owing to the crisis in international shipping fares) which has caused stagnation in this once active segment of the Croatian balance of payments.

These trends have resulted in a high deficit in the current account. In 1997 the current account deficit reached its highest level at USD 2.34 billion. It decreased to USD 1.54 billion in 1998, and remained at the same level in the first nine months of 1999. The current account deficit amounted to 4.5 per cent of GDP in 1996, and reached 12 per cent of GDP in 1997, dropping to 7.5 per cent of GDP in 1998, and then to 7.1 per cent of GDP in 1999 (see Table 12.1). This deficit in the liquid payment balance has been covered in the last few years (1996–98) through the sale of shares in Croatian companies to foreign entities (portfolio investments – USD 1.3 billion), the direct investment of foreign capital (foreign direct investment – USD 1.6 billion) and by the growing indebtedness of Croatia to foreign entities (other investment – USD 4.4 billion).

Table 12.1 *Main economic indicators of the Croatian economy, 1994–1999*

	1994	1995	1996	1997	1998	1999
Nominal GDP (USD bn)	14.6	18.8	19.9	20.0	21.3	21.0
Real GDP (USD bn)	5.9	6.8	6.0	6.5	2.3	–1.0
Real industrial production	–2.7	0.3	3.1	6.8	3.7	–2.0
Real private consumption	13.2	12.5	8.9	11.0	3.5	–2.0
Real gross fixed investment	16.1	–25.1	15.0	12.0	2.5	–2.0
Consumer prices (% change)	–3.0	3.7	3.4	3.8	5.4	4.2
Producer prices (% change)	77.6	1.6	1.5	1.6	–2.1	2.5
Broad money (M2) (in %)	90.7	16.9	37.5	25.8	9.6	–5.9
Unemployment rate (in %)	14.8	14.5	16.4	17.5	17.6	19.2
Merchandise exports (USD bn)	4.3	4.6	4.5	4.2	4.6	4.3
Merchandise imports (USD bn)	5.4	7.9	8.2	9.4	8.8	7.8
Trade balance (USD bn)	–1.0	–3.3	–3.7	–5.2	–4.2	–3.5
Current account (USD bn)	0.8	–1.3	–0.9	–2.4	–1.6	–1.5
Gross foreign debt (USD bn)	2.8	3.3	4.8	6.7	8.5	9.5
Gross foreign debt (% of GDP)	21.0	17.5	24.1	33.5	38.5	45.2
Budget balance (% of GDP)	1.7	–0.9	–0.5	–1.3	0.5	–2.7
Interest rate (avg. annual, %)		20.3	22.5	15.5	15.8	16.5

Sources: *The Croatian National Bank Bulletin*, No. 37, 1999; CROSTAT, *Monthly Statistical Report*, 4/1999; Ministry of Finance, *Monthly Statistical Review*, March 2000.

Croatia's foreign debt has almost quadrupled in the period under analysis, growing from USD 2.5 billion in 1993 to USD 9.5 billion at the end of 1999. The total outstanding debt of Croatia, which surpassed USD 9.3 billion in the autumn of 1999 corresponds to 45 per cent of the country's GDP (it was only 21 per cent in 1994). A sizeable portion of foreign loans has been allocated for infrastructure projects (roads, bridges, and so on) which might cause some difficulties in repayment since the inflow of foreign currency from these projects will be gradual and indirect. The official calculation of the future payment of medium- and long-term foreign debts shows that repayment levels will rise in 2000 and 2001. This situation will demand an extensive effort to launch the export of goods and services in order to service these obligations successfully. Foreign-debt servicing in 2000 and 2001 will be in the region of USD 1.8 billion annually, that is, five times higher than in 1999 when it amounted to USD 274 million. In lieu of this, it seems that the rescheduling of these debts will be necessary in the near future.

THE SEQUENCE OF BANKING REFORM IN CROATIA

The dynamic developments in Croatia after the Second World War (in the period from 1952 to 1989 the average annual GDP growth rate was 4.6 per cent) entailed the development of a banking system since the entire system was destroyed in the period between 1945 and 1948. Not a single bank founded before 1945 continued its business operations. The establishment of new banks was a lengthy and extremely difficult process. It should be emphasised that the monobanking system, which was so common among socialist economies, was broken up in Croatia in the mid-1960s. Thus Croatia's commercial banks have operated separately from the central banking system and from direct government control for a considerably longer period than other transition countries. Nevertheless, under the socialist system Croatian banks were exposed to strong social and political influences. It was after 1974, with the introduction of the new constitution and the Associated Labour Act (which created a special type of self-managed community and firm), that the growth of the banking system found itself on its specific course. The banks were organised as 'Basic Organisations of Associated Labour' according to the law of 1977. There were three types of banks: internal banks, basic banks and associated banks.[1] According to statistical data, in 1985 there were about 107 banking institutions in Croatia. Of these, 37 were so-called 'internal banks' in large enterprises; 46 were 'basic banks'; one was an 'associated bank' and almost 23 were 'other financial organisations'. The relative importance of these banks is evidenced through the structure of their expenditures (all banking institutions = 100). That is, internal banks participated with 8.6 per cent, basic banks with 87.8 per cent, the associated bank with 2.8 per cent and all other financial institutions participated with only 0.8 per cent. In other words, proliferating banking institutions were not all that important for the balance sheet of banking.

Inherited instability was the main economic issue at the time of the creation of the independent Croatian state. The average monthly rate of inflation had reached almost 28 per cent when the Stabilisation Programme was implemented in October of 1993. The implementation of this programme resulted in a sudden drop in the inflation rate, thereby ensuring stability on the domestic market. The rate of inflation in the 1995–98 period was under 4 per cent per year. A high deficit in the current balance of payments, however, sparked a 5.4 per cent rise in retail prices in 1998 and a 4.5 per cent increase in 1999.

Immediately following Croatia's independence, the Croatian National Bank (CNB) began accumulating foreign reserves within the framework of the Stabilisation Programme, and this had a crucial impact on the money supply. The formation of international reserves in the early 1990s was largely the product of unrecorded capital inflows. The increase in the CNB reserves during 1992–94 enabled Croatia to have, at the end of 1995, approximately 10 per cent of GDP in its reserves which had risen to 15 per cent of GDP at the end of 1999 (see Table 12.1). When taking its initial step, the CNB tightened its monetary policy and liberalised the foreign exchange market, while the government realigned the prices of public utilities in order to eliminate losses burdening the budget and placed controls on wages in the public sector. Monetary and credit policies remained neutral and hardly restrictive, and the real exchange rates appreciated in the period up to the middle of 1999. The exchange rate was the main tool of stabilisation in the first phase of the Stabilisation Programme. The second phase of this programme – that is, after 1995 – involved a number of structural reforms: fiscal changes, the speeding up of privatisation, and the restructuring of loss-making public sector enterprises and banks with the development of the financial system. There is a danger that inflationary pressures might manifest themselves from attempts to restore export competitiveness through devaluation.

The break-up of the monetary system of the former Yugoslavia caused Croatian banks to become insolvent in technical terms. The freezing of household foreign currency savings deposits in 1991 resulted in the creation of a public debt commonly referred to as 'frozen foreign currency deposits'. In addition, numerous companies found themselves in serious difficulties and were unable to repay their debts to banks. Consequently, the government recapitalised a number of major companies through the issue of so-called 'big bonds', which were used by these companies for the repayment of their debts. This explains the large share of public debt, that is, claims on the government, in bank assets.

In December 1991, Croatia took a step towards currency reform by replacing the Yugoslav dinar, which it had been utilising, up to that point, as the national currency, with the temporary 'Croatian dinar'. The new currency, the kuna (HRK), was introduced in May 1994, only six months after the implementation of the Stabilisation Programme. At that time, inflation was well under control and the central bank's reserves were on the rise. The central bank has made considerable changes in its methods for allocating credit to the central government and to commercial banks. Since 1993, credit to the central government has been restricted by law to 5 per cent of budgetary revenues. The state can borrow only in the short term from the CNB, and these loans must be repaid by the end of the fiscal year. Thus, the CNB cannot finance budget deficits. Furthermore, the deposits of the central government with the commercial banks were transferred to the central bank (Škreb, 1998, p. 5).

The Banking Law was adopted by parliament in 1993. The minimum capital adequacy ratio was set at 8 per cent. This law created three types of banking institutions: banks with full licence (with minimum capital equivalent to DEM 15 million), banks with limited licence (with minimum capital equivalent to DEM 5 million) that have no international payment service as well as saving banks (with minimum capital equivalent to DEM 1 million). The 1993 law liberalised the entry of new banks; newly entering private banks were very aggressive in their policies and achieved a large market share.

The new Banking Law was announced in December 1998. The minimum capital adequacy ratio was raised from 8 per cent to 10 per cent. This new law was more restrictive in the fields of risk exposure, examination, licensing and in the authorisation of bank management. The new Banking Law strengthens supervision and CNB control, thus giving greater authority to the central bank. New measures were implemented on the micro- and macroeconomic levels in order to restore confidence in the banking system and in order to increase the efficiency and competitiveness of banks and savings institutions.

The banking system in Croatia was concentrated on a small number of large banks that controlled a relatively extensive share of total assets and revenues. With the appearance of new banks, the system has gradually become less concentrated. The entry of banks owned by foreigners and the burgeoning of smaller and medium-sized banks contributed to this process. The share of the nine largest banks in the total revenue of the Croatian banking sector fell from 92 per cent in 1994 to 72 per cent in 1996. The structure of the banking industry was transformed from an oligopoly with pronounced monopolistic elements to an oligopoly with observable elements of competition.

THE STRUCTURE OF THE BANKING SYSTEM

The banking system in Croatia was made up of 60 banks and 33 savings banks in 1998. The total assets of the banking sector were HRK 93.3 billion (with banks holding 98.5 per cent and savings banks holding 1.5 per cent). All of the banks are of the universal type (56 are joint-stock companies while four are limited liability companies). Most of the banks are privately owned (85 per cent in 1998), while the four largest banks, which accounted for about 34 per cent of the total banking assets, were owned by the government. Fifty-three banks and one branch of a foreign bank have full licences. The banking system remains highly concentrated, with four big banks dominating the market. Their share, however, in the total banking assets has fallen in recent years: in 1996 it was 59.9 per cent, while in 1997 it had fallen to 53.1 per cent and remained at that level through 1998. (See Table 12.2.)

Table 12.2 *Number of banks in Croatia, 1993–1999*

Year/ Dec.	Deposit money banks (DMBs)	Savings banks	Total	Assets of DMBs (HRK m.)	Foreign assets of DMBs (USD m.)
1993	43	0	43	47,332	13,232
1994	50	33	83	54,620	9,111
1995	53	21	74	62,654	11,980
1996	57	22	79	67,483	12,419
1997	60	33	93	85,309	13,856
1998	60	33	93	93,326	14,669
1999	53	30	83	93,252	12,193

Source: *The Croatian National Bank Bulletin*, No. 44, 1999; No. 48, 2000.

Between 1994 and 1998, the number of deposit money banks (DMBs) increased by 20 per cent. The foreign assets of those banks went up from USD 9.1 billion to USD 14.7 billion (an increase of 60 per cent). In 1999, however, there was a decrease of those assets in dollar terms and a stagnation of the national currency. New criteria introduced in 1999 resulted in the disappearance of a number of DMBs and savings banks. This process is set to continue.

In 1998, the majority of banks (85 per cent) were predominantly privately owned. Their share in the total banking assets was 70.2 per cent. The other nine banks were state-owned banks (at least by majority), and managed the remaining 29.8 per cent of total banking assets. The privatisation process in

Croatia has developed in two ways: the first was the privatisation of existing banks and the second was taking steps to establish new banks with private or entity assets. An important feature was the rapid entry of foreign banks. Before 1996, only one bank had entered the Croatian market, but during 1996 and 1997 some six foreign banks opened branches or subsidiaries. This prompted an ensuing atmosphere of intensified competition. In 1999, foreign banks obtained majority shares in some large state banks.

Credit rates were extremely high before the Stabilisation Programme in 1993, as can be assessed from Table 12.3. The Croatian National Bank's discount rate was gradually reduced to 5.9 per cent, but it then rose again in 1999 to 7.9 per cent. A similar tendency was observed in the interest rates of DMBs. Credit interest in kunas (sometimes indexed to the foreign currency parity of the kuna) went down, but still remain high. However, what is most interesting is the falling interest rate for credit in foreign currency which declined from 15.7 per cent in December 1995 to 6.3 per cent in October 1999.

Table 12.3 *Credit rates of Croatian banks, 1993–1999*

Year (Dec.)	CNB discount rate	Deposit interest rate	Lending money banks credit rates on:		
			credit in kunas	credit in kunas (indexed to f. currency)	credit in foreign currency
1993	34.5	27.4	59.0	21.8	–
1994	8.5	5.0	15.4	12.0	–
1995	8.5	6.1	22.6	19.6	15.7
1996	6.5	4.2	19.3	19.0	19.3
1997	5.9	4.4	14.1	14.4	13.6
1998	5.9	4.1	16.1	13.0	7.0
1999, Oct.	7.9	4.4	13.3	12.7	6.3

Source: *The Croatian National Bank Bulletin.*

The high interest rates are partly the result of high expenditures on mandatory reserves and other obligatory expenditures. The CNB immobilises over 30 per cent of all domestic deposits in obligatory reserves. As a result of this, the banks must immobilise a significant part of their foreign currency deposits, once again for the purpose of securing the liquidity of accepted deposits.

The interest rate spread (lending deposit rate) is very large, but the tendency is to lower this spread as a result of competition. It was 16.5 points in 1995 and has gone down to 8.9 points in October 1999. Enterprises are willing to borrow at very high rates in order to avoid illiquidity. Since neither investors nor the central bank have real-time information on the solvency of individual banks, higher interest rates may attract depositors and creditors, thereby boosting the lending capacity of bad banks, and encouraging the reallocation of scarce resources to risky transactions. The nature of the competition in the market is such that the existence of moral risk may induce otherwise solvent banks to adopt similar patterns of behaviour as their insolvent rivals, which results in a general rise in interest rates and a slowdown in economic activity.

The interest rate spread is very large, which enabled banks to afford high salaries for their staff in 1998 (72 per cent above the average level of wages in the total economy). According to data from the Payments Institute for 1998, within the framework of the profit structures of banks, savings and other financial institutions, the greatest share was that of interest earned on approved credit (67.5 per cent). Profits from provisions and compensation amounted to 13.6 per cent, while the remaining profits totalled 18.9 per cent (profits from securities, and so on). Nearly half of the profits from interest (49.5 per cent) were collected from enterprises, followed by those from private individuals with 26.1 per cent. The remaining 24.4 per cent came from other sectors.

The relatively low share of investment in GDP is the result of a small marginal propensity to save (MPS). The MPS level was 7.4 per cent in 1994/95. By the following autumn, it was registered at 5 per cent, and in the 1997–99 period it was even negative (–10.5 per cent). Table 12.4 shows the data on the volume and structure of the savings of citizens in current accounts and time savings in kunas and foreign currencies. The data indicate that citizens are more and more concerned when it comes to saving their income. This has caused the proportion of term deposits in the number of total deposits to deteriorate.

The rise in kuna and foreign currency deposits between 1995 and 1998 resulted from the fact that Croatia's citizens, attracted by high domestic interest rates, transferred their savings from foreign to domestic banks. For example, in neighbouring Austria the interest rate varied from 2.5 per cent to 4 per cent, while Croatia offered up to 12 per cent on time deposits. The bank shake-up once again initiated the tendency of saving in foreign banks and in 'socks under mattresses'. The crisis in domestic banks in 1999 caused citizens to withdraw their deposits.

Savings in domestic currency increased at a relatively fast rate between 1993 and 1997 (especially after 1995). Between 1995 and 1997 it nearly tripled, while time deposits grew faster than 'at sight' deposits. The causes were: (a) the stability of the national currency (the kuna) in relation to the basket of the most important foreign currencies (stability primarily in relation to the DEM); (b) higher interest rates for long-term savings deposits than for 'at sight' deposits. However, these trends suddenly stopped in 1998 and 1999.

Table 12.4 *Savings of citizens in Croatia (at the end of the year, in HRK bn), 1994–1999*

	1994	1995	1996	1997	1998	1999 Oct.
1. Total deposits in HRK bn	0.8	1.0	1.8	3.1	3.1	2.6
Savings deposits	0.4	0.5	0.7	1.1	1.1	1.1
Time deposits	0.4	0.5	1.1	2.0	2.0	1.5
2. Total Forex deposits	18.1	21.5	25.7	32.0	37.4	35.0
Forex savings deposits	4.0	6.4	7.4	8.6	10.0	9.7
Time deposits	2.6	5.3	11.2	18.8	24.0	22.5
Blocked Forex deposits	11.5	9.8	7.1	4.6	3.4	2.8
3. Total deposits	18.9	22.5	27.5	35.1	40.5	37.6
4. Exchange rate	5.63	5.32	5.54	6.30	6.25	7.32
5. Total deposits (USD m.)	3.3	4.2	5.0	5.7	6.5	5.1
6. GDP	87.4	98.2	108.0	124.9	138.4	143.2
1/6 (in %)	1.0	1.1	1.7	2.5	2.3	1.8
2/6 (in %)	20.5	21.8	23.9	25.7	27.0	24.4

Source: *The Croatian National Bank Bulletin*, 4 (43), 1999.

Savings in kunas at the end of 1998 remained at practically the same level as had been reached in the previous year, but decreased by 16 per cent in the first nine months of 1999. If we take into consideration the depreciation of currencies towards the US dollar, the decline is even greater in real terms. The bankruptcy of some banks has weakened the confidence of investors, who have moved towards 'good' banks. The share of foreign exchange deposits in good banks rose from 74.9 per cent in the first quarter of 1997 to 77.2 per cent in the first quarter of 1999.

It is especially important to emphasise the drastic decline in total savings that occured after 31 December 1998, when they decreased by USD 1.35 billion or by 21 per cent. This was a result of citizens becoming more free in the use of their foreign currency deposits (old 'frozen' savings decreased from 75.6 per cent of the total sum of savings in December 1993 to 7.5 per cent of the total sum of savings in September 1999).

The bank crises were the main reason for the withdrawal of money from savings accounts. The share of foreign currency savings in total savings (93 per cent) shows how deeply rooted the fears of the population actually are. Citizens tend to judge the merits of saving through past experience (in the former Yugoslavia), regardless of the relative stability of the domestic currency over the past six years. The bankruptcies in the savings and banking industry in 1998 call for the extensive regulation of banks and an improved regard for the safety of depositors. These steps might stop the withdrawal of deposits and re-establish confidence in the banking sector. At the time of the introduction of the Limited Deposit Insurance Programme, it was declared that up to HRK 30,000 (USD 4,800) per savings account is 100 per cent insured and an additional HRK 20,000 per account is 75 per cent insured. In 1998 the insured amount was raised to HRK 100,000. Only household sector savings accounts are insured.

THE MAIN FEATURES OF CENTRAL BANK REFORM

The Croatian National Bank (CNB) has existed as a part of Yugoslavia's federal system of monetary authorities since the mid-1970s. As a result of the political independence gained with the new constitution of the Republic of Croatia (in 1990), Croatian monetary independence got under way. The CNB operates as an independent institution and is solely responsible to parliament, to which it submits biannual reports on its activities. Parliament also sets the limits on borrowing from the CNB. According to the Croatian National Bank Act, the CNB Council and the governor of the CNB make up this bank's governing body. The CNB Council is composed of the governor (the president of the council), the deputy governor and vice-governor by virtue of their position, as well as independent experts. The CNB Council is responsible for implementing the decisions, which are made by a two-thirds majority vote among its members.

Currently, the primary responsibility of the CNB is to promote currency stability through a sound monetary and foreign exchange policy. The CNB is responsible for determining the money supply, the general liquidity of banks, maintaining the general liquidity of payments abroad, issuing banknotes and coins, supervising banks and regulating, organising and adjusting the information technology system required for the normal functioning of the CNB, in addition to maintaining gold and foreign currency reserves. (See Table 12.5.)

Table 12.5 *International reserves of the CNB and the DMBs (USD m.), 1993–1998*

Year/Month	Int. reserves CNB	Exchange reserves DMB	Total
1993 Dec.	616	713	1,329
1994 Dec.	1,405	902	2,307
1995 Dec.	1,895	1,370	3,265
1996 Dec.	2,314	1,992	4,306
1997 Dec.	2,539	2,333	4,872
1998 Dec.	2,816	1,949	4,765
1999 Dec.	3,025	1,608	4,633

Source: *The Croatian National Bank Bulletin*, 4 (43), 1999.

Only three measures remained unchanged in CNB policy between 1992 and 1999. These are in relation to: short-term credits to the government, the reserve requirement and the discount rate. With regard to monetary policy instruments, there were many changes between 1992 and 1999. The policy instruments abandoned during this time were: selective refinancing credit for specific economic activities (such as agriculture), general and earmarked quotas, short-term loans as the basis of commercial papers and bills, uncollateralised loans for withdrawals from household sector savings and cheque accounts, compulsory CNB bills and the minimum liquidity regulation.

New policy instruments are currently coming into force. For example, the CNB has begun to issue its own bills and has developed indirect monetary policy instruments: repo arrangements (repurchase agreements), foreign exchange swaps, and Lombard credit. In 1998, the CNB used modified instruments of monetary policy with a major feature being the increased use of repo auctions of CNB bills and Ministry of Finance treasury bills, as well as the reactivation of the interventive loan instrument. Another innovation in 1998 was the introduction of the pre-rehabilitation loan (preparing for bank restructuring). The CNB used auctions of CNB bills and required reserves to neutralise the possible negative effects of monetary creation. The CNB imposes restrictions on short-term capital inflows.

The most important change in the Lombard loan instruments came about in December 1998 when the Lombard and daily loans were unified (in order to make the role and significance of collateral more transparent). In December 1998 it was decided that Lombard loans would be granted up to 50 per cent of the nominal value of CNB bills in kunas, foreign exchange, Ministry of Finance treasury bills and other bills of exchange.

Internal Audit has been in service, as an independent organisational unit, since its foundation in 1995. It reports directly to the governor of the CNB, and its main task has been to audit the organisational units of this bank, in particular those areas where potential risks exist. Special emphasis was placed on the management of the foreign exchange reserves of the CNB through regular monthly audits and occasional targeted audits. The Treasury Department was audited to ensure the timely documentation of business transactions, banking supervision and the internal costs of the CNB.

Figure 12.1 *Money supply, deposit money and cash balances in Croatia, April 1994 to February 2000*

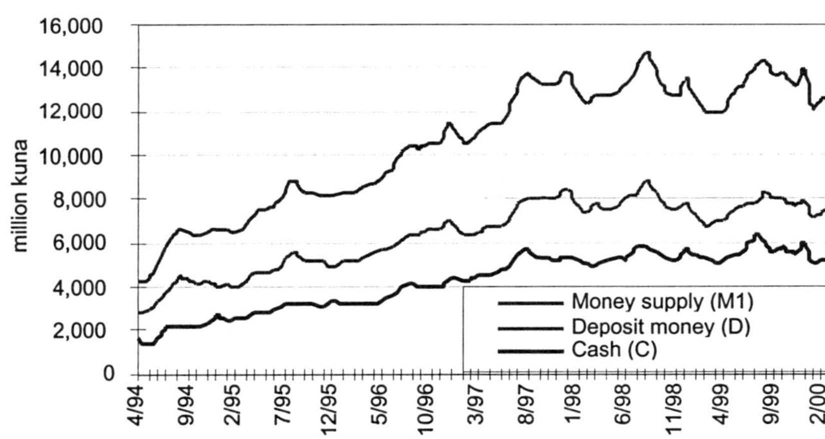

Source: *The Croatian National Bank Bulletin*, No. 48, 2000.

In 1998, the Payments Operations Department of the CNB worked on the transformation of the domestic payments system in two phases. The Croatian System of Large Payments (CSLP) was introduced during the first phase. It is a system that allows interbank payment transactions through the accounts of banks and savings banks at the CNB in real time and on the gross settlement principle, that is, that every payment transaction be executed individually when presented. The system began functioning on 6 April 1999 and payment operations were transferred from the Payments Institute to the CNB (transactions through giro accounts, settlements accounts, required reserve accounts and required deposit accounts) for 54 banks and five savings banks. The creation of the CLSP brings the Croatian payments system closer to the payments systems of European Union members.

Figure 12.2 *Monetary aggregate M4 in Croatia, April 1994 – February 2000*

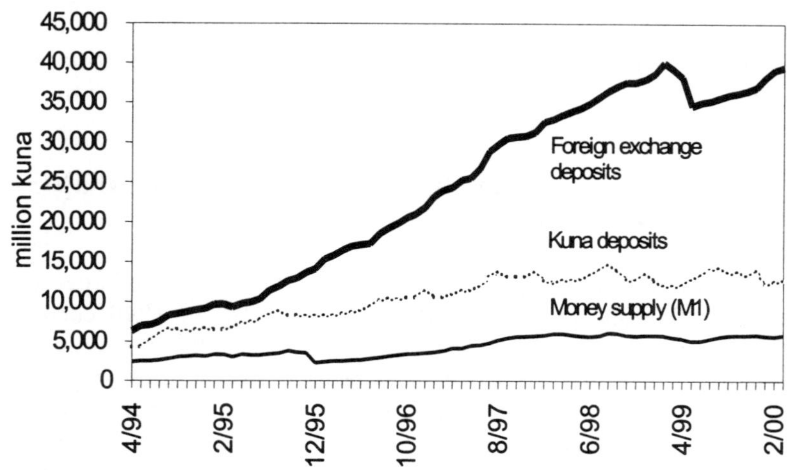

Source: *The Croatian National Bank Bulletin*, No. 48, 2000.

The second phase in the reform of payments is the transfer of payments through client accounts (individuals and legal entities) from the Payments Institute to deposit institutions. Within the framework of these developments, the total available foreign currency assets stopped growing, and in fact decreased between December 1997 and December 1999 by USD 139 million or –5 per cent. The net foreign currency reserves were used to intervene on the foreign currency market, in foreign debt repayment and in the restraining of depreciation in the exchange rate.

Money supply M1 doubled in the first year after the stabilisation with no impact on prices which were down in 1994 (see Figure 12.1). The money supply increased to HRK 13.8 billion until stagnation in 1997, caused by an increase in the amount of currency in circulation at the same time that deposit money shrank. Along with the monetary multiplier (about 1.4) and the high level of obligatory reserves (30 per cent), the influence of credit activity on changes in the monetary base were weak. Since 1993, the share of cash money in the structure of the monetary base has been increasing, which points to the presence of a grey economy.

In contrast to this, the money aggregate M4, despite its growth, had little influence on managing liquidity since its structure is dominated by foreign currency deposits. Banks increasingly turned towards the general public, who proved to be more reliable than firms were. The slowing velocity of broad money (M4) from five in 1994 to three in 1996 and 2.4 in 1998, prompted banks to extend their activities to the population, granting credit for home and other expenses, the purchase of cars and so on. As of 1997, banks have come to the realisation that there is a danger of having bad loans in their portfolios if they continue to grant credit to illiquid companies. (See Figure 12.2.)

THE FINANCIAL RESTRUCTURING OF THE BANKING SYSTEM AND OF INDIVIDUAL BANKS

The process of bank rehabilitation started in 1996 with four large banks: Slavonska, Splitska, Riječka and Privredna. In 1997 the CNB conducted detailed interviews with 55 banks. The results suggest that the older banks (those that existed before 1990) have better credit policies (arguably a product of far more experience). The banks recognise that they cannot trust an assessor paid by the client. However, in the smaller banks a member of the management may be in direct contact with clients. Personal contacts still remain crucial in lending.

The main problems that the interviewers noted relating to documentation and the assessment of credit applications are that:

- most clients' financial statements are unreliable;
- land records are inaccurate and out of date;
- banks cannot find out whether a client has outstanding loans from other banks; and
- banks cannot find out if a co-debtor or guarantor is simultaneously guaranteeing more than one loan.

The Croatian banking system experienced its second crisis in 1998. The key causes were: (a) the bad credit policies of certain banks, is that, those not based on commercial criteria and risk assessment, (b) extremely high interest rates and (c) insufficient experience in mergers, acquisitions, bankruptcies and the insolvency of banks. In 1998, several banks were declared bankrupt by the government. Among them were a few large ones: Dubrovačka, Županjska, Glumina and Gradska. The preliminary calculation of the losses of these four banks amounts to about USD 600 million. These failures were followed by some other small and medium-sized bank bankruptcies. In the period between March 1998 and March 1999, the CNB Council initiated bankruptcy proceedings in eight institutions (out of which two are deposit-taking institutions), which represent 7 per cent of the total assets of the banking system. The cost of bank rehabilitation up to 1998 is assumed to be about 22 per cent of the 1997 GDP and the total costs will probably increase this ratio to 24 per cent if we take into account the case of Dubrovačka banka (Babić et al., 1999, p. 102).

There are no precise data on bad assets. According to the decision of the Classification of Balance Sheet Assets and Off-Balance Sheet Items of Banks and Saving Banks, banks are required to estimate the level of credit risk for each borrower quarterly. Borrowers are classified into risk groups A, B, C, D and E. Loans for which there is minimal risk of non-payment are classified in category A, while loans with the highest level of risk are placed in category E.

Table 12.6 *Classification of bank credit portfolios in Croatia, 1995–1998*

Year	1995	1996	1997	1998
Total assets	64,494	66,730	85,892	103,200
Credit classified as:				
A	55,731	58,747	76,379	89,061
B	3,910	2,602	4,511	5,132
C–E	5,213	5,381	5,002	9,007
Off-balance sheet items	12,639	14,792	17,188	18,093
Total credit vol.	77,493	81,522	103,080	121,293

Source: CNB, *Annual Report*, 1995–98.

As Table 12.6. shows, the share of bad assets out of total assets (those classified in categories C through E) rose from 6.8 per cent in 1995 to 7.4 per cent in 1999. That is 5.2 per cent of GDP in 1995 and 6.9 per cent in 1998. Only a part of these were inherited from the past. It is important to note, however, that the volume of bad credit over four years almost doubled in spite of all of the government interventions that have partly covered some of the bad debt in certain banks. The internal control of banks has been strengthened in the past few years by new rules giving additional powers to the CNB for the auditing of a bank's assets and liabilities.

THE CURRENT STATE OF NATIONAL BANKING SECTOR REFORM

The capital market remains undeveloped. According to the data of the Zagreb Stock Exchange, the Croatian capital market is going into the 21st century with a lower level of development than five years ago. The market capitalisation (the 'weighed' value of represented shares which were traded) of the Zagreb Stock Exchange in the last quarter of 1999 varied between 13 and 14 per cent of GDP. The situation remains adverse when taking into account the level of business at the stock exchange which amounted to an insignificant 4 per cent of GDP in 1999 (a mere third of its business in 1997).

In October 1999, the first phase of the privatisation of the state telecom firm (Hrvatske telekomunikacije) was completed. The sale of 35 per cent of the shares of the company (to Deutsche Telecom) brought USD 850 million. This transaction improved liquidity since the government used the inflow to decrease its liabilities in the banking sector. The central bank increased its deposits with banks, but there was no conveyance of liquidity to the enterprise sector.

Similar privatisation acts followed. In mid-1998, the Republic of Croatia announced in *The Financial Times* that it would hold a public auction for the sale of Privredna banka. The Italian Banca Commerciale Italiana from Milan made an offer which was accepted, and on 15 December 1999, 66.3 per cent of the shares of Privredna banka were sold to them. The Italian bank accepted as assets the bonds that the agency issued, and which the state will pay over the course of the next 15 years. The bonds carry an average 6.25 per cent annual interest rate. Zagrebačka banka's share of foreign capital was 39.64 per cent by the end of 1998, and since its shares are traded on the London Stock Exchange, it is estimated that the share of foreign capital could total 42.85 per cent by the end of 2000. Thus, foreign capital will greatly increase its share in capital with the sale of national banks. The situation in the largest Croatian banks is reflected in Table 12.7.

In two years, foreign capital increased its share in the nine largest banks from 24.2 per cent to 59.6 per cent according to official estimates. The resources gained by the sale of the state's share in national banks should provide money to be used in the payment of insured savings deposits in bankrupt banks. The arrival of foreign capital in the large banks has been followed by the strengthening of the share of Austrian banks in the capital of regional banks (Bjelovarska, Trgovačka, Čakovečka and others). The Croatian market has been attractive for foreign capital since loans in Croatia are granted with high interest rates, for example, in September 1999, the rates were 14 per cent for short-term credits and up to 13 per cent for long-term credits. These are nearly three times higher than those offered in banks within the European Union.

Table 12.7 *Percentage of foreign assets in the nine largest Croatian banks, 1998 and 2000*

	in 1998 (HRK m.)		1998	2000
Bank	Assets	Founder's capital	Foreign share (in %)	
Austria	1,071	249	100.0	100.0
Dalmatinska	2,487	276	24.0	43.7
Hypo	1,110	226	100.0	100.0
Poštanska	–	384	0.0	0.0
Privredna	16,950	1,663	0.0	66.3
Splitska	7,651	381	0.0	75.0
Riječka	5,594	449	2.7	75.0
Raiffeisen	2089	280	100.0	100.0
Zagrebačka	24,852	1,859	39.6	42.9
Total	61804	5,767	24.2	59.6

Sources: *CNB Annual Reports*, various issues; Author's estimates.

The process of banking system reform has not yet been completed. It is obvious that Croatia will continue with the further privatisation of banks and to steadily increase the level of foreign capital in the banking industry. It is quite possible that there will be a continuation of the process of liquidating small, insolvent banks with the aims of improving the health of the banking system in general and of regaining the trust of depositors.

CONCLUSION

Croatian banking is characterised by a surplus of employees, factionalism, the outdated organisation of labour, a low level of technological equipment and weak leadership techniques, all factors that raise unit costs. The creation of the new banking system in Croatia was played out under exceptionally difficult circumstances (economic transition in a war situation). The monetary policy of 1993/94 suppressed inflation, but its restrictiveness together with the fixed exchange rate reduced both employment and production. The increase in foreign indebtedness did not succeed in sparking the expansion of production (or even employment for that matter) and, as a consequence, the exhausted economy will have a tough time servicing its foreign debts.

In Croatia, where citizens hold about 93.3 per cent of their savings in foreign exchange deposits, confidence in the banking system is of great importance. The interest rate spread is very large, which enabled banks to afford high salaries for their staff in 1998 (72 per cent above the average level of wages in the total economy).

Banking reforms in Croatia were undertaken primarily by legal regulations (the new Banking Law in 1998). This improved the existing monetary instruments and introduced new ones. It also strengthened the interventional capabilities of the CNB with regard to the control and audit of banks. Namely, banks were too susceptible to the activities of individuals, or groups of mutually connected individuals. Banks, as a result, took exceedingly high risks. This has been a negative experience in the banking practice of Croatia. The new law regulates, more restrictively, the susceptibility of banks to well-connected dominating interest groups. The banking reforms, however, did not increase the total liquidity of the economy. This illiquidity was created by the bankruptcy of banks whose greatest problems were caused by risky speculation, ignorance and bad management.

Only nine foreign banks (holding 60 per cent of the total banking assets) were operating in Croatia in 1998. The arrival of foreign banks did not, however, have the expected effect of increasing the competitiveness and efficiency of domestic banking. The profits from the sale of the state's share in the large banks were for the most part used to cover deficits in the budget, the Pension Fund and in health insurance (all of which are chronically underfunded). Economists believe that these sums would be more effective if used to fund economic growth. It is obvious that the profits from sales in the forthcoming period will not achieve sums as large, and a decrease in budgetary spending is an inevitability. Turnaround in economic policy in general should be based on encouraging exports and savings (of the state, the population and of firms).

At the beginning of the 21st century, globalisation is imposing new challenges in banking that are prompting banks to enlarge in order to cope better with growing competition. Contemporary banking is introducing new products: swaps, options, futures, derivatives and so on, while Croatia is still operating with traditional banking products. The banking crisis showed that there are still a number of factors mitigating against the trend to enlargement and the introduction of foreign capital. This has been mainly due to ignorance or in order to protect monopolistic positions. Therefore, intellectual capital (skills and modern management) is of inestimable importance to the transformation of the Croatian banking system.

NOTE

1. Internal banks were the financial subsidiaries of enterprises. These banks were not designed to acquire deposits or grant credit outside their own membership; basic banks were socialist enterprises and other legal social entities which signed a self-management contract of association with the basic banks; associate banks were two or more basic banks with obligations in activities of common interest.

BIBLIOGRAPHY

Babić, M., P. Jurković and V. Šonje (1999), 'Banking System Development in Croatia', *Zagreb Journal of Economics*, **3**, pp. 75–113.

Claessens, S., A. Demirgüç-Kunt and H. Huizinga (1998), 'How Does Foreign Entry Affect the Domestic Banking Market', Policy Research Working Paper No. 1918, Washington, DC: World Bank.

Craft, E., M. Curavić and M. Tepuš (1998), 'Report on the Credit Policies of Croatian Banks', *Surveys*, **8**, Zagreb: CNB.

Croatian National Bank (CNB), *Bulletin*, various issues, 1994–2000, Zagreb: CNB.

Croatian National Bank (CNB) (1997), 'Banks at the Crossroads', A Report on the Banking System in the Republic of Croatia, **4**, Zagreb: CNB.

Croatian National Bank (CNB) (1998), *Annual Report*, Zagreb: CNB.

Croatian National Bank (CNB) (1999), 'Croatia in the Second Stage of Transition 1994–1999', Working paper.

Jovančević, R. (1998), 'Globalna ekonomija na početku 21. stoljeća i hrvatsko gospodarstvo' [The Global Economy at the Beginning of the 21st Century and the Croatian Economy], in R. Jovančević (ed.), *Gospodarska politika Hrvatske i Europska unija* [The Economic Policy of Croatia and the European Union], Zagreb: University of Zagreb, Faculty of Economics and Mekron promet, pp. 1–55.

Republic of Croatia, Central Bureau of Statistics, *The Statistical Yearbook. 1999*, Zagreb: Central Bureau of Statistics.

Republic of Croatia, Central Bureau of Statistics (1998–2000), *Monthly Bulletin Report*, various issues, Zagreb: Central Bureau of Statistics.

Rohatinski, Z. (1999), *Macroeconomic Forecasts*, **3**, Zagreb: Privredna banka d.d, pp. 27–9.

Škreb, M. (1998), 'Economic Transition in Croatia', *A Survey of the National Bank of Croatia*, **11**, Zagreb: CNB.

Stiglitz, J.E. and K. Hoff (1999), 'Modern Economic Theory and Development', Symposium on Future of Development Economics in Perspective (mimeo), Dubrovnik.

Stipetić, V. (1998), 'The Economic Development of Central Europe 1879–1996', in Symposium on Integration of the Central European Countries with the Adriatic, Zagreb: HAZU.

13. Banking Reform in Macedonia

Gligor Bišev

INTRODUCTION

In contrast to other command economies, Macedonia, within the former Yugoslav Federation, has had a two-tier banking system since 1964.[1] The National Bank of Yugoslavia (NBY) assumed the role of the monetary authority, with multiple sets of quantitative goals: to support economic growth and employment, to maintain price stability and to achieve a sustainable balance of payments position. The central bank, NBY in this case, also had selective (qualitative) goals: to finance agricultural sector activity and the production for export. In the 1980s, the selective goals became dominant, and quantitative monetary targets lost their importance. This led to uncontrolled monetary expansion and hyperinflation in 1989. As a result of the monetization of the huge Federal government deficit, hyperinflation re-emerged in 1992. Bank supervision barely existed: the National Bank of the former Yugoslavia focused mainly on whether banks were using funds properly for selective purposes.

Extending credit and collecting deposits were the main bank activities in the 1964–92 period. Banks did not offer payment services, which were supplied by a special centralised financial institution. The banks' activities were in accordance with the main characteristics of the economic system based on associated labour. Banks were owned by a number of enterprises, each enterprise having one vote. The main function of a bank was not to make a profit by undertaking normal risks, but to extend as much credit as possible to enterprises at the lowest possible interest rate. Generally, net debtors were managing banks, and misallocation of resources was a permanent feature. Thus, in the 1980s the Macedonian economy as a part of the Yugoslav Federation was faced with stagflation and the banking sector was heavily burdened with bad loans, due to resource misallocation.

Macedonia's monetary independence from the former Yugoslav Federation occurred in April 1992 with the introduction of the Macedonian denar as legal tender to replace the Yugoslav dinar. At the same time, new institutional regulations for the central bank of Macedonia (National Bank of the Republic of Macedonia – NBRM) and the banking industry were adopted. The central bank was established as an independent monetary authority with the unique goal of maintaining price stability. Simultaneously, the central bank has become responsible for banking supervision. The hyperinflation in 1992 was swiftly reduced through effective money supply control, based on monetary targets. Due to the fact that Macedonia is a small and open economy (2.1 million citizens and a share of foreign trade in GDP above 80 per cent in the period after monetary independence), an exchange rate target replaced the monetary target in mid-1995. This strategy has proved efficient in maintaining price stability. Since that period the rate of inflation in Macedonia has converged to the German one. The exchange rate target imposed firm discipline on all macroeconomic policies. The fiscal deficit of 13.4 per cent in 1993 was brought down to 1.2 per cent in 1995 and stayed at less than 2 per cent in the following years. In 1999 a small budget surplus was recorded. Except in July 1997, when the exchange rate of the denar against the German mark was devalued by 16.2 per cent, it remained stable. Strong external shocks[2] have heavily undermined the growth potential of the economy. A slowdown in the restructuring of the real and financial sector in the last three years has strengthened the negative effects of the unfavourable climate created by the external shocks. Modest economic growth re-emerged in 1996. The average growth rate of GDP in the 1996–98 period was 1.7 per cent. Despite the Kosovo crisis in 1999, the growth of GDP accelerated to 2.7 per cent. This was not enough to reduce high unemployment, which in 1998 reached 34.5 per cent.

A universal type of banking system was inaugurated after monetary independence. The number of banks has increased rapidly (from four before monetary independence to 23 at the end of 1999), and 17 savings banks were established. The main features of the current banking system are: overbanking, high bank concentration, dominance of the classic bank activities, weak competition and inefficiency.

The current coalition government (composed of three parties) was established after the elections in November 1998. In articulating its economic policy the government had proclaimed three basic goals: opening up and liberalising the economy, rapid restructuring of the enterprise and banking sectors, and harmonising the institutional framework in accordance with the European Union (EU) directives with a view to joining the EU.

SEQUENCE OF BANKING REFORM

The concept of a universal banking system was adopted as a basis for reform. Banks were defined as institutions that collect deposits and extend credit in order to make a profit. However, it was stipulated that they had to be solvent and liquid, and other supervisory standards were prescribed for the first time. The central bank was to be the main supervisory body. It was possible to establish a bank as a joint-stock company with a minimum of ten shareholders. The voting power per shareholder depended on the number of subscribed shares. The minimum capital for establishing a bank was not prescribed by law. This right was given to the National Bank of the former Yugoslav Federation, which set a limit of dinar 6 billion (USD 500,000).

The tradition of a two-tier banking system had existed for almost 25 years, prior to the banking reform in the late 1980s. The main goal of that reform had been bank concentration and at the end of 1989 only eight financial institutions existed in the country. Two of these were banks with headquarters in Macedonia, two were branches of banks with headquarters in other republics of the former Yugoslavia, and there were four insurance companies (Table 13.1). Three new banks were established by the end of 1991, mainly as offshoots of the largest bank. Just before monetary independence the two bank branches were transformed into joint-venture banks. The number of non-banking financial institutions remained unchanged.

Table 13.1 *Number of financial institutions (FIs) in Macedonia, 1992–1999*

Type of FI	92	93	94	95	96	97	98	99
Banks	7	19	19	21	22	22	24	22
Foreign bank branches	0	0	1	1	1	1	2	1
Savings banks	n/a	n/a	23	22	27	20	18	16
Exchange offices	0	351	540	729	757	395	341	370
Explicit deposit insurance funds	0	0	0	0	1	1	1	1
Insurance companies	4	4	4	6	8	8	9	9
Stock exchange	0	0	0	0	1	1	1	1
Total no. of FIs	11	374	587	779	816	448	396	420

Source: National Bank of the Republic of Macedonia.

An explicit deposit insurance scheme did not exist. Banks were obliged to redeposit the foreign exchange deposits of households with the National Bank of former Yugoslavia. Thus, foreign exchange deposits of households were part of the international reserves. As a result, there was a guarantee from the Federation of the former Yugoslavia for the foreign exchange deposits of households. These deposits, denominated in the national currency, were guaranteed by the Federal Central Bank of former Yugoslavia. The guarantee either for foreign or for domestic currency household deposits covered the total amount. This created a high degree of moral hazard risk within the banking industry.

The new monetary order of the Republic of Macedonia was proclaimed on 26 April 1992 when parliament adopted the Law on the Means of Payment in Macedonia and the National Bank of the Republic of Macedonia Act. The Macedonian denar was proclaimed as legal tender. The exchange of the former Yugoslav dinar for Macedonian denar at a rate of 1:1 was effected during a three-day period (28–30 April 1992). Thus, on 30 April 1992 at 8 pm, the former Yugoslav dinar ceased to be legal tender in Macedonia.

The Macedonian denar started as a pure paper currency in a hyperinflationary whirlpool. In the month of its appearance the rate of inflation rose to 83 per cent per month. There was no coverage of international reserves which were concentrated at the Federal level. In order to defend the purchasing power of the denar and to create a viable currency, an orthodox stabilisation programme with some heterodox elements was launched. The main orthodox elements of this programme were a very tight fiscal and monetary policy in combination with a fixed exchange rate of the denar against the German mark. The two heterodox elements were a wage freeze and the introduction of price control for energy and the main foodstuffs, which accounted for 28 per cent of the total value of goods and services. The outcome was a very swift reduction in inflation, which after four months was brought down to 8 per cent per month. Thus, the main goal of the first stabilisation programme was fully achieved: to secure acceptability/viability of the new currency through stabilising its domestic and external values.

The National Bank of the Republic of Macedonia (Central Bank) Act, has secured the full institutional and functional independence of a central bank. The institutional independence of the central bank can be observed through the institutional arrangements for electing the governor of the bank, the term of office of the governor, and the relations of the bank with the government, the Ministry of Finance and parliament.

The functional independence of the National Bank of Macedonia has meant that it is fully independent in selecting the monetary strategy to maintain price stability. It is independent in setting intermediate targets and in the unlimited usage of the instruments of monetary policy, including changes in interest rates. In order to prevent fiscal dominance over monetary policy, legal bands for government borrowing from the central bank have been established.

The main goal of the National Bank of Macedonia is to maintain price stability.[3] Thus, it can be ranked among the central banks that do not select their main objective. The central bank can select only the degree of price stability as its ultimate goal and the strategy for achieving and maintaining it. The central bank has also been performing a supervisory and settlement function, in accordance with its responsibility for the stability of the financial system as a whole.

The central bank remained responsible for setting the minimum capital required to establish a bank until mid-1993. In the period from April 1992 to May 1993 the central bank established a very low level of minimum capital for starting a bank. The licensing procedure was also very liberal. This led to the creation of 13 new, private banks within a period of ten months. During this period, one of the old banks went bankrupt. Thus, at the end of 1993 the number of banks increased to 19, and the number of total financial institutions to 23. The newly established banks have very little capital strength. The average level of shareholders' capital of the 13 newly established banks was USD 0.5 million. These banks were unable to break down the oligopolistic position within the banking sector or to increase efficiency. They were unable to compete with the old large banks of which the top two banks have an average share capital of USD 35 million. Thus, small banks were created, which in the long run were unviable and unable to secure profitable and efficient operations.

In May 1993 an act relating to banks and saving banks was enacted. The power of the central bank to set the minimum capital required for establishing a bank was abolished. The minimum capital was prescribed by law and was considerably higher than that established by the central bank in the period from April 1992 to May 1993. The Bank and Savings Banks Act sets supervision standards, in line with the Basle Capital Standards, to which banks and savings banks had to conform. There are requirements for: a capital adequacy ratio (8 per cent); a single large loan (10 per cent of the capital); the total loan exposure to a single client (30 per cent of the capital); the total large credit exposure of a bank (300 per cent of the share capital); credit to shareholders and bank insiders (10 per cent and 1 per cent of the share capital, respectively); provisions and loan classification (in five categories – A, B, C, D, E); non-performing assets (D and E); and capital links among shareholders. Off- and on-site supervision has become the responsibility of the central bank. However, because of the lack of skilled staff, banking supervision remained weak until the end of 1995.

A combination of small private banks and large old, insolvent and illiquid banks did not restore confidence in the banking industry. Confidence was further damaged in the process of disintegration of the former Yugoslavia, when foreign exchange household deposits valued at USD 1.4 billion were seized by the National Bank of former Yugoslavia. The level of financial intermediation was very low and misallocation of resources continued. The bad loans in bank portfolios reached 85 per cent of the total loan portfolio of the four banks that had existed before monetary independence. In order to address these problems, in the beginning of 1995, policy makers undertook decisive measures for the rehabilitation and restructuring of the banking system, specifically, of the financial[4] and operational[5] set-up.

There was no special programme for the privatisation of the old banks. Under the privatisation of enterprises programme, banks were automatically privatised. By the end of 1995 the four old banks had 62 per cent of their equity privatised.

The number of banks remained fairly constant after 1995, and by 1999 the number of banks was almost the same as when the reconstruction of the banking system started. The inefficient allocation of resources continued, as reflected through the following indicators: the proportion of bad loans remained high (one-third of total bank assets); very high nominal and real lending interest rates; and very high interest rate margins. Considerable consolidation occurred in the savings bank sector, where the number was reduced by one-third in the 1996–99 period (see Table 13.1).

STRUCTURE OF THE BANKING SYSTEM

The Macedonian national currency area is itself not an optimum currency area; indeed, it is a very small currency area. The total population is 2.1 million and total GDP in 1999 was USD 3.4 billion. Macedonia is a low-income country with a GDP per capita at a market exchange rate of USD 1,635 in 1998. However, it has very open economy. Export and import of goods in 1999 accounted for some 85 per cent of GDP.

The financial market is very shallow (Table 13.2). A standard measure for the depth of the financial market is the proportion of the broader definition of money supply M2 to GDP. The average proportion of M2 to GDP in the 1992–99 period was 11.9 per cent. This proportion rose from 11.4 per cent in 1992 to 15.3 per cent in 1999. The proportion of M2 to GDP of the most advanced transition economies is 45 per cent and the proportion of M2 to GDP in the matured market economies is 75 per cent.

Table 13.2 *Total assets of banks and the depth of the financial market in Macedonia, 1992–1998*

	Total in million denars	Assets in million USD	Share of total assets in GDP in %	Share of M1 in GDP in %	Share of M2 in GDP in %
1992	n/a	n/a	n/a	9.1	11.4
1993	75,162	2,253	88.0	6.2	13.2
1994	95,920	2,363	65.5	5.5	10.7
1995	44,123	1,162	26.0	6.8	10.8
1996	41,546	1,003	23.5	7.0	10.6
1997	50,912	919	27.5	7.1	11.1
1998	59,093	1,140	31.0	7.6	12.8

Source: National Bank of the Republic of Macedonia.

Monetisation of the economy is also very low. The proportion of the narrow definition of money supply (M1) to GDP in 1999 was 8.9 per cent (the average for matured market economies is 20 per cent and for advanced countries in transition the average is 16 per cent).

The financial intermediation through the banking system was very small. The total share of banks' assets to GDP in 1999 was only 33.1 per cent. The proportion was artificially high in the years before the cleaning of the banks' balance sheets (1993 and 1994) when the claims on the National Bank of former Yugoslavia based on redeposited foreign currency households deposits were presented in the total assets.

The financial system consists of: the monetary authority; banking institutions (deposit money banks, a development and export promotion bank, savings banks); and non-banking financial institutions (exchange offices, deposit insurance fund, insurance companies and the stock exchange).

The monetary authority is the National Bank of the Republic of Macedonia. Its main goals are to safeguard the domestic and external value of the Macedonian denar and to maintain the stability of the banking system as a whole through pursuing the function of banking supervision.

The main features of the banking system were set up in 1993 with the enactment of the Banks and Saving Banks Act. Banks were defined as universal-type financial institutions that collect deposits and extend credits. With respect to the level of minimum capital requirement, banks were classified into two categories: those that can extend credit and collect deposits in the country (with a minimum capital requirement of DEM 3 million) and those that in addition can make payments abroad and undertake external capital operations (with a minimum capital requirement of DEM 9 million). In 1996 the minimum capital requirement was increased to DEM 7 million for the first type of bank, and to 21 million for the second type. Besides these banks, the existence of savings banks was recognised. They were designed as small bank-like institutions that can collect deposits and extend credit only to households. The minimum capital requirement for establishing a savings bank was set at DEM 150,000, which was increased to DEM 300,000 in 1996. The minimum capital requirement for the Postal Savings Bank was set at DEM 500,000 in 1993 and raised to DEM 1 million in 1996.

Savings banks flourished after the legal framework was set up. In 1996 their number reached 27 (Table 13.1). The small scope of work and strong competition coming from banks led to considerable consolidation of the savings bank sector. By the end of 1999 their number was reduced to 16.

Banks are the core institutions of the banking system. The role of savings banks is relatively insignificant. The share of savings banks in the total assets is 1 per cent, whereas from the total savings of households, they attract some 3 per cent. Within savings banks, the role of the Postal Savings Bank, which accounts for more than half of the total savings within the savings bank industry, is more significant. It is a fully state-owned financial institution, where the main shareholders are two public enterprises, the Post Office and Macedonian Telecommunications.

At the end of 1999 there were: 21 universal-type banks (of which 16 held a licence for domestic operations, and a licence for external capital operations and external payments, and five had only a licence for domestic operations), one bank for development and export promotion, and one branch of a foreign bank. The bank for development and export promotion was established in the second half of 1998 with a share capital of DEM 30 million, fully in state ownership. The other banks are owned by the private sector. The private shareholders at the end of 1999 accounted for 86.7 per cent of total banks' share capital. Individually per bank the degree of private sector ownership ranged from 46.5 to 100 per cent (Table 13.3). Until the end of 1999, the ownership structure had little foreign participation. The foreign shareholders had 19.3 per cent in total banks' share capital at the end of 1999. This reached 54 per cent after the entry of the three foreign strategic investors in the largest Macedonian bank (Stopanska Banka Skopje) at the beginning of 2000.

Table 13.3 *Ownership structure of Macedonian banks as of 31 December 1999*

Banks	No.	Capital		Assets		Foreign *	No.
		USD mil.	%	USD mil.	%		
1.Domestic	18	221	89.3	1,060	88.5	–	13
Private	17	206	83.3	1,045	87.2	–	9
State-Owned	1	15	6.0	15	1.2	0.1–10	4
2.Foreign							
Below 50%						11–50	5
Above 50%	5	26	10.7	138	11.5	51–100	5
Total	23	247	100	1,198	100.0		23

Note: *Ownership, in per cent.

Traditional products dominate in the operation of the banking industry. On the assets side, credits account for 64.2 per cent of total activity. Loans to enterprises and funds on the correspondent accounts at foreign banks account for almost all banks' loan activity. Loans to households and mortgage credits are negligible. On the liability side, deposits account for 60.6 per cent of total activity. Household deposits account for 37.4 per cent of total deposits, and their share in GDP is just 4.7 per cent. Household deposits denominated in denars comprise 23.6 per cent in total denar deposits, and 2.5 per cent in GDP. Foreign exchange household deposits account for 51.3 per cent of total foreign deposits, with a share in GDP of 2.2 per cent (Table 13.4).

High nominal and real interest rates have been a permanent feature of the banking system. Between 1996 And 1999, the average nominal and real interest rate was 21.1 per cent and 19.5 per cent, respectively, in relation to lending. This implied highly risky projects being selected and financed by banks. The average denar deposit rate was 11.7 per cent in nominal and 9.4 per cent in real terms. The interest rate spread between denar and foreign currency deposits has fluctuated around 6–7 percentage points. The interest rate spread between lending and deposit rates was 8.5 percentage points, which implies, on the one hand, inefficiency of financial intermediation, and, on the other hand, lack of competitiveness in the banking system. The effective interest rate margin based on the collected and paid interest income was 2 percentage points. (See Figure 13.1.)

The non-banking financial institutions consist of foreign exchange offices, the Deposit Insurance Fund, insurance companies and the stock exchange.

Until the end of 1999 there was no legal framework to deal with investment funds. Foreign exchange offices were established after 1992; their number increased rapidly to 757 in 1996; but by the end of 1999 had declined to 370.

Table 13.4 *Total deposits and savings of citizens in Macedonia (in million USD), 1994–1999*

Deposits	1994	1995	1996	1997	1998	1999
1. Total denar deposits*:	293	326	288	248	303	369
Demand	139	172	132	125	155	192
Short term	92	87	91	74	96	117
Long term	62	67	65	49	52	60
2. Total denar household deposits:	98	113	112	80	90	87
Current account	12	17	17	12	19	22
Giro account	1	3	3	2	3	3
Other demand	0	0	0	0	0	0
Short term	30	37	41	29	29	27
Long term	55	56	51	37	39	35
3. Total Forex deposits:	88	111	93	96	144	148
Short term	87	108	90	92	137	139
Long term	1	3	3	4	7	9
4. Total Forex household deposits:	21	23	31	43	70	76
Short term	20	22	29	39	63	67
Long term	1	1	2	4	7	9
5. GDP	3,389	4,348	4,412	3,712	3,504	3,433
2/1 (in %)	33.4	34.7	38.9	32.2	29.7	23.6
4/3 (in %)	23.8	20.7	33.3	44.8	48.6	51.3
2/5 (in %)	2.9	2.6	2.5	2.1	2.6	2.5
4/5 (in %)	0.6	0.5	0.7	1.1	2.0	2.2

Note: * Non-banking and non-government.

Source: National Bank of the Republic of Macedonia.

The Deposit Insurance Fund was created at the end of 1996. Its purpose is to compensate depositors of banks and saving banks that have gone bankrupt, in order to build confidence and to prevent a run on the banks. In order not to undermine the competition among financial institutions and to prevent the development of moral hazard-related problems, the coverage ratio of household savings deposits is only 75 per cent, and the total compensation cannot exceed DEM 10,000 in denars. The Fund is a shareholding company, where the banks and savings banks are the main shareholders. A bank or a savings bank cannot collect household deposits if they are not insured by the Fund.

Figure 13.1 *Lending, deposit and interest rate spreads in Macedonia, 1995 – 1999*

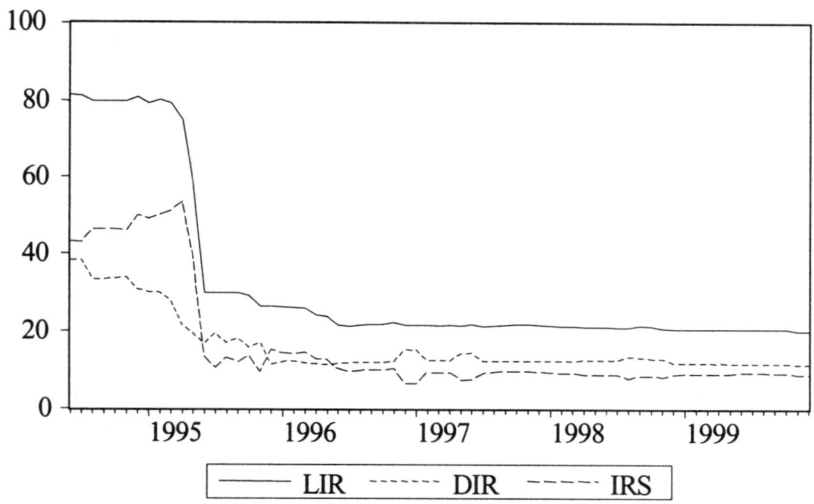

Notes:
LIR = Lending interest rate.
DIR = Deposit interest rate.
IRS = Interest rate spread.

Source: National Bank of the Republic of Macedonia.

The Macedonian Stock Exchange was founded in March 1996 and is still in its initial stages. The current trading is on the floor, and it is expected that from mid-2001 it will become an electronic stock exchange. No companies are permanently listed on the stock exchange. Trading is on a case-by-case base, with a total turnover of 0.8 per cent of GDP in 1999.

The insurance market is very shallow and heavily concentrated. At the end of 1999 there were nine insurance companies established as private companies. Two out of the nine are engaged in representing and intermediating in the insurance business, two deal with life and property insurance, and two are engaged only in property insurance. One of the insurance companies is also involved in reinsurance. The largest insurance company accounted for 77 per cent of the total insurance services in 1999.

CENTRAL BANK REFORM

Before the monetary independence of the country the National Bank of Macedonia was part of the system of national central banks in the former Yugoslavia. After April 1992 it became the monetary and supervisory authority of the country. Its institutional set-up was based mainly on the organisational and legal structure of the German Bundesbank. The Macedonian Central Bank has three main responsibilities, of which the key function is monetary policy. There are two other basic functions which are closely connected to monetary policy, namely, banking supervision, and supervision and participation in certain segments of the payments system. These are the functions, but the overall theme is stability – stability of the purchasing power of the national currency and stable functioning of the financial system, including the payments system. The other functions of the central bank are: issuance of banknotes and coins; management of the international reserves of the country; foreign exchange control; and serving as the bank for the central government.

The central bank is fully independent from the government and responsible only to parliament. The term of office of the governor, who is elected by parliament, is seven years – which is much longer than the political election cycle. Thus, the central bank is oriented to long-term goals in designing and pursuing monetary policy. In principle, the government cannot monetise its fiscal deficits; the exception is that it is possible in the short run when government deficits are of a seasonal nature. Even in such cases, government borrowing from the National Bank of Macedonia can only be short term, cannot be more than 5 per cent of the central government budget, and cannot exceed the monetary capacity of reserve money issuance determined by the monetary projections of the central bank. The final maturity of such borrowing cannot extend beyond the end of the current fiscal year. Since monetary independence, the government has never availed itself of this opportunity. On the contrary, because of the need to sterilise the considerable increase in net foreign assets of the central bank, the government has continued to augment the bank's deposits. (See Table 13.5.)

The National Bank of Macedonia has in the main used two different strategies for maintaining price stability in the period from April 1992 to December 1999. From April 1992 to September 1995, the central bank had used a monetary targeting strategy for maintaining price stability, in combination with a flexible exchange rate regime. Since October 1995, an exchange rate targeting strategy has been adopted for maintaining price stability. The exchange rate target has been fixed but there is an adjustable exchange rate of the Macedonian denar against the German mark. Since October 1995 the exchange rate has been devalued only once (in June 1997, by 16.2 per cent). Although the exchange rate targeting strategy was in place, the central bank has continued to publish monetary targets as it did during the period of monetary targeting strategy: from 1992 to 1996, targets for M1, and since 1997, targets for M2-denar.

Table 13.5 *Projected and achieved growth rates of inflation and money supply in Macedonia (in per cent, annually), 1992–1999*

Year	Infla-tionary goal	Achieved inflation	Differ-ence (4=3–2)	Inter-mediate target	Achieved growth	Differ-ence (7=6–5)
1	2	3	4	5	6	7
1992	2,408.4	1,925.2	–483.2	755.1	704.5	–50.6
1993	434.2	229.6	–204.6	268.3	239.7	–28.6
1994	70.0	55.4	–14.6	80.7	83.2	2.5
1995	8.0	9.2	1.2	23.0	25.3	2.3
1996	2.0	0.2	–1.8	8.3	–1.7	–10.0
1997*	4.5	5.0	0.5	8.9	13.2	4.3
1998	–1.0	3.0	4.0	9.2	11.1	1.9
1999	2.3	3.0	0.7	11.4	33.5	22.1

Note: * A year in which exchange rate devaluation occurred under the regime of a fixed exchange rate of denar against the German mark.

Source: National Bank of the Republic of Macedonia.

From April 1992 to September 1995, a deceleration of money supply growth was achieved through the monetary targeting strategy. The growth rate of money supply was reduced from 704.5 per cent in 1992 to 27 per cent in September 1995. As a consequence, the rate of inflation decreased from a hyperinflationary level (1,925.2 per cent in 1992) to below 10 per cent in September 1995. Since October 1995, the exchange rate targeting strategy harmonised the growth rates of money supply and inflation with those in the anchor currency country, Germany. (See Figure 13.2.)

Price stability on the level of the highly industrialised countries has been creating favourable conditions for financial system soundness, an increasing propensity to save and efficient allocation of resources. However, even in such circumstances, the credibility of the banking system has remained low and misallocation of resources has remained high, bringing the economic recovery to a standstill. Economic growth resumed in 1996 (0.8 per cent), and remained moderate (average growth rate during 1996–99 was 2 per cent). Low economic growth was mainly due to the slow pace of the restructuring of the real and financial sectors and to very strong negative non-economic external shocks. In 1999, despite the negative effects of the Kosovo crisis, GDP growth was 2.7 per cent.

Figure 13.2 *Money supply, exchange rate and rate of inflation in Macedonia, 1995–1999*

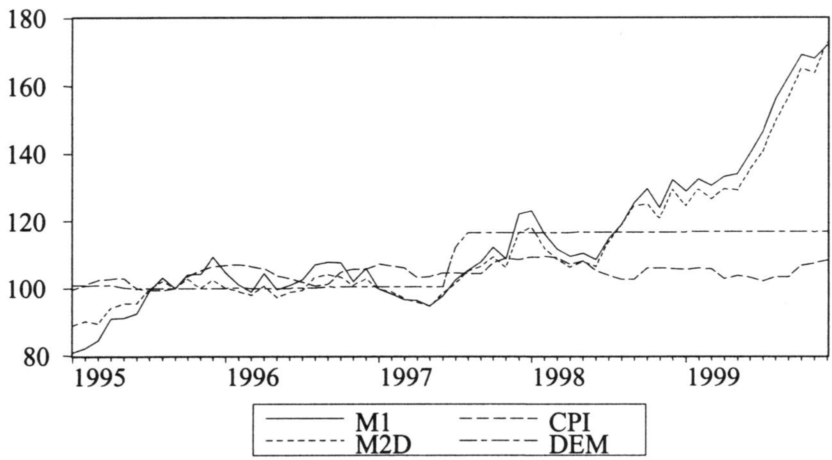

Source: National Bank of the Republic of Macedonia.

The central bank used a broad variety of instruments in order to maintain efficient control over the money supply growth. After 15 months of monetary independence the inherited selective credits for export, production for export and agricultural support were ended. The main monetary policy instruments for money supply control became the indirect, market-based instruments of control in the form of open-market operations of the following types: credit auctions, with market-determined interest rates as a monetary policy instrument for the issuance of reserve money, and auctions of central bank bills at a fixed interest rate as a monetary policy instrument for withdrawal of reserve money and for sterilisation of the effects of the increase in net foreign assets (NFA) of the central bank. In order to increase the demand for reserve money, the reserve requirement has also been used as a monetary policy instrument. At the end of 1999 the rate of reserve requirement on bank deposits was 8 per cent, which is the lowest rate among the countries in transition. The discount rate was the lowest interest rate in the financial system, while the Lombard rate was the highest. Money market rates, and credit and central bank bill auction rates fluctuated between these limits.

In the 1994–99 period the direct monetary policy instrument of credit ceilings was in place. In order to avoid distortionary effects, the ceiling per bank was adjusted for the increase in long-term deposits and change in the market share of the bank. However, the credit ceilings did not constrain credit growth effectively. That is, liquidity management was mainly conducted by indirect instruments of monetary control. The credit ceiling was a safety valve, which was never reached by the banks. The actual growth of credits, on average, was lower by ten percentage points than the one allowed for by credit ceilings.

The NFA increase was the main source of the growth of the reserve money and injection of the liquidity in the economy between 1996 and 1999. This was especially the case in 1998 and 1999 when the NFA increased by USD 37 million and USD 128 million, respectively. In order to sterilise these effects the central bank sold a considerable number of central bank bills. The sterilisation was also supported by the funds deposited by the government in the National Bank of Macedonia (USD 27 million in 1998 and USD 17 million in 1999). Thus, the increase of interest rates for sterilisation purposes was avoided.

FINANCIAL RESTRUCTURING OF THE BANKING SYSTEM AND INDIVIDUAL BANKS

The financial restructuring of the banking system started at the beginning of 1995. Its main goal was to clean the bad loans from the portfolio of the old banks. These loans had reached 85 per cent of total bank loans. Measures for financial restructuring were a combination of centralised and decentralised approaches, and they included:

1. linear rehabilitation of all four old banks in order to increase their solvency;
2. rehabilitation of the largest bank – Stopanska banka Skopje – in order to increase its solvency and liquidity;
3. measures for reducing the monopolistic position of the largest bank;
4. privatisation of the banks; and
5. creation of a bank rehabilitation agency to deal with the collection of bad loans from enterprises and, on a case-by-case basis, link the rehabilitation of banks with the rehabilitation of enterprises.

Through linear rehabilitation measures, the old banks were released from their obligations pertaining to the assets and liabilities based on the foreign exchange household deposits which had been seized as international reserves by the National Bank of Yugoslavia (USD 1.4 billion) and the assets and liabilities based on credit to some official and commercial foreign creditors (Paris Club of Creditors and Zurich Club of Creditors, amounting to USD 330 million). By the end of 1999, the government had repaid USD 0.8 billion of the total amount of so-called 'frozen' foreign currency household deposits, mainly through these deposits being used as means of payment in the process of privatisation. With respect to the remaining USD 0.6 billion, at the beginning of 2000, the government issued bonds denominated in euros with a 12-year maturity, including a two-year grace period, and an interest rate of 2 per cent.

The measures for increasing the solvency and liquidity of the largest bank in addition to the linear measures include: the replacement of the non-performing denar loans with government bonds, amounting to 4.9 billion Macedonian denars (MKD)(USD 123 million); an injection of liquidity through the special-purpose deposit from the government of MKD 600 million (USD 12 million); and a special credit line from the central bank of MKD 800 million (USD 16 million).

The monopolistic position of the bank (before the rehabilitation it had a market share of 65 per cent) was reduced by transforming five major branches into independent commercial banks. Thus, the market share of the largest bank was reduced to 34 per cent.

There was no special programme for the privatisation of the old banks because they were socially owned enterprises. Banks were automatically privatised along with the privatisation of enterprises. By the end of 1995, 62 per cent of the share capital of the four old banks was privately owned.

The collection of the domestic enterprises' bad loans (accepted by the government) was transferred to the Bank Rehabilitation Agency, which was established in the beginning of 1994. The agency assumed the management of claims on more than 240 enterprises on the basis of the transformation of bank bad loans into government bonds. In the process of the management of the claims, priority was given not only to the collection of the loans from the companies, but also to the restructuring of those companies. The main methods used in this process were: (a) prompt sale of the claims, with discount; (b) debt rescheduling; (c) sale of the claims to interested investors; and (d) conversion of the claims into equity. (See Table 13.6.)

Table 13.6 *Bad-debt ratios for Macedonian banks (in million denars), 1992–1999*

	1	2	3	4	5	6	7	8
1992	85.2	53.0	n/a	n/a	n/a	n/a	n/a	n/a
1993	82.3	48.0	11.4	6,730	n/a	n/a	n/a	n/a
1994	79.9	43.6	4.3	6,301	n/a	n/a	n/a	n/a
1995	44.4	23.7	7.4	12,491	4,563	10.3	n/a	n/a
1996	42.7	28.5	8.1	14,272	6,683	16.1	8,485	8,497
1997	35.6	26.1	8.7	16,115	6,870	13.5	10,429	10,755
1998	32.8	24.2	8.6	16,412	9,378	15.9	8,119	8,758
1999	41.3	28.9	10.7	20,934	10,751	14.9	11,326	11,424

Notes:
1 = Bad debts* as a percentage of bank loans.
2 = Bad debts* as a percentage of total assets.
3 = Bad debts* as a percentage of GDP.
4 = Total loans in C, D and E.
5 = Total net loans in C, D and E.
6 = Total net loans in C, D and E (as a percentage of total bank assets).
7 = Allocated provisions.
8 = Potential losses.
* Bad debts are defined loans classified in risk categories C, D and E.

Source: National Bank of the Republic of Macedonia.

In addition, the process of rehabilitation of the banking system included liquidation of the second largest bank and three smaller recently established new private banks, as well as a permanent strengthening of the supervisory standards (for credit and market risks, foreign exchange exposure, sensitivity to risks, internal control and so on), and their strict enforcement.

The costs of the rehabilitation of the banking system were extremely high. Total costs reached 42.3 per cent of GDP, of which 12.1 per cent refers to the cleaning of bad loans from the banks' balance sheets and 30.2 per cent of GDP refers to the costs for payment of 'frozen' foreign currency household deposits. This was one of the most costly operations of bank restructuring, taken as a percentage of GDP.[5]

The share of bad loans remained high even after bank restructuring: 44.4 per cent of total loans at the end of 1995 or 7.4 per cent of GDP. Until the end of 1998 the share of bad loans in the total loan portfolio continued to decrease (32.8 per cent). Total loan provisions covered 49.5 per cent of total bad loans. The loan portfolio deteriorated in 1999. The bad-loan share increased by 8.5 percentage points, mainly in the context of the Kosovo crisis, when enterprises responded to the shock by refusing to service their debts; as a result the ratio of provisions to bad loans increased to 54.1 per cent.

Unfortunately, the financial restructuring of the banking system in 1995 was not immediately followed by operational restructuring through the introduction of new client-oriented banking products, the implementation of efficient techniques of risk management, the reduction of costs for financial intermediation, the implementation of efficient credit and liquidity policies and so on. Competition in the financial sector remained weak, which has not created pressures for consolidation and higher efficiency in the banking industry.

Table 13.7 *Statutory ratios and Cook ratio (ratio of capital to weighted assets) in Macedonian banks, 1994–1999*

Ratio	Prescribed	1994	1995	1996	1997	1998	1999
1	8%	19.09	39.60[b]	33.03	27.30	25.90	28.70
2		7.06	22.15	26.18	23.78	23.98	20.70
3	10%	n/a	n/a	n/a	n/a	n/a	n/a
4		[a]	1.09	2.49	3.37	2.72	6.75
5		[a]	1.61	2.32	2.39	2.44	2.10
6	25%	32.73	31.08	29.35	30.05	26.41	27.8

Notes:
1 = Capital adequacy ratio.
2 = Capital/total liabilities.
3 = Coefficient of big loans (as a percentage of bank's capital).
4 = Coefficient of long-term investments in companies (as a percentage of bank's capital).
5 = Coefficient of long-term investments in banks (as a percentage of bank's capital).
6 = Coefficient of investments in fixed assets (as a percentage of bank's capital).
[a] There are no data for capital investments in banks and companies for the end of 1994. Total capital investments of the banks as of 30 September 1994 represents 9.4 per cent of the capital of the banks.
[b] Not including Stopanska Banka, Skopje, which was in the process of rehabilitation.

Source: National Bank of the Republic of Macedonia.

Operational restructuring of the banking system started at the beginning of 2000, when the largest bank, Stopanska Banka Skopje, was sold to three foreign institutional investors: National Bank of Greece S.A. Athens with a stake of 65 per cent, and the European Bank for Reconstruction and Development, London and the International Finance Corporation, Washington, with a stake of 10 per cent each in the bank's capital. The precondition for this development was a second financial reconstruction of the bank, which occurred at the end of 1999 with the replacement of USD 122 million of bad loans by government bonds. This created additional costs of 3.5 per cent of GDP for rehabilitation of the banking industry. Thus, the total costs since 1995 for the rehabilitation of the financial system reached 45.8 per cent of GDP.

Bank soundness as seen through the capital adequacy ratio was very high (28.7 per cent at the end of 1999 – see Table 13.7). In some cases, the high capitalisation is a result of accounting effects rather than economic solvency. For some banks, the high capitalisation is also a structural feature associated with the low deposit base. That is, banks with small deposits tend to maintain higher-than-average capital adequacy ratios.

OBSTACLES TO BANKING REFORM

The dependence of enterprises on banks' funds is very high. Because of the undeveloped stock market, almost all of the externally required funds for enterprises comes from the credit market of banks. The bond and equity markets are of modest means. On the credit market, enterprises borrow 98.5 per cent of their total external funds. The remaining 1.5 per cent of external funds used by companies comes from equity and bond markets.

In addition to funds available on the credit market from banks, there is access to credit lines from international institutions: a credit line of USD 22.5 million from the World Bank, targeted to private companies; one of USD 12 million from Taiwan; and one of USD 6.5 million from the KFW for the development of small and medium-sized companies. A few micro-credit lines also exist, mainly for small self-employed businesses.

The high number of companies dependent on banking industry funds indicates that bank soundness and efficiency is closely connected with the private investment and economic growth in the country. Improved bank efficiency in combination with high macroeconomic stability secures cheaper financing of companies. At this stage the most flexible form of risk capital – equity finance – is woefully underdeveloped.

Corporate governance and restructuring of the real sector is still poor. The loss-making enterprises still have access to bank funds. Thus, profitable projects and small and medium-sized enterprises are crowded out by big loss-making companies. Soft-budget constraints almost tripled the inter-enterprise debt in the 1996–99 period. At the end of 1999, inter-enterprise debt reached MKD 30 billion and exceeded the stock of money supply M1 by 55.1 per cent.

At the end of 1999, banks in Macedonia had 106 branches and agencies. Thus, there were 18,868 citizens per bank agency or branch, which is 11 times higher than the average number (1,682) in the EU. This is an indicator that banks are not client-oriented institutions. Such a situation is supported by the institutional set-up of the domestic payment system. That is, banks are still not receiving payment orders from or issuing statements of accounts to their clients. This is done by a separate specialised institution for payment services (the Payment Office), which has branches and agencies all over the country. Thus, although banks do not have their own offices nationwide, they can have clients all over the country based on the facilities provided by the specialised Payment Office. It was projected that this institution will cease to function in the second half of 2001 and banks would then undertake to offer payment services to their customers. This was to be a strong impetus for banks to increase their branch and agency network, significantly.

At the end of 1999 there were 53,846 citizens per bank or saving bank. This indicates that there is overbanking, and the process of concentration and consolidation in the banking industry will begin soon. Of the total number of banks and savings banks, only six of the former and four of the latter had headquarters outside of the capital (Skopje). The combined assets of the banking institutions located out of the country's capital, account for only 10 per cent of total assets.

The entry of foreign investors into the banking industry has been fully liberalised. The participation in bank capital per shareholder is limited to 20 per cent (from mid-2000 up to 33 per cent). The participation of a foreign bank in a domestic bank's capital is unlimited and can be as much as 100 per cent. With the entry of foreign strategic investors in the largest domestic bank at the beginning of 2000, foreign ownership in the banking industry reached 54 per cent. Considering the high degree of interest of some foreign banks in the second and third largest banks in the country, it is expected that in the near future foreign ownership will increase to 80 per cent.

The takeover of domestic by foreign banks is accelerating the process of operational restructuring of the banking sector, increasing its efficiency, introducing new client-oriented products, especially securitisation and marketable products, introducing new techniques for risk management, improving internal control systems and so on. Thus, the financial system in Macedonia is becoming more integrated in the international financial system and international flows of capital. In the long run, efficient allocation of resources will boost the growth and prosperity of the country.

CONCLUSION: LESSONS AND THEIR RELEVANCE

Although there had been a tradition of a two-tiered banking system for more than three decades, the reconstruction of the Macedonian banking system involved all the phases characteristic of transition economies. However, because banks were state-owned enterprises, they were privatised automatically under the general enterprise privatisation scheme. Thus, the government had to bear the costs for bank rehabilitation, but did not receive any revenue from the privatisation of the banking system.

Although macroeconomic stability existed for several years, major weaknesses in the banking and enterprise sectors have hampered more rapid economic growth and development. A large share of non-performing assets in the portfolio of large banks, stemming from losses in the enterprise sector, has been a key impediment to development in the financial sector. The banking system has been crippled by a low level of intermediation, high cost of capital, severe lack of financial discipline, and poor allocation of credit. Reforms aimed at strengthening lending practices, encouraging foreign bank participation, improving bank supervision and, above all, a consolidation process that breaks away from the past, are helping to pave the way to economic recovery.

The sequence of bank rehabilitation did not follow a logical path. Financial reconstruction in 1995 was not succeeded by the operational restructuring of the banking system. Thus the efficiency of the banking system remained low. Misallocation of resources and bad bank practices continued. This led to another financial restructuring of the largest bank in 1999. The mistake of misalignment of financial and operational restructuring was not repeated again. The bank was sold to foreign strategic investors, which immediately began the process of operational restructuring.

The problems of overbanking and underbranching remain unsolved. However, along with increased efficiency, the banking system will witness consolidation and an increase in branch offices throughout the country in the near future. This process will be facilitated by the aggressive entry of foreign banks into the domestic market, which is now highly liberalised. Foreign participation in banks' capital stands at 54 per cent. In the process of consolidation it is expected that this share will increase further and the national banking system will become a part of the global financial system in which a few mega-banks will dominate.

NOTES

1. Two-tier banking system is characteristic for a market-based economy. The first tier consists of the central bank (performing primarily monetary policy duties), while the second tier is made of commercial banks. In contrast, in a monobank system, the state bank performs both central bank and commercial bank functions. Thus only one tier exists.
2. The main external shocks, which severely damaged the Macedonian economy and its growth potential, were the following: the break-up of former Yugoslavia in 1991; the UN embargo in the 1992–95 period against the neighbouring country, Yugoslavia, which

accounted for 18 per cent of the total Macedonian foreign trade; the unilateral informal Greek embargo on movement of goods and services across the border of the two countries from April 1994 to November 1995; the Kosovo crisis in the first half of 1999 and its lasting effects; and EU sanctions against the authoritarian regime of Slobodan Milošević in Yugoslavia imposed at the beginning of 1999.

3. 'The National Bank of the Republic of Macedonia is independent and responsible for the stability of the domestic currency (denar), for the monetary policy and for the global liquidity of external payments', Article 3, National Bank of the Republic of Macedonia Act, *Official Gazette*, No. 26/96.
4. The main purpose of financial restructuring is the renewal of the bank's solvency (net worth). The bank could improve its balance sheet by inflow of new capital (from the present and new shareholders), by reducing the liabilities (for instance, some liabilities to be written off), or by increasing the value of the assets (for instance, by improving the collection of bad claims, by accelerating the realisation of collateral for bad loans and so on). This phase of the bank's restructuring usually includes government intervention by: replacement of bad claims with government bonds, establishment of a government agency for the collection of bad claims undertaken from banks, liquidity support from the central bank, acceleration of the privatisation process in banks and so on.
5. Operational restructuring includes: audit of the business strategy of the bank; improvement of corporate governance; establishment of sound management and accounting systems; adoption of better techniques for risk evaluation and assets and liability management; efficient liquidity management; and implementation of an efficient internal control and audit system as a prevention against different kinds of risks. Operational costs in banks could be reduced by the implementation of new technologies, closing some branches, opening agencies, and reducing the number of employees. Usually this phase begins with a change of management of banks under the rehabilitation programme.
6. The financial restructuring of the banking system has considerable fiscal implications, with the costs being borne by taxpayers. There is empirical evidence that these costs range from 4 per cent of GDP in the case of bank restructuring in the Philippines to 45 per cent of GDP in the case of restructuring of the banking system in Kuwait. The average costs for restructuring of the banking systems in the transition economies were about 8 per cent of GDP (the Czech Republic in 1993: 7.8 per cent of GDP; Hungary in 1993: 12.2 per cent of GDP; Poland in 1993: 5.7 per cent of GDP).

BIBLIOGRAPHY

Balino, T.J.T. and C. Cottarelli (eds) (1994), *Policy Issues and Country Experiences*, Washington, DC: International Monetary Fund.

Beattie, V., P. Casson, R. Dale, G. McKenzie, C. Sutcliffe and M. Turner (1995), *Banks and Bad Debts*, New York: John Wiley & Sons.

Bišev, G. (1997), 'Basic Information of the Emerging Banking System in Macedonia', Vienna Institute Monthly Report, No. 2, Vienna: Vienna Institute.

Bišev, G. (1999), 'Banks' Soundness and Economic Growth', in Ž. Šević (ed.), *Banking Reform in South East European Transitional Economies*, Sofia and London: University of Greenwich Business School, Balkan Center for Public Policy and Related Studies, Humanities Research Centre, 395–405.

Boonstra, W.W. and C.W. Eijffinger Sylvester (eds) (1997), *Banks, Financial Markets and Monetary Policy*, Amsterdam: Nederlands Instituut vor het Banken Effectenbedrijf.

Borish, M.S., M.F. Long and M. Noel (1995), 'Restructuring Banks and Enterprises, Recent Lessons from Transition Countries', World Bank Discussion Paper No. 279/1995, Washington, DC: World Bank.

Caprio, G., D. Folkerts-Landau and T.D. Lane (eds) (1994), *Building Sound Finance in Emerging Market Economies*, Washington, DC: International Monetary Fund/World Bank.

De Gregorio, J. and P. Guidotti (1992), 'Financial Development and Economic Growth', IMF Working Paper No. 101/92, Washington, DC: IMF.

Enoch, C. and J.H. Green (eds) (1997), *Banking Soundness and Monetary Policy, Issues and Experiences in the Global Economy*, Washington, DC: International Monetary Fund.

Galbis, V. (1994), 'Sequencing of Financial Sector Reforms: A Review', IMF Working Paper 101/94, Washington, DC: IMF.

Group of Banking Supervisors from Central and Eastern Europe (1998), BSCEE Review.

Johnston, B.R. (1997), 'The Speed of Financial Sector Reform: Risks and Strategies', in A. Harwood and B.L.R. Smith (eds), *Sequencing? Financial Strategies for Developing Countries*, Washington, DC: Brookings Institution Press.

Johnston, B.R. and V. Sundararajan (1999), *Sequencing Financial Sector Reforms, Country Experiences and Issues*, Washington, DC: International Monetary Fund.

Llewellyn, D. (1999), 'The New Economics of Banking', *SUERF Studies*, No. 5, Amsterdam: Société Universitarie Européenne de Recherches Financières.

Lindgren, C., G. Garcia and M. Saal (1996), *Bank Soundness and Macroeconomic Policy*, Washington, DC: International Monetary Fund.

World Economic Outlook (May 1998), *Financial Crises, Causes and Indicators*, Washington, DC: International Monetary Fund.

14. Banking Reform in Romania

Claudiu Doltu

INTRODUCTION

The centrally planned economic system in Romania had collapsed by the end of 1989. At the beginning of 1990, the new democratically elected power – the former communists – had chosen gradualism as a general philosophy for transition. The first steps of reform – price liberalisation, trade liberalisation, free enterprise, privatisation and restoration of property rights – were taken, but progress has been slow. As a consequence, macroeconomic imbalances threatened the country's general stability. A political change took place at the end of 1996 and since 1997, the structural reforms have been accelerated. As a consequence, Romania's GDP contracted significantly, unemployment increased, and many companies and banks (state owned and private) were declared bankrupt. At the end of 1999, Romania was still lagging behind Central and East European countries in the process of transformation, but the first good effects of the structural reforms undertaken so far, indicate that the country is on a sensible track. (See Table 14.1.)

Before the Second World War, Romania had a competitive banking system regulated by an independent central bank. The National Bank of Romania (NBR), many of whose constituent principles and functioning mechanisms were inspired by the legislation in Belgium, was founded in 1880. According to its founding law,[1] the NBR was established as a central bank with private capital, but the state also had a share in its capital. In July 1948, the communist regime nationalised the NBR along with most of the private commercial banks. The other commercial banks were closed. At the beginning of 1947, 2,062 banking entities – 383 commercial banks and 1,679 credit co-operatives – existed in Romania. At the end of 1947 only 70 of these had survived, but all were nationalised (Negrea, 1991). Some 44 years later only eight banks remain in existence.

Table 14.1 *Romania's GDP growth (in per cent), 1990–1999*

1990	1991	1992	1993	1994	1995	1996	1997	1998	1999
–5.6	–12.9	–8.8	1.5	3.9	7.1	3.9	–6.1	–5.4	–3.2

Source: National Commission for Statistics.

At the end of 1999, 41 commercial banks were registered in Romania, 34 of which were chartered in Romania and seven were branches of foreign banks. Of the total number of banks, one had fully state-owned capital, three had majority state-owned capital, four had fully Romanian private capital, seven had majority Romanian private capital, eleven had majority foreign private capital and eight had fully foreign private capital. Although the number of banks has increased by almost five times in nine years, the quantity and quality of banking products are low compared to Western practice. At the end of September 2000, the total number of bank entities (branches, offices) was about 3,448. Since Romania has an estimated population of about 22.5 million people, on average, a bank entity provides services for 6,526 inhabitants.

The main macroeconomic indicators that show Romania's development in the last ten years are as shown in Tables 14.2–5.

Table 14.2 *Inflation rate in Romania (end of year), 1990–1999*

Year	Inflation rate	Year	Inflation rate
1990	37.7	1995	27.8
1991	222.8	1996	56.9
1992	199.2	1997	151.4
1993	295.5	1998	40.6
1994	61.7	1999	45.9

Source: National Bank of Romania.

Table 14.3 *Romanian exchange rate ROL/USD (annual average), 1990–1999*

Year	Exchange rate	Year	Exchange rate
1990	22.43	1995	2,033.26
1991	76.39	1996	3,082.60
1992	307.95	1997	7,167.94
1993	760.05	1998	8,875.55
1994	1,655.09	1999	15,333.00

Source: National Bank of Romania.

Table 14.4 *Romanian government fiscal position (per cent of GDP), 1990–1999*

	1990	1991	1992	1993	1994	1995	1996	1997	1998	1999
A	39.8	41.9	37.4	33.8	32.0	32.1	29.8	30.7	34.8	34.8
B	37.7	38.7	42.0	34.2	34.5	35.0	33.8	34.6	39.2	36.8
C	2.1	3.2	–4.6	–0.4	–2.5	–2.9	–4.0	–3.9	–4.4	–2.0
D	–	–	3.7	2.1	2.5	1.9	5.0	6.0	8.0	12.5
E	–	–	0.3	0.9	1.3	1.3	1.6	3.7	4.9	5.5

Notes:
A = Revenue.
B = Expenditure.
C = Balance.
D = Public debt (domestic public debt).
E = Interest (interest expenditure for domestic public debt).

Source: Ministry of Finance.

Table 14.5 *Current account deficit in Romania (per cent of GDP), 1990–1999*

1990	1991	1992	1993	1994	1995	1996	1997	1998	1999
8.7	3.5	8.0	4.5	1.4	5.0	7.3	6.1	7.9	3.8

Source: National Bank of Romania.

THE SEQUENCE OF BANKING REFORM

The first phase of banking system reform in Romania started at the end of 1990 when a two-tier banking system was established. In April 1991, parliament adopted the Law on Banking Activity (Law No. 33/1991) and the Law on the Statute of the National Bank of Romania (Law No. 34/1991). The NBR assumed the traditional central banking functions and all its previous commercial operations were transferred to the commercial banks. Although, according to the central bank law, the NBR should have had a high degree of independence, being accountable only to parliament, political pressures influenced its important decisions. The low level of NBR independence was evident until 1997, when monetary policy was applied to finance the government's quasi-fiscal deficits. It is also noteworthy that the NBR – in its capacity as a regulatory and surveillance authority – did not succeed in closing down any commercial bank until 1999 although many banks were practically bankrupt, and survived only by refinancing from the central bank and borrowing daily from other banks. A flagrant example of political interference in NBR policy was the law (adopted by parliament) which obliged some state-owned banks to offer huge credits for 'strategic' activities, such as agriculture and energy imports. The central bank had to cover these credits, which were never paid back by borrowers. The NBR's independence increased after 1997 and according to its new Statute (Law No. 101/1998), its main permanent objective is price stability. The present legislation (the new Banking Act – Law No. 58/1998 – and the Norms added to the Bank Insolvency Act – Norms No. 9/27 September 1999) creates conditions for avoiding excessive refinancing to banks in trouble and the strengthening of fiscal discipline.

The second phase in banking reform was characterised by an increase in the number of licensed banks and accumulating tensions. The general policy regarding the number of new banks involved a trade-off between the entry of new banks and the quality of banks. In an attempt to avoid excessive entry of banks into the market, and given the limited enforcement capacity of the regulators, a second-best solution (that is, restrictions on entry) was adopted. This approach maintained both an oligopolistic market structure, which inhibited the development of a competitive system, and also the 'too-big-to-fail' problem.

Although the number of banks increased significantly in this phase, the banking system still had a high degree of concentration and segmentation. Also, no bankruptcy proceedings were completed. The banking system provided poor bank intermediation of savings and investment. The range of banking services increased very slowly. The weakness of some state-owned banks and the authorities' hesitation to resolve bank failures created excellent opportunities for lending to banks with chronic liquidity problems. From 1996 the government ensured profit opportunities for banks by issuing huge volumes of treasury bills and offering high interest rates. These factors explain the low degree of competition in the banking system and indicate why the banks were not oriented to serve the customer.

The economic, political and institutional environment in Romania has made it difficult for regulators to act decisively regarding banks in trouble. There have been strong political pressures placed on state-owned banks to sustain large state-owned companies. The bad loan problem started to increase in 1995–96 but, because of the lack of transparency, it became evident only after 1997. There are also other factors that contributed to the bad-loan problem, beyond the political pressures on banks and banking regulators. Often, banks themselves preferred simply to roll over bad loans to conceal the extent of their problems and to avoid a reputation as hard creditors by attempting to recover non-performing assets. On the one hand, bank bankruptcies were a politically unacceptable solution in Romania before 1997. On the other hand, the too-big-to-fail problem became the strongest argument for delaying decisive action. As a result, the moral hazard problem increased significantly because the managers and shareholders of several banks (both state owned and private) had considered themselves protected from the consequences of their investment decisions. At present, the bad-debt problem is still a significant feature in the Romanian banking system. A centralised approach to this problem was adopted at the beginning of 1999, when the Bank Asset Recovery Agency (AVAB) was established. The AVAB is entrusted with taking over doubtful and loss-making loans and off-balance-sheet items from the state-owned banks undergoing restructuring and/or privatisation in order to recover these assets from debtors.

The third and the fourth phases in banking reform began, more or less concurrently, during 1999. The biggest state-owned bank (Bancorex) was closed down at the beginning of 1999. Its non-performing loans were transferred to AVAB and the Romanian Commercial Bank (a majority state-owned bank) incorporated the remaining assets through a merger operation. In 1999, the NBR appointed a new managing committee to oversee Banca Agricola's restructuring and to prepare the bank for privatisation.

Two private banks, Banca Albina (1999) and Bankcoop (2000) were declared bankrupt by the Commercial ward. The NBR filed a lawsuit against another private bank (Banca Internationala a Religiilor) in the summer of 2000. Bank privatisation started in 1998, when the French bank Société Générale acquired a majority stake (51 per cent) in the Romanian Bank for Development. In 1999, General Electric Capital Corporation and Banco Portugues de Investimento bought 45 per cent of the total shares of BancPost. In little less that two years (1999 and the first nine months of 2000), eight banks exited the market.

STRUCTURE OF THE BANKING SYSTEM

In the early stages of banking reform, all existing specialised banks (that is, the bank for agriculture, the bank for foreign trade, the bank for investments) became universal banks. All newly created banks (private Romanian, foreign and joint ventures) adopted the same strategy.

The core of the Romanian banking system is represented by the NBR, which is an independent central bank.[2] Its main goal is to ensure the stability of the domestic currency in order to contribute to price stability. The NBR draws up and implements the monetary policy and foreign exchange, credit and payment policies, and is also responsible for the licensing and supervision of the banking system.

All commercial banks provide both retail and corporate banking. A special position is held by Casa de Economii si Consemnatiuni (CEC), a savings bank, which is organised as a public limited company and regulated by a special law (Law No. 66/1996).

Although the CEC is entitled to carry out the whole range of banking activities, this institution has a large degree of autonomy with regard to central bank powers of supervision and control. Also, since 1996, other institutions can provide banking services – the so-called credit co-operatives.

The activities of these institutions are not yet supervised by the NBR, but according to a law adopted in 1998 (Law No. 58/1998), the existing legislation shall be modified so as to allow the NBR to supervise the activities of these institutions, as well as the CEC's activity. The credit co-operatives proliferated quickly after 1997 and acted very aggressively in the next few years. In 1999, many of them experienced serious liquidity problems, which increased public distrust of the whole banking system. Taking advantage of the public's inexperience, and the authorities' lack of action, credit co-operatives included the word 'bank' in their commercial name, and so created a false image of their position in the banking system. Rumours about their financial position triggered pressure from depositors and increased problems for some of them. The NBR announced that in 2000 they would modify legislation in order to force these institutions to adopt the required safety conditions.

Table 14.6 *Number of Romanian banks by type of capital, 1991–1999*

	1991	1992	1993	1994	1995	1996	1997	1998	1999
A	7*	7*	4*	1	1	1	1	1	1
B	0	0	3	6	6	6	6	6	3
C	3	5	5	8	9	14	13	13	11
D	2	5	2	5	8	10	13	16	19
Total	12	17	14	20	24	31	33	36	34

Notes:
* Including CEC.
A = Fully state-owned capital; from 1994, the only bank with fully state-owned capital is the CEC.
B = Majority state-owned capital.
C = Fully or majority private Romanian capital.
D = Fully or majority foreign capital.

Source: National Bank of Romania.

For many years, state-owned banks did not increase in number, but they continued to dominate the market, even though between 1994 and 1999 the number of private banks increased by 13 to 30. At the end of 1999, four banks were fully owned by domestic private capital and eight were fully owned by foreign investors. The changes in the number of bank, incorporated and chartered in Romania are shown in Table 14.6.

The year 1999 can be considered as the year of change in the evolution of the Romanian banking system. Both the number of state-owned banks and their market share decreased. The hesitation in restructuring state-owned banks and political reluctance regarding privatisation in the banking system seriously threatened the stability of the Romanian financial sector in early 1999.

During the last decade, the main characteristics of the banking system have been concentration and segmentation. Three segments could be identified in the banking system: state-owned banks, small banks with foreign and/or Romanian capital and foreign banks. At the end of 1999, state-owned banks were still dominant on the market, holding 50.33 per cent in total bank net assets. From 1998 to 1999, banks with a majority foreign capital increased their share in total bank net assets significantly from 15.12 to 43.56 per cent. This rapid increase is explained by the privatisation of two state-owned banks (Romanian Bank for Development and BancPost).

Table 14.7 *Position held by state-owned banks in Romania, 1991–1998*

Year	Total assets	Total credits %	Total deposits %	Year	Total assets	Total credits %	Total deposits %
1991	83	94	68	1995	64	76	56
1992	76	93	60	1996	66	76	62
1993	76	87	61	1997	61	63	61
1994	69	82	61	1998	62	73	59

Sources: National Bank of Romania, *Annual Report 1998*.

State-owned banks enjoyed a permanent and comfortable dominant position in the market (see Table 14.7). After 1991, they maintained their influence through political and diffuse private interests. Their management did not develop clear strategies (either profit or customer oriented). Instead, the focus was mainly on financing state-owned companies, the public sector and often the pursuit of unclear political and private interests. In accordance with the Medium-term Economic Strategy for Integration in the European Union,[3] up to the year 2002, three of the four remaining state-owned banks (Banca Agricola, Romanian Commercial Bank and CEC) have to be privatised, preferably by a strategic investor.

Small banks (with Romanian and/or foreign capital) are more oriented towards lending to private companies. In a short period of time, foreign banks or banks with foreign participation have proved to be the most profitable motivations (Popa, 1997, pp. 217–28). At the same time, newly formed banks received higher net revenues than state-owned banks. The explanation is simple: a newly formed bank is strongly motivated to attract customers and to expand its business. In order to do so, such a bank offers a better quality of service.

Foreign banks are focused on financing major foreign companies operating in Romania. In 1999 and 2000, foreign banks have become more interested in increasing the number of branches in the country. This development is interesting because, generally, big foreign banks have been reluctant to extend their own branch networks in the region.

Table 14.8 *Segmentation of the Romanian banking system as of 31 December 1998*

Banks/segments	Leu deposits[c]	Forex deposits[c]	Leu loans[d]	Forex loans[d]	Total assets (%)
State owned[a]	70.8	52.6	59.9	61.4	64.2
Private	29.2	47.4	40.1	38.6	35.8
Domestic owned	13.1	14.7	17.3	18.4	15.7
Foreign banks and joint ventures[b]	16.1	32.7	22.8	20.2	20.1

Notes:
[a] Romanian Commercial Bank, Bancorex, Banca Agricola, BancPost, CEC and Eximbank.
[b] Domestic and foreign capital.
[c] By customers (percentage).
[d] To non-government (percentage).

Source: World Bank, *Romania Financial Sector Review*, March 1999.

Important events occurred in 1999 and 2000: the privatisation of the Romanian Development Bank and BancPost, the merger between the Romanian Commercial Bank and approximately 10 per cent of Bancorex, and the bankruptcy of Banca Albina, Bankcoop and Banca Internationala a Religiilor. This will have changed the segmentation of the banking system (see Table 14.8). However, there are no recent data available about the effects of these events on segmentation.

The aggregate total assets of banks expressed in local currency (the Romanian leu: ROL) increased between 1990 and 1999, but show a decrease if they are denominated in US dollars. A simple comparison of figures expressed in US dollars is not relevant because the interbank market did not determine the exchange rate until 1994.[4] The spectacular decrease in total bank assets (if they are expressed in US dollars) could be explained by the permanent strong depreciation of the leu between 1990 and 1998. More significant is the decrease in total bank assets in 1999 compared to 1998. This decrease is certainly explained by the acceleration of the restructuring in the banking system that involved the closure of the most important state-owned bank (Bancorex), the taking over of bad debts from Banca Agricola by AVAB and also the closure of some small private banks.

Table 14.9 *Total assets in the Romanian banking system, 1991–1999*

Year	Million ROL	Million USD	Exchange rate* (ROL/USD)
1990	1,071	48	22.43
1991	2,290	30	76.39
1992	4,002	13	307.95
1993	9,843	13	760.05
1994	20,415	12	1,655.09
1995	32,440	16	2,033.26
1996	55,023	18	3,082.60
1997	100,188	14	7,167.94
1998	148,005	17	8,874.81
1999	182,178	12	15,332.93

Note: * Annual average.

Source: National Bank of Romania, *Annual Report 1999*.

Due to high rates of inflation, interest rates have remained at high levels. Over time, the net interest margin (the difference between interest revenues and interest expenses scaled by total assets) decreased from 6.31 per cent in 1994 to 3.72 per cent in 1997. In 1998, the net interest margin was negative (–2.21 per cent) and this could be explained by the chronic liquidity problems of two state-owned banks (Bancorex and Banca Agricola), which had borrowed significant amounts from the interbank market (Doltu, 1999). So, for the whole banking system, the interest paid exceeded that received. (See Figures 14.1–3.)

Figure 14.1 *Average Interest for non-banking customers (1991–2000)*

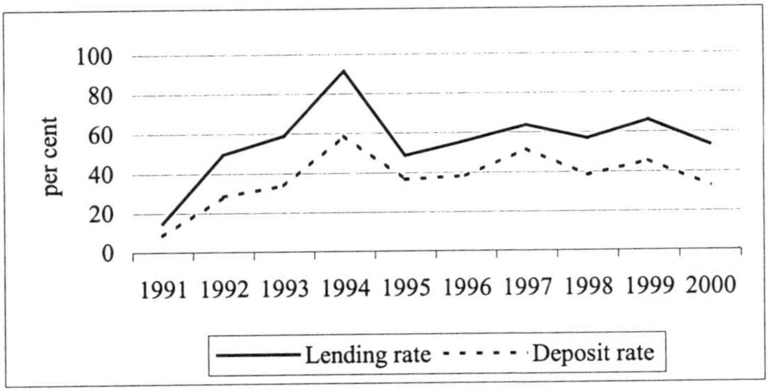

Source: Data released by NBR.

Figure 14.2 *Average interest rate (1996–2000)*

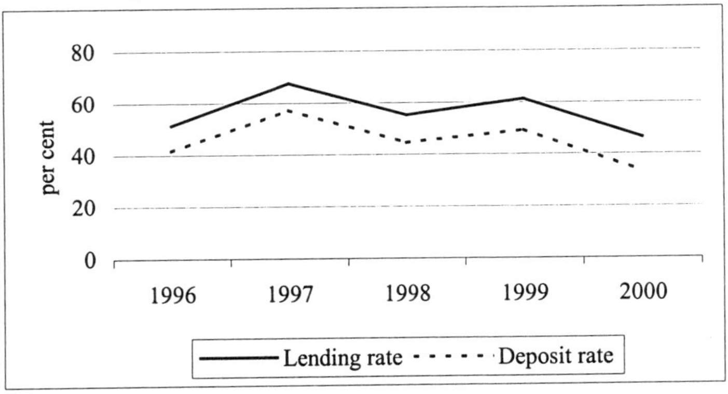

Source: Data released by NBR.

Figure 14.3 *Average interest rate for interbank operations (1996–2000)*

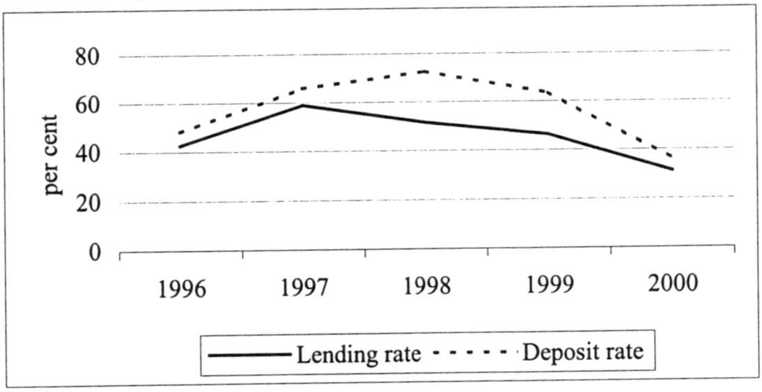

Source: Data released by NBR.

The decrease in the net interest margins can be explained by the progress in macroeconomic stability – first at all, a decrease in inflation – and it also indicates the beginnings of structural reform in Romania. For the 1994–99 period, household deposits in national currency increased by 4.03 per cent of GDP to 7.9 per cent of GDP. Household deposits in foreign currency also increased by 1.3 per cent in 1993 to 4 per cent in 1999. This evolution shows an increasing public confidence in the banking system. (See Table 14.10.)

Table 14.10 *Household savings in Romania, 1994–1999*

Deposits	1994	1995	1996	1997	1998	1999
ROL billions						
Household savings	2,728	5,136	8,808	20,166	30,967	39,238
o/w demand	359	496	789	1,599	1,403	1,357
Household demand	183	183	183	183	183	183
Total	3,270	5,815	9,780	21,948	32,553	40,778
Forex (USD, thousands)						
Demand	227	328	380	318	382	330
Time	43	129	231	521	846	1,042
Total	270	457	611	839	1,228	1,372
A	6.57	8.06	8.98	8.76	8.84	7.82
B	0.90	1.29	1.73	2.40	2.96	4.03

Notes:
A = Total deposits in national currency/GDP.
B = Total Forex deposits/GDP.

Source: Calculations based on data released by the National Bank of Romania.

CENTRAL BANK REFORM

The NBR was founded in 1880 as a central bank with private capital, but the state also owned a proportion of its capital. In July 1948, the communist regime nationalised the NBR, thus halting the banking system's development on market principles. At the end of 1990, a two-tier banking structure was introduced, involving the central bank – the National Bank of Romania – and commercial banks. At present, the NBR's legal framework is based on the National Bank of Romania Act (Law No. 101/1998) which modifies the previous Law No. 34/1991.

Under the central bank law, the NBR has a high degree of independence, being accountable only to parliament. The governor and the board of directors – consisting of nine members – are appointed by parliament upon the recommendation of the prime minister for a renewable eight-year term, and they can only be removed by parliament at the request of the prime minister.

The NBR's main goal is to ensure price stability in the domestic currency, which will contribute to price stability generally. The NBR draws up and implements the monetary policy concerning the control of the money supply, and is also responsible for the conduct of the exchange rate policy, the management of official international reserves, and credit and payment policies. At the same time, the NBR is the sole bank licensing and supervisory authority and is empowered to act as lender of last resort for the commercial banks.

The NBR has a small number of instruments to conduct monetary policy. In 1992, credit ceilings were replaced by the refinancing of commercial banks in order to control the monetary base. Since 1992, minimum reserve requirements (a different reserve requirements ratio applied to leu deposits as opposed to that applied to foreign currency deposits) were introduced, followed in subsequent years by standing facilities such as Lombard credit and currency swaps.

Before 1997, the main monetary instrument used by the NBR in monetary policy was refinancing credit, extended through four windows:[5] structural credit, auction credit, Lombard credit and the so-called special credit. After 1997, the NBR used only Lombard credit and special credit for refinancing – for banks in distress.

Open-market operations are not a very common practice in Romania, because the secondary market for government securities started to operate only in 1999. In 1999, for instance, liquidity management through government securities operations was kept at a very low level. This is explained by two factors: first, the liquidity surplus did not allow new purchases of treasury certificates from the market and, second, banks are reluctant to buy government securities issued for bank restructuring – the only category of government securities held in the NBR's portfolio.

After 1997, deposit taking and minimum reserve requirements were the most commonly used instruments in conducting monetary policy. The NBR made extensive recourse to deposit-taking operations in order to counteract the net impact of the operations providing monetary injections induced by the government securities operations and Forex market operations. This is why the interest rate on deposit taking was the most representative interest rate applied by the central bank as a monetary policy instrument post-1997.

There is a legal restriction on credit being provided to the government. The ceiling is twice the central bank's capital reserve fund and up to 10 per cent of the state budget. The central bank is also prevented by law from buying government securities in the primary market and can purchase them only in the secondary market. In 1999 an exception was made when, based on a government emergency ordinance, the NBR provided money for the banking system's restructuring and accepted treasury certificates in its portfolio.

The government encroached upon NBR's independence by forcing it to provide funds to the public sector, and persuading parliament to pass laws in its favour. In 1996 for instance, parliament adopted a special law in favour of agriculture. According to this law, the NBR granted credit to one state-owned bank (Banca Agricola), which then provided funds for agriculture. Although such practices stopped after 1997, the NBR continued to provide special credit for state-owned banks in distress and for the Bank Deposit Guarantee Fund, which has been under pressure because of the successive bankruptcies of some private banks. In March 2000, for instance, the government decided that the credit line granted by the NBR to guarantee funds to the banking system, amounting to ROL 2,000 billion, would be used for payments to the deposits at Bankcoop (a private bank).

Because of the systematic failure in achieving its goals regarding inflation during the last decade, the NBR's credibility has remained weak. There is a negative expectation by the public that inflation will exceed official targets. Often, companies design their balance sheets assuming inflation rates to be 50 to 100 per cent higher than NBR targets. (See Figure 14.4.)

Figure 14.4 *Growth rates of M1 and M2 monetary aggregates in Romania, 1990–2000*

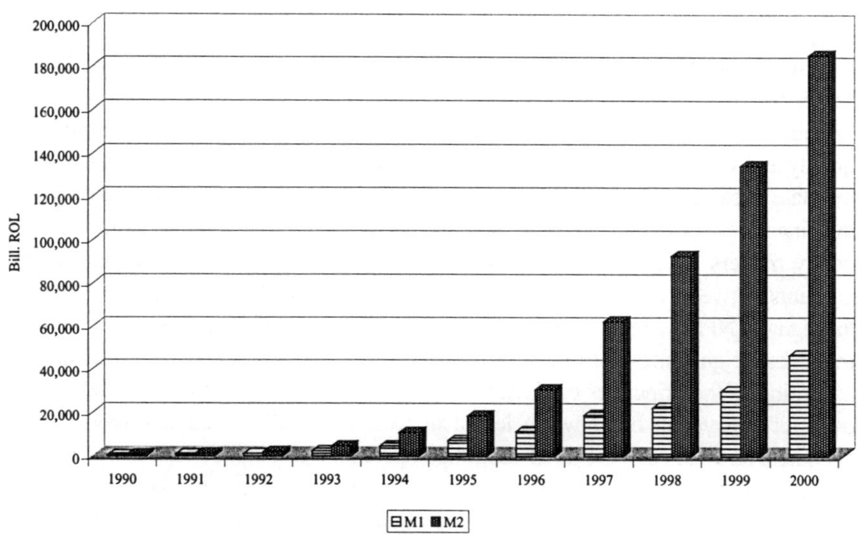

Source: Data released by the National Bank of Romania.

Progress has been achieved by the NBR in adopting prudential rules that address the following areas: capital adequacy, large exposures, insider lending, foreign currency exposure, investments in non-banking companies, ownership of banks by non-bankers, loan classification and general and specific reserves. Also, its supervisory capabilities have strengthened. The NBR has begun an on-site inspection both of state-owned and private banks. On-site examinations are complemented by off-site supervision. From a technical point of view, the NBR's supervisory activities have improved inn efficiency in recent years. Further improvement will depend on an increase in political independence of the supervisory authority rather than on any technical changes.

The current deposit insurance scheme is based on the Bank Deposit Guarantee Fund, which has been operational since 1996. This is an independent institution, financed by the compulsory contributions of the commercial banks. At present, only the deposits of private individuals are insured. The level of insured deposit is about USD 2,700 and the equivalent in Romanian lei. In order to preserve the real value of insured deposits, the maximum level of insured amounts is indexed quarterly in accordance with the inflation rate for the previous period. At the beginning of 2000, the government passed an emergency ordinance to amend Ordinance No. 39/1996 regarding the setting up and operating of the deposit-guarantee fund in the banking system. According to this normative act, the banks' contribution to the fund is double the annual contribution, as previously regulated. In spite of the pressure exerted by some powerful business groups in Romania, a system of full deposit insurance is not justified. Such a system is extremely costly and it can also maintain disincentives for market discipline. Large depositors (corporations and other banks) should not be included in a formal insurance scheme. Instead, they should be encouraged to be address the issue of bank solvency.

The payment system has developed rapidly in recent years, both in terms of quality and value of the payment documents settled through the banking system and the state Treasury. The National Payment System (NPS) links the real economy to the financial and banking sectors and allows the NBR to intervene in monetary policy matters. The system allows permanent monitoring of the use of in-transit amounts between banks. In 1999, the total value of final settlements performed through the NPS was about ROL 4,095 trillion (ROL 16,000 billion daily), which is more than eight times the GDP. The settlement period for payment, standardised according to the principles established by the European legislation, was about 3.6 days for a payment order worth less than ROL 500 million and five days for a cheque. The final settlements of securities operations through settlement accounts opened with the NBR for the stock and OTC (over-the-counter) markets amounted to about ROL 841 billion. The electronic payment system has started to develop. The final settlements through the settlement accounts of EU/CEMEA VISA INTERNATIONAL and EUROPAY reached ROL 88 billion, four times greater than in 1998.

Information on the payment instruments rejected, lost, stolen or destroyed is conveyed by banks and NBR branches and is managed through the electronic data-collection system. The Payment Incidence Bureau facilitates access to information on account holders with potential high risk, who have been involved in major payment incidents. Credit risk information is disseminated, both on the initiative of the NBR and at the request of the banks, in their own name or in the name of their customers. In 1999, the Payment Incident Bureau recorded 127,697 incidents worth about ROL 4,044 billion. More than 99 per cent of these were debit payments rejected for lack of deposits. The remainder consists of lost, stolen, destroyed and cancelled debit payment instruments. Of the total number of account holders involved in the incidents, 91 per cent are enrolled in the Credit Risk National File, of which 43 per cent are banned from issuing cheques.[6]

A simplified scheme of the national payment system is presented in Figure 14.5 (Savoiu, 1988).

FINANCIAL RESTRUCTURING OF THE BANKING SYSTEM AND INDIVIDUAL BANKS

The bad-debt problem increased significantly after 1994, mainly because the state-owned banks continued to focus on financing state-owned companies and the public sector. At the end of 1996, the four state-owned banks held 66 per cent of total assets and about 75 per cent of total credit in the market. In spite of their importance in the market, some of these banks were heavily burdened with non-performing loans, dating mainly from the pre-1997 policy which required them to provide low-interest (and largely unrecoverable) credit to the agriculture, mining and energy sectors. In the light of increased interest rates and the general decline in the economy, the problem of debt intensified in 1997, and by mid-year over one-half of total state-owned credits were classified as doubtful or losses. Another peak in bad debts was recorded in 1998. This seemed to trigger the restructuring process and, finally, in 1999, the authorities opted for a centralised approach regarding bad debts in the banking system, at least regarding those with the state-owned banks. (See Table 14.11.)

Table 14.11 *Bad-debt situation in Romania's banking system, 1994–1999*

	1994	1995	1996	1997	1998	1999
Doubtful and loss/total credit to non-govt (%)	22.57	47.41	42.84	58.70	66.26	36.45
Doubtful and loss/total bank assets (%)	10.48	24.02	20.90	21.04	26.45	11.55
Doubtful and loss/GDP (%)	4.30	10.80	10.56	8.41	10.63	4.03

Sources: National Commission for Statistics and the National Bank of Romania (author's calculations.

Figure 14.5 *Key elements of the Romanian central bank's payment system*

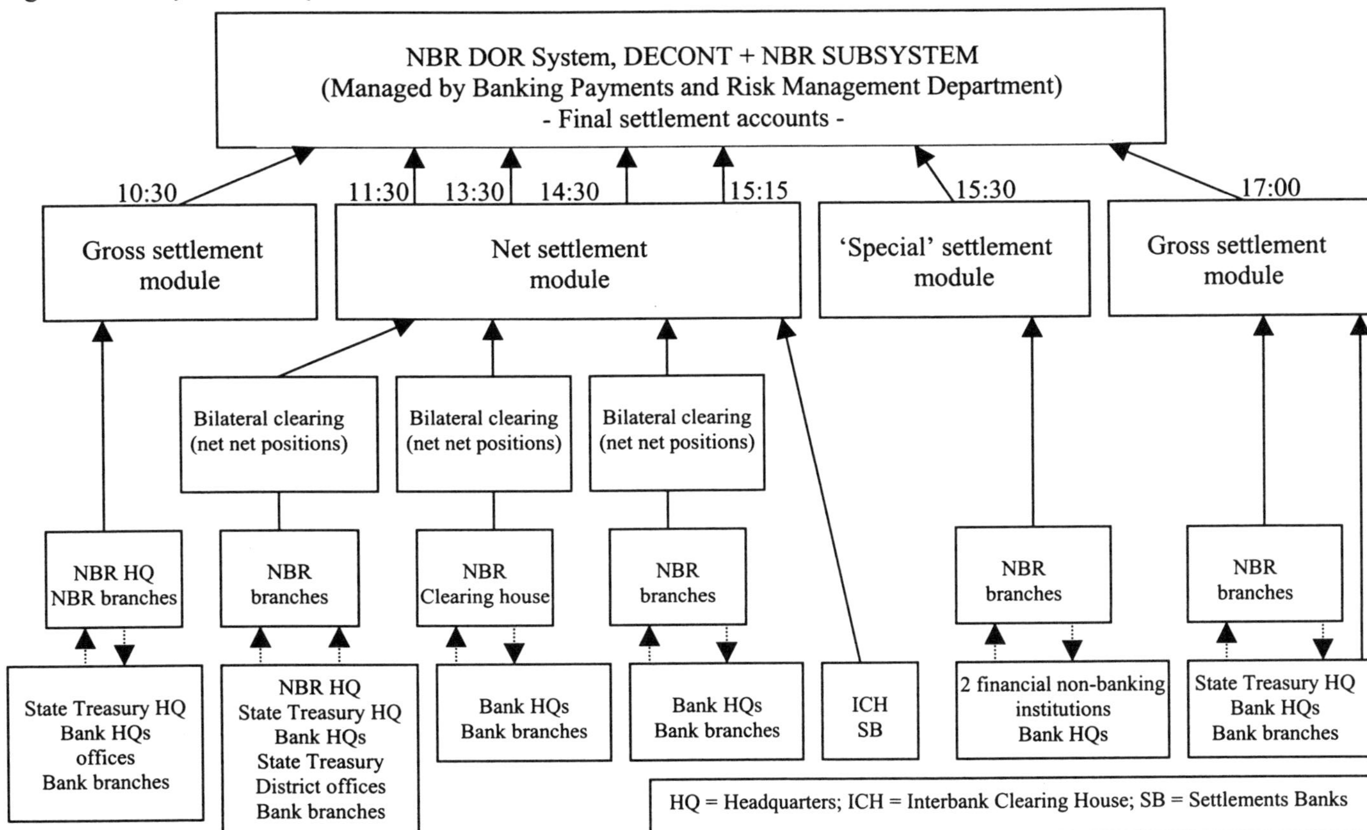

Usually, loan quality reflects risk taking. An indicator for loan quality is the growth rate of lending (adjusted for inflation) of the banking system as a whole. The rapid increase in bad debts of the biggest state-owned banks appears to confirm this hypothesis that for a bank, the rate of loan growth is negatively correlated with the bank's capacity to evaluate and monitor lending. This is why, in most cases, the higher the growth rate of the loan, the more rapid the deterioration in the quality of new loans. This assumption also holds for the whole banking system because of decreasing returns to investments.

Banks are more likely to make risky loans when less of their equity is at risk. In Romania's case, this fact has been exacerbated by two additional elements. First, at least two of the biggest banks with chronic liquidity problems were state owned and highly political. Second, until 1999, the Romanian authorities did not accept bank bankruptcy, regardless of whether the banks were state owned or private. Therefore, a moral hazard problem developed in the banking system.

There is a positive correlation between the real rate of loan growth and the ratio of equity to total assets (see Figure 14.6). This could suggest that loan growth is not necessarily based on the government guarantee, except for 1997 and 1998. However, this evidence has to be interpreted with caution because the accounting measure of equity can overstate the strength of a bank when non-performing loans have not been classified and therefore provisions have not been made. In the Romanian economy, details on a bank's off-balance-sheet exposures are not disclosed in its financial statements.

Figure 14.6 *Real loan growth and bank capitalisation in Romania, 1991-1999*

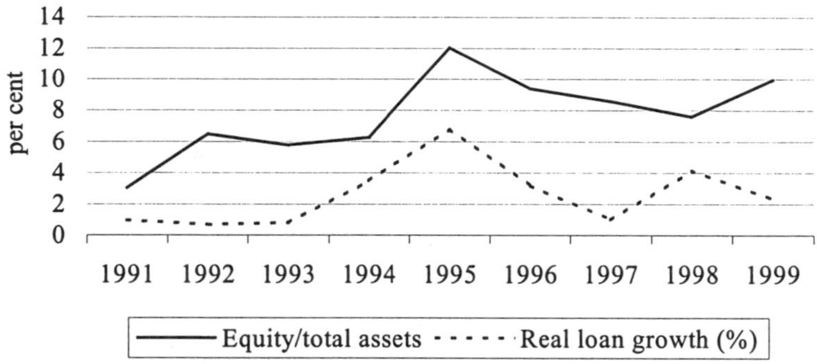

Source: Calculations based on data released by the National Bank of Romania.

The financial strength of banks is reflected by the ratio of equity to total assets (see Figure14.6). There has been a degree of variation over time in this average ratio in the Romanian banking system. Starting from 6.5 per cent in 1991, it reached a peak of 12 per cent in 1995 and fell in the next three years. In 1999, the restructuring process started at the beginning of the year and this explains the increase of capitalisation. From 1991 to 1999, this ratio averaged 7.7 per cent. By comparison, from 1993 to 1997, the average ratio in transition countries was 9.6 per cent and, in general over time across transition countries there was an upward trend.[7]

Romanian banks provide standard banking products (see Table 14.12). Also, since 1997, new banking products – for instance, Internet banking – have appeared on the market.

Table 14.12 *Standard banking products offered by Romanian banks*

Banking products	Wholesale banking	Retail banking
Current accounts	√	√
Term deposits	√	√
Money transfers	√	√
Standing orders	√	√
Loans	√	√
Bankcards and related services	√	√
Cheques	√	√
Safe deposit boxes	√	√
Custody services	√	X
Certificates of deposit	√	√

Source: Author's.

The scale of banking in the Romanian economy is significantly lower than in Western economies (see Table 14.13). This is true regardless of whether it is measured in terms of broad money, which reflect deposits, or in terms of total domestic credit to the private sectors, which shows lending.

Bank lending to the public sector in the Romanian economy is higher than the average of Western economies. From this perspective, the Romanian economy suffers from an underprovision of bank intermediation and a lower efficiency in mobilising savings and in allocating credit to the private sector. This underprovision can be explained at least in part by the macroeconomic instability that has existed in the Romanian economy (Croitoru, 1993).

Table 14.13 *The scale of banking in the Romanian economy (per cent), 1992–1999*

	1992	1993	1994	1995	1996	1997	1998	1999	Average
A	31	22	21	25	28	25	25	26	28
B	7	8	7	12	17	12	14	10	11

Notes
A = Ratio of broad money to GDP.
B = Ratio of private sector credit to GDP.

Source: Calculated from data released by the National Bank of Romania.

The restructuring measures taken by the authorities in 1999 have had positive results on the key financial indicators of banks. Overdue claims, loans and interest classified under doubtful and losses, the capital adequacy ratio, the overall risk rate and other financial and prudential indicators indicate a positive trend (see Table 14.14).

Table 14.14 *Developments of the key financial indicators in Romanian banks, 1998–1999*

Indicator	31.12.1998	31.12.1999
Capital adequacy ratio	10.25	17.90
Overdue loans (gross value)/total assets	32.21	14.76
Doubtful and overdue claims (net value)/total assets	14.54	2.36
Overall risk rate	53.54	40.66

Sources: National Bank of Romania, *Annual Report 1999*.

CURRENT STATE OF THE BANKING SECTOR

In recent years, Romania has been caught in a vicious circle of saving. Deterioration in enterprise competitiveness leads to low savings in the economy and high real interest rates. In turn, the reduction of savings and the persistence of real interest rates at relatively high levels discourage investments and postpone the improvement of enterprise competitiveness (Croitoru and Tarhoaca, 1999.) The real economy continued to register deficits. In 1998, retained profits and savings financed 65 per cent of investments (see Table 14.15). The other sources of finance for investments were domestic credit (8 per cent), external credits (6 per cent), state and local budgets (8 per cent) and other sources (13 per cent). Therefore, the banking system is not significantly involved in providing credits for investments in the real sector. In other words, the banking system does not perform well its basic function of intermediation between savings and investment in the economy.

At this moment, any significant state initiative to assist small and medium-sized enterprises (SMEs) with micro credits is not only premature, but is also undesirable as long as public finance continues to be one of the most important factors of macroeconomic instability. The European Union and USAID has initiated some international programmes aimed at providing micro credits for SMEs. Also, the Romanian government has tried to provide micro credits for those who lost their jobs in the restructuring of some industries. These micro credits were aimed at helping workers to start their own small business but, until now, the results have not been convincing.

Table 14.15 *Sources of finance for real sector investments in Romania, 1994–1998*

	1994	1995	1996	1997	1998
Total investments	100	100	100	100	100
Source of financing:					
Savings	46	63	63	65	65
Domestic credit	17	9	7	7	8
External credit	11	5	8	8	6
State and local budgets	20	17	15	14	8
Other sources*	6	6	7	7	13

Note: * This includes foreign capital, special funds, financing from the State Ownership Fund and the general public.

Source: Romanian Centre for Economic Policies.

Continuing bank restructuring is also a necessary condition for restructuring the economy as a whole. Banks should become strict creditors, which will help to improve the financial discipline in the economy. Improving the efficiency of resource allocation will not be possible without introducing hard-budget constraints and improving corporate governance in the whole economy. Even if, from this perspective, the situation in the banking system seems to be better than in the rest of the economy, a real improvement in economic behaviour depends on the continuing restructuring in the economy.

With respect to bank privatisation, the Romanian authorities have adopted the principle of selling to a strategic investor – a foreign bank with reputation.

As the major shareholder of state-owned banks, the State-owned Fund (SOF) is the institution responsible for bank privatisation. International consulting companies are selected to prepare state-owned banks for privatisation and then the SOF takes a final decision regarding the privatisation tenders. In 1999, revenues from bank privatisation were used only for servicing the foreign public debt, but no special decision has yet been made concerning the future revenues from this source.

During the last few years, foreign bank entry has become more important. The number of foreign banks increased from five to 19 between 1994 and 1999. The increasing presence of foreign banks (banks with full or majority foreign capital) is revealed by the consolidation of their position expressed by their proportion in total share capital and total net assets. The foreign banks' proportion in total share capital and total net assets increased by 24.47 per cent and 15.12 per cent, respectively, in 1998 to 39.58 per cent and 43.58 per cent, respectively, in 1999. An increase in the importance of the foreign banks in the market is expected, since the privatisation will continue in the future.

This foreign entry helped to improve the performance of the banking sector, mainly because foreign institutions can more easily satisfy capital adequacy ratios and they have access to a funding source from abroad. Foreign banks also have a good reputation and more transparent financial accounts; they bring better technologies and banking skills and raise the level of investment. Romania has already signed the European Union Association Agreement so it is expected that it will continue to open up banking system to non-discriminatory access by foreign banks.

Banking reform has developed slowly in Romania mainly due to the general approach adopted in the transformation process – so-called gradualism. If the general institutional framework of the banking system is, generally speaking, compatible with Western practice, then increasing the independence of the central bank and completing the privatisation of the remained state-owned banks is the way forward for strengthening the banking system, increasing its efficiency, and reducing intermediation costs. Effective restructuring in the banking system started only in 1999, and the market structure has not changed radically so far. Behavioural changes of banks are at an early stage, but the competition in the market is increasing. The most significant positive result of the restructuring measures adopted so far is the decrease in moral hazard in the banking system.

CONCLUSION

The Romanian banking system provides less bank intermediation of savings and investment than banking systems in the more advanced economies in transition. This is why, along with factors outside the financial sector (degree of macroeconomic stability, privatisation and so on), it is important to consider the specific conditions that are required for promoting the stable expansion of the banking sector. These specific factors are resolving bank failures, managing entry into banking, and bank privatisation.

In the long run, healthy competition in the banking system means that only those institutions that are best able to serve customers at lower cost will survive. The difficulty of poorly performing banks exiting the market arises from the fear about the spillover effects that the closure of a bank can have on other banks. Romania has already experienced such a scenario in early 1999, when the second biggest state-owned bank (Bancorex), finally exited the market. After years of debt accumulation (the total losses of Bancorex are estimated to be about 2 per cent of Romania's GDP) the authorities accepted that it was necessary to close down the bank.

One of the main sources of the too-big-to-fail problem is that the larger the bank, the larger the interbank exposures tend to be. An additional source is the fact that a large bank has a large number of depositors who might create a banking panic and exert political pressure for depositor protection. Another factor that can explain the reluctance of regulators to resolve the problems of banks in difficulty is the lax incentives for the regulatory authority. Practically, the economic, political and institutional environment in Romania has made it difficult for regulators to act decisively. There have been and still are, for example, strong political pressures placed on state-owned banks to sustain large state-owned companies. This problem can be solved only by the privatisation of state-owned banks and companies.

Given the existing obstacles to efficient bank liquidation, a key challenge is to detect banks that are in difficulty as early as possible, and to deal with them promptly. An immediate intervention needs accurate financial reporting by banks so that the regulators can ascertain when a bank is in trouble. If such a bank is identified early, the regulators can impose remedial action so as to restore its capital adequacy or to impose a recapitalisation plan. If a bank's balance sheet has deteriorated beyond all hope of recovery and no recapitalisation is possible, the regulator must instigate liquidation proceedings as soon as possible.

In order to respond to the problems of regulatory and political inference, the NBR has improved mandatory corrective action measures. This implies a set of rules for actions that the regulators must take in specific situations. It will be useful to disseminate these rules so that the general public could better understand the significance of the decisions and actions adopted by regulators.

Reducing concentration is a primary condition for avoiding the too-big-to-fail problem that is still present in Romania's banking system. Policies aimed at curbing increases in concentration through mergers of private banks are also desirable in the long run. This is not in contradiction with the present NBR policy of encouraging mergers of small banks in order to increase their capital, and eliminate undercapitalised banks to avoid major shocks. In the short term, the privatisation of the remaining state-owned banks should be one of the priorities in restructuring the banking system.

From the beginning of the banking system reform, the NBR has tried to avoid excessive entry of banks in the market. Nevertheless, maintaining an oligopolistic market structure inhibits the development of competition and it preserves the too-big-to-fail problem. Indeed there is a trade-off between the entry of new banks and the quality of banks. At least in the short term, given the limited enforced regulatory capacity regulators, a second-best solution (that is, restrictions on entry) seems to be sensible.

The empirical evidence throughout the world shows that benefits of privatising outweigh the costs. It is also true that there are significant differences between the privatisation of banks and the privatisation of non-financial companies. The main difference arises from the fact that with the privatisation of a large bank an important constraint is not to weaken the confidence of depositors. This is not the case in Romania.

The success of bank privatisation in 1998 and 1999 shows that the important depositors did not lose confidence in privatised banks. Indeed, the privatised banks attracted more depositors. In both cases, the main reason for this is that the new major shareholder was a reputable foreign bank.

Obviously there is a strong case for involving outside interests in privatisation and ensuring the participation of strategic investors. Importing managerial skills and improving the bank's reputation are central to bank privatisation.

NOTES

1. *Monitorul Oficial*, from 17/29 April 1880.
2. The independence of the central bank is laid down in the Law on Statute of the National Bank of Romania (Law No. 101/1998: the National Bank of Romania Act).
3. The government of Romania has published the *Medium-term Economic Strategy for Integration in the European Union*. This strategy, which also includes an Action Plan accepted by the European Commission, was adopted by the government in May 2000. The document designs the general action framework for the Romanian authorities in the next four years (2000–2004).

4. In Romania, the interbank market started to operate only in August 1994. Previously, the exchange rate was established through Forex auctions held daily at the NBR head office.
5. Structural credit is granted for specific end users, at a 'floor' or reference – discount – rate. For auction credit, banks bid weekly; the interest rate is the market one. Lombard credit is granted for overnight liquidity shortages within a certain per cent of the bank's own funds, at a higher rate. Special credit is generally granted to banks in distress.
6. See NBR, *Annual Report*, 1999, p. 93.
7. See EBRD, *Transition Report*, 1998.

BIBLIOGRAPHY

Croitoru, L. (1993), 'Liberalizarea financiara si functionarea sistemului bancar romanesc 1991–1993', [Financial Liberalisation and the Function of the Romanian Banking System 1991–1993], *Oeconomica*, **3/4**, 1994, Bucharest, pp. 55–82.

Croitoru, L. and C. Tarhoaca (1999), 'Fiscal Policy in Romania: Three Vicious Circles of the Romanian Economy' in C. Rűhl and D. Daianu (eds), *Economic Transition in Romania: Past, Present and Future*, Proceedings of the Conference: Romania 2000. Ten Years of Transition – Past Present and Future, Bucharest: Romanian Centre for Economic Policies and World Bank, pp. 443–56.

Doltu, C. (1999), 'The Development of the Banking System in Romania', in C. Rűhl and D. Daianu (eds), *op. cit.*, pp. 245–60.

Government of Romania (2000), *Medium-term Economic Strategy for Integration in the European Union*, Bucharest: Government of Romania.

Isarescu, M. (1996), *The Romanian Banking System: Recent Development and Perspectives*, Bucharest: NBR, pp. 45–55.

Negrea, R. (1991), *Spoliatorii* [Spoliators], Bucharest: Aureus.

Popa, C (1997), 'Romania's Banking Sector Reform: A Comment', in E. Thiel Blommestein (ed.), *The New Banking Landscape in Central and Eastern Europe: Country Experience and Policies for the Future*, Paris: OECD, pp. 217–28.

Savoiu, V. (1998), *Banca Centrala si sistemele de plati de interes national* [The Central Bank and the Relevant Payment System], Bucharest: Editura Enciclopedica, Colectia Bancii Natiionale a Romaniei, Bucharesti, pp. 821.

15. Reforming the Banking System in Yugoslavia

Yoji Koyama, Goran Pitić, Jelena Galić and Aleksandar Šević

INTRODUCTION[1]

Yugoslavia's post-Second World War development has had three phases: (i) central planning (until the mid-1950s), (ii) socialist self-management and collective bargaining (until the mid-1980s), and (iii) economic transition (the end of the 1980s and the 1990s). Until the beginning of the last phase, Yugoslav business practices were characterised by 'self-management', semi-planned markets, and the prevalent influence of political factors. In the setting of wages and prices, as well as in foreign trade and investment, there were more liberal manifestations of economic laws. At the very beginning of the transition process numerous economic and non-economic shocks impeded progress. Now, although the intention is to introduce a market economy and to democratise social and political life, there is no real readiness on the part of either the government or rent-seeking lobbies to develop parliamentary democracy and accept far-reaching economic reforms.

During the last decade of the 20th century, Yugoslavia made little progress with regard to its economic development. The Yugoslav economy has been exposed to a number of economic and non-economic shocks that have negatively affected its performance.[2] The break-up of the former Yugoslavia in 1991 was the first non-economic shock that accelerated the GDP decline in the 1990s. In 1991, GDP fell by 11.6 per cent. In 1992, UN sanctions contributed to a further decline: GDP fell by 27.9 per cent. Finally, the hyperinflation during 1992–93, which ended in a complete monetary collapse, further reduced GDP. In 1993, the GDP level was just 40 per cent of its level in 1989. In 1999 one of the lowest levels of GDP in the last few decades was recorded. In the light of this fact it is evident that the downward trend in the GDP level, which has lasted for more than a decade, is continuing. (See Table 15.1.)

Table 15.1 *Yugoslavia's main economic indicators, 1994–1999*

Economic indicators	1994	1995	1996	1997	1998	1999*
Real GDP (USD bil.)	13.862	14.681	15.548	17.000	18.150	13.300
Real GDP growth	5.5	6.1	5.9	7.5	2.6	–19.3
GDP per capita (USD)	1,318	1,392	1,471	1,600	1,800	–
M1 (USD bil.)	1.6	0.7	1.1	1.5	1.1	1.4
Unemployment rate	23.1	24.6	25.3	26.1	26.5	30.0
Inflation – CPI	0	74.1	93.1	18.5	44.3	50.1
Trade balance (USD)	1.1	2.1	2.3	2.4	2	1.8

Notes: * Estimated data; CPI = Consumer price index.

Sources: Federal Statistical Office and authors' estimates.

The Yugoslav economy also faces a number of internal limitations to growth. These are a shortage of working capital, a low level of capacity utilisation (approximately 45 per cent) and low levels of labour productivity, accompanied by low share of both savings and gross domestic investment in GDP. There is also an extremely high level of public consumption (close to 60 per cent of GDP in both 1997 and 1998), which represents a long-term destabilising factor for the Yugoslav economy. In addition, the amount of outstanding state debt has reached 14 per cent of GDP. Moreover, overall debt expressed as a per cent of GDP in 1998 was at the GDP level of that year. Since there was a huge drop in GDP in the following year, these debts were estimated at 140 per cent of GDP in 1999. A number of big loss-making enterprises, amounting in 1998 to about 58 per cent of GDP, and increased inter-enterprise arrears (25 per cent of GDP in 1998) as a result of an enterprise liquidity problem, fostered high unemployment. Officially unemployment amounts to 25 per cent, not including a further 25 per cent of the redundant labour force, a high number of pensioners (1.4 million), and refugees and displaced people (566,000 and 250,000, respectively). However, the main external limitations are Yugoslavia's exclusion from international trade and financial markets and the unresolved situation with key international financial organisations.

In the 1989–93 period, the Federal Republic of Yugoslavia (Serbia and Montenegro) experienced two hyperinflations. Accordingly, two programmes were subsequently introduced to combat high inflation. While the former was heterodox, the latter programme was rather orthodox in its character. The last stabilisation programme was launched on 24 January 1994. The immediate result was price stabilisation. Furthermore, since 1994 real GDP has shown steady recovery with the exception of the year 1999. In the real sector nothing substantial has changed, as investment and employment continue to decline. There is also a high foreign trade deficit (USD 2 billion yearly on average) due to the lack of competitiveness of Yugoslav exports, and the high import dependence of its economy. The foreign exchange rate on the black market is currently more than three times higher than the official exchange rate. Monthly inflation rates in 1999 were highly volatile and within the range of 0.5 per cent to 12.4 per cent. Finally, for the year ended December 1999 the annual inflation rate amounted to 50.1 per cent.

It can be said, six years after the launch of the stabilisation programme, that the economic policy initiated in 1994 was the combination of a populist policy and a policy to encourage production – at all costs – and not, in essence, a stabilisation policy.

Yugoslavia's financial system is fairly well developed, comprising banks and other financial institutions, and financial (capital and money) markets. The Yugoslav banking system has been two-tiered since the inception of the first significant market reforms in 1965. The National Bank of the Federal Republic (FR) of Yugoslavia was established in June 1993 by the Law on the National Bank of Yugoslavia, when the centralisation of monetary authority at a federal level occurred. In mid-July of 1999 there were over 80 commercial banks in FR Yugoslavia, almost two-thirds of which were in Central Serbia. Apart from banks, there are a number of insurance companies and brokerage houses. Financial markets are characterised by a high degree of financial repression (direct budget subsidies; selective credit; non market-clearing interest rates; inflation tax through high legal reserve requirements and so on).

SEQUENCE OF BANKING REFORM

Yugoslavia has had a two-tier banking system since 1965. From 1965 until the end of the 1980s only *socially-owned* banks existed in the Socialist Federal Republic of Yugoslavia, established on principles of worker self-management. Despite the dominance of social property, the development of the financial sector was remarkable. An interbank market was established at the end of the 1960s, while the establishment of the Forex market followed shortly afterwards, in the early 1970s. The capital and money markets commenced their operations in 1989. During the same period, the National Bank of Yugoslavia (NBY) functioned as a decentralised system of central banks. In June 1993 a new Law on the National Bank of Yugoslavia was adopted, which proclaimed the centralisation of the highest monetary authority. The NBY was proclaimed an institution of the Federation, acting in the public interest with authority for conducting monetary policy and performing banking supervisory functions.

Doubtful claims and other problems burdening the Yugoslav banking system are mostly vestiges of the past. In the socialist period, the Yugoslav banking system functioned in a semi-market environment, in which bank management was autonomous in business decision making and the conduct of business policy (in contrast to banks in 'real socialist' Eastern Europe). However, the business operations of banks were subordinated to the interests of credit beneficiaries and not to the profit motive of their owners. As a result, Yugoslav banks were characterised by low profitability and business inefficiency.

With the introduction of economic reforms in 1988, the process of banking sector transformation began. Existing state-owned banks were transformed formally into joint-stock companies. Further market liberalisation allowed for the establishment of a great number of new banks. Among 'new' private banks (for example, Dafiment and Jugoskandik banks), institutions emerged which atracted new depositors with the promise of enormously high interest rates that in the hyperinflationary economy were supposed to be real; however, these were not sustainable. These banks disappeared rapidly, leaving behind a huge number of cheated depositors. This can be attributed to the poor supervisory standards of the central bank and inefficient legal protection under the poorly performing legal system. An additional problem of 'new' banks was chronic illiquidity. On the other hand, 'old' state-owned banks ceased servicing households' foreign exchange accounts and simultaneously started having problems with collecting extended loans. Accordingly, bad debts kept accumulating.

The Law on Banks and Other Financial Organisations of 1993 brought about a new regulatory framework for the functioning of the banking system. In compliance with this law, a bank may be founded only as a joint-stock company, by at least two founders. Founders may be Yugoslav citizens or legal entities, or foreign nationals or legal entities. A bank must obtain a licence from the NBY in order to become operational, and it must be issued within 60 days of submitting the application and the required documentation.

After 26 June 2000, the monetary element of the initial capital must not be less than USD 5 million at the exchange rate valid on the day of the payment of these funds. Foreign founders also have to submit proof of the origin of their assets, as well as the fulfilment of the reciprocity condition. According to the Law on Foreign Exchange Operations of 1995, banks may conduct foreign exchange operations only on the basis of the authorisation given by the NBY, which includes three levels of authority (licence):

- authority to engage in international foreign exchange payment and foreign exchange credit operations – 'big licence';

- authority to engage in international foreign exchange payment operations – 'medium licence';
- authority to engage in foreign exchange and foreign exchange operations in the country – 'small licence'.

To date, there are only a few foreign banks, which are represented through their own branches and involved in corporate banking.

Far-reaching and efficient privatisation of the state-owned banks has not yet been implemented, and foreign banks are barely represented. The Yugoslav government has not officially adopted a programme of banking sector reform. At the same time, in economic theory, it is generally accepted that a combination of the centralised and decentralised models of restructuring is most appropriate, and such a system should be implemented. Nevertheless, the restructuring of the banking sector must be carried out within the framework of the reform of the whole financial sector, as part of a set of structural reforms.

STRUCTURE OF THE BANKING SECTOR

The Yugoslav banking system comprises the central bank (National Bank of Yugoslavia) as the key monetary institution (which has *de jure*, a high level of institutional independence but a very low level of real independence in practice), and the commercial banking sector consisting of more than 80 licensed banks.

In 1989 state-owned banks ('old' banks) were transformed into joint-stock companies, while at the same time, a great number of 'new' private banks were founded. It should be noted that all Yugoslav banks operate as universal banks, which means that they may perform non-traditional in addition to traditional banking operations. (See Table 15.2.)

The Yugoslav financial sector has a traditional structure since non-bank financial institutions (insurance companies, savings and loan institutions, pension funds, health-care funds and stock exchanges in Belgrade and Podgorica) possess assets amounting to only 1.64 per cent and 1.92 per cent of total assets of both banks and other financial institutions in 1995 and 1996, respectively. Following the revocation of licences for certain banks at the beginning of 1997, the ratio has increased significantly, to the benefit of other financial institutions. (See Figure 15.1.)

Table 15.2 *Banking products offered in Yugoslavia*

Banking products	Wholesale banking	Retail banking
Current accounts	✓	✓
Term deposits	✓	✓
Money transfers	✓	✓
Standing orders	✓	✓
Loans	✓	✓
Telephone banking	–	–
Bankcard and related services	✓	✓
Cheques	✓	✓
Selling of securities	–	–
Safe deposit boxes	✓	✓
Custody services	–	–
Certificates of deposit	✓	✓

Source: Authors' findings.

Figure 15.1 *Relative weight of assets of Yugoslav banks and non-bank financial institutions, 1994–1999*

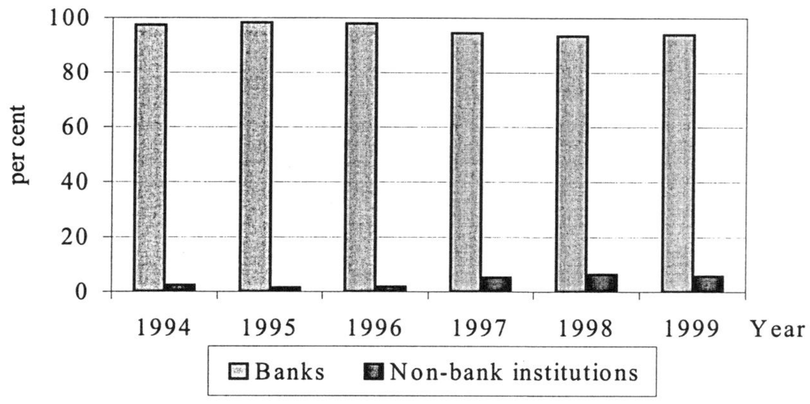

Source: National Bank of Yugoslavia.

The Yugoslav banking sector is also characterised by an oligopolistic market structure. Six large banks dominate the sector, accounting for about 60 per cent of the total balance of Yugoslav banking on average. At the same time, there are a relatively large number of small banks, with modest financial potential.

Figure 15.2 *Comparison of 'old' and 'new' Yugoslav banks in terms of assets, equity and profit*

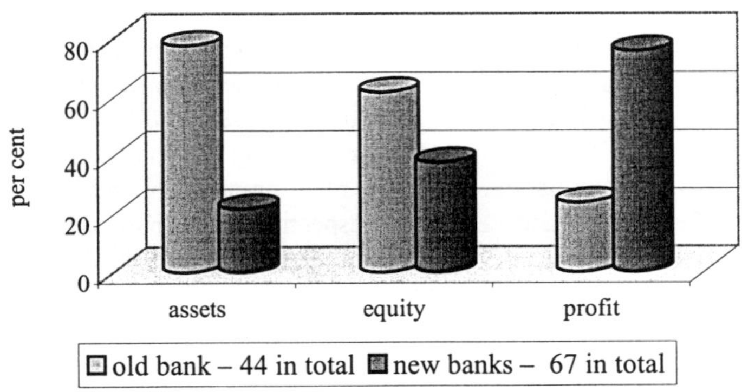

Source: National Bank of Yugoslavia.

The main characteristic of the Yugoslav banking sector is division into 'old' and 'new' banks[3] (see Figure 15.2). The essential difference between them lies in the fact that 'old' banks have: (a) foreign exchange savings deposits in the National Bank of Yugoslavia on the assets side; (b) so-called 'old' foreign exchange savings deposits of the general public on the liabilities side, which they are unable to service; and, as a rule, (c) heavy external debt originating from long-term loans and guarantees, the servicing of which is problematic. Apart from that, even though both old and new banks are joint-stock companies, the 'new' banks are as a rule privately owned, while the 'old' ones are stateowned (because their owners, that is, stockholders, are state-owned companies or 'privileged monopolies' derived from state-owned companies).

CENTRAL BANK REFORM

The evolution of the central bank in post Second World War Yugoslavia had the following phases: National Bank of the Federal Peoples' Republic of Yugoslavia (1946–65), National Bank of the Socialist Federal Republic of Yugoslavia (1965–93), and National Bank of the Federal Republic of Yugoslavia (1993 to date). Until 1947 the National Bank of Yugoslavia was a joint-stock company, and then it became a public institution which continues to exist. Until 1971 the central bank was unified, and in the 1971–93 period it operated a system of central banks, where the members were the central banks of republics and autonomous regions. It was a decentralised system, which provided an original solution not seen elsewhere in the world, and it did not have parallels in contemporary federal states. This solution actually embraced the concept of national economies in Yugoslavia, within the domain of monetary policy (Šević, 1996).

The NBY is the only note-issuing bank in FR Yugoslavia; it has its head office in Belgrade, and its obligations are guaranteed by the Federation. National banks of republics and autonomous provinces have lost their status as legal entities. In 1993 the National Bank of Serbia and the National Bank of Montenegro were transformed into the main branches of the NBY with head offices in Belgrade and Podgorica, respectively, and national banks of autonomous provinces became branches of the NBY with head offices in Novi Sad and Priština. An organisation for issuing banknotes and minting coins (the Note Printing Office) is a part of the NBY, but it has no separate legal identity of its own.

By law, the National Bank of Yugoslavia performs the following functions:

- it sets monetary policy;
- it regulates the money supply;
- it carries out transactions on behalf of the federal state (FR Yugoslavia);
- it regulates the liquidity of banks and other financial institutions;
- it sets the dinar exchange rate policy and the dinar exchange rate itself (in co-operation with the Federal government);
- it regulates liquidity in external payments;
- it sets the conditions for and controls payment operations in the country; and
- it issues banknotes and coins.[4]

The principal obligation of the NBY *vis-à-vis* the Federal Assembly is the submission of the annual report on its activities for parliamentary discussion. It further submits, if necessary, quarterly reports on its conduct of monetary policy and on the state of banking and the overall financial system in the country. The NBY also co-operates with the Federal government in setting basic goals of economic policy and supports the realisation of these goals. In the domain of setting the policy of the dinar exchange rate, the law prescribes that the NBY and the Federal government co-operate. Exchange rate policy is set forth by the Federal government, following proposals by the NBY.

The Constitution of the Federal Republic of Yugoslavia prescribes that the NBY be managed by the governor, elected by the Federal Assembly, on the recommendation of the president of FR Yugoslavia, for a period of five years. Another governing organisation of the bank is the NBY' Council, which has seven members comprising the governor and six members nominated by the Federal Assembly for a period of five years. Three members of the NBY Council are appointed by the governor, while the other three are nominated by the Federal government. The Council's decisions are made by a majority of votes. The NBY is represented by the governor, and in order to improve efficiency, the NBY Council has one deputy and one or more vice-governors, whose duties are defined by the Statute of the NBY.

Figure 15.3 *Placements of the NBY, 1994–1999*

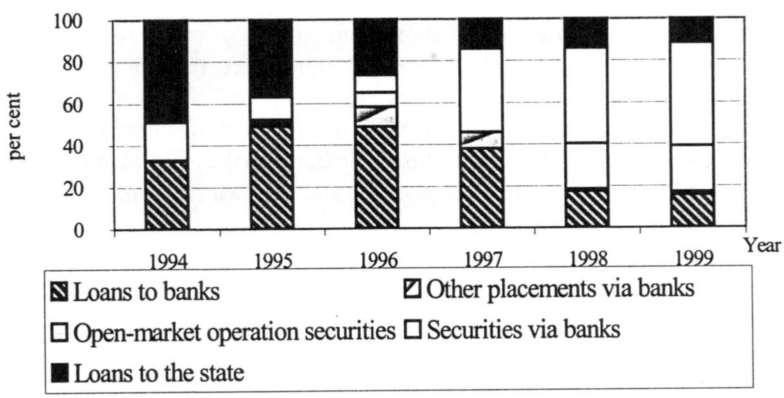

Sources: National Bank of Yugoslavia.

Institutional independence of the National Bank of Yugoslavia is best measured by the limit on the volume of government borrowing from the National Bank of Yugoslavia (see Figure 15.3). FR Yugoslavia and its republics may only raise loans from the NBY for bridging the budget deficit gap, but not more than 10 per cent of the projected annual budgetary revenues, provided that the total amount of credit does not exceed 15 per cent of NBY investments, denominated in dinars. The government is obliged to repay all short-term loans by the end of the fiscal year at the latest in order to prevent direct monetisation of the budget deficit. The NBY also acts as a fiscal agent for the Federation, since it can issue short- and long-term securities at home and abroad on behalf of and for the account of the federal state.

In addition, the NBY is authorised to perform transactions relating to the raising and repayment of foreign loans, as well as to foreign payment operations on account of the Federation. The Law on the National Bank of Yugoslavia of 1993 gives a high degree of institutional independence to the bank. However, institutional independence is only a necessary, but not a sufficient condition for the efficient functioning of a central bank. Factual independence of the central bank requires personnel and financial independence, as well as its independence in pursuing monetary policy.

As for personnel independence, it should be noted that since the beginning of 1992 the average term of office of the governor of the NBY has been among the shortest in the world. This points to a very low degree of *de facto* independence for the bank. With regard to financial independence, it should be emphasised that during the post-hyperinflationary period the NBY continued to finance the government above the legal defined limits. During this period, the bank also granted a substantial amount of credit for financing quasi-budgetary operations, which implied the direct financing of state-owned enterprises and certain public services.

In pursuing monetary policy, the NBY is independent in selecting its aims and objectives and instruments for monetary policy implementation. Otherwise, the basic goal is price stability and the central bank is free to select the relevant *de jure* instruments:

- open-market operations;
- refinancing policies;
- reserve requirements;
- discount rates;
- intervention in the foreign exchange market.

Open-market operations have been performed in Yugoslavia since the 1970s, while they have been resumed in FR Yugoslavia since 1993, when the NBY began to purchase and sell short-term securities in the secondary money market. This has occurred more seriously since 1995.

Insufficient bank liquidity and unattractive interest rates have depressed the demand for the securities used in open-market operations. Due to existing restrictions, refinancing policies have remained the major source of dinar-denominated loans to banks. During the previous period (prior to 1993), such policies were used selectively and largely in specified priority areas: agriculture, power supply and export promotion. Another questionable practice was the use of a substantial amount of credit for making up a deficit in the government budgets (that is, in the non-banking sector).

The discount-rate policy (NBY interest policy) conducted in the pre-1993 period was very static. Real interest rates became positive only at the end of

1995. In the case of Yugoslav banking, a very low discount rate also brought about an excessive demand for primary-issue loans, whereby it stopped being an efficient instrument in regulating the amount of money and credit in circulation (the discount rate amounted to 2.5 per cent until March 1999 and 2 per cent thereafter).

Reserve requirements are still one of the key instruments used by the NBY to regulate monetary aggregates. At the end of March 1999, the compulsory reserve rate was 23 per cent. Until September 1999 it fluctuated around 20 per cent, at which time it was finally set at 17 per cent. In comparison with international standards, this rate is very high.

Figure 15.4 *M1 and M2 annual growth in Yugoslavia, 1995–1999*

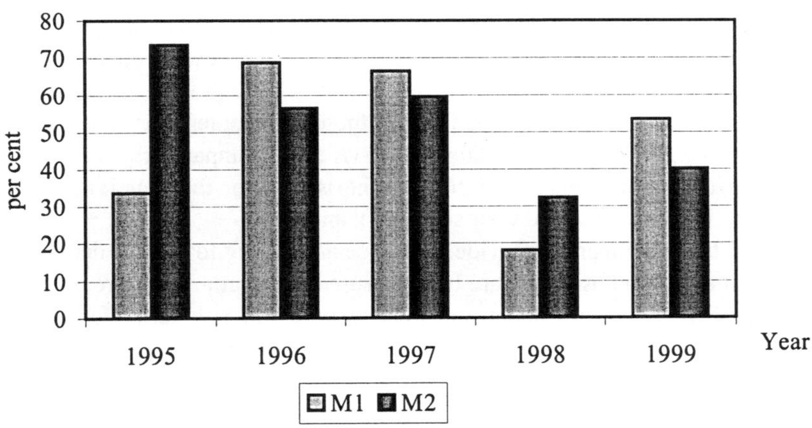

Source: National Bank of Yugoslavia.

While the projected M1 growth over the last few years was approximately 15 per cent annually, average growth between 1995 and 1999 ranged between 20 and 70 per cent (see Figure 15.4). A drastic departure of the actual movement of the money supply from the projected one in monetary policy shows that, in fact, the NBY is not independent in regulating the money supply. A low rate of collection of approved principal and interest points to the bank's lack of independence in pursuing a policy of primary-issue loan allocation. All this suggests that, despite a high degree of formal institutional independence, the independence of the NBY is very limited in practice.

One of the most important functions of the NBY as required by the law is the 'control and supervisory function'. According to the Law on the National Bank of Yugoslavia, the bank has the authority to perform two types of control: those relating to solvency and those relating to the fulfilment of legal requirements. The NBY performs control and supervisory functions through continued monitoring and fulfilment of prudential control requirements, which are in compliance with international standards. If irregularities have been detected, the NBY undertakes specific measures and gives orders to the financial institutions concerned to improve their stance. Finally, the NBY can decide to revoke licences for banks and other financial institutions and initiate procedures for their bankruptcy (that is, liquidation).

Under the existing system, there is no efficient scheme of deposit insurance. In compliance with the Law on Banks and Other Financial Institutions, a bank (or other financial institution) is obliged to insure its deposits and pay an insurance premium either to the Agency for Deposit Insurance and Bank Rehabilitation (an independent Federal government agency) or to another insurance company, under the following conditions:

- that a bank is not the founder of these companies nor does it have management or property claims *vis-à-vis* these companies;
- that these companies have NBY authorisation for these activities (after careful examination of their solvency); and
- that these companies provide insurance amounting to no less than 20 per cent of the deposits that are being insured. The sum of the premium and payment terms are set in accordance with the risk level for specific banks.[5]

For the time being, deposit insurance schemes applied in developed market economies would not be efficient under Yugoslav banking practice, because there is insufficient confidence in any funds.[6] In time, with the restoration of credibility and improved functioning of the state, it will be necessary to define and restore the functioning of certain types of deposit insurance (similar to those in developed market economies).

The payments system has been organised in a unified manner, through the specialised organisation that is part of the NBY: the Institution for Accounting and Payment (ZOP). Under the authority of the NBY, the institution carries out payment activities, business recording and financial statistics collection, as well as business control for financial entities in FR Yugoslavia. Payment activities are performed in the following way: ZOP accepts payment orders along with the special document from legal entities and other payment agents. Banks, other financial organisations and postal savings banks receive money from individual persons.

The NBY gives and retains authorisation to payment agents, prescribes the method for the carrying out of payments and implements control of payment activities. Payment agents are accountable to the NBY; that is, ZOP submits daily reports on payments and balances of accounts that are subsequently processed. Payments are honoured up to the limit represented by the amount of money in payers' accounts. If there are insufficient funds to cover the payment, agents alert the NBY and ZOP, on the same day, to any payments that cannot be honoured and institute procedures for enforced reimbursement. If debtors are illiquid they are expected to pay contracted interest rates, penalty interest rates and cover damages, if the damage was higher than penalty interest rates.

From 1 January 2001,[7] payment agents will represent the NBY, commercial banks, postal savings banks, other financial organisations, and postal enterprises. By law, banks will be authorised to perform payment system operations, rather than the Payments System Administration (SPP). At the same time, ZOP will become a type of clearing house.

The transfer of the authorisation to banks should preserve the SPP's efficiency and effectiveness, which implies a so-called 'real-time gross settlement'. However, the weak banks (that is, those with chronic illiquidity problems) fear that their situation may not support 'money in transfer' and this will impair the efficiency and effectiveness inherited from the previous system. On the other hand, there could be problems related to technical inadequacies present in the vast majority of banks, which would create certain monopolistic advantages for those capable of carrying out payment activities immediately.

FINANCIAL RESTRUCTURING OF THE BANKING SYSTEM AND INDIVIDUAL BANKS

The Yugoslav banking system has a rather unusual balance structure because, in contrast to the foreign exchange sub-balance, four-fifths of which is non-performing and mostly immobilised, actual transactions are recorded in the sub-balance denominated in new dinars (YUD). Therefore, the latter sub-balance alone indicates the real potential of Yugoslav banking. During the period of hyperinflation in 1992–93, the banks' liabilities denominated in dinars almost melted away but were restored through a process of remonetisation, after the implementation of the Programme of Monetary Reconstruction (1994). The share of the dinar sub-balance of all banks ranged from 20 to 27 per cent (of which demand and short-term deposits accounted for 17 to 20 per cent). However, the actual potentials are below this amount because: (a) a large amount of capital is tied up in fixed assets, as it is difficult to find other profitable investments; (b) clients' deposits have stagnated, due to inflationary pressures, and (c) private savings are almost negligible (the share of dinar savings deposits in GDP during the 1994–97 period was below 1 per cent, while the share of sterile 'old' foreign exchange savings deposits in GDP amounted to 22.5 per cent at the end of 1997). (See Table 15.3.)

The asset structure seems rather fragile. The sources of bank liquidity are mostly the clients' demand deposits, which fluctuate on a daily basis. On the other side, the manufacturing cycles in specified industries require long-term sources of finance, but these credit beneficiaries are usually unable to repay their credits on the due date. As a result, in the balance sheets of banks, long-term investments are on the assets side, while short-term financial means are mostly on the liabilities side, implying that banks have a liquidity problem.

Over the years non-performing assets have continued to accumulate in the Yugoslav banking system. Economic agents used loans from banks to finance inefficient business operations, but, at the same time, they were unable to service their debts on time. In such circumstances banks were forced to reschedule their loans, which further aggravated the position of the banking sector. This also points to a significant presence of a non-market credit allocation and, simultaneously, raises the question of priority in the order of restructuring (that is, what should be restructured first – debtor enterprises or banks). It is estimated that commercial banks regularly collect about 50 per cent of approved principal and about 60 per cent of computed interest.

Yugoslav banks are largely undercapitalised. Capital adequacy is actually worse than reported by banks, because banks do not make a realistic evaluation of the collection rate of foreign currency loans (at present, these loans are not repaid); as a result, capital is artificially inflated, since actual and potential losses are not deducted.[8] Large loans manifoldly exceed the set limit, which points to an inadequate client structure, whereby the largest amount of credit (mainly in foreign currency) is concentrated on large debtors who, as a rule, are in financial difficulties. And finally, fixed investments as a percentage of banks' capital are much larger than prescribed and are made at the expense of the monetary part of capital; this points to an irrational use of capital, which is frozen in real assets (non-performing assets). On the other side, banks are lacking a mobile credit potential.

Owners of banks do not pursue profitable opportunities since their aim is to buy bank shares in order to be extended credit by the bank. Thus, we are faced with the situation that the debtors of a bank are actually its owners. This contributes to the lack of adequate credit policy since personal contacts and political meddling exclude any relevant evaluation of potential borrowers. Such a policy helps to perpetuate the bad-debt situation. The government should therefore end this malpractice by breaking up the debtor–owner vicious cycle.

Table 15.3 *Savings of citizens in Yugoslavia (USD m.), 1994–1999*

Deposits	1994	1995	1996	1997	1998	1999
1. Total dinar deposits	122.13	73.29	129.27	180.95	146.67	150.75
Current account	76.91	48.56	89.71	117.65	77.39	84.25
Giro account	19.71	9.72	10.74	14.44	16.82	23.30
Other demand deposits	12.05	8.03	17.01	20.14	23.88	18.27
Short-term deposits	1.67	1.24	5.83	21.14	22.15	18.88
Long-term deposits	11.79	5.74	5.98	7.58	6.43	6.05
2. Total Forex deposits	4,134.81	4,467.21	4,131.60	3,822.05	4,133.24	3,843.73
Short-term Forex	2,110.66	2,240.81	2,031.92	1,875.19	78.48	47.26
Long-term Forex	2,024.15	2,226.40	2,099.68	1,946.86	112.58	6.13
Old Forex deposits	–	–	–	–	3,942.18	3,790.34
3. GDP	13,862	14,681	15,548	17,000	18,150	13,300*
YUD/USD exchange rate	1.55	4.74	5.13	5.91	10.03	11.66
Ratio of 1/3 (in %)	0.88	0.50	0.83	1.06	0.81	1.13
Ratio of 2/3 (in %)	29.83	30.43	26.57	22.48	22.77	28.90

Note: *Estimated data.

Source: National Bank of Yugoslavia.

Operating costs in 1997 amounted to 13.11 per cent while 50 per cent of the interest margin was used to cover them. With high interest margins, banks attempt to compensate for all the irrationalities in banking operations. The bulk of these operating costs were for labour, which points to the fact that Yugoslav banks are also burdened by redundancies. Operating costs can be reduced through increased competition. Accordingly, the government should encourage the entry of foreign banks to address this issue, but not without close supervision.[9]

Finally, poorly performing bank managers are not accountable and cannot be penalised. This refers, above all, to the lack of internal control over business operations and management in a large number of banks, as well as to inconsistency in conducting bankruptcy proceedings against insolvent banks. Financially stronger banks tend to establish internal audit groups that are directly responsible to shareholders and can be called to account at the

Annual General Meeting. These banks tend to implement a system of quality supervision. Smaller banks, on the other hand, tend to organise these systems *ad hoc* with the aim of forming them into a particular body in the future.

Table 15.4 *Statutory ratios in Yugoslav banks, 1994–1999*

Ratio	Prescribed	1994	1995	1996	1997	1998	30.09.99
A	Min 8 %	7.74	5.58	9.53	9.96	9.77	10.63
B	Min 20 %	9.19	7.78	10.60	11.23	10.24	12.42
C	Max 80 %	450.25	558.78	366.17	377.69	398.31	312.70
D	Max 15 %	7.73	7.91	10.18	10.48	9.95	8.86
E	Max 51 %	8.47	9.14	10.24	11.26	11.33	12.72
F	Max 20 %	53.82	43.65	43.58	35.51	36.00	36.58

Notes:
A = Capital adequacy.
B = Capital/total liabilities.
C = Coefficient of big loans (as a percentage of bank's capital).
D = Coefficient of long-term investments in companies (as a percentage of bank's capital).
E = Coefficient of long-term investments in banks (as a percentage of bank's capital).
F = Coefficient of investments in fixed assets (as a percentage of bank's capital).

Source: Law on Banks and Other Financial Organisations, Articles 26 and 27.

In general, the Yugoslav banking regulations have, to a large extent, been brought into line with the European Union (EU) standards and requirements. In practice, however, there is a significant difference between adopted legislation and banks' behaviour. This refers, above all, to shareholding, recapitalisation and the computation of capital. As for 'old' banks, it should be noted that their shareholders are mostly socially owned enterprises that are not interested in the banks', results, thus adversely affecting the quality of bank control and management. On the other hand, 'new' banks are mostly mixed and private; however, they still encounter the cross-shareholding problem. According to local solvency standards, which are in conformity with EU legislation, the minimum capital adequacy ratio is 8 per cent. In Yugoslav banks, this ratio ranges from 5.5 to 12 per cent. The majority of banks have met this requirement. However, a more thorough analysis shows that the figures are inflated and that the real values reveal an unfavourable capital structure, inadequate risk dispersion and insufficient reserves to cover bad loans. We assume that it would be appropriate to increase the capital ratio by 15 per cent in order to take account of a higher risk exposure in the Yugoslav economy.

The profitability of Yugoslav banks is generally low. Compared to the return on capital in EU countries, which ranges from 12 to 15 per cent on average, the rate of return on capital of those Yugoslav banks declaring positive financial results, ranges from 0.1 to 2 per cent. The reason for such a low level of profitability should be sought in bad loans, the fact that the owners are not profit motivated (that is, in the form of a dividend), high operating costs, and high write-offs.

Figure 15.5 *Banks' interest rate margin in Yugoslavia, December 1998 to December 1999*

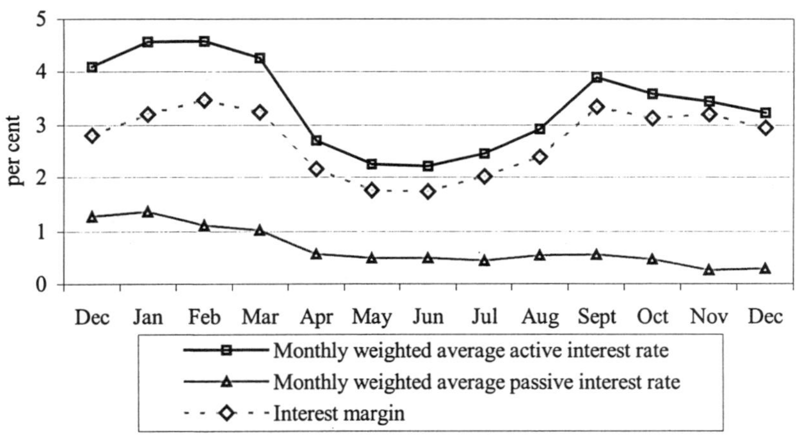

Source: National Bank of Yugoslavia.

The illiquidity of Yugoslav banks is the result of their heavy indebtedness, the poor performance of banks and the economy as a whole, the lack of financial discipline, an inadequate rate of credit collection and bad corporate financial strategy, in addition to higher operating costs relative to revenues. Since mid-1996, as a result of illiquidity, 12 commercial banks have had their operating licences revoked. Despite all this, the liquidity of large commercial banks is mostly maintained due to credits extended by the central bank. In 1996, liquidity credits accounted for approximately 40 per cent of the total credit extended by the NBY. Likewise, an increasing number of banks use a substantial part of their total reserve requirements to maintain their liquidity. Moreover, credits extended for the liquidity of banks or, indirectly, for making up the quasi-budget deficit, are coupled with the use of a considerable part of the reserve requirements for maintaining the short-term liquidity of commercial banks. This reduces, to a large extent, the efficiency of monetary policy, since the NBY often oversteps its authority as the lender of last resort for the purpose of maintaining the liquidity of the banking sector. (See Figure 15.6.)

Figure 15.6 *Banks' liquidity rate in Yugoslavia, December 1997 to December 1999*

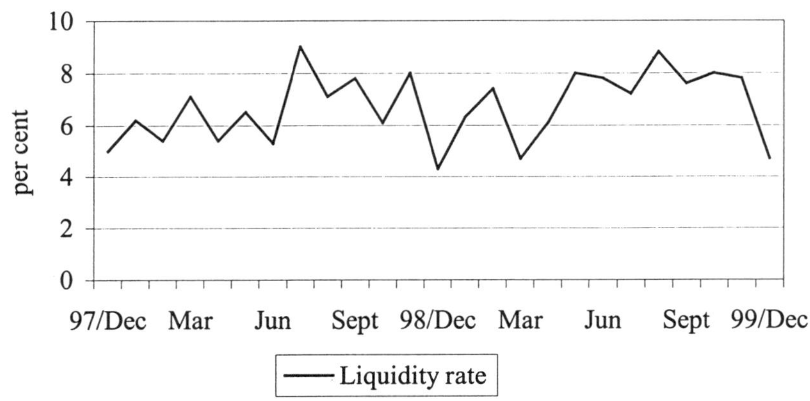

Source: National Bank of Yugoslavia.

In FR Yugoslavia there are no professional banking bodies. It is expected that increased competition in the future will lead to the establishment of such institutions. There exists only the Association of Banks, membership of which is not compulsory. Nevertheless, banks have a set of incentives to become members (contacts with the NBY, clarifications concerning monetary policy and so on). The Association of Forex Dealers and a foreign exchange market operate within the Association of Banks. Earlier, there was a Banks Association of Serbia, which ceased to operate in 1992 when it merged with the organisation at the Federal level.

CURRENT STATE OF NATIONAL BANKING AND OBSTACLES TO BANKING REFORM

The Yugoslav government has not yet adopted a programme of rehabilitation and consolidation of the banking sector. The implementation of a rehabilitation programme for four banks is underway, led by the Federal Agency for Deposit Insurance and Bank Rehabilitation. In our opinion, a further restructuring process should go through several phases. The most important question is whether one should opt for a centralised or decentralised model.

In the case of the Federal Republic of Yugoslavia, the centralised model will bring great relief to the banking sector, since non-performing assets will be transferred to the Federal Agency for Deposit Insurance and Bank Rehabilitation. Bearing in mind the magnitude of the fiscal deficit, a centralised approach may have negative fiscal and monetary implications, thus affecting macroeconomic equilibrium.

In a decentralised model, banks solve the problem of non-performing assets by themselves. The advantage of this model lies in the fact that budgetary funds are not used, and that macroeconomic performance is not adversely affected. In the Yugoslav case, however, non-performing assets exceed the banks' ability to cover them by relying on their own funds. Banks have no shareholders who would be able to undertake their recapitalisation.

It is imperative to carry out an impartial audit of bank balances according to international standards in order to get a true picture of the real potential of banks (actual assets, bad debts, risk investments). So far, auditing practices have been deemed to be somewhat secret, in order to conceal bad conditions within the banking sector. Depending on the audit results it is important to carry out the recapitalisation of banks with actual and potential losses of up to 30 per cent, between 30 and 80 per cent, and up to 110 per cent. Banks with actual and potential losses above 110 per cent should be declared bankrupt.

Privatisation and the promotion of competition are cornerstones of efficient bank reform. The methods of 'cleaning' bank balances are evidently linked to the process of bank and enterprise privatisation, which implies a simultaneous restructuring of both banks' assets and liabilities. A change in the ownership structure of banks will also bring about a change in managerial structures. At the same time, it is necessary to provide incentives to foreign banks to appear on the domestic market, whether independently or together with a domestic partner in the form of mixed ownership.

The whole process of rehabilitation and restructuring of the banking system has to be carried out with a continuous monitoring of bank operations (with respect to their adherence to the requirements of prudential control). Continuous control and supervision of banks has a preventive function or, in other words, should alert the rehabilitated banking system to unfavourable indicators. The ultimate responsibility in this process of supervision and continuous monitoring lies with the central bank. Currently, statutory ratios are the basic means of prudential control, which are defined in the Law on Banks and Other Financial Organisations, Articles 26 and 27.

CONCLUSION: LESSONS AND THEIR RELEVANCE

In general, it can be concluded that the problems of the Yugoslav banking system are:

- *'old' foreign exchange savings deposits*;[10]
- *foreign debt*, which is linked to the regulation of relations with international financial institutions (heavy indebtedness abroad arising from long-term loans and guarantees, the servicing of which is problematic);
- *the need for the cleaning of bad loans from bank assets and the choice of the modality of assuming these obligations* (that is, the problem of old debts and the problem of stopping the renewal of bad debts, which is linked to a change in the system practices and the imposition of hard-budget constraints); and
- *a need for privatisation*, that is, reorganisation of the banking system and the provision of an optimal volume and structure, which implies the minimisation of the costs of banking infrastructure (above all, the transformation of the debtor, quasi-shareholding types of banks into genuine joint-stock banks, as well as a change in their ownership and management structure, thus bringing about a radical change in the method of their operation).

These problems can be tackled by the combination of centralised and decentralised approaches, bearing in mind the seriousness of the situation and the specific circumstances in Yugoslavia. Also, bank restructuring makes sense only when coupled with a restructuring of the real sector in which non-viable firms are closed and viable but troubled firms are restructured.

Even though the restructuring process of the banking sector has not really started in FR Yugoslavia, there are certain positive points that should be noted: (a) the two-tiered system has been refreshed by the introduction of so-called new banks that are mostly privately owned and relatively more efficient than the old state-owned banks; (b) the efficiency of the current payments system involving the NBY, the SPP, banks and other non-bank institutions as well as the postal savings banks should be preserved, even if in the future banks and other financial institutions become the main pillars; and (c) improved paid-in capital standards will reduce the number of banks with short-term business goals, which will improve the functioning of the banking sector.

The strong influence of the political factor in the economy and EU sanctions, fortified further by the so-called 'external wall of restrictions', has contributed to the strengthening of the viewpoint not to introduce banking reform. Populist policies presented by the current governments (Šević and Rabrenović, 1999) in a highly impoverished surrounding imply the centralisation of financial resources and their equitable distribution. However, in such a case excessive bureaucratic practices will be imposed, with all the anomalies (corruption, crime, inefficiency, market distortions and so on) that accompany them.

NOTES

1. The empirical foundation of this country study has been based on comparable data ranging from 1994 to 2000. Data from the previous period are not comparable, because of hyperinflations in 1989 and 1993.
2. The strongest non-economic shock hit Yugoslavia on 24 March 1999, when the North Atlantic Treaty Organisation (NATO) forces attacked the country and caused huge damage to its economy. Direct and indirect war damage and costs are estimated at tens of billions of US dollars.
3. 'Old' banks account for about 90 per cent of the total balance of Yugoslav banking and constitute half the number of registered banks.
4. See Article 24–52, Law on the National Bank of Yugoslavia (*Official Gazette of the Federal Republic of Yugoslavia*, No. 32/1993).
5. Citizens' dinar-denominated deposits that are held at banks and the Postal Savings Bank are guaranteed by the National Bank of Yugoslavia, while foreign exchange deposits are guaranteed by the Federation directly.
6. In conditions when the state as the guarantor of old foreign exchange deposits has lost credibility, it is likely that some deposit insurance funds established by banks, or independent funds will also have no credibility.
7. In compliance with Article 2 of the Law on Changes of the Law on Payment Operations (*Official Gazette of the Federal Republic of Yugoslavia*, No. 74/99).
8. A high proportion of the capital in the liabilities of 'new' banks stems from the fact that these new banks do not have more significant deposits; instead, a substantial part of their credit potential is created out of capital. The liabilities of 'old' banks are inflated by fictitious claims (exchange rate differentials from the earlier period and frozen old foreign exchange obligations at home and abroad). If a realistic evaluation of potential losses were made and if banks were obliged to maintain their reserves at the full amount necessary for their cover, then the degree of banks' undercapitalisation would become evident.
9. If uncontrolled, foreign banks would have an absolute advantage and become dominant in all three lender categories: agent, co-agent and participants (through participation in loan sales markets). In the second phase, licences would be granted to small banks, whose primary target would be to take over and restructure state-owned banks. This would reap the benefits not only of capital infusion, but also of technological and managerial know-how.
10. 'Old' foreign exchange savings deposits of the general public are private foreign exchange savings deposits made in commercial banks, which 'old' state banks are unable to service, and which have remained 'frozen' on the balance sheets of 'old' banks. 'New' banks are not burdened with this item on their balance sheets because, since the early 1990s, as a result of a loss of confidence in the banking system, the general public have been keeping their savings 'under the mattress'.

BIBLIOGRAPHY

Buch, C. (1995), 'Monetary Policy and the Transformation of the Banking System in Eastern Europe', Kiel Working Paper No. 676, Kiel: Kiel Institute of World Economics.

European Bank for Reconstruction and Development (EBRD) (1996), *Transition Report*, London: EBRD.

European Bank for Reconstruction and Development (EBRD) (1998), *Transition Report*, London: EBRD.

Federal Statistical Office (1999), *Statistički godišnjak SR Jugoslavije* [Statistical Annual Bulletin of FR Yugoslavia], Belgrade: Federal Statistical Office.

Goodhart, C.A.E. (1995), *The Central Bank and the Financial System*, London: Macmillan.

Koyama, Y. (1999), 'Direction of the Banking System Reform in Yugoslavia in the Light of Japanese Experience', in Ž. Šević (ed.), *Banking Reform in South East European Transitional Economies*, Sofia and London: University of Greenwich Business School, Balkan Center for Public Policy and Related Studies, Humanities Research Centre, pp. 291–308.

Labus, M. (1998), 'Financial Sector in Yugoslavia', in G. Pitić (ed.), *Challenges and Opportunities for the Economic Transition in Yugoslavia*, Belgrade: USAID, Economics Institute, Chesapeake Associates, pp. 32–48.

National Bank of Yugoslavia, *Bilten NBJ* [Bulletin of the NBY], various issues, Belgrade: National Bank of Yugoslavia.

Pitić, G., N. Fabris and J. Galić (1999), 'Yugoslav Banking Sector – Main Obstacles and How to Tackle them in the Restructuring Process', in Ž. Šević (ed.), *op. cit.*, pp. 331–56.

Šević, A. and A. Zamberlin (1999), 'Banking Restructuring in the FR of Yugoslavia', in Ž. Šević (ed.), *op. cit.*, pp. 357–76.

Šević, Ž. (1996), *Centralna banka: Položaj, organizacija, funkcije ...* [Central Bank: Position, Organisation, Functions ...], Belgrade: Čigoja štampa.

Šević, Ž. (1999), 'Central Banking in South East European Transitional Economies: A Comparative Perspective', in Ž. Šević (ed.), *op. cit.*, pp. 103–30.

Šević, Ž. and A. Rabrenović (1999), 'The Civil Service of Yugoslavia: Tradition vs. Transition', in T. Verheijen (ed.), *Civil Service Systems in Central and Eastern Europe*, Cheltenham and Northampton, MA: Edward Elgar, pp. 47–82.

Šević, Ž. and A. Šević (1998), 'Monetary Policy in a Transitional Economy: Some Open Questions and Experiences', *Economic Systems*, **22** (3), pp. 299–304.

Sheng, A. (ed.) (1996), *Bank Restructuring, Lessons from the 1980s*, Washington, DC: World Bank.

Živković, B., M. Arsić and S. Rikanović (1999), 'Crisis of the Banking Sector in Yugoslavia and Possible Improvements of the Banking Restructuring Model', in Ž. Šević (ed.), *op. cit.*, pp. 309–29.

Index

Agency theory 83, 184-200
Albania 2, 4, 7, 11, 12, 20-21, 25-26, 28-29, 34, 36, 38, 40, 42-43, 54, 56-58, 60, 67, 70, 100, 104, 113, 115-16
Auditors 83, 86, 88, 92, 95

Bad debt 5-6, 8, 107, 147, 160, 232-33, 249, 270, 281, 291, 293, 305, 316, 320-21
Balance of payments 56, 112, 126, 235
Bank Consolidation Corporations 218-19, 225, 234, 236
Bank insolvency 280
Bank liquidity 43, 311, 315
Bank of Albania 4, 100, 105, 118-20, 188-204
Banking performance 176-77
Banking reform 4-5, 9, 12, 23, 57, 62, 103, 118, 164, 166, 175, 177-79, 181, 188, 204, 210, 217, 236, 251, 256, 272, 279-81, 298, 304, 320, 322
Banking regulation 177, 179, 317
Banking sector 5, 7-13, 23, 41, 54, 58-59, 65, 72-73, 76, 103, 110-11, 113-14, 118, 147-49, 151, 153, 159-60, 177-78, 188, 204, 211, 217, 219, 221, 225, 227, 237, 243, 249, 254-55, 258, 272-73, 290, 296, 298, 305-08, 312, 315, 319, 320-22
Banking supervision 6-7, 14, 60, 102-03, 110, 171, 190-91, 211, 221, 230, 245, 255, 259-60
Bankruptcy 6, 10, 14, 31, 67, 74, 81-82, 91-92, 94, 96, 101, 115, 164, 171, 173-75, 182, 189, 211, 220, 226, 235, 248, 251, 280-81, 284, 293, 313, 317
Banks and Saving Houses Act 260
Basle Capital Standards 258
Basle Committee 75
BCC , see: Bank Consolidation Corporations
Big-bang 61,
BISERA 229
BNB, see: Bulgarian National Bank 222-23, 225, 227, 229-30, 239
Bosnia and Herzegovina 1, 5, 11-12, 20-21, 30, 33, 56-60, 65, 67, 70, 109, 114, 116, 118-20, 203, 207-09, 211, 213-214, 217
Bretton Woods 133, 142
Broad money 44, 191, 235, 247, 295
Budget deficit 40, 108, 120, 126, 135, 168, 188, 198, 235, 310, 319
Bulgaria 1-2, 8, 11-13, 20-22, 25, 28-29, 33-40, 42-43, 54, 56-59, 67, 72-73, 164-65, 167-69, 171-73, 176, 178-80, 213-232
Bulgarian National Bank 215, 217-29, 232
Bulgarian Stock Exchange (Sofia) 29, 73, 237

Capital adequacy ratio 42, 152, 155, 224, 230, 258, 271-72, 295-96, 298, 318
CAR, see Capital adequacy ratio
CEC, see: Central European Countries
Central bank reform 196, 201, 206, 265, 287
Central European Countries 13, 19-22, 25, 27-28, 37-38, 42, 104, 284
Central planning 22, 27, 35, 58-59, 213, 220, 232, 302
Centralised 5-6, 12, 36, 148-54, 158-59, 171-74, 188, 206, 254, 268, 281, 291, 306, 313, 320-21
CNB, see: Croatian National Bank

CNB policy 244
Competition policy 22, 42, 53, 96
Competitiveness 12-13, 24, 32, 124, 128, 132-34, 136,138, 168, 176, 229-30, 235-36, 251, 262, 296, 304
Concentration 73, 99, 117, 173, 178, 233, 255-56, 273, 280, 299
Conflict of interest 83, 86, 90, 93
Consolidation 9, 12, 49, 59, 71, 73, 75, 151-52, 154-55, 157, 160, 206, 219, 225, 233, 235, 259, 261, 271, 273-75, 297, 320
Corporate banking 282, 306
Corporate governance 7, 9, 11, 34, 43, 76, 79, 83-86, 89, 164, 173-76, 179, 272, 297
Corruption index 37,
Credit Co-operative 6, 186, 277,
Credit rates 240
Croatia's economic indicators 235
Croatian National Bank 235, 237-251
Currency board 11, 29-30, 40, 51, 112, 121, 125-231, 133-42, 203-4, 211-12, 220, 222, 227, 229-32, 234-36, 238
Czech Republic 5, 13, 19, 22, 34-35, 39-40, 148, 151-52, 154, 160, 162-65, 169, 171-72, 174, 177, 179, 275

Dayton Peace Agreement 5, 12,
Decentralised 5-6, 12, 36, 148-49, 153-59, 171-72, 174, 178, 268, 304, 306, 309, 320-21
Deposit insurance 8, 55, 77, 153, 160, 205, 211, 216, 230-31, 243, 256, 290, 313, 320, 322
Deposit Insurance Fund 231, 257, 262, 264
Deregulation 24
Direct monetary instruments 111-12, 114
Directors 85-89, 91, 95, 287
Dollarisation 12, 43-44,
Doubtful debt

EBRD, see: European Bank for Reconstruction and Development
Economic development 22, 55, 79-80, 100, 103, 126, 178, 190, 214, 302

Estonia 6, 37, 121, 126, 136, 141
EU Directives 230, 255
EU, see: European Union
European Bank for Reconstruction and Development 5, 8, 19-23, 25-27, 32-36, 39-40, 42, 49, 51, 54-55, 57-59, 64-65, 67-70, 72-76, 165-70, 172, 175-77, 180, 187, 239, 271, 300
European Central Bank 14, 51-52, 66-67,
European Monetary System 64,
European Union 1-2, 11, 20, 47, 49-51, 53-54, 56-57, 64-67, 72, 75, 140, 145, 215-16, 222, 246, 250, 255, 273, 275, 296, 300, 317-18, 322
Eurosystem 51, 52
Exchange rate regimes 140

Federation Banking Agency 204-5, 209-10
Financial crisis 50, 145, 177, 180, 213-16, 219-20, 222, 226, 228, 232, 237-38
Financial development 163-67, 178-79, 186
Financial restructuring 8, 153, 171, 178, 204, 215, 233, 247, 268, 271, 274-75, 291, 314
Financial sector reform 48-49, 52-54, 56, 57-59, 62-64, 66, 116, 193, 204
Financial system 6-7, 9, 31, 38, 41-44, 49, 51-52, 55, 57-61, 66, 98-99, 101, 103, 109-11, 114-18, 164, 170, 188, 190, 204, 206, 217, 220-22, 227-29, 232, 238, 258, 265, 267-68, 272, 274-75, 304, 309
Fiscal policy 40, 100-1, 235
Fixed exchange rate 52, 127, 133, 137, 142, 228-29, 251, 257, 266
Floating exchange rate 51, 128, 141, 143-44, 182
Foreign assets 126-27, 214, 239, 250, 265, 268
Foreign assets in banking
Foreign banks 8-9, 43, 61, 64-65, 70, 76, 118, 177, 187, 194, 206, 216, 220-21, 225, 227, 232, 236, 238, 240, 242, 251, 262, 273-74, 278, 284, 297-98, 306, 317, 320, 322

Foreign direct investment 38, 170, 204, 217, 223, 235

G-8, see: Group of Eight
GDP, see: Gross domestic product
German Bundesbank 265
Gold standard 228
Governance 11, 22, 28, 33-34, 43, 51, 53, 76, 79, 80-86, 153, 155, 159, 164, 173-76, 179
Gradualist 38-39, 61
Gross domestic product 20-31, 35-38, 40, 43, 69-70, 72-77, 165-70, 175-76, 181, 188, 196, 200, 206, 209-10, 221, 223, 226, 235-37, 241-42, 248-49, 255, 259, 262-64, 267, 270-72, 275, 277-79, 287, 290, 293, 295, 298, 302-4, 315-16
Group of Eight 47, 68, 71-76,

Hong Kong currency board system 129
Hungary 5-6, 13, 19, 21-22, 33-35, 37, 39, 44, 58, 141, 148, 154-55, 157-60, 164-69, 171, 176-77, 179, 275
Hyperinflation 109

IMF, see: International Monetary Fund
Inflation control
Inflation rate 26, 28, 32, 40, 132-33, 152, 168, 176-79, 200, 228, 237, 278, 289-90, 304
Infrastructural networks 47, 65
Insolvency 150, 154, 248
Insolvency laws 82, 280
Institutional investors 90, 271
Interest spreads 176-77
Intermediation 8, 43, 55, 59, 70, 72, 75, 131, 164, 176, 179, 206, 259, 262, 271, 274, 280, 295-96, 298
International Monetary Fund 20, 49, 54-57, 59, 64, 67, 121, 142, 159, 165, 188, 211, 220
International reserves 125-26, 237, 244, 256-57, 265, 269, 288
Investment compact 48, 54, 64, 67,

Late reformers 163-64, 171-73

Latvia 141
LCA, see: Loan Collection Agency
Legal and regulatory framework 59
Legal tender 255-56
Lender-of-last-resort 97, 106-7, 114
Liberalisation 19, 22-25, 28, 29, 32, 35, 38-39, 42, 44, 50, 58, 165, 169, 171, 277, 305
Lithuania 127, 136, 141
Loan Collection Agency 198

Macedonian Stock Exchange 264
Market discipline 29, 86, 290
Modified currency board system 130, 136
Monetary aggregates 109, 117
Monetary policy 4, 11, 40-41, 44, 55, 79, 81, 99-100, 102-03, 107-08, 110-15, 117-21, 129, 132, 139, 142, 188,190, 196-98, 203, 206, 208, 211, 220, 228, 244, 251, 257-58, 265, 267-68, 275, 279, 281, 288, 290, 305, 309, 311-12, 319
Money supply 35, 40, 44, 112, 126, 191-92, 208, 214, 219-20, 223, 228, 235, 244-45, 247, 255, 259-60, 266-67, 273, 288, 309, 312-13
Monopolistic 23, 252, 269, 314
Moral hazard 6, 79, 107, 158-59, 164-66, 170-72, 178-79, 233, 256, 264, 280, 293, 298
Moral suasion 111, 114

National Bank of Romania 106, 118-20, 277-79, 285-89, 293-96, 300
National Bank of the Republic of Macedonia 116, 255-57, 271, 275
National Bank of Yugoslavia 5, 13-14, 101-05, 118-20, 304-314, 316, 318-322
National Payment System 290-91
NBRM, see: National Bank of the Republic of Macedonia
NBY, see: National Bank of Yugoslavia
Non-performing loans 8, 41, 44, 77, 147, 160, 167, 171-73, 178-79, 181, 194, 206, 213, 281, 291, 293

OECD, see: Organisation for

Economic Co-operation and Development
Organisation for Economic Co-operation and Development 36, 82, 86, 229, 232
Overdue loans 76, 296

Payment Bureau 60, 202, 204-5, 207-9, 211
Poland 5, 13, 19, 24, 35-37, 39, 58, 141, 154, 160, 163-66, 168-72, 176-78, 181, 196, 275
Price stability 38, 100, 111-12, 127-29, 133, 190, 254-55, 258, 266-67, 280-81, 288, 311
Private banks 10, 42-44, 50, 59, 65, 77, 186, 196, 198-99, 205-6, 209, 212, 216, 219, 226, 233, 258-59, 270, 281, 284-85, 289-90, 293, 299, 305-6
Private sector credit 165, 295
Privatisation 5, 7-10, 13, 19, 22, 24, 29-33, 38, 40, 51, 53, 60-61, 63, 67, 69-72, 74-76, 115, 151-52, 155, 165, 167, 173-75, 176, 178-80, 182-83, 187, 189, 193, 205, 209, 211, 215-16, 219-20, 222-23, 225, 227, 235-37, 240, 249-50, 259, 269, 274-75, 277, 281, 284, 297-300, 306, 320-21
Pyramid saving schemes 43

Real Time Gross Settlement 196-97
Recapitalisation 6, 64, 69, 149, 151, 155, 171-73, 176, 178-79, 234, 299, 317, 320
Recession 24-27, 34, 42, 171
Rehabilitation 5, 12, 31, 45, 49, 63-64, 74, 148-60, 226-28, 245, 247-48, 259, 268-72, 274-75, 313, 320
Remonetisation 315
Reserve requirements 113, 116-17, 121, 191, 288, 304, 311-12, 319
Restructuring 6, 8-9, 22, 29, 42-44, 49, 52, 55, 63, 65, 76-77, 154-60, 163, 166-67, 170-73, 175, 178-80, 204, 206, 215, 220, 224-25, 227, 232-34, 237-38, 245, 247, 255, 259, 267-68, 270-75, 281, 285, 288-89, 291, 293, 295-99, 306, 314-15, 320-21
Retail banking 61, 64, 282, 295
Roll-over 280
Romania 1-2, 6, 8, 10, 12-13, 20-22, 25, 28, 30, 33, 35-40, 42, 54, 56-60, 77, 101-02, 106, 116, 118-20, 141, 163, 165-66, 168, 171, 176, 277-300
RTGS, see: Real Time Gross Settlement

Savings Bank 2, 14, 69-70, 72, 77, 183, 186-88, 209-10, 217, 230, 240, 282, 314, 322
Savings of citizens 194-95, 241-42, 263, 316
SEECs, see: South-East European countries
Segmentation 3, 115, 280, 284
Shareholder capital 156
Shareholders 59, 83-96, 148, 150, 156-57, 167, 173-74, 180, 217, 224, 237
Slovakia 13, 19, 35, 37, 40, 141, 256, 258, 261, 275, 281, 317, 320
Slovenia 1, 3-5, 8, 11, 13, 19, 21-22, 33-35, 37, 39-40, 104-05, 116, 118-20, 141, 160, 163, 165-66, 168, 171, 176
Social capital 21, 34
Social ownership 34, 209
South-East European countries 1, 5, 8, 20-22, 25, 27-28, 31-33, 36-38, 40-44, 52-57, 65, 117
Spill-over 298
Stabilisation 19, 23-28, 30-32, 39-40, 44, 53-56, 109, 132, 138, 237-38, 240, 247, 257, 304
Stability pact 11, 47-51, 54, 53-59, 61, 64-67
State bank 4, 42-44, 60, 68, 99-101, 103-04, 109, 116, 216, 240, 323
State enterprises 29, 33, 36-37, 79, 81-82, 96, 153, 155, 213, 220, 228, 232, 235, 238
State entity 148, 150, 153-54
State-owned banks 5, 7, 9-10, 30, 42, 70-72, 74, 76, 118, 121, 175-79, 189, 202, 205, 216, 219, 220, 226-27, 232-33, 236, 240, 280-84, 286, 289, 291, 297-99, 305-6, 322
Structure of the banking system 182,

186, 205, 212, 223, 227, 259, 281
Supervisory board system 88, 95

Takeovers 89, 93-94, 273
Tirana Stock Exchange 185
Too-big-to-fail 280, 299
Total lending targets 114
Transition economies 58, 62, 92-93, 148, 152, 154, 159, 163-64, 166, 168-71, 173-76, 178-79, 274-75
Transition indicators 19, 22-23
Transition report 35, 39, 51, 57, 300
Twin deficit 163
Two-tier banking system 4, 101, 103, 116, 119, 213, 220, 224, 237-38, 254, 256, 304

Vested interests 62, 175, 177

Working table II (Stability Pact) 48-49, 52-53, 63-64, 67
Workout unit 149, 158
World Bank 20-22, 24. 29-30, 32, 42, 44, 49, 52-55, 64, 67, 155, 160, 173, 188, 206, 209-10, 212-13, 216, 272, 284

ZUNK bonds 227-28